THE OUTLAW YOUNGERS

A Confederate Brotherhood

a
biography
by

Marley Brant

MADISON BOOKS

Lanham • New York • London

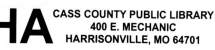

Published by Madison Books
4720 Boston Way
Lanham, Maryland 20706

3 Henrietta Street
London WC2E 8LU England

Distributed by National Book Network

The paper in this publication meets the minimum
requirements of American National Standard for
Information Sciences—Permanence of Paper for
Printed Library Materials, ANSI Z39.48–1984. ⊗™
Manufactured in the United States of America.

Library of Congress Cataloging-in-Publication Data

Brant, Marley.
The Outlaw Youngers : A Confederate brotherhood : a
biography / by Marley Brant.
p.   cm.
1. United States—History—Civil War, 1861–1865—
Underground movements.   2. West (U.S.)—History—
Civil War, 1861–1865—Underground movements.
3. Younger, Cole, 1844–1916.   4. Younger, James,
1848–1902.   5. Quantrill, William Clarke, 1837–
1865.   6. Guerrillas—West (U.S.)—Biography.
7. Outlaws—West (U.S.)—Biography.   8. Missouri—
Biography.   I. Title.
E470.45.B7   1992
973.7'092'2—dc20   92-25023   CIP
[B]

ISBN 0-8191-8627-9 (cloth: alk. paper)
ISBN 1-56833-045-6 (pbk.: alk. paper)

This book is dedicated in loving memory to my father
Herbert B. "Red" Olmstead, Jr.

and
with love and appreciation for their assistance, support and
encouragement, *my* gang:

my guys Dave and Timothy Bruegger, my right hand, Kathie
Montgomery, and my mom, Gladys M. Olmstead

With special thanks for the spurrings of Bob and Jesse.

Contents

Contents

Contents

Preface

After years of research into their story, it at last became clear to me that what motivated the Younger brothers of Missouri was commitment. Regardless of the object of their commitment, be it family, friends, their homeland, or their undertaking of the special task of becoming the most well known, feared, and ruthless of desperado gangs, the Youngers grabbed life by the shirtfront and held on for all they were worth. The manifestation of their passion resulted in unique rewards, such as occasional large sums of money and a fame that has endured over a century. Along the way, however, they paid a heavy price: the death of dear friends and family members, the loss of the ability to experience life as free members of society, their self-respect and finally, for three of them, their own young lives.

As my study of their lives and times grew from a passing interest into a maddening obsession, I realized that the Youngers did not fit the stereotypical definition of the outlaw. Desperate they were, but the reasons behind their isolation and hatred were shared by the society in which they lived. It was not their motivation that was unique, it was their approach to meeting their frustrations head-on in a manner their community was not able to accept. Yet paradoxically, social mores were often overlooked by respected members of society when "The Boys" needed shelter or an airtight alibi.

The Youngers' struggle to maintain the sanctity of their family was certainly not an isolated instance in postwar Missouri. If an attempt is to be made to understand the family's identity and the prestigious position it held in the pioneer days of Missouri history, it becomes necessary to isolate the Younger family to examine a second layer of anti-Confederate action by the state's power structure. The intricacies of Missouri's 1865 Drake Constitution were far-reaching and affected nearly every aspect of postwar adjustment. My key to revealing the underlying motives of the Younger brothers' antisocial convictions was to attempt first to understand why they chose to fight their enemies with such vengeance that their lives would be placed in jeopardy and engulfed in turmoil decades after the official end of the War Between the States. While I studied their determination to seize what they felt was rightfully theirs, I became aware of my own growing compulsion to find ways to explain their actions while neither condoning nor condemning them. I finally realized that the Youngers and I shared a passion for truth, although, as with most facts, the "truths" revealed were often oblique or self-serving.

Whether the Younger brothers were on the side of good or evil is a question that depends on one's perspective of their times. It cannot simply be determined through an overview of their lives or outlaw careers. There were certainly times when they were motivated by a desire to make their political statement in the hope that those who had chosen to disagree with the country's establishment might be served as well as those who shared the beliefs of the "winners." Yet many times they were motivated by simple greed and a sinister desire to be recognized as career rebels, lightly dismissing the fact that their premeditated acts against authority might cause death or destruction. Eventually, even they realized they fit no conventional category of good or bad, right or wrong. While struggling to convince themselves of their inner virtues, they were unable to rise above their selfish deeds to fulfill their own desires to reform. The question remains: was it that they did not want to end their criminal careers, or did they simply not know how?

The Younger brothers remembered only too well what life had been like before the Border War, before the War Between the States, before they stepped into their first bank. Their family beginnings displayed a healthy respect for society and the law through the careers of their grandfather the judge, uncles who served in the state legislature, and their own father, a respected public servant. It is hard to accept that, with such a background, the sole reason the four brothers chose to live lives of outlawry was because their father had been taken from them when they were young and impressionable. No, the story is far more complex than that. Possessing high intellects and strong personalities, Cole, Jim, John, and Bob Younger were motivated in varying degrees by revenge, frustration, greed, ego, and blind family loyalty. While not responsible for the actions of the Younger brothers, Frank and Jesse James played an influential and instrumental role in their lives. The chemistry demonstrated in the coalition of the two sets of Confederate brothers was explosive. It was also lucrative and fatal. There is strength in numbers and vulnerability through dissension. The James and Younger brothers were not strangers to either of these propositions.

Whether offered as a reason or dismissed as an excuse, the fact is that the Youngers seemed to find it impossible to adjust to a structured life within society. What lay beyond young lives devoted to the fight was terrifying to them. With ideas of assimilation into the quiet lives of ranchers and farmers, they chose to defy convention to demand rewards that they felt they were entitled to, that they had somehow earned, one last time. Another group of disbelievers in their cause unwillingly crossed their path, and yet another innocent man died. The scorecard was tallied, and the Younger brothers of Missouri had failed to win the game or even tie the score.

I invite you to examine the lives of Cole, Jim, John, and Bob Younger. I have attempted to present the particulars of their individual stories without prejudice or judgment. I freely admit a sympathy for the people of western Missouri who struggled through the devastating times of the Border War and the War Between the States and who suffered the adjustments and tribulations of the period of Reconstruction. By virtue of the fact that the Younger family was a viable part of that community, they, as a whole, are included in my sympathies. However, since most people involved in that historical drama chose to accept their fate and the Youngers did not, we must at that point set the Youngers aside from their community and examine their individual actions and reactions. Surprising conclusions will be drawn by both author and reader. Some actions will be revealed to be acceptable while others will not. I have chosen to write this book as an informal narrative rather than as a structured academic presentation in the hope that the reader will be drawn into the events depicted as a less than casual observer. What's promised is an in-depth biography of four strong-willed individuals who, along with Frank and Jesse James, managed to capture the interest of total strangers and fascinate a nation. More than a hundred years after their reign as America's most notorious outlaws, they continue to enthrall.

Acknowledgments

I offer my Very Special Thanks to the members of the Younger Family who so generously shared their files, scrapbooks, Bibles, family records, photographs, family stories and recollections. Your friendship will be a treasured part of my life always: Bessie Collins, Sylvia Creek, Zudora Von Demfange, Delores Reed Fozzard, Carolyn Hall, Jack Hall, Charlene Johnson, Donald Lambkin, Leola O. Mayes, Diana Peairs Rawlins, F. M. Rawlins, Nora Lee Smith, June Spicer, William Talley, Ruth Whipple, Verne Whipple, Harriet Baird Wickstrom, John Younger and that master story-teller, Dreat Younger.

Thanks so much to all of you who shared your interest, time, materials and family stories: Mildred Addy, Betty Barr, Thelma Barr, Ione Bowman, Claude Bronaugh, George Chadwick, Naohm Hoffman Coop, Carol Cooper, Mary B. B. Crouch, Mary Withrow Davidson, Milton E. Edmonson, Chris Edwards, Vera Eldridge, William Eldridge, Jean Forney, Edwin Grube, Carl S. Hage, Harold Hage, Donald Hale, Margarette Hutchins, J. W. Lercher, Othor MacLean, C. E. Miller, Richard Miller, John Mills, Ethelrose James Owens, Chuck Parsons, James R. Ross, Monika and Michael Scklore, Marjorie Settle, Phillip Steele, Joseph Stevenson, George Warfel, Florence Wiley, Jack Wymore and Ted P. Yeatman.

Many thanks to Armand De Gregoris for the use of his unpublished photographs and to W. C. Bronaugh, Dallas Cantrell, B. J. George and Harry Hoffman for their special contributions.

A big thanks goes out to copy editor Faith Hanson, whose

proficiency not only enhanced the manuscript but provided me with a much needed refresher course in English.

Thanks always to Willie and Carol Olmstead, my aunts and uncles, Aunt Francie O., John Delgatto and my family and friends, especially those who showed such great interest in my work and encouraged me to "stay on the trail" every step of the way.

My heartfelt thanks to the following people without whom this book would never have been written, with appreciation for their support, encouragement, friendship, hours of research and assistance and for always being there for me and my work: Kathie Montgomery, Milton F. Perry and Dr. William A. Settle, Jr. . . . and to Wilbur A. Zink, "Keeper of the Younger Flame," for his inspiration, support, sharing of materials and for his very special friendship.

Additionally, I would like to thank the following institutions and their conscientious employees and volunteers, without whom the research of this book would have been impossible: The State Historical Society of Missouri, Columbia (Kathleen McIntyre, Jo Ann Tuckwood, Fae Sotham, Laurel Boeckman, Juanita Tillman, Rhonda Peske); The Minnesota Historical Society (Steven Eric Nielson, Dallas Lindgren, Tracey Baker, Bonnie Wilson, Ruth Ellen Bauer); The Ancient Free and Accepted Masons (William E. Wall); The Blue Earth County Historical Society (Denise Schmidt Hudson, Marcia Schuster, Audrey Hicks); Brookings Public Library (Anne Trump); Buckham Memorial Library, Faribault (Robert Kaupa); The Buffalo Bill Historical Center (Paul Fees); Bushwhacker Museum (Patrick Brophy); California Historical Society (Judy Sheldon); California State Library (Thomas Fante); Cass County Historical Society (Irene Webster, Anita East, Katherine Kenagy); Clay County Archives (Vera Eldridge); Clay County Recorder (William Eldridge); City of San Jose (Nancy C. Martin); Clerk of the District Court, Faribault (Diana Hering); College of William and Mary (Kay J. Domine, James W. Oberly, Laura Frances Parrish); Dallas Historical Society (Casey Greene); Dallas Public Library—Texas/Dallas History and Archives (Jean Hudson); Dennison Area Chamber of Commerce (Anna Wegar); Douglas County Historical Society—Lawrence, Kansas (Judy M. Sweets); Faribault Chamber of Commerce; Goodhue County Historical Society (Orville Olson); Historic New Orleans Collection (John T. Magill); Historical Society of Southern California (Jack Moore, Carol Daugherty); Independence, Missouri—Jackson County Recorders Office; Jackson County Historical Society (Nancy Ehrlich, Patrick O'Brien, Sarah Schwenk, Gerald Motsinger); James Farm (Milton Perry, Pam Banner, David Smith); Jesse James Museum—Adair (Jackie Wilson); Kansas City Public Library—Missouri Valley Room (Virginia Wright); Kansas District Court (Phyllis Barnard); Kansas State Historical Society (Eugene Decker, Darrell Garwood); Kentucky Commonwealth Archives (Lynn Lady); Lee's Summit Public Library; Logan County Clerk's Office (Welson Frantz); Louisiana State Archives (Vernell Murphy); Louisiana State Museum (Rose Lambert); Maryland Historical Society (Frances P. O'Neill); Maryland State Archives (Richard Richardson); Missouri State Archives (Billie Smith); National Archives and Records Service; New Orleans Public Library (Jean Jones); Northfield Historical Society (Mary Ellen Frame, Caroline de Mauriac); Northfield Public Library (Marston Headley); Pioneer Museum of Butler (Eleanor Lynch); Ray County Museum (Pauline E. Brown); Rice County Historical Society (Dale Maul, Susan McKenna); San Jose State University (Dr. Benjamin F. Gilbert); Santa Clara County Historical Society (Louise Sumpter, Lee Ingraham); Sherman Library (Jacqueline Banfield); Society of California Pioneers (Grace Baker); Stillwater Public Library (Sue Collins); Tilson Club of Kentucky (Nettie Watson); Transylvania University (Kathleen Bryson); Tulane University Library (Wilbur E. Meneray); United States Naval Academy at Annapolis (Dr. William W. Jeffries); University of Oklahoma—Western History Collection (John R. Lovett); Washington County Historical Society (Anna Engquist, Louise Johnson, Joan K. Daniels); Watawon County Historical Society (Ruth Anderson) and the Wayne County Historical Society (Wilma West, Audrey Kinser.)

1

Beginnings

It is not improbable that retaliation for the recent
great outrage at Lawrence, Kansas may extend to
indiscriminate slaughter on the Missouri border unless
averted by very judicious action. (signed) A. Lincoln

During the last week of August, 1863, a special dispatch to the
President of the United States was sent through the *Missouri
Democrat*:

General Lane has returned to Lawrence. A meeting was held on his
return. Lane said the citizens had killed 41 of Quantrill's men.
Majors Clark and Plumb were denounced. The people of Baldeoin
disputed Quantrill in passing a ford and say if Plumb had done his
duty they could have whipped the Rebels. Lane is organizing forces
and says he will go into Missouri on the 9th of Sept. He left Gen.
Ewing only on a pledge that Ewing would issue an order directing
all the citizens of Jackson, Cass, Bates and part of Vernon Cos.
except those in Kansas City, Westport, Harrisonville and Independence, to leave the county within 15 days. Ewing has issued the
order and the people of Kansas are going into Missouri to see the
order executed. The people have demanded the order issued by the
general commanding and the people will see it executed. They say
they will have no more of the Schofield-Ewing orders. Ewing is
frightened, and in the chase after Quantrill was in a complete
quandary. He is looked upon as being a general without a heart and
brains. About 50 of the most noted secesh of Platte County have

subscribed from $1 to $10 each for the Lawrence fund. By so doing they expect to escape the anticipated devastation of Western Missouri. General Ewing has returned to Kansas City. Quantrill had with him Sam. Hays, brother of Up. Hays, Dick Yeager, Holt, George Todd and Younger, with 150 men, on whom they could depend in a fight with about 150 more of the citizens of Platte, Clay, LaFayette, Jackson, Cass and Bates Cos., not over 300 in all. One thousand Kansas men will be in Missouri this week. Up to this morning 183 bodies were buried in Lawrence. The remains of 7 more bodies are found. One hundred and eighty-two buildings were burned; 80 of them brick; 65 of them were on Massachusetts St. There are 85 widows and 240 orphans made on Quantrill's raid. Lane has commenced rebuilding his house. Three men have subscribed $100,000 to rebuild the Free State Hotel, known as the Eldridge Hotel. Several merchants have commenced rebuilding. All the laboring men in town will set to work tomorrow to clear off the ruins. In spite of the terrible calamity, the people are in good spirits. All the towns in the state have sent in large sums of money. Even the men burned out on Quantrill's retreat have sent in loads of vegetables and provisions. A man was to-day tried in Lawrence and found guilty of being a spy for Quantrill and was hung. The Chiefs of the civilized Indians of the Delawares and Sacs and Foxes offered their services to Lane. Reports just in say the buildings in Cass County, Missouri are on fire and over 100 of the sympathizers are killed. A fearful retribution no doubt awaits Missouri. In view of these facts, your memorialists respectfully, but most earnestly, pray your Excellency to rescind the order by which a part of Missouri is attached to the District of the Border and to order that it be reattached to the Central District of Missouri and be placed in command over the soldiers and people in the counties of the border—some officer whose sense of duty and of love to his country rises far above his political aspirations and party ties and prejudices, and whose sole desire and efforts will be to guard and foster the interests of the government in that region, and to bring law and order out of the chaos that now prevails. This is all that the masses of the people desire and for this your memorialists will ever pay, etc." (signed) A. A. King, R. C. Vaughn, A. Comingo.[1]

The Kansas-Missouri border was in shambles. Law and order, as defined by anyone who had ever believed in a democratic society, was an ideology of the past after the devastation of the

Kansas town of Lawrence on August 21, 1863. The guerrilla warriors of Missouri, led by a man named William Clarke Quantrill, ensured that things would never be the same for anyone who had ever even heard of "The Border." The reply to the dispatch read:

> It is not improbable that retaliation for the recent great outrage at Lawrence, Kansas may extend to indiscriminate slaughter on the Missouri border unless averted by very judicious action. I shall be obliged if the General-in-Chief can make any suggestions to General Schofield upon the subject. August 31, 1863 (signed) A. Lincoln[2]

The reports of what happened in Lawrence that day and why Quantrill's guerrillas chose that town to demonstrate with finality their determination to end any further encroachment on the farms and fields of the Missouri-Kansas border are extensive and varied. The ties to the pioneer-developed land of both states' forebears were, by 1863, held tight with bloodstained hands. The Kansans claimed that they had been waiting for a devastating event such as the destruction of Lawrence from those whom they regarded as the lawless renegades of Missouri. The Missourians felt equally as strong about what they believed to be the immoral misdeeds of the Kansans. According to some historians, the raid on Lawrence was in direct retaliation for the September 23, 1861, raid on the small town of Osceola down in St. Clair County, Missouri. Jim Lane, leading Kansas troops, had nearly destroyed that county seat, which served as the supply base for Sterling Price's Confederate Army. Regardless of the purpose of the attack, emotions ran so high on these matters that sometimes little reasoning was evident in many of the actions of either group of loyalists. The men, women, and children of the border found they were entrenched in a fight for the land that they held as dear as life itself and, in fact, for their very lives themselves.

Whether or not Cole Younger ever knew that he had been mentioned by name in a dispatch to the President of the United States is not known. Had he known, it undoubtedly would have been the highlight of his life. While reports indicate that it was a fact that Cole Younger made an appearance in Lawrence that fateful day, he was not among the men who decided to take on more than the original plan of finding Jim Lane, hanging him, and burning down his town. Murdering innocent townspeople was not on the agenda, but with the capture of Lane unfulfilled, tempers ignited and chaos reigned. Cole, a young man of only nineteen, was said to have been most actively involved in the search for Lane. Ironically, it was at Lawrence that Cole began to make a name for himself as a fearless soldier and a fair man. He assisted many men and women out of the way of imminent danger as the other guerrillas laid waste to their town and ruthlessly killed over 150 men. His participation at Lawrence was an event in Cole's life of which he was not proud, although at the time he welcomed the notoriety of being associated with Quantrill. Cole Younger, even at that early age, had begun to build himself into a legend.

Life before the border war was fairly predictable for Thomas Coleman "Cole" Younger. Named after his uncles, Missouri legislator Coleman Younger and Thomas Fristoe, Cole was born on January 15, 1844. His family was affluent, and Cole and his four brothers enjoyed the sort of foolhardiness that can accompany the rearing of fourteen children. The family Younger not only was quite respected and extremely well liked but had been an established part of western Missouri society for several years by the time they settled in Harrisonville, Cass County. After his incarceration for bank robbery, Cole often referred to the prestige enjoyed by his grandparents, both socially and politically. The family background of the Younger brothers was indeed an integral part of their life story. The family was extremely influential throughout the pioneer years before the Civil War and remained so during the Reconstruction years that followed. Many of the Younger and Fristoe aunts and uncles would later step forward to influence, aid, and abet their nephews as they made their individual decisions to step outside the accepted boundaries of law and order. To know the outlaw Younger brothers it is important to know something of their personal roots.

Originally coming to the United States from Strasbourg on the Rhine and arriving in eastern Maryland, the first of the American Youngers settled in Virginia. Once here, they were considered to be among the aristocracy of the time, counting in their number relations to the very highest echelon of American society.

On December 28, 1783, in Hampshire County, Virginia, Cole's paternal grandfather, Charles Lee Younger, was born. Charlie, as he was known, was the son of Joshua Logan Younger and Elizabeth Lee. His father was with George Washington's army at Valley Forge, and his mother was related to Revolutionary War general "Light-Horse Harry" Lee, the father of Robert E. Lee. "Light-Horse Harry" was said to be a remote descendant of Lady Godiva of Coventry. One of his father's seventeen children, Charlie evidently believed in the sanctity of the large family and sired nineteen children of his own.

After the death of his first wife, Nancy Toney, Charlie and his children settled in Crab Orchard, Kentucky, where he bred and raced fine horses. He married Sarah Sullivan Purcell in 1807, and six more children were born, including Henry Washington, who was to become the father of the outlaws.[3] Younger family history records that Charlie grew weary of his involvement with horses and, seeking more excitement, joined with a volunteer group that left for eastern Missouri to fight Indians sometime around 1808. That same history reports that Charlie became a captain in the Missouri Volunteers and, at one point, served alongside Daniel Boone. In any event, by 1822, he was living in Callaway County, Missouri, on the Auxvasse Creek. Charlie joined a mule-driving expedition and after traveling to Colorado with the mules and making quite a profit, he settled in Clay County, Missouri, to gather his family together in one location. As his children began to leave home and become successful on their own, Charlie and Sarah relocated south to Cass County, where Charlie evidently purchased several hundred acres of farmland. With this purchase, he became one of the wealthiest landowners in the western part of Missouri.

After his move to Cass County, Charlie became involved with a neighbor named Parmelia Wilson. Although Charlie was still married to Sarah, and would be until his death, he fathered nine children with Parmelia.[4] Most notable of these children was Adeline, whose sons, Grat, Bob, and Emmett Dalton, would become the notorious Dalton Gang. The Dalton Gang, while involved in many robberies throughout the West, Oklahoma, and California, are best remembered for their ill-fated attack on the town of

Coffeyville, Kansas, in 1892. The Daltons attempted to show the world that they were more talented at bank robbery than their Younger cousins, who were then serving life sentences at Stillwater Prison, by attempting to rob two banks simultaneously. The attempt failed miserably, and Bob and Grat, along with their gang members, were killed. Emmett, seriously wounded, was captured and served a long sentence in prison. On his release, Emmett moved to Hollywood, California, where he sold real estate and wrote a book chronicling his adventures entitled *When the Daltons Rode*.

Charlie was very well known in Cass County and neighboring St. Clair County, where he additionally owned several hundred more acres. With his children growing in number every year and the size of his landholdings, Charlie was creating a veritable dynasty in western Missouri. Although his children with Parmelia were born "Wilsons," before Charlie died in 1854, he stipulated in his last will and codicil that each of his Wilson heirs was free to use the Younger last name.[5] All the children used their father's name.

A few years before he died, Charlie fathered two more children with his mulatto slave, Elizabeth Simpson. Their son Simpson was fourteen when he served as a corporal in the 27th Colored Infantry of the Union Army.[6] After the war, he was sent to Oberlin College in Ohio to be educated as was stipulated in his father's will. While attending Oberlin he played baseball for the Resolute Baseball Club, a championship team.[7] In later years, while living in Kansas City, Simpson attempted to attend a performance at the Ninth Street Theater owned by A. Judah. Although they held tickets for the orchestra circle, Simpson and his guest were refused seating there. They were informed that the rules of the theater did not allow colored persons to sit anywhere other than in the balcony. Simpson brought suit against the theater, and the case of *Younger v. Judah*, July 2, 1892, reached the Supreme Court of Missouri. Although the case was decided against Simpson Younger on the basis that the state could not determine the management policies of theaters, it stood as one of the first segregation tests in Missouri.[8]

Cole Younger's maternal grandfather was Richard Marshall Fristoe. Named after United States Chief Justice John Marshall, who was said to be an uncle, Richard was born on March 22, 1789, in Knoxville, Tennessee. Born to the wealthy and social Elizabeth Lovell and the Reverend Robert Fristoe, Richard was considered to be quite a catch for any of the charming young women of eastern Tennessee. Richard evidently had little time for courting ladies, however, and on October 6, 1814, he joined Capt. Daniel Price's Company of Mounted Volunteer Infantry from East Tennessee. He soon was appointed a lieutenant and was active in what became known as the War of 1812. He served under Maj. John Chiles and was present at the Battle of New Orleans.[9]

Fristoe returned home to Tennessee about May of 1815 and began courting the lovely Mary "Polly" Sullivan of nearby McMinnville. Polly was from a wealthy and prestigious family herself. She was said to be a grandniece of future United States President Zachary Taylor. Richard and Polly were married in August of 1815. In June, the following year, their first daughter, Bursheba Leighton, was born. In 1817, Richard's pioneer spirit directed him to follow the hundreds of other adventurers from Kentucky and Tennessee to the frontier of Missouri. Living in Lafayette County, the Fristoes added five more children to their family. Richard enjoyed his successful work as a farmer, but he learned quickly to invest his profits in land and property. He bought and leased a store and owned and operated Fristoe's Fish Trap on the Little Blue River. The fish trap was very popular, as the steamships used the spot where it was located as a landing when new residents began to pour into the newly developed area.[10] Settlement in the area was popular, and eventually a county needed to be created. Richard Fristoe suggested that the county be named after Andrew Jackson, whom he had admired since serving under him at the Battle of New Orleans. Whether this was the sole reason for the naming of Jackson County is doubtful, but Jackson County it was and the future metropolis of Kansas City was under way.

Now that the county was established, the people living within the settlement decided that they needed to name the town. Richard Fristoe had been appointed one of the first three judges of Jackson County and, along with Abraham McClelland and Henry Burris, he named the "Town of Independence." Known for many noteworthy events and residents over the next 150 years, Independence is probably best known as the hometown of President Harry S. Truman.

In 1832, Judge Fristoe and his family moved to Independence and resided in a large, beautiful home in the center of town. They owned hundreds of acres of lush farmland by now, and their pastures and cornfields stretched for miles. Their last daughter, Frances, was the first female born in Independence. Judge Fristoe continued to serve on the county court, and in 1833 he was elected a member of the Missouri State Legislature, in which he served two terms. He also was postmaster for several years. A well-respected and socially prominent man, Richard died on one of the several farms that he owned just outside Independence on November 21, 1845. He was buried in Independence, but his marker was destroyed during the Civil War and the exact location of his grave has become unknown.[11]

That the matching of Henry Washington Younger to Bursheba Leighton Fristoe was a merging of old money and new pioneer spirit cannot be denied. Known as two of the best and brightest in Jackson County society circles, the young couple brought to their engagement prestige of both name and accomplishment.[12] Young Henry was already involved with local politics, and the quiet Miss Fristoe was the respected judge's daughter. Henry and Bursheba were married in 1830. They enjoyed fourteen children: Laura, Isabelle, Anne, Richard, Mary Josephine, Caroline, Thomas Coleman, Sally, James Hardin, Alphae, John Harrison, Emma, Robert Ewing, and Henrietta. By the year of the birth of their last child, life for the Henry Younger family of Missouri looked promising indeed.

2

A Missouri Family

"No trees were there on the prairie
And long and heavy the grass
Few were the settlers and scattered
On the western frontier vast."
—"Lee's Summit" by Miss Dollie Breitenbaugh, 1894

Henry Washington Younger was a man of ambition. Development of western Missouri was still in its infancy when he came of age. With an astute sense of the future, Henry realized that the men with power and property would soon be the forces of this new frontier. When his family moved from Crab Orchard, Kentucky, to eventually reside in Clay County, Missouri, Henry had already begun planning for prosperity. Henry's older brother Coleman became active in Clay County politics as soon as he was of an age to do so. Although Coleman was only ten months older, he was extremely dynamic and often tutored Henry in both business and politics. Henry learned quickly and realized that the county of his father-in-law, Jackson County, would soon be open to many new ventures. Hopefully, hand-in-glove with the new ventures would come fortune.

Henry borrowed a small amount of funding from Richard Fristoe in order to start up an enterprise near Fristoe's Fish Trap. Henry created a ferry business near the town of Randolph on the Little Blue River. The proceeds from the ferry business enabled him to buy a small piece of land in Jackson County and acquire a few slaves. One of the slaves was left to operate the ferry business

in his name as Henry concentrated on expanding his property.[1]
He had his father's knack for recognizing the finest of horses and
began a side business of buying and selling horses to the new
residents of Jackson County. By 1850, Henry was wealthy enough
to purchase over a hundred acres of prime farmland in a settlement
called Strother. Strother would be incorporated as the "Town of
Lee's Summit" in 1868.[2] Working alongside one another, Henry
and his sons and sons-in-law erected a large, two-story house on
their new property. By the time the house was finished, however,
Henry had decided he wanted to master the business aspects of
landownership and he leased the land and house to tenant farmers.
Parcels of this land would remain in the Younger name for the next
couple of decades. Henry's next move was to buy an additional
several hundred acres northwest of his original Jackson County
farm. Henry and Bursheba decided to live here with their growing
family.

Henry was also developing his political expertise and aspirations
at this time. A controversy continues today regarding whether or
not Henry did, indeed, serve as part of the Missouri State General
Assembly. His name appears in some county and personal records
as having been a "rep," yet a detailed look at the official records
of the Assembly fails to turn up his name.[3] His brother Coleman
is listed, however.[4] A Democrat after the dissolution of the Whig
Party in Clay County, Coleman served as Clay County's
representative in the Missouri General Assembly in 1846.[5] Coleman's third wife, Augusta Peters Inskeep, was the aunt of outlaw
Johnny Ringo. Additionally, it is Coleman's marriage to Augusta
that brings the only "family" link between the Youngers and the
James family. Benjamin Simms, the second husband of Zerelda
Cole James, the mother of Frank and Jesse, was part of Augusta's
family.[6]

Land was free and plentiful when the neighboring territory of
Kansas came into existence. Previous to the second election in the
new territory, Missourians were anxious to obtain the powers that
would enable them to participate in the new area's direction and
operation. The issue of whether or not the new territory would
become a free or slave state was at the core of many burning
debates. The thought of two states so closely bound by an anxious

border unnerved many citizens in the communities of the border. Their loyalties were drawn, but they wanted to possess the bounties that each side enjoyed. Many Missourians crossed the border before Kansas's second election and staked out a small square of land. "I claim this spot of ground as my residence" was all that needed to be said or done to give them the right to vote in any Kansas election.[7] Many of the Missourians didn't even go through that exercise and, without ceremony, simply voted. On March 30, 1855, although he had never lived in Kansas, Henry Younger, a conservative Unionist with slaves, was elected to the Shawnee Mission Legislature along with A. M. Coffee and David Lykins.[8] It is perhaps from this membership that Henry's name was mentioned as "rep" in some of the annals of county history.

By 1856, Henry owned several thousand acres of Jackson County. He and Bursheba were very happy in Strother and had earned the respect of their neighbors easily. Their children were well liked and several attended the school that stood on the property of one of the town's founding members, William B. Howard.[9] The boys often hunted and fished on the property around the original homestead. Interestingly, whether due to the family name or not, this land would be a constant source of legal entanglement even decades after Henry's death. In fact, Mrs. Hada M. Frey filed suit against Henry, Bursheba, and their heirs in 1929 over some of the land her family purchased in 1854 so as to clear the title.[10]

The Younger parents and children enjoyed the popularity which befalls a wealthy, well-mannered family. Only the death of eighteen-month-old Alphae cast a shadow over the time the family lived in Jackson County.

Sometime in the late summer of 1856, Henry decided to expand his landholdings into neighboring Cass County. Having already scouted the area extensively, he purchased several hundred acres of farmland in the center of the county. A house was erected, and the Younger family, minus the girls, who had already married by that time, relocated to the new community. On leaving Jackson County, Henry deeded some of his property to his daughters Laura Kelley, Belle Hall, and Anne Jones. The remainder was divided for lease or sale to both tenant and other farmers. Previously, on April 15, 1852, the Jackson County Court purchased 160 acres of Henry's land for $2,000 so that a county poor farm could be established.[11]

The area in which the Youngers settled, known as Grand River Lodge, was prime to become a city. Congressman Albert G. Harrison was very popular with his constituents in the area, and to show their respect, the city was named Harrisonville. In 1857, the men of Harrisonville met at a scenic spot on the Younger property popularly called Younger's Grove. Harrisonville needed a new mayor, and the host of the event was among the candidates.[12] By 1859, Henry Younger would become mayor of the City of Harrisonville.

Since his arrival in Harrisonville, Henry had become a merchant. He opened a dry goods operation and later ran a successful livery in partnership with his son Dick and his half-brother C. Frank Younger. Henry was not only very successful but very popular, as well. The Youngers moved to a house in the center of Harrisonville purchased from Dr. Henry D. Palmer in 1859.[13] Henry would frequently travel into Independence and Kansas City to attend to business and act as mail contractor. On these trips he would carry letters and messages to the larger population centers as men did in those days whenever they had occasion to travel any distance.

Although Henry's political involvement took back seat to his businesses during his early days in Harrisonville, he was known always to share his opinion on the various situations involving the people of Cass County whenever he was asked. Of course the Kansas situation was never far from the minds of the Missourians living on the Kansas-Missouri border.

While in Harrisonville, the Younger girls, along with their brothers Cole and Jim, attended classes taught by their cousin Stephen Carter Ragan.[14] Education was very important to the Youngers.

Caroline was considered the prettiest and most outgoing of the Younger girls. She was called by the nickname "Duck" and was the pet of her father and brothers. Caroline married the Youngers' wrangler, George Clayton, and they had two children.[15]

Charles Richard Younger was the eldest son of Henry and

Bursheba. Named after both his paternal and maternal grandfathers, he was the pride and joy of his parents and was held in awe and reverence by his brothers and sisters. Called Dick, Richard Younger was a handsome, intelligent young man with his father's interest in civic affairs and his mother's genial nature. Dick attended prestigious Chapel Hill College in Lexington, Missouri.[16] The college was highly recommended to Dick by his Fristoe relatives and counted as some of its eminent graduates U.S. Senator F. M. Cockrell, Governor John S. Marmaduke, Joseph W. Mercer, and Col. John T. Crisp.

The Youngers were a tight-knit family, and each member paid close attention to the others' successes and failures. Isabella Frances was born in 1834, the second daughter. She married Richard S. Hall in Jackson County in 1856. Richard Hall was a shopkeeper who later expanded his business to become a blacksmith as well.[17] The family lived in Lee's Summit, original home of the Younger family. Belle and Richard were quite popular there. Richard owned the first breech-loading shotgun in town, and Belle was one of the first ladies to possess a modern sewing machine, a folding-leaf Singer.[18]

Upon graduation from Chapel Hill, Dick Younger returned home to Harrisonville and, influenced by Richard Hall, started his own small livery business with his brother-in-law, Will Kelley.[19] Laura Helen, the eldest child of Henry and Bursheba Younger, married William H. Kelley before the Border War and the Civil War. Before they were married, Kelley was a freighter over the Santa Fe Trail.[20] Laura and Will raised three children, one of them Kelley's by his first wife.[21]

Dick was extremely well liked in Harrisonville and was expected to fare exceedingly well in the county's business and society circles. He became involved with the Masons and joined the Grand Lodge of Missouri, Prairie Lodge Number 90, raised in 1860.[22]

In March of 1860, a lawsuit was filed against Dick and Will claiming that they were in the debt of M. D. Lrefner for goods purchased. The judgment went for Younger and Kelley, however, and the "debts" were left to Lrefner.[23]

Cole Younger idolized his brother Dick. In Cole's eyes, Dick was everything a Younger should or could be. At the same time, the feisty young Cole felt that he would always stand in his brother's shadow. Cole was a very good-looking young man himself but without the polish and gentility of Dick. The young men each exhibited an air of outward confidence, yet Cole's thoughts and ideas always seemed to be relegated to second opinion whenever his brother was involved in the conversation. Born in 1838, Dick was six years older than Cole. By the time Dick was twenty-one and Cole fifteen, both young men were actively developing and honing their charm and persuasiveness. Where Dick was rational and calm, Cole was high-spirited and impulsive. Henry Younger could only hope that young Coleman would follow in the steps of his son Dick, of whom he was extremely proud. Regardless of how Cole felt about Dick's high esteem within the community, as well as the family, the competition served him well. Always striving to maintain the level of achievement and respect of his brother, Cole started to develop a quick mind and captivating personality of his own.

It was with shock and disbelief that the Harrisonville community learned of the sudden death of Charles Richard Younger on August 17, 1860. The Harrisonville *Democrat* reported: "It is with great pain that we chronicle the death of our young friend C. R. Younger." The article goes on to describe how Dick had voted in the city election two days prior to his death and was seen in town during the following day. On the night of the third day, however, he was dead at his parents' home at the age of twenty-two. The cause of his sudden death has never been explained, although appendicitis has been mentioned. The *Democrat* report reflects the extreme amount of respect the young man had earned: "His remains were followed to the grave by a large concourse of friends and relations and by the brothers of the mystic eye who took charge of the corpse and had it interred with the usual ceremonies of that ancient order."[24] Dick Younger's remains have never been located, but it is very possible that they lie along with those of his father somewhere on the property that was once the Younger farm. It is also possible that both men are buried somewhere in the Orient Cemetery in Harrisonville.

The Younger family was devastated. Henry Younger was so distraught he temporarily turned his businesses over to the management of his brother Frank. Although Bob Younger was only six at the time of Dick's death, Dick was his hero. Bob would always resent his brother Cole's attempts at replacing Dick in Bob's esteem.

Cole was unbelieving of the event and undoubtedly felt in a total quandary as to his future course. Cole had applied to Chapel Hill College at the urging of Dick but had felt uncomfortable with the idea of spending his formative years inside a brick institution. Cole didn't want to go to college. With Dick's passing, Cole wondered if his father would introduce him, also, into the business life of Harrisonville. Cole Younger felt that perhaps his turn as the favored son had arrived, and he threw himself into an aspect of their lives that he knew would draw his father's interest: local politics.

3

The Border

Them Kansans ordered my family to come outside
and said right now
While the house was burned, all the goods were
packed and without a sound our home was burned
to the ground.
And I swore to hell that I'd fight you back
You Kansas thieves can't steal like that
You got us freezing in our own fields
It's the blade of my knife I'll make you feel
I'll fight you 'hawkers and kill with ease
You've ruined my life, I'll make yours grieve.
　　　　　—"Jayhawking" by James C. Edwards

The plantation system of slavery was not the rule in Missouri.
Although many of the farmers of Missouri came from slave states
and attempted to utilize the slave system, the farms were considerably smaller and the farmers most often worked alongside their
slaves. The principal crop in many areas of western Missouri was
hemp. Hemp was of great use to the Southern states because,
among other things, it was used as rope to tie the cotton bales.
Farming the hemp product was long, hard labor best accomplished
by the collective efforts of many workers. This in itself was one of
the main incentives for the continued use of slaves in western
Missouri and why the Missouri farmers were so threatened by the
"Free State" abolitionists of Kansas. In retrospect, however more
desirable it would have been to have them free their slaves and pay
them for their work, these Southern pioneers were availing them-

selves of the system that their families had known and successfully
employed for decades. For the most part, the farmers didn't fully
realize they were usurping basic human rights by holding slaves.

The Kansas-Nebraska Act of 1854 was designed to allow settlers
the freedom of choice as to whether or not the new territory of
Kansas should be slave or free. At the same time the measure
incorporated the rule of popular sovereignty, which allowed
"squatters" to come into Kansas and claim land. The Missourians
crossed the border in great numbers at this time as a means of
influencing the pro-slavery vote. The act repealed the Missouri
Compromise of 1820, which had served to outlaw slavery in the
Kansas Territory. The current act established the principle of
congressional nonintervention in the Kansas and Nebraska terri-
tories. Yet with all the Missourians crossing the border to vote on
the issues at hand, the newly elected Kansas legislature of 1854–55
issued its statement from Lecompton legalizing slavery in Kansas.
As far as the longer-established Kansans were concerned, the
matter was not settled. Since it was evident that the question of
slavery would be decided by the number of bodies available to vote
one way or the other, the Kansas Free Staters began to bring in
homesteaders from other states who agreed with their beliefs.

Emotions ran high, and by 1855 violence was occurring on a
regular basis as the Missourians and Kansans crossed the border in
an attempt to drive out the opposing factions. Crusaders and
opportunists emerged to take advantage of the explosive issue.
John Brown, with his single-minded fanaticism, drove relations to
a fever pitch. Looting and murder were not uncommon acts on
either side of the border as committed by the Jayhawkers of Kansas
and the Bushwhackers of Missouri. Two men in particular would
rise to power to encourage and escalate the chaotic border resent-
ments.

On January 29, 1861, James H. Lane was elected to the U. S.
Senate representing the new free state of Kansas. Lane's hatred of
Missourians was legendary, and he had been fighting along with
the other Kansans nearly from the beginning of the troubles. Soon
after the new senator's arrival in Washington D.C., Lane succeeded
in gaining the favor of Abraham Lincoln by organizing protection
for the capital immediately after Fort Sumter. Within months,

Lincoln granted Lane the authority to raise troops in Kansas by appointing him a brigadier general in the Union Army. Lane proceeded to gather together the Jayhawkers who had previously been involved with him as they had engaged in daily battle with the Missourians. He formed the 3rd, 4th, and 5th Kansas Regiments, known as Redlegs for the blood-colored leggings they wore.

While Lane was conducting raids into Missouri, by legal means or not, Charles R. Jennison was also rising to prominence within the Jayhawker movement. Jennison, originally from the East, was a doctor with a fierce belief in abolition. He formed a vicious vigilante group known for plundering and murdering those not in his favor up and down the Missouri border. Finally, in 1861, Kansas governor Charles Robinson persuaded the federal authorities to commission Jennison a colonel so as to place him and his volunteer troops under military discipline. "Jennison's Jayhawkers" became the 7th Kansas Volunteer Cavalry Regiment. Interestingly, "Buffalo" Bill Cody, as a young man, was a member of the 7th Kansas organization.[1]

In September 1861, the troops of Confederate general Sterling Price defeated federal forces in a major battle at Wilson's Creek, Missouri. After their victory, Price began leading his soldiers north through Missouri. They were cheered by the Missourians in nearly every town they passed through in the southwestern part of the state. Lane was infuriated. He decided to gather his staunchest troops, cross into Missouri, and meet the Southern supporters on their own ground. Over 1,500 Jayhawkers, led by Lane, crossed the fields of Missouri, destroying the farms and settlements of all those who they had decided were in agreement with the Southern sentiments. On September 22, Lane and his men plundered and then destroyed the Missouri town of Osceola in St. Clair County. The banks, stores, and homes were unmercifully looted and nearly a dozen civilians were killed as they tried to save their belongings. The courthouse was completely razed, and nearly all possessions of any worth, including family heirlooms, money, and livestock, were taken by the Jayhawkers on their retreat. The sacking of Osceola would be remembered by the Missourians for a very long time.

In the summer of 1861, Henry Younger's livery in Harrisonville was looted by the Jayhawkers. In the dead of night, nearly everything that could be carried or driven was taken by the Kansas troops. Forty fine saddle horses and wagons and carriages worth over $4,000 belonged to Kansas before daybreak. While this was the most effective and costly raid Henry's business would endure, it was not the last. Several times in the next twelve months Henry lost horses and livery supplies to small groups of Kansas raiders.

Recovering from looting and destruction had become a way of life for the people on the border by the end of the year. Retaliation was a word that was beginning to claim a prominent place on the lips of nearly every farmer in western Missouri. While the farmers and businessmen gathered in clusters to decide what means should be employed to stop the Kansans from crossing the border and attacking their settlements, the young men of the border formed to talk of other, perhaps more effective, ways of stopping the Jayhawkers. The methods they discussed were not much different from the acts of the Jayhawkers as they decided to fight fire with fire. These young "bushwhackers" were dead serious and beyond "legal" means would fight as brutally and as absolutely as their opponents. The day of the Missouri guerrilla had arrived.

Missouri Enters the War

1857	The Supreme Court of the United States announces the Dred Scott Decision. Scott was a Missouri slave who was determined by the court to be property without any rights of citizenship.
1861	Kansas becomes a Free State.
1861	The Missouri Convention votes to stay in the Union.
April 1861	Missouri governor Claiborne F. Jackson refuses President Lincoln's call for troops.
June 17, 1861	First confrontation between Union soldiers and the Missouri state militia under Governor Jackson at Booneville.
August 10, 1861	The battle of Wilson's Creek.
July 22, 1861	The state convention meets to remove pro-Confederate leaders and appoint those who support the Union. Hamilton R. Gamble is appointed governor.
September 1861	Jackson attempts meeting of legislature. Attendance not adequate to be determined a "legal session." Those attending vote to secede.
March 1862	Confederate troops defeated at Pea Ridge.

4

The Murder of Henry Younger

When the guerilla awoke he was a giant! He took in,
as it were, and at a single glance, all the immensity of
the struggle. He saw that he was hunted and
proscribed; that he had neither a flag or a
government; that the rights and amenities of civilized
warfare were not to be his; that a dog's death was
certain if he surrendered even in the extremist agony
of battle: that the house which sheltered him had to
be burnt; the father who succored him had to be
butchered; the mother who prayed for him had to be
insulted; the sister who carried food to him had to be
imprisoned; the neighbor who witnessed his combats
had to be laid waste; the comrade shot down by his
side had to be put to death as a wild beast—and he
lifted up the black flag in self-defense and fought as
became a free man and a hero.
        —John Newman Edwards in *Noted Guerillas*

John Newman Edwards would attempt to immortalize the Missouri guerrillas and justify their every action with prose so sympathetic and florid that his words would be difficult to discount. Yet, as with the Jayhawkers, many of the Bushwhackers were not moral or honorable men. William Clarke Quantrill, informally called Charlie, was born in 1837 in Canal Dover, Ohio. It seems he was never one to represent himself with absolute honesty, and the stories that circulated about Quantrill were a far cry from fact.

23

He claimed to have come from Maryland and to have become involved in the border war because of his need to avenge the death of his brother at the hands of James Montgomery's Jayhawkers while the brothers were crossing Kansas on a trip to California. Reality was a different story.

In 1859, Quantrill settled in Kansas, where he taught school briefly. He became involved with the Jayhawkers, stealing horses to sell for profit. In 1860, along with five other men, he attempted to steal slaves from a farm in Jackson County. Whether by design or accident, the group of raiders was ambushed and several of the men were killed.[1] Quantrill, possibly an informant according to some researchers, was spared, and he was next seen in Missouri at the Battle of Wilson's Creek fighting with Price's army, although he was not affiliated with any official military group. He also is said to have been present at other skirmishes and battles immediately following Wilson's Creek.

By the fall of 1861, when the border problems had erupted into serious hostilities, Quantrill was the leader of a small group of Jackson County youths who were anxious to engage in physical negotiations with the Jayhawkers. After the young men were made to see that there was no other organized group to deal specifically with the border situation and the wanton destructiveness of the Jayhawkers, the band under Quantrill doubled, then tripled, in number. Eventually, when the Quantrill organization was full grown, 43.5 percent of the troops had a least one relation active in the group. Ninety-six percent of the leaders had brothers or cousins who were also involved with Quantrill.[2] No matter that Quantrill had a questionable background and no real military experience; he was able to gather a group of dedicated "troops" bent on revenge and anxious to become part of an organized effort to confront the Jayhawkers in defense of their homes and farmlands. Enfolding into his ranks such determined personalities as George Todd and William Gregg, Quantrill secured his leadership by providing these men with immediate action through merciless raids on Union sympathizers throughout Jackson County.

Mary Josephine was considered the most adventurous of the Younger daughters. As a young girl she would ride her horse at breakneck speeds over the fields of Strother. Near her twentieth birthday, Josie married an unbridled young man named John Jarrette. The marriage was not particularly popular with her parents or sisters, but Josie's brothers, especially Cole, found Jarrette fascinating. John and Cole became fast friends, and it was Jarrette who suggested to Cole that he become involved with Quantrill during the border troubles. Cole had been urging his father to take a more active role in the fight against the Kansans, but Henry Younger resisted, choosing instead to attend political meetings and trying to proceed with business as usual. Although his businesses were the target of the raiders on several occasions, Henry and his family were able to keep control of their wealth during this time due to their own protective efforts and those of their friends and neighbors. In a letter written eighteen years later, Cole explained his family's interaction with the other citizens of their community:

> At the most critical period of the great strife, in 1862, we had five different farms in Cass and Jackson Counties, with corn cribs full of corn. When food became difficult to obtain, I told all the poor people to help themselves and take what corn they needed without charge. I made no distinction then between Federals and Confederates.[3]

Cole's inaccurate reference to "I" instead of "my father" is typical of the ego that developed through Cole's victories and successes during his time with Quantrill. Regardless of who was given credit, such was the Younger policy. The Cass and Jackson county communities were greatly appreciative of Henry's generosity.

In the fall of 1861, a dance was given for Martha Mockbee at the home of her parents, Cuthbert and Sarah, in Harrisonville.[4] The Mockbees were well respected in the city and were close friends of the Youngers. Originally from Kentucky, the Mockbees were in sympathy with the Southern cause but had yet to officially align themselves with any organized movement. Two of the Younger girls attended the party, along with their brothers Cole and Jim. During the evening, one of the girls, either Sally or Caroline, was approached by Irvin Walley. Walley was one of the militiamen stationed at Harrisonville. Walley asked the young lady to dance, but she refused, as she was not impressed with the soldier's strong-arm attempts to force other young women to dance with him. Rebuffed, Walley likely had some unkind words to say to the girl. Defending his sister, Cole demanded that Walley leave her alone. Turning the situation to his favor by using his military position, Walley asked Cole where Quantrill was. Cole claimed he didn't know, which was likely the truth. Walley responded that Cole was a liar. Cole immediately struck the soldier, and the two were soon wrestling on the floor. Walley drew his pistol, but the fight was immediately ended by the other young men at the party.

Cole returned home with his sisters to tell his father what had transpired. Henry was disturbed by the incident, as he knew that Cole's loyalties were strong and the young man was not usually of a mind to let unfavorable events fade into the past. Henry felt that the safety of his son was now at stake and that the Union troops would look for any excuse to physically harm Cole. Henry suggested Cole leave immediately for one of the Younger farms in Jackson County and stay away from Walley and his friends.[5] That night after Cole left, Walley did indeed show up at the Younger house demanding that Henry turn Cole over to him. Walley said that Cole was a spy for Quantrill. Henry denied such an allegation, and the soldiers left, vowing to find Cole on their own. Concerned for Cole, Henry sent word that he should stay in the "bush" until the incident blew over. Cole decided that he would be better able to protect himself if he were armed and somehow secured a shotgun and a revolver. By arming himself, whether in self-defense or not, Cole was in violation of John C. Fremont's orders that no one not affiliated with an organized group of recognized militia bear arms. Cole Younger, at the age of seventeen, was now an outlaw. Since it was now impossible to return home, Cole felt that it was time to align himself with those attempting to bring the local upheaval under control through military means. With the single-minded determination of a young man anxious to prove his worth and, additionally, his independence from his father, Cole joined with Jarrette. By the first of the year, 1862, the two were members of Quantrill's band of Missouri guerrillas.

During the first five months of 1862, Cole engaged in many skirmishes with the Quantrill organization. In his autobiography, he wrote that several of the encounters with militiamen that winter were in the vicinity of Independence and that nearly all of them were victories for the guerrillas. The cost in lives was great on both sides. Quantrill's men, many of them under the age of twenty-one, were not to be denied. Each victory spurred their desire for greater conquests. Allen Parmer, the future brother-in-law of Frank and Jesse James, as well as several others who would be associated with the postwar activities of the Jameses and Youngers, was a member of Quantrill's group at this time.

The inability of Sterling Price to hold Missouri for the Confederacy caused Quantrill's ranks to swell as former Confederate soldiers returned home in defeat. In February of 1862, Maj. Gen. Henry Halleck of the Union Army provided these men with the opportunity to post bond and take loyalty oaths, thus being "paroled." Many took advantage of the opportunity to return home to check on their families and immediately join groups of irregular soldiers such as Quantrill. Frank James was one of these men. Having fought under Price in several battles, James took his oath and within weeks was riding with Cole and the others of Quantrill's soldiers.[6]

Quantrill disbanded his followers in May of 1862 in order to reorganize and replenish their supplies. Cole, Quantrill, and George Todd went to Hannibal, Missouri, attired as Union soldiers in an attempt to secure ammunition. Their mission successful, they returned to Kansas City, where they were engaged in the planning of their future assaults on June 20, 1862.

John Newman Edwards's attempt to glorify the James and Younger brothers as mighty warriors during the war resulted in several tales of either heroic or horrific proportions. One of the stories that Edwards told in his essay "A Terrible Quintette" concerned Cole and the Enfield rifle. Cole is said to have tested the new rifle by lining up fifteen federal soldiers and attempting to shoot through them to test the firepower of the rifle. When the first attempt failed to see the ball pass through all the soldiers, Cole is quoted as having said, "Cut them loose. The new Enfield shoots like a popgun." Cole is reported to have then shot the remaining soldiers one by one. This story is undoubtedly not true and evidently was created by Edwards or believed by him in order to make Cole out to be the ruthless guerrilla that Edwards painted Jesse James to be. Cole's respect for the lives of both his enemies and his comrades was noted throughout the guerrilla and Confederate network, and such disregard for humanity is completely uncharacteristic of Cole's nature.

Henry Younger desired to continue with his life as if everything was going to return to normal after the Kansas-Missouri difficulties were settled. This was apparent when he traveled to New York in the early spring of 1862. Cole was with Quantrill, and that organization was beginning to be well known and feared throughout Missouri and Kansas. The eldest son at the Younger home was now Jim, who was only fourteen. Strangely, Henry left his family amid all the terrorism running rampant in their area to go to New York to buy spring and summer goods to sell at his dry goods store. The selling of hats and notions hardly seems appropriate in light of his neighbors' fears of losing their farms and possessions due to the continuous raids of the Jayhawkers. Henry's actions demonstrated how important he felt it was to convince the people in his community that the border hostilities would soon be over and to encourage them to continue to live the lives they had before the turmoil had started. Henry was gone only a short time and advertised the success of his trip in May when he took out an elaborate notice soliciting business in the local newspaper. After the dry goods business was back in full operation, Henry devoted his energies to reorganizing his livery.

In mid-July, Henry and several of his employees traveled to Kansas City to sell the stock they had on hand in the Harrisonville livery. This was done to gain funds to replenish Henry's stables of fine horses. Horses were in great demand, and Henry continued to sell to soldiers and sympathizers of either cause. He preferred to stay "neutral" as an example to his neighbors of how they could best get along with the opposing factions as they continued to strive for a return to the tranquil existence they had known before the troubles escalated. Although much talked about in Harrisonville, Cole's alignment with Quantrill was not something that Henry discussed. Cole claims that there was an additional reason for Henry's trip north to Kansas City. While Henry had been in the East (Cole writes that he was in Washington on business relating to his mail commission), several more Jayhawker raids had occurred in Harrisonville which affected Henry's business. Cole claims that Henry went to Kansas City to talk to someone in the headquarters of the state militia to see what could be done about the continuous raids.[7] Perhaps Henry did speak to someone about the political situation in Cass County, but the raids by Kansas in that part of the state were certainly nothing new and the state militia had already demonstrated that it had little interest in becoming involved as peacemaker.

On July 20, Henry left his employees in Kansas City for a few days of recreation. There was little activity that went unnoticed during those tumultuous days. Henry's business transactions had been quite successful that week, and he hid over $1,500 in cash in a money belt. He placed it around his waist beneath his clothing for safekeeping on the long ride home. Henry boarded a buckboard and began his trip back to Harrisonville.

There are several versions of what happened next. The accounts of Henry's death, based on popular speculation, have been passed down through many generations. Rufus Burris of Washington Township told a story of how Henry was aware of being followed at some point and stopped at the Mockbee home. Not heeding his friends' advice to stay with them, Henry believed he could out-travel his pursuers and continued on. Soon, Burris claimed, William Mockbee saw seven soldiers in pursuit of Henry. Minutes later, the soldiers were seen retreating at high gallop toward Kansas City. The Mockbees rode in search of Henry and found his body lying on the Harrisonville Road.[8] This is an interesting story, but it is doubtful that Henry was close to Harrisonville when the ambush took place.

Jacob T. Palmer of Jackson County claimed that Henry was killed at the top of the Blue Hill beyond Dodson and that the soldiers removed his body to the town of Olathe, Kansas.[9] What is fact is that Henry's body was almost immediately found and returned to his widow, presumably by those in charge at the militia headquarters in Kansas City.

Cole's version of the murder of his father is perhaps the most accurate. Cole wrote that Henry was about one mile south of Westport, a suburb of Kansas City, when he was shot three times and killed. He continues that Mrs. Washington Wells and her son, Samuel, recognized the body and that Mrs. Wells guarded Henry while her son returned to Kansas City to inform the federal commanding officer, a Colonel Peabody, of the murder.[10] While it was probably known that Henry Younger was returning home to Cass County with a substantial amount of profit from his transactions, his murder was, most likely, political. There seems little doubt that Irvin Walley was the leader of the group of soldiers who killed Henry. Walley had sworn vengeance on Cole Younger, and the unsuspecting Henry had driven his buggy directly into that vengeance. Although some accounts say that $500 was taken from Henry, his body did not seem disturbed in any way after it fell from the wagon. The shots came from behind, as evidenced by his fatal wounds, but it is unlikely that theft was any motive for the ambush. Everyone who had any knowledge of the obviously cold-blooded crime assumed that whoever was responsible had deliberately and knowingly murdered Henry Washington Younger that June day of 1862.

Cole claimed that after Colonel Peabody came into possession of his father's body he found and removed nearly $2,000 from the hidden money belt. The money was returned to the Youngers along with Henry's body. Other accounts say that it was Henry's widow, Bursheba, who knew of the hidden belt and removed it from her husband's body herself. Regardless of who found it or how it was removed, the money remained with Bursheba and Henry was prepared for burial in Harrisonville.

Although he was with some of Quantrill's men that day in Kansas City, it is doubtful that Cole had occasion to visit with his father before Henry's death. Cole never mentioned seeing Henry in Kansas City. Yet within hours of the murder, the soldiers responsible were heard bragging about the murder of "Cole Younger's pappy." While Henry's body was being returned home, Cole was contemplating what would happen to his father's murderers.

In his autobiography Cole claims that Walley was formally charged with the murder of his father yet was released when his fellow soldiers provided him with an alibi. In a letter to Maj. Gen. Samuel R. Curtis from the headquarters of the Central District of

Missouri at Jefferson City dated January 27, 1863, Benjamin Loan, a brigadier general in the Missouri State Militia, wrote:

> Recently, I had arrested a Captain Walley, who had murdered one Harry Younger, in Jackson County, for his money. The evidence of his guilt was so clear and conclusive that he confessed it. Preferring that he should be regularly tried and punished, I directed a court to be held in Independence for that purpose. The witnesses, soldiers in the Fifth Regiment Missouri State Militia, who were stationed at Harrisonville, in Cass County, were sent to attend court. When on their way, they were bushwhacked by a band under Bird Younger, a son of the murdered man, and the court was not held.[11]

The "Bird" Younger referred to was no doubt Cole, who was sometimes called "Bud." Why Cole would kill the men who were to testify against Walley is questionable. It could have been that he did not know that the men were on their way to the court-martial. It's also possible that Cole believed that Walley was with them and planned to kill all the men who were in any way responsible for his father's death in one attack.

Cole wrote in a letter:

> In relation to Walley I will say: if I were what the world paints me, there could be no excuse except cowardice for my neglect to kill him. During the war I did everything in my power to get hold of him, but failed. . . . When I returned home from the war I could have killed Walley nearly any time but only by assassination. . . . I could not pollute my soul with such a crime.[12]

Cole Younger, trained and active as a guerrilla in one of the most aggressive and deadly companies of the war, undoubtedly would have found a way to kill Irvin Walley had he so desired. Bearing in mind the background and breeding of Bursheba Fristoe Younger, it is probable that Cole's mother asked him, and her other sons as well, to end the feud that had resulted in the death of her husband. Walley would be allowed to live with his own guilt over the murder of Henry. Such a request would likely have been honored by the Boys, as they loved and respected their mother above all else. Besides, they would know full well that Irvin Walley would be looking over his shoulder for the rest of his life awaiting the Youngers' retribution for the death of their beloved father.

Walley is mostly identified with the Jayhawker movement. Yet what his exact involvement was with either the Kansans or the Missouri militia at the time of Henry's death is shrouded in mystery. Irvin Walley was born on December 7, 1833, in Franklin County, Ohio. He grew up in Grundy County, Illinois, where his father, George, was a farmer.[13]

For some reason, Walley moved to Bates County, Missouri, in 1855. He bought a small parcel of land and worked as a farmer until he joined the Cass County Home Guards. Walley was enrolled as a private in Company B on June 27, 1861. From that point forward, Walley's military record becomes most interesting. He was appointed sergeant on July 25, 1861, and began serving as a scout. Walley served in this position until August 25, 1861, when he was appointed a captain in Company G.[14] It would have been at this point in his military involvement that Walley first met Cole at the ill-fated Mockbee party. For reasons not specified on his official military records, Walley resigned as captain in Company G and was mustered out of the Home Guards on October 31, 1861. He evidently rejoined Company B, serving as a private once again until he was mustered out a second time on February 28, 1862, allegedly due to an injury he sustained while engaged in a skirmish with Bushwhackers. If this is true, and it is according to Walley's military records and application for pension, who was he serving with when he and a group of Missouri militiamen ambushed Henry Younger? At the bottom of his papers appears this notice:

> Companies E.F.G. and H. Cass County (Missouri) Home Guards were attached to 9 Reg't Kansas Infantry as Companies E.F.H. and I. This transfer was made without proper authority.[15]

In his letter from the Missouri State Militia headquarters, Brig. Gen. Benjamin Loan referred to him as "a Captain Walley." Would this have been an official title or one retained from his days as a captain in Company G?

The mystery does not end there. According to a pension application by his wife in 1894, Walley's death was eventually caused by injuries he had received while serving with the Missouri Home Guards. In a letter to the pension committee dated December 26,

1894, E. F. Rogers, who had enlisted with Walley and served at the same time, claimed that Walley was injured sometime before January, 1862, when he fell from his horse during an engagement with Bushwhackers. According to Rogers, he was "struck in the belly" by the pommel on his saddle, badly "rupturing" him. Walley eventually died of problems relating to his prostate and urethra. Yet at the bottom of this affidavit is the following statement:

> This affiant was formerly a D. Ey. of this office. See his private letter to Comm. in 1882, in which he says he knows nothing about the particulars of his disability.[16]

If Walley was arrested by the Missouri Militia for the crime of killing Henry Younger, and if he did confess, as stated by Loan, he seems never to have been punished for his crime in any way. It appears that after the witnesses failed to show up, the case against Walley was simply dropped. Walley returned home to Bates County, settling in Butler, at the conclusion of the war. Soon after his return, he opened the first public house (hotel) in that town. Called the Walley Inn, the house remains standing at its original location today. The inn also served as a post office and a tavern. Interestingly, the following was once noted about the house when it was described for historical purposes: "Heavy iron rings found in the upstairs baseboards were said to have been used to restrain overnight prisoners, and possibly to chain runaway slaves seeking their freedom."[17]

Across from the inn, Walley developed some land which was eventually called "Walley's Addition" to the town of Butler. Politically, Walley was called a "staunch Republican and a fearless advocate of its principles." Walley, who would have been twenty-eight years old when he killed Henry Younger, married Mary E. Long of the Rutledge family of Virginia, on August 31, 1863, forty-three days after Henry's murder. The couple eventually had five children. The men of his command dead, by the hand of Cole or otherwise, Irvin Walley remained untouched. Walley died peacefully, with or without guilt regarding the death of Henry Younger, on April 28, 1894.

Rumors about Henry's murder circulated for decades. After the

Youngers were sent to Stillwater Prison, this affidavit was found in the diary of James Madison Smith (1811–1872) by his family:

> That three men of said name Cole, Bud and John Younger stopped at the house of Mr. Knight and in conversation informed him that they would kill Mr. J. Smith on first sight, but also told me that Mr. Smith was the cause of the death of the old man Younger. Cole Younger told Mr. Knight that the said Smith sent a party of soldiers to follow his father out of Kansas City and shot him in his carriage on his way home, etc. Signed, Augustus Quailes, dated 27 July, 1869.

J. M. Smith was a neighbor of the Youngers, living in Harrison-ville for many years. He served in the Missouri Home Guards from 1861 to 1864 under a Captain Robinson. No specific cause of his death has been found.

Another statement adds an extra dimension to the Walley story. A quote attributed to Gen. Jo. O. Shelby appeared in a newspaper several years after the Youngers had begun serving life sentences in prison. Shelby allegedly said that T. Jefferson Younger, half-brother of Henry, told him that Walley was not the man responsible for the murder. According to Shelby, T. J. said that the crime was committed by a Captain Stephens.[18] No action was undertaken to prove or disprove this claim, and none of the Youngers had any comment about this allegation.

The death of Henry Younger devastated his family and left a bleeding, open wound among his widow and children. Bob Younger, although still a boy, swore that he would follow in his father's footsteps of respect and honor by becoming the best farmer in Missouri. Henry's body was laid to rest in an unmarked grave for its protection. It was painfully clear that the war was really just beginning for the celebrated Younger family.

5

Quantrill Visits Lawrence

*Men at war never war with women, but women from
the South they take
To an ancient cell which killed as it fell with the aid of
the Union's weight.
We're gonna ride and track you down. We're gonna
burn Lawrence to the ground.*
— James C. Edwards, "Lawrence Massacre"

So many tall stories seem to be told about Cole Younger's military career that it is hard to decide which, if any, are based in fact. One of the more incredible tales appears to actually be true.

By August, 1862, Cole was deeply entrenched with the Quantrill band. His father buried, Cole had returned home long enough to warn his family not to engage in business with anyone not known to them. It was decided that Henry's dry goods store and livery were to be run by Frank Younger and various friends of Henry's until something more permanent could be decided on. Jim Younger, although only fourteen, felt obligated to join Quantrill and avenge the murder of his father. Cole, acting now as head of the family, told Jim that his responsibility was to watch over their mother and direct the activities of their two younger brothers. Both John and Bob, eleven and nine by now, were anxious to join the fray but knew that their place was at home with their mother and sisters should there be any further attacks on the family.

Having assured himself that the home front was secure, Cole returned north to Quantrill. On his arrival, Cole discovered that he was "on loan" to Confederate colonel Upton B. Hayes. Hayes was temporarily ensconced with his men at the Cowherd Farm at Lee's Summit. The Hayes group was being closely watched by the men of Col. James T. Buel's 7th Missouri Cavalry, which was stationed at the federal post in nearby Independence. Hayes's men were low in number, yet their presence made Buel nervous and he decided that action should be taken against them. His first move was to issue an order on August 10 that all citizens of Jackson County should be disarmed. His men would begin to carry out his command the next day. Hearing this, Hayes and Quantrill decided to attack the troops in Independence. If such a siege were successful, it would provide the guerrillas and soldiers with badly needed food and ammunition. A successful surprise attack would also serve to discredit Buel to his superiors. The troops and citizens of Independence knew that the Confederates at the Cowherd Farm would be angered by Buel's command and would likely make immediate plans of their own.

Buel decided to casually proceed with his plans to attack the Cowherd Farm while ignoring reports that Hayes and Quantrill were soon going to make their presence known in Independence. Either unbelieving of such a threat or simply lax, Buel allowed the Confederates to slip into Independence at dawn the morning of August 11 and catch the sleeping Union soldiers unaware.[1] One of the major reasons this was possible might have been because of the actions of Cole Younger two days previous to the attack. Hayes and Quantrill had both expressed their desire to embarrass Buel, yet knew that Buel's troops far outnumbered theirs. Having decided that they would need more information as to the size and location within Independence of the Union troops, it was suggested that one of their men would need to go inside the town, somehow, to provide them with the answers to their questions. Cole Younger volunteered.

Dressed as a "granny," complete with dress, shawl and bonnet, Cole mounted his horse sidesaddle, picked up some apples and vegetables and headed toward Independence. He rode through the town selling apples from his splint basket and recording his sales in a notebook. He made his way through the soldiers and civilians, noting their placement and number as he pretended to update his bookkeeping. He finally aroused the suspicions of a Union picket, and a confrontation occurred. The picket, while not suspecting that the apple woman was a man, did think that "she" might be doing something other than selling apples. He asked several times for the vendor to halt her activities. When he was ignored, the soldier commanded her. The "woman" encouraged her horse, and the picket attempted to grab her reins. Finally, unable to avoid this action, Cole pulled a large cap-and-ball revolver from under his shawl and shot the picket. As the man fell dead, soldiers were alerted to the fraud and began to chase the "apple woman." Guns exploding loudly and dust flying through the air, Cole made his escape and returned to Hayes and Quantrill with his report.[2] Two days later, the Confederate soldiers were in Independence. By the end of the battle, Buel had surrendered and the Confederates were in possession of wagonloads of food and ammunition. While only about 100 federals surrendered or were killed, over 200 Union soldiers fled Independence rather than face the deadly rebels.

Cole claimed that it was shortly after his appearance as the "apple woman" that he was enrolled in the Army of the Confederate States of America. He wrote:

> It was within a day or two after the surrender of Buel at Independence that I was elected as first lieutenant in Captain Jarrette's company in Col. Upton B. Hays' regiment, which was a part of the brigade of Gen. Joseph 0. Shelby.[3]

Cole said that he was sworn in by Col. Gideon W. Thompson and that he began serving as a "regular" on that day. Within days of Cole, several men who had been riding with Quantrill for a length of time were sworn into the army as well. Jarrette was not the only Younger relative serving with Quantrill. Others included brother-in-law George Clayton and cousins John Harris, Nathan Kerr, John McCorkle, and George and Tom Talley.

Hayes scouted the area of Strother for reinforcements shortly after the Independence confrontation. Union troops under the command of Col. Henry Foster were sent to Lone Jack to stop Hayes from being successful. Hayes had already made plans to take the town of Lone Jack prior to the arrival of Foster and his men. The battle, on August 16, which again began about dawn, was the fiercest in western Missouri. In his private account, Quantrill guerrilla Hiram George wrote:

> This was one of the hardest contested and bloodiest battles fought in Missouri, taking into consideration the numbers engaged. For three solid hours the conflict raged, and it was almost a hand to hand fight most of the time. Both parties had to fight on foot, there were so many hedge fences we could not use our horses. Finally the enemy withdrew, but very sullenly. I want to tell you we were as glad as they were.[4]

Cole, as well as others, said the battle lasted at least five hours. Cole was not injured. Colonel Foster was shot and captured. He was placed in a bed alongside his brother and told by one of the guerrilla leaders that he was going to be put to death. Cole, overhearing this statement, disagreed that Foster should be killed in such a manner, as the combat had ended. He pleaded Foster's case to the Confederate commanding officer and Foster was spared. Henry Foster later recounted this incident in a letter of appeal regarding Cole's pardon from Stillwater Penitentiary.[5]

After his experience at Lone Jack, Cole returned home to Harrisonville to check on his family. He was unaware that his family had been once again victimized by yet another Union captain.

Sarah Anne Younger was known to her family as Sally. Born in between her brothers Cole and Jim in 1846, Sally was a calm, level-headed girl with a staunch disposition. Cole told Harry Hoffman, his close friend in later years, that upon his return home he found his sister (presumably Sally, who was about eighteen years old at the time) distraught and crying in her room. When he asked her what the matter was, she said, "Brother, I am afraid to tell you." Prying the story out of her, Cole discovered that Sally had been assaulted by a federal captain who had invited himself and his fifteen soldiers to a get-together of the women of the neighborhood at Bursheba's house. The captain had taken a liking to the young lady and had asked her to walk outside with him. Out of fear, Sally accompanied him only to have him physically attack her. Cole told Sally to be brave and swore to her the captain wouldn't ever bother her again. Cole told Hoffman, "I had decided that minute to make him pay, and after he paid he would never be able to return to persecute my sister, or any other virtuous girl again."

Cole continued to tell Hoffman how he located the captain shortly afterward in Kansas City. Gathering twelve of his friends, Cole went after his enemy. He told the others that none of them must shoot the captain. The captain in the lead, the group of soldiers traveled up the road where Cole and the others were waiting. Cole said:

> When they reached the top of the hill, I fired. Immediately every gun in our hands seem to explode at once. When all was over there were fourteen dead men in the road. Only one escaped. He was riding in the rear. He turned his horse and speeded away. I walked out and stood beside the Captain. I said out loud, "Sister, I have kept my word."[6]

It is possible that the events of this incident were later confused with Cole's alleged ambush of his father's murderers.

Cole Younger was a young man known to be quite popular with the ladies of Cass and Jackson counties. Girls, and later women, were drawn to his warm and self-depreciating charm. One of the young women whom Cole was quite friendly with in his teenage years was Elizabeth Brown. Elizabeth, or Lizzie as she was called, was the daughter of Robert and Mary Jane Brown of East Tennessee. The Brown family moved to Cass County with over forty slaves in 1842. Robert Brown became one of the most successful landowners in the county. He eventually constructed the first steam gristmills and sawmills in Cass County and established a tannery. In 1851, the Browns moved into one of the loveliest homes in the area, which became known as Wayside Rest.

Cole became good friends with Lizzie's four older brothers, in particular Tom Brown. He often visited Wayside Rest, where Lizzie would entertain the boys by playing the piano and singing. Referring to one of those recitals, Cole wrote to Lizzie in later years: "You plaid and sang ever so many pieces and we enjoyed it better than we have enjoyed the best singing in the land in after years."[7] During the border conflicts, Robert Brown voted against Missouri's succession, but he resigned as a delegate to the state's convention in May, 1863, rather than vote for the emancipation ordinance that was presented. Lizzie was sent to the Independence Female College, but at the end of the term the Battle of Independence was fought and the college was closed. Lizzie then attended Howard Female College at Fayette and finally was a student at Christian College in Columbia until the close of the war. While at Christian College she met Henry Clay Daniel, whom she married in 1868. Daniel became an attorney and eventually a judge. He served as mayor of Harrisonville in 1887. One of their daughters married writer John Trotwood Moore.

Tom Brown was critically wounded at the Battle of Pea Ridge and died shortly after. Cole continued to be friends with the Brown family, although he saw little of them after the war. Cole wrote to Lizzie that her family was "the family of all other's on earth that outside of Mother's I loved the best."[8] Cole renewed their friendship after thirty-five years when he wrote to Lizzie from Stillwater prison the year previous to his parole. They remained friends until Cole's death.[9]

Upton Hayes joined General Shelby in the south that fall. Jarrette was told to bring his able-bodied men with the group, and those unable to travel were left in Jackson County under Cole's care. The wounded guerrillas were actively sought during the winter, but no major battles occurred.

Cole's involvement in one event that happened during this time has never been proven or disproved. The family of Reason S. Judy was well known in Cass County. Originally from Kentucky, Reason was a descendant of John J. Judy, a Swiss immigrant who had fought and died in the Revolutionary War. After a childhood spent in Indiana, Reason married and moved to Cass County, where he was a farmer. He enlisted in Captain Brigg's Company C, Second Battalion of the Home Guards, in February, 1862, and participated in the Battle of Lone Jack. Also serving in the militia at this time were two of Judy's sons, John and James. These sons may have been at Lone Jack also. In October of 1862, Reason Judy was discharged from the militia due to an injury.[10] Cole claimed that during one of Quantrill's raids that occurred at the time when Cole was relocating the wounded guerrillas, one of Reason Judy's sons was killed. Cole wrote that all the guerrillas knew that the young man was killed by Dick Maddox and Joe Hall at Paola while Cole was in Austin, Missouri.[11] The other son was also killed by the Quantrill group that year, again without Cole's participation. In March, 1863, Reason Judy was appointed Sheriff of Cass County, a position in which he served five and a half years. Cole wrote that Judy swore out a warrant for his arrest, claiming that Cole was the one who killed Judy's son (although which son is not clear). A search of the circuit court records of Johnson and Cass counties and various counties in Kansas failed to reveal any such indictment. Cole, however, swore that this action by Judy affected him "so that from 1863 to 1903 I was never in Cass County except as a hunted man."[12]

Throughout the rest of the winter of 62–63, Cole stayed with the smaller guerrilla bands in the area. He was involved in many of the skirmishes when the wounded men were moved as they recovered. It is unlikely that he was involved with many of the planned attacks by Quantrill, if any at all. His name was well known in the border counties by this time, and the militia was very anxious to get their hands on him. The federal soldiers had been making regular unannounced appearances at the Younger home in Cass County trying to catch Cole on one of his visits to check on the welfare of his family.

It was not uncommon for the teenaged Jim Younger to be accused of being a spy for his older brother. That made Jim question more than ever whether or not he should join Quantrill. Cole continued to discourage Jim as he felt that Jim was still not old enough. It is probable that Quantrill would not have accepted Jim into his ranks, at any rate. Jesse James, also anxious to join his brother Frank in Quantrill's service, was rejected on the basis of age. Cole thought that the militia's harassment of Jim was potentially dangerous and that it might be safer if the family were to move from Cass County, where they were well known, to one of their farms in Jackson County. Also, Cole would be in a better position to look after them, as he was working in the area of Independence at the time. Taking only necessary provisions and clothing, the family moved north to Strother for the winter. The militia easily found them by February.

While Jim hid in the backwoods, the militia questioned Bursheba as to the whereabouts of her two sons. Claiming that she didn't know, Bursheba asked that her family be left in peace. The response to her plea was an order by the commanding officer to burn the farm. Over the protests of John and Bob, the soldiers prepared the house for burning. Bursheba was allowed to make one trip inside to gather what she could, and the house was torched.

Nearly twenty-five years after the war, Reuban Smith, who had served under Capt. William A. Long, recalled the burning of the Younger house that day:

> Mrs. Younger lived about four miles from Pleasant Hill and she informed me that Cole had been there that day, and that she should feed him or harbor him at any other time he might come. A few days later I found that another of her boys had been there and that she had fitted him out with clean socks and under clothing. She talked as though she were running the whole Confederacy, and she said she would give aid and comfort to the boys in the brush at any and all times. Reporting this to Captain Pinger, who outranked me, he instructed me to send out a detail to burn the house.[13]

This order was legal inasmuch as the militia's General Order Number 3 contained the following clause:

> 2. That all persons who shall knowingly harbor, conceal, aid or abet by furnishing food, clothing, information, protection or assistance whatever, to any emissary, Confederate officer or soldier, partisan ranger, bushwhacker, robber or thief, shall be promptly executed by the first commissioned officer into whose hands he or they may be delivered, or under whose control he or they may be placed. The houses at which these persons receive food, protection or assistance in any way, shall be destroyed.

Bursheba was lucky to be alive.

By the end of February, the family was once again back in Cass County. The spring was spent attempting to dissolve Henry's businesses as the Youngers tried to raise only enough crops to feed themselves without becoming involved in major business transactions. Although Cole continued to stay in Jackson County, whenever any of the guerrillas were in Cass County Jim would risk his mother's displeasure by taking them food and ammunition. Bursheba didn't oppose Jim's helping the soldiers but feared retaliation upon him and the others of her children.

A new force rose within the guerrilla scene in 1863. William Anderson from Randolph County, Missouri, had been making periodic raids with Quantrill and his men. While seeming to enjoy the confrontations more than just a little, Anderson was hesitant to join as a full-time member. Perhaps he was uncomfortable with the leadership of Quantrill, as Anderson seemed to be of a mind to promote all-out warfare with words so strong they caused even Quantrill's group of uninhibited warriors to wince. Anderson began to spend more and more time with the guerrillas by the summer of 1863.

By this time, the irregulars were more determined than ever and their actions were swift and effective. Union Brig. Gen. Thomas C. Ewing was given the important task of either bringing the guerrilla movement to an end or rendering it unable to continue its vendetta against the federals. The first thing that Ewing decided was necessary was the arrest of many of the female relatives of the guerrillas so that they were unable to aid their fathers, brothers, or husbands in any way. Over a hundred of the young women were identified and taken to a makeshift prison in Kansas City. Josie, Caroline, and Sally Younger were included in the roundup and taken to the jail. Bursheba was perhaps excluded because she had four small children at home who seemed to pose no threat.

The jailing of their loved ones served only to infuriate the guerrillas even more. They began to plan for a raid on the jail, but on August 14, an event occurred that made their plans unnecessary. The three-story building owned by G. C. Bingham that was serving as the jail collapsed. Several young women were killed and several others injured. The Younger girls were fortunate enough to escape serious injury, but their cousin, Charity Kerr, was killed. Interestingly, Charity Kerr and another of the Youngers' cousins, Nannie Harris, had spoken to their "Uncle Harry" minutes before his murder. It was their thought that their subsequent imprisonment in the makeshift jail may have been because they had seen Henry's murderers.[14] It was the belief of the guerrillas that Ewing had deliberately caused the building to be undermined, causing the collapse. This seems unlikely, because Ewing would have figured that the guerrillas would have been enraged to the point of an even greater commitment to revenge, as was, eventually, the case. The guerrillas also believed that Ewing's action was planned and supported by Jim Lane and Kansas general James C. Blunt. Lane was known to be spending his time in the area of Lawrence, Kansas. One of the girls killed was the sister of William Anderson. A second sister of Anderson's was severely injured. Grief-stricken and infuriated, Anderson soon became one of Quantrill's most dependable yet blood-thirstiest lieutenants.

While Caroline and her sisters escaped the worst consequences of the experience, the trauma of the time spent in Kansas City would obsess Caroline for the rest of her life. She died of undetermined causes in 1865.

The Missouri guerrillas had had enough. A general consensus was taken, and it was decided that what was needed was an absolute and spectacular show of force that would send an explosive message to the federals. The irregular soldiers found it necessary to demonstrate that they were not to be taken any less seriously than any full-fledged army, regardless of their number. Remembering the destruction of Osceola, they decided that the entire body of guerrilla fighters would gather together and descend upon Jim Lane's town of Lawrence. Lane was to be captured and no quarter was to be given the town: it was to be leveled by whatever means possible. "Remember Osceola!" was the cry. On the morning of August 19, Quantrill and all the Missouri guerrillas, including Cole Younger and Frank James, set out for Lawrence, Kansas.

The fervor that drove the guerrillas to plan their devastation of Lawrence was ghastly to behold as they joined together under an improvised flag carried by one of the men to signify their commitment. Three to four hundred guerrillas joined Todd, Anderson and Jarrette to ride under Quantrill that day. Farmers who had the misfortune of living along the route of the determined guerrillas were enlisted as guides. Some were killed. Support for the all-out warfare that William Anderson had been advocating rose to a fever pitch. The soldiers had been whipped into such a frenzy by Quantrill, Anderson, and Todd that self-control seemed to be nonexistent and cries for complete devastation of the enemy were prevalent. It would have been apparent to anyone observing the group that reason was being forfeited in the name of revenge. The swollen ranks of tired, war-ravaged irregulars was out of control.

The enraged group hit the town of Lawrence early on the morning of August 21. Screaming the now-famous guerrilla yell, the Missourians confronted the 3,000 inhabitants of the town. Without quarter, any man or boy who was seen was killed. Men were pulled from their houses and other hiding places and mercilessly slain before the eyes of their wives, mothers, and children. The Union soldiers within the town pleaded to be taken prisoner but were killed on the spot. Stores were emptied and burned. Homes were put to the torch, and screaming families ran aimlessly about. The search for Jim Lane had begun.

Cole's mission was to find and capture Lane. The plan was to take Lane back to Missouri, where he could be publicly beheaded. As he rode toward the Free State Hotel, Cole was sickened by the actions of his fellow guerrillas. Even his years of ruthless battle had not prepared him for this. He yelled to the women and children to run to the cornfields so that they would be spared witnessing the gruesome sight. Little did he realize that on first hearing the guerrilla yell, that was precisely where Jim Lane had gone. Hiding in his nightshirt, Lane was not found by Cole and his men. Cole, anxious to depart from the madness that had overtaken the town, began to think that Lane was not in Lawrence. He started to lose control of his men as their search for the hated leader left them frustrated and angry. In his private account, guerrilla Hiram George wrote: "The officers in the hotel begged to be taken prisoner, but Quantrill reminded them of General Halleck's, and of the hundreds of old men they had killed in Missouri. We left the town in ashes at ten o'clock."[15]

After nearly three hours of terror and horror, a large group of Union soldiers appeared on the town's horizon. The guerrillas rounded themselves up and successfully fled the devastated town. Cole wrote that on the way out of Lawrence he stopped to help his brother-in-law John Jarrette when his horse was shot from under him. It was said that Jarrette had over $8,000 in saddlebags, which he was forced to leave behind. Cole also makes an interesting statement in regard to the famous "Black Flag" under which it is claimed the guerrillas rode:

> One of the treasures that we did bring out of Lawrence that day, however, was Jim Lane's "black flag" with the inscription "Presented to General James H. Lane by the ladies of Leavenworth." That is the only black flag that I knew anything about in connection with the Lawrence raid.[16]

Kansas was appalled by the events at Lawrence. Back in Missouri, Gen. Thomas C. Ewing prepared for his most desperate and despicable action to date.

The Wartime Activities of Frank and Jesse James

May 4, 1861	Frank enrolls in the Centerville Home Guard.
August 10, 1861	Frank fights in the Battle of Wilson's Creek under General Sterling Price.
August, 1861 to February 12, 1862	Frank joins General Price in various battles. Meets Cole Younger, who also works with Price through Quantrill.
February 12, 1862	Frank captured in Springfield. Has measles and is paroled home.
April 26, 1862	Frank signs oath of allegiance; continues to support Confederacy.
May, 1863	Though undocumented, it is believed that Frank is arrested while visiting his family and is taken to Liberty and jailed for three days.
Late May, 1863	Frank joins the Quantrill organization.
Late May, 1863	Looking for Frank, Union soldiers hang Dr. Samuel and whip teenaged Jesse.
August 21, 1863	Frank present at raid on Lawrence, Kansas.
June–July, 1863	Zerelda James Samuel taken to prison in St. Joseph and released after a short time.
Winter, 1863–64	Frank goes to Texas.
May, 1864	Jesse joins guerrillas through Fletch Taylor.
August 12, 1864	Jesse wounded in skirmish.
September 20, 1864	Jesse participates in the Centralia encounter. Kills Maj. A.V.E. Johnson in battle.
October 27, 1864	"Bloody Bill" Anderson killed during encounter. Frank and Jesse present. Jesse swears revenge on Anderson's killer.
Winter, 1864–65	Frank and Jesse to Texas.
January, 1865	The Samuel family relocates to Nebraska.
January, 1865	Frank goes to Kentucky with Quantrill group.
May, 1865	Jesse returns to Missouri.
May, 1865	Jesse surrenders at Lexington, shot while leaving area. Seriously wounded, he makes his way to Nebraska.
July 26, 1865	Frank surrenders at Samuels Depot.

6

The War at Home

*We have seen these refugees passing through our
streets going they know not whether.*
—Lexington *Union* report on Order No. 11, 1863

When Lane finally emerged from the cornfield, he saw the utter
devastation of his town and the cloud of death that hung over it.
Extolling the fallen townsmen as heroes, he spoke not at all of his
own flight and consequent escape. Calling upon his past success as
the great Kansas orator, Lane attempted to rouse the remaining
citizens of Lawrence and the Union soldiers who entered the town
to help restore order and bury the dead. Demanding an immediate
siege of Missouri, Lane tried to gather an impromptu army to
leave immediately for the neighboring state. He told anyone who
would listen, and all ears seemed to be open to him, that he wanted
to see Jackson, Cass and Bates counties burned over and "everything laid waste."[1] Lane was not the only one calling for such
action. A notice went out through the Kansas newspapers that
anyone wishing to assist in clearing out the Bushwhackers and
their supporters should meet in Paola (Kansas) on September 8.[2]
Efforts to gather the forces needed to accomplish such a task might
have been successful.

General Schofield informed General Halleck that Lane's actions
would be checked. Regardless of what Lane was planning or would
attempt, all Kansas troops and citizens would be kept out of
Missouri. A Union picket line was standing ready at the border to

ensure that no one crossed. There would be no vigilante slaughter. There were other ways to approach the issue, the military suggested. Any actions recommended or ordered by the federal militia would be valid and legal. One of the military's first actions was giving Charles Jennison, the most feared of the Jayhawker leaders, the authority to recruit Union soldiers. The Missourians knew that they were in imminent danger and began to meet to discuss ways in which they might escape retaliation by the Kansans. Some sought to gain the sympathies of the Kansans by contributing large sums of money to a Lawrence fund. For the most part, the Missourians simply waited, many nearly paralyzed with fear.

Within the week, Lane met with General Ewing at Morristown, Missouri. It has been written that Lane threatened Ewing with Ewing's removal from command as soon as Lane could meet with the authorities in Washington. Ewing, anxious to hold on to his position, regardless of public sentiment against him, bargained with Lane. Lane had proposed a general evacuation some weeks prior to this August 22 meeting. Ewing was ready to commit to such an endeavor if Lane would stop bad-mouthing him.[3] All eyes had fallen on Ewing as being responsible for what had happened at Lawrence. Had he been more effective at removing the guerrillas or, at the very least, capturing and holding them for trial, they would never have been able to raise the troops that had so decimated the city. On August 25, 1863, acquiescing to the demands of Lane and other Kansans, Gen. Thomas C. Ewing issued General Order Number 11.

The central demand of the order was addressed to the citizens of Jackson, Cass, Bates, and a part of Vernon counties: they would remove themselves from their homes and properties within fifteen days. Those who could prove their loyalty to the satisfaction of the commanding officer nearest their residence (how this could be done was left ambiguous) would be allowed to stay within the confines of the military stations or any part of the state of Kansas except counties of the eastern border. All were to surrender their crops to the military. What the military didn't want would be destroyed. Regardless of their political sympathies, some 20,000 families would eventually be affected by this order.

A giant exodus began as men, women, and children were forced to comply. Few knew where to go other than somewhere beyond the counties that they had lived in since first coming west to Missouri. On September 5, an article in the Lexington *Union* stated:

> We have seen these refugees passing through our streets, ill clad, often times barefooted, leaving their only shelter, and their only means of substance during the approaching winter, the crops now maturing, in numerous cases without money to buy food or pay rent, going they know not whether.[4]

While the order did have the immediate effect of removing aid, shelter, and access to food for the guerrillas, the federals were forced to feed the displaced masses and help them find shelter. Great amounts of time would need to be devoted to this purpose if it were to be successful. Since the number one priority of the militia was the pursuit of the guerrillas, the federals simply herded the people through the district and encouraged them to find places to stay outside the district. Finding new homes for these people would not be the militia's problem.

It would have been extremely difficult for Bursheba Younger to claim loyalty to the Union even if she had been of a mind to do so to accommodate her family. Because thousands of people were leaving the counties en masse, appearances by the militia at homes not yet vacated took time. Jim Younger, the eldest at home, told his mother that he would find somewhere for the family to go, as such a move was inevitable lest harm come to some or all of them. John and Bob adamantly refused to surrender their father's home and kept sentry at the windows with weapons almost too large for them to handle. Bursheba pleaded with her two youngest boys to accept the advice of their older brother and make preparations to leave Cass County. The dissension became so great that Bursheba fell physically ill with worry and apprehension. The young boys, deeply disturbed by the condition of their distraught mother, quieted their objections and discussed privately what they might do. Cole later said that his mother was simply "trying hard to keep her home together until after this terrible war was over" and, like the others around her, was undeserving of such a fate.

Before Jim had the opportunity to return home with suggestions as to where the family might relocate, the militia visited the Younger farm. Cole said to Harry Hoffman:

> On the day the Federals came to execute the order, my mother was bedfast, weak, worn and sick. The captain in charge said, "Mrs. Younger, why haven't you complied with Order Number 11?" My mother said, "I am sick; I have no place to go, and it seems impossible for me to leave." The captain said, "Mrs. Younger, you refuse to obey Military Order Number 11. We are going to burn your buildings."[5]

Bursheba pleaded with the authorities to no avail. Finally, out of desperation she asked if she could remain for the night. The condition would be that she would burn the home and buildings herself in the morning. This was agreed to. Said Cole:

> On the following day my mother had the Negroes place a bed in a farm wagon and carry her out of the house. She set it afire with her own hands. She was placed on the bed in the wagon. They drove away, my mother, four children, and two Negroes. Seven persons were in that wagon; not one among them had ever done anyone a wrong in their lives.[6]

Still not having had any communication from Jim, John suggested that the family start toward Lafayette County, as Bursheba had relatives there. They could stay with "kin" until they decided what they were going to do. The sentiment was great: whatever was decided for the future, the boys declared they would never even consider living anywhere other than their beloved western Missouri. There were many things that would need to be taken into account, and the minds of the Younger family, as they slowly progressed toward Lafayette County, were troubled and full.

After the Lawrence attack and the issuing of Order Number 11, the guerrillas were in a quandary as to what to do next. It was certainly not in their favor to stay within Ewing's district, as the militia was everywhere, carrying out the demands of the order. Any confrontations with soldiers engaged in this venture would have involved citizens already traumatized by their forced relocation. Although all of those present at Lawrence had participated in some form or another, many of the guerrillas were disheartened that a situation such as had occurred at Lawrence had been necessary. Additionally, most of these men had been farmers before the war. Killing unarmed men was not something that they felt comfortable about, regardless of how they had been told and had accepted that such acts were necessary to the guerrilla movement. The men began to examine their consciences and question their commitment to Quantrill's philosophy as they watched their loved ones reel from the trauma of being forced from their homes. The first signs of dissension began among the irregulars.

William Anderson, now known as "Bloody Bill" because of his commitment to the annihilation of his enemies, refused to curtail his activities in any way. A group of rebels who wholeheartedly supported his demolition tactics remained loyal to his command. Within a short time, a teenaged boy named Jesse James would be welcomed into Bill Anderson's fold. Quite a fold it was. There was no question about Anderson's group of fighters: they would go anywhere at any time and would commence each encounter with a no-holds-barred enthusiasm that would place their mark of hatred on all those with whom they battled. Jim Cummins was one of Anderson's men. Cummins wrote:

> Having looked the situation over I determined to join the worst devil in the bunch. Frank James had joined Quantrill's band. While he was fierce, he was nothing to compare with that terrible Bill Anderson, so I decided it was Anderson for me as I wanted to see blood flow in revenge for the outrages the Jayhawkers had committed.[7]

Anderson's group dedicated themselves to continuing the fight from central Missouri. Many of Quantrill's men left to join Shelby in Texas within weeks of the events at Lawrence. Quantrill had decided that regrouping, both in spirit and rank, was greatly needed. Those who wanted to continue the fight without interruption either followed Anderson and Todd to central Missouri or started winding their way down to Texas to serve under the command of General Shelby. Among the guerrillas, Shelby was the most respected of the Confederate leaders and they were honored to be welcomed among his troops.

John Jarrette was one of those who elected to join Shelby. In his absence, Cole was made captain of their company. Jarrette, always restless, appeared back in Missouri in a very short time. Subsequently, Cole was once again reduced to lieutenant. Jarrette and Cole talked incessantly about their immediate future. By this time, Bursheba and the family were living at the home of Bursheba's sister, Nancy Campbell, in Waverly. For the moment, they appeared safe. Jarrette talked with Cole about the inability of the guerrillas to move about as freely as they had in the past. He suggested that perhaps the war, although the war of which he spoke was not the war of the border, would be better fought in the southern regions for the time being.

Quantrill liked Cole and had allowed him many privileges as a soldier of only nineteen. Cole had been seduced by such "power," as most young men of that age might have been. He believed that his calling as a soldier and a leader would have met with his father's approval and that his actions would have made Henry proud. He felt he certainly had reached the level of respect that his brother Dick had enjoyed at the time of his death three years before.

Jarrette laid out plans already approved by General Shelby. Cotton thieves were prevalent in the area of the Mississippi River near Louisiana. They were wrecking havoc with the Southern sympathizers in the area, as their activity was approved by the Union Army. Shelby wanted to send down a group of men who could end this problem. Cole would once again become a captain of a company, this time without having to revert to any former rank. He would join Dave Poole, who would also be given a command, and ride under Jarrette to Louisiana to handle the situation.[8] Cole jumped at the opportunity. He was anxious to leave the reminders of the massacre at Lawrence as far behind him as he could. Yet Cole wasn't ready to abandon the reputation and action he had enjoyed as a soldier. After briefly visiting Waverly to check on his family, Capt. Cole Younger headed for Louisiana with Jarrette and Poole.

In the meantime, those who remained in Missouri made their plans. Some of the men had chosen to stay in Jackson, Cass, and Bates counties, which were now known as the "Burnt District" because of the militia's actions in burning the countryside in compliance with Order Number 11. Periodic raids were conducted by some of those who had stayed behind, but none of these confrontations was anything in comparison to what had been a regular occurrence in the past. Quantrill had already planned to winter in the South. Order Number 11 simply changed his time frame. He would take his group to Sherman or Denison, Texas, earlier than expected, but after the winter they would return to Missouri. The border at Kansas was too well guarded to attempt any raids after Lawrence, but the militia was always a welcomed target. Instead of returning to western Missouri, as planned, they too would relocate to central Missouri.

Cole says that he was hand-selected, along with forty other Missouri boys, by General Shelby's adjutant general, John Newman Edwards, to handle a special assignment.[9] These men were sent on a scouting mission to Arkansas to determine whether or not the Union soldiers in that area were going to move against the Confederate troops of Price, also in the area. Their mission was successful, and Cole enjoyed immensely the praise of Shelby and Edwards.

Hundreds of other families in the area were forever affected by the war. The family of David Talley was very close to the Youngers. David arrived in Independence from Oensville, Kentucky, in 1835. He became a store clerk and later proprietor. David married Bursheba's sister Mary Anne, and they eventually were the parents of ten children. As his family grew, David bought and operated a farm that stood along the Independence and Harrisonville stage route. The Younger and Talley cousins often kept company. Tom and George Talley served alongside Cole with Quantrill. During one surprise ambush (an informant was involved) Cole and the Talleys were forced to flee on foot. Tom had only one boot on at the time of the first warning and his other foot was stuck in his boot. He was immobilized. Cole stopped to yank Tom's boot off so that the two could escape the federals who were in pursuit. They got away safely, but Tom's brother George was not as fortunate and was killed during this encounter.[10] While living in Jackson County, Bob Younger often spent time with his cousins and two of the Talley boys.

Jim Younger was not displeased that Cole had left the area. He had decided that he would be held back no longer and if things went smoothly for the family through winter, he would join what was left of Quantrill's group in Missouri. Jim knew that Quantrill would return in the spring and decided that he would finally fulfill his obligation to become involved in the military aspects of the war. He surely had experienced enough of the civilian involvement. With Cole in Texas, or wherever it was that he might be in the South, Jim waited for spring and the realization of his need to become one of Quantrill's "men." Jim was sixteen years old.

In May of 1864, about the time that Jim was introducing himself to Charlie Quantrill, Cole was sent to Colorado with Col. George S. Jackson. Their mission was primarily to render useless the transcontinental telegraph line. After this assignment Cole claimed that he and Jarrette were given the job of escorting an Officer Kennedy to British Columbia to deliver papers for the purchase of two "vessels."[11] Cole was back in Texas and parts of Mexico by the fall of 1864.

By this time, Quantrill had returned to Missouri, where Anderson and George Todd were beginning to take over the leadership of the organization. Quantrill decided to discontinue his activities for a while and secluded himself in the home of his alleged wife, Kate King.[12] Many of Quantrill's regulars were disenchanted by the fact that the war seemed to be nearly ended in their enemy's favor. Some of the men decided either to return home to lie low until after the war ended or to return to Shelby. Others joined with Anderson and Todd to get in the last few licks before their cause was defeated. These were men who would fight until the end and beyond.

Shortly after Jim began assisting Quantrill with some scouting endeavors, the federal militia visited the Younger family in Waverly. The militia had heard that Jim had joined with the guerrillas, and his absence confirmed their information. Claiming that the Youngers didn't seem able to get the message the federals had been trying to deliver in the past, the commanding officer ordered the Campbell farm burned. John and Bob had been fishing along one of the streams that ran from the Missouri River when they saw the flames from the farm begin to rise to the sky. Running home, they arrived just as the solders were beginning to leave the property.

While John ran to comfort his mother, young Bob threw himself against the soldier who was last to mount. The soldier pushed Bob roughly to the ground, saying that it wasn't their fault that General Ewing had failed to teach the Youngers a lesson. As the soldiers rode toward Lexington, Bob wiped bitter tears from his boy's face and demanded that his mother grant him just one thing. He refused to carry the middle name of Ewing any longer. In the future he would be known as Robert O. Younger.[13] The Youngers left the farm and went to nearby Missouri City, where they stayed at another Fristoe residence. They wondered what was going to happen next.

The remaining guerrillas began to lose their purpose. They were unsure of what they wanted to accomplish at this point, and their cause seemed to turn inward. Their need to express their individual feelings of loss and frustration became paramount. They would not be defeated without showing the "Blue Bellies" the Confederate stock of which they were made. They would not go down easily.

Although neither Cole nor Jim participated, an encounter at Centralia turned brutal. On September 25, 1864, two hundred and twenty-five men under Anderson and Todd rode toward Columbia. The group camped several miles from the town. The day after their arrival, Anderson rode with a few dozen of his men into the nearby town of Centralia. The guerrillas enjoyed great sport screaming their guerrilla yells and terrorizing the people of the town. After they had been there awhile, a train pulled up to the Centralia station with many civilians on board, as well as twenty-five unarmed Union soldiers on furlough. Anderson's men made the soldiers relinquish their uniforms, as Union jackets and pants were used often by the irregulars. One by one, the soldiers were executed as they stood in front of the station. Their bloody deed concluded, Anderson and his men returned to the encampment.

Maj. A.V.E. Johnston later arrived in Centralia and viewed the slaughter. He and his men set out to find those guilty of such a dastardly deed. For some unknown reason, once Johnston met up with the guerrillas, he ordered his troops to dismount to do battle. The result of this order was disastrous: over one hundred Union soldiers were killed. Included among the dead was Major Johnston. It has been said in subsequent years that Jesse James, fairly new to the Anderson organization, was responsible for the death of the major. This may have been the start of young Jesse's "career."

Shortly after this encounter, George Todd was killed in a guerrilla skirmish near Independence. Some of those riding under Todd transferred their allegiance to Anderson. Others, further disheartened, returned to wait out the end of the war with their families, who had been scattered about the state of Missouri. Within a month, another blow to the guerrilla movement occurred. While passing through Ray County, the group with Bill Anderson was surprised by Union troops led by Maj. S. P. Cox. Although most of the guerrillas escaped harm, Jesse James among them, Anderson was killed. Left behind, Anderson's remains turned up at a federal post shortly after. Major Cox had posted a sign near Anderson's body claiming that such would be the fate of the other guerrillas should they decide to continue the fight. The guerrilla movement was falling apart. Quantrill, who had come out of his temporary retirement, decided to take the remainder of his soldiers to Kentucky. He knew, and his irregulars were starting to accept the fact also, that the rebel forces would soon be forced to face the eventuality of defeat.

Jim Younger joined with Quantrill to travel to Kentucky. Jim wasn't keen to go to another state but finally had the opportunity to be accepted as a fighting member of the organization. Perhaps his "official" involvement would be brief, but when the war was over he would at least be able to say that he had been a guerrilla and had attempted to avenge the wartime atrocities committed by the federals.[14]

Only a small band by this time, Quantrill and his men neared Louisville on May 10, 1865, and decided to stop for the night. They knew of a Southern sympathizer in the area named Jeremiah Wakefield, and many of them boarded in Wakefield's barn. Others continued on to find other lodging. Hours later, Union Capt. Edwin Terrill passed on the main road alongside the farm and saw the tracks of over a dozen horses leading into the barnyard. The Union patrol advanced on the barn and caught the sleeping guerrillas unaware. That no picket had been posted was further evidence of the fatigue and sense of hopelessness the group was experiencing. The fighting men of Quantrill had at last let their guard down. The area of the barn erupted with gunfire. When the surprise attack had ended, many of the guerrillas lay wounded. Quantrill, with his face in the mud, was unconscious. He was taken from the barn as the surviving guerrillas were arrested. According to John McCorkle, guerrilla cousin of the Youngers:

> And they captured Dick Glasscock, Jim Younger, Bill Gaugh, Vess Aker, Jack Graham, Dick Burns, George Robinson, Tom Evans and Andy McGuire. These last nine named were taken to Lexington and placed in jails and on three different occasions were taken out into the jail yard to be hung, but each time the boys would come out of the jail cheering for Jeff Davis and daring them to hang them, telling them their deaths would be avenged.[15]

Regardless of whether McCorkle's account is accurate or not, the captured guerrillas were spared the noose and were taken to the federal prison at Alton, Illinois. Jim Younger's military career was brief. Shortly after his first official engagement, Jim was a prisoner of war. Charlie Quantrill was taken to the military prison hospital at Louisville, and he died there several days later. Although first buried in Louisville, Quantrill's remains were eventually relocated to Dover Cemetery in Dover, Ohio. Other guerrillas who had traveled to Kentucky with Quantrill but had not been with the group that fateful night later surrendered at Samuel's Depot, near Louisville.

On April 9, 1865, Lee surrendered at Appomattox and the War Between the States was officially over. Cole was not in Missouri to hear of either the end of the war or the capture and imprisonment of his brother. It is unlikely he even knew that Jim had traveled to Kentucky with Quantrill. Having first visited Los Angeles, Cole was on the Pacific Coast at the home of his uncle, Coleman Younger, when the news arrived of the end of the war. Uncle Coleman lived in San Jose, and Cole had been enjoying the sights of San Francisco as his Missouri comrades fought their last battle. Cole, anxious to relieve himself of the trauma of war for a short while, had found his way to Victoria, apparently under the guise of locating specialty supplies for General Shelby. When Uncle Coleman offered his brother's son California hospitality, Cole eagerly accepted. He would stay in California until the fall of 1865.

GENERAL ORDER NO. 11

Headquarters
District of the Border
Kansas City, Missouri
August 25, 1863

First,—All persons living in Cass, Jackson and Bates Counties, Missouri, and in that part of Vernon included in this district, except those living within one mile of the limits of Independence, Hickman's Mills, Pleasant Hill and Harrisonville, and except those in that part of Kaw Township, Jackson County, north of Brush Creek and west of the Big Blue, embracing Kansas City and Westport, are hereby ordered to remove from their present places of residence within fifteen days of the date hereof. Those who, within that time, establish their loyalty to the satisfaction of the commanding officer of the military station nearest their present places of residence, will receive from him certificates stating the fact of their loyalty and the names of witnesses by whom it can be shown. All who receive such certificates will be permitted to remove to any military station in this district, or to any part of the State of Kansas, except the counties on the eastern border of that State. All others shall remove out of this district. Officers commanding companies and detachments serving in the counties named will see that this paragraph is promptly obeyed.

Second,—All hay and grain in the field, or under shelter in the district, from which the inhabitants are required to remove, within reach of the military stations, after the 9th of September, next, will be taken to such stations and turned over to the proper officers there; and reports of the amounts so turned over made to district headquarters, specifying the names of all loyal owners and the amount of such produce taken from them. All grain and hay found in such district after the 9th of September, next, not convenient to such stations, will be destroyed.

Third,—The provisions of General Order No. 10 from these headquarters will be at once vigorously executed by officers commanding in the parts of the district, and at the stations not subject to the operations of paragraph first of this order, especially in the towns of Independence, Westport and Kansas City.

Fourth,—Paragraph 3, General Order No. 10, is revoked as to all who have borne arms against the government in this district since August 20, 1863.

By order of Brigadier General Ewing,
H. Hannahs, Adjutant

7

A Family Divided

*I will, to the best of my ability, protect and defend
the Union of the United States, and not allow the
union to be broken up and dissolved . . .*
—Oath of Loyalty, 1865

After so many years of debilitating discontent, devastating raids,
and horrific battles, it was hard to believe that the war had finally
ended. The people of western Missouri didn't know how they
would be treated or just what direction their lives would now take.
Even those who had remained neutral or had quietly sided with
the federals were unsure of what would become of the land that
had been ripped from their possession following Order Number
11. Certainly those who had believed in the Confederacy or had
supported the irregulars had cause for concern now that the federal
government had emerged victorious.

Slowly, the people of the devastated Missouri border counties
began to return home. They were anxious to put the past five years
behind them and rebuild their war-ravaged families. Farms needed
to be renovated immediately, but the economic suffering was
nearly as great as the human suffering. Yet these were strong
pioneer families: they would do whatever needed to be done. They
would go forward, continuing their individual sagas.

Bitterness flowed through the veins of many of those who had
supported the guerrilla movement. It was felt that the irregular
soldiers, not having had a strong Confederate organization with

61

which to join, had simply acted to defend their homes and loved ones. Whether this was the case or not, the war had been exhausting, and even among the guerrillas who had already returned home, the sentiment was that "enough was enough." Attempting to put their experiences behind them and begin anew without malice, they began rebuilding their farms and communities. Others felt that they could never forgive or forget any wartime activities, but these men didn't know how to continue the fight. They vowed to keep in close touch with each other should any further action be needed to defend their homeland. All in all, the war may have been "over" in Missouri but the borderland was far from peace and tranquility.

As both the civilians and former guerrillas began to settle into the newness of "peacetime," politics were being discussed in the state capital. The Republicans were the group in power, and the call was for a new constitution. There were many issues that needed to be dealt with, and one of them was the Southern (Confederate) sympathizers. One of the leaders of the Radical Republican Party was a St. Louis lawyer named Charles D. Drake. So many of his ideas became incorporated into the new state constitution of 1865 that it became known as the Drake Constitution. Drake suggested that one way to keep the anti-Union faction from causing further problems was to enact certain restrictions. The restrictions were direct: former Southern sympathizers could not vote, hold any office, or be employed in any professional position, including those of the church. Additionally, while no one would be prosecuted for any civil or criminal acts while in the military service of the United States or the state of Missouri committed after January 1, 1861, those who had acted against these governments would be exempt. There would be no amnesty for any anti-Union activists or supporters.

As many of the guerrillas sighed in the relief that they would not be hung without trial, others realized just what this meant. They could not engage in activities to rebuild their farms if they were to be arrested and tried. What would be their fate if they were convicted? Even if they were left untried, they would not be able to take jobs or even freely serve God in their places of worship. What were they to do? As most had in the years previous, they would "make do." This was, evidently, going to be the new direction of their lives.

Cole was still in California at Uncle Coleman's when the Drake Constitution was voted on and approved. Knowing that he would be arrested on sight should he return to Missouri at this time, he decided to stay in the company of his uncle until the newness of the situation wore off. Jim was being held in the prison at Alton. The Younger family, consisting of Bursheba, John, Emma, Bob, and Retta, returned to Jackson County. They decided to stay in the house that had been previously leased to tenant farmers in Strother. They, too, wondered what the future would hold.

In the months immediately following the enactment of the new constitution, carpetbaggers from Kansas and other states began moving into Missouri. They were allowed to hold office and take over professional institutions such as banks with little interference from the Republicans running the state. Posses were raised to deliver vigilante justice to those Southern sympathizers who had not had the "sense" to give themselves up for trial. Lynchings were not uncommon. There seemed to be little difference in the area between the newly arrived law and order and the "justice" that had been the norm for the past five years.

A partial amnesty was made available for those who had supported the Confederacy. They could take a loyalty oath, swearing their allegiance to the new constitution of Missouri and to the United States. Those who would take this oath would be "paroled." One clause, which specified that those taking the oath had never been involved in actions against the government, would be virtually ignored. Many took the oath, knowing that there was no other way they would be allowed to continue peacefully with their lives. In an age when a man was considered to be as good as his word, many men who had dedicated the last few years of their lives fighting to uphold the beliefs of their individual families were forced to swear allegiance to something they did not believe in. In the hearts of many, the war would continue.

With her two eldest boys still away, Bursheba wondered what she should do to provide the safest environment for her other children. The depressed area of Jackson County, with its burned fields and the grief-stricken faces of returning families, seemed unacceptable to her as a place to begin a new life. John and Bob continuously talked about their desire to return to Cass County. Bursheba couldn't bear the thought of going back to Harrisonville and confronting the town that had been her home with Henry. As a man, Bob Younger reflected on this time when he said:

> My brother John and I wanted our lives to return to the way they had been when our Pa was alive more than anything. We knew that would never happen, though, so the least we thought should happen was we would return to Harrisonville. It hurt Mother greatly to even think about that so we decided to go along with whatever she wanted us to do.[1]

The boys wondered aloud what had become of their father's businesses? They had yet to hear that the livery and dry goods store had been virtually destroyed and that their Uncle Frank had been forced to sell the remaining inventory to provide the Youngers with badly needed funds to enable them to pick up the pieces of their shattered lives. Even though the Younger house in the center of town had been spared destruction, Bursheba felt that she could never return to Harrisonville. With this in mind, the first thing the family would need to decide would be where to live. Although several of their farms had been destroyed, they would need to sell all the remaining property to recoup some of the money lost during the years since Henry's death. Bursheba had been on the run for the past three years, and now, feeling overwhelmed, she decided that their selection of a new home base could wait a little longer. Emma and Retta Younger, aged thirteen and eight at the close of the war, had been deeply affected by the hostilities. The young girls had not known a stable home life for over three years. Although first-hand witnesses to everything that had happened to the family, they had nothing to say about any future plans. They looked to their mother and brothers for all decisions. Bursheba and the other Younger daughters worried as to what the toll would eventually be on Emma and Retta's impressionable young minds. It would come to pass that the constant turmoil of their early years would provide both girls with a strong dedication to family. Emma would find security through her life with her husband, Kitt Rose, and her own three daughters. Retta

forever dedicated herself to the life of her Younger family, centering on her brothers long after the death of her mother.

The molestation of the Younger family had not stopped with the
end of the war. The various posses that had been formed returned
to the Younger residence often, awaiting the return of Cole and
Jim so that they could be arrested. Bursheba and her daughters
almost dreaded the return of the boys, for they were now more
vulnerable without an organized group behind them. John and
Bob, on the other hand, were anxious to hear of their brothers'
recent adventures. Before the winter of 1865 began, both Cole and
Jim would find their way home to Missouri.

Jim realized that the only way he was going to be released from
the federal military prison was to take the loyalty oath of Missouri.
His captors acknowledged that Jim had not been with Quantrill
very long and were lenient inasmuch as they decided to send him
back to Missouri and let the state decide what to do with him. He
was told that if he were to take the oath, he could return to his
family. He would still be subject to the provisions of the Drake
Constitution, but Jim had served his time and that would be
sufficient. Jim returned to Strother, where he was welcomed with
open arms and loving hearts. His swearing an allegiance to principles that had not served the best interests of his family upset Jim
greatly, however, and the loyalty oath would leave a great scar on
Jim's sensitive spirit.

Cole decided to brave the political climate and return to his
family as well. He had not seen them for quite some time. While
his family was very happy to see Cole, the consequences of his
return home caused them to become gravely uncomfortable once
again. After all, Cole had not surrendered and had not taken the
oath of loyalty. He was still a wanted man. The vigilante posses
had visited the Younger home so often in the recent past that it
was just a question of time before they would come again while
Cole was at home. Cole was not anxious to expose his family to
further danger and decided that he should stay elsewhere, away
from his family, while he decided what next to do with his life.
Cole had enjoyed his military service and the "position" he had
obtained. He was now confused as to his future direction. Bursheba suggested he visit his great-uncle Thomas Fristoe in Howard

County. Cole agreed, believing that both he and his family would thus be safe. Jim was now at home to look after the family, and both John and Bob had grown to be quite self-sufficient young men. Cole returned home briefly to participate in the family's first Christmas together since the death of Henry, but for all his enemies knew, Cole Younger was more likely than not somewhere outside Jackson County.

By the first of the year, the family was still in a quandary. Jim suggested they start a crop in their Strother fields, but the energy level was low within both the family and the community as the struggle to begin lives anew got under way. Besides, since slavery had been abolished, the supply of field hands had been depleted. Jackson County would be adjusting to a new way of farming. Cole returned to Jackson County a few times to check on the family, but his presence caused a certain disharmony among the brothers. Where it was Jim's nature to attempt to keep peace among the family members, Cole was unable to resist John and Bob's verbalized resentment of Cole's efforts to become the head of the family. John and Bob argued that Cole had not been an active member of the family for several years. They proposed that they themselves had kept the family together and operational since, first Cole, and then Jim, had left to fight with Quantrill. This angered Cole, who still saw the young men as boys, and arguments would ensue whenever Cole was around. Though irritated, the boys still loved their brother and would often do things for him to make his temporary exile easier.

Bursheba also had an important female helpmate at this time. One of the "members" of the Younger family was a black woman named Susan. Called Suze, she was first their slave and later, when slavery was abolished, their helper and companion. Suze first came to live with the Youngers about 1850, right after their move to Jackson County. She was only about fourteen at the time but would remain with the family for decades. Suze was with the family through the births of several of the children and was a confidant to both the girls and the boys as they grew older. She was tremendously loyal and helped the family through many crises. Suze was with the Youngers when Henry was murdered, each time one of the family's homes was burned, through the move to Texas and the death of Bursheba. One story concerning Suze claims that once during the war, Kansans came looking for Cole while he was visiting at home. Having to act fast, Cole wrapped himself around a stump. Suze sat over the stump, and her voluminous skirts hid him. He was not found, and his life was spared.

In January, 1866, John and Bob drove Bursheba north to Independence to buy additional supplies for the winter. Cole had asked John to pick up a revolver that he had left with an Independence gunsmith. Having done so, John began to load this and the other of the family's purchases into the rear of the wagon. While John was at work, a former Union soldier named Gillcreas approached the Youngers and made scurrilous remarks about Cole and Jim in the presence of their mother. Taking offense, John told the older man to be quiet. Claiming that they would see who was made to be quiet, the man slapped John across the face with a frozen wrapped mackerel that he had just purchased at the market. The impact caused the boy to drop to the ground. His temper flaring, John struggled to his feet. It has been said that at this point Bob, demonstrating that he was now a product of his environment, suggested to John, "Why don't you shoot him?" As John moved to the back of the wagon to retrieve the loaded gun that he had just picked up from the gunsmith, Gillcreas began to move his hand toward his hip. John grabbed the gun and shot in Gillcreas' direction. The bullet hit Gillcreas between the eyes. The incident occurred outside the sheriff's office at the Independence jail, and a crowd immediately fell upon John, moving him quickly to the sheriff's office before he could be harmed by Gillcreas' friends. John was held overnight in the jail. In the morning, a coroner's inquest determined that the man was just seconds away from using a large slingshot when the fifteen-year-old shot him. Since the slingshot was considered a lethal weapon, the incident was ruled self-defense and John was released.

Bursheba wondered if life would ever return to normal for her family. Since Henry Younger had died without a will, his estate was in shambles. Bursheba knew that she would have to return to Cass County in order to petition the estate to allow her to withdraw money to "educate" her minor children. While Bursheba had been educating her children at home during the war, she knew that this "intent" would be received favorably by the court and would thus enable her to withdraw funds to relocate her family. Because Henry had died with his businesses fully operational, many of his business affairs, credits and debts, were still outstanding and the entire estate was disorganized. It would take years to straighten it out, and it would never be satisfactorily settled. The minor children would be allowed to withdraw funds on a fairly regular basis, however, providing they supplied an explanation.[2] Most of the Younger fortune was gone, the real property having been stolen or burned long before.

Bursheba stayed with friends in Cass County just long enough to try and accomplish something with the estate. Emma and Retta went to Pleasant Hill to stay with their sister Anne. John and Bob were sent down to St. Clair County, once the home of their grandfather. They first stayed with their Uncle Frank, who had relocated to Appleton City. They also spent time under the influence of their uncles Littleton and T. J. near Osceola. Events temporarily at a standstill, the Younger family attempted to regroup.

The Oath of Loyalty

I, _____, do solemnly swear that I am well acquainted with the
terms of the third section of the second Article of the Constitution
of the State of Missouri, adopted in the year eighteen hundred and
sixty-five, and have carefully considered the same: that I have
never, directly or indirectly, done any of the acts in said section
specified: that I have always been truly and loyally on the side of
the United States against all enemies thereof foreign and domestic:
that I will bear true faith and allegiance to the United States, and
will support the Constitution and laws thereof, as the supreme law
of the land, any law or ordinance of any state to the contrary
notwithstanding: that I will, to the best of my ability, protect and
defend the Union of the United States, and not allow the same to
be broken up and dissolved, or the Government thereof to be
destroyed or overthrown, under any circumstances, if in my power
to prevent it: that I will support the Constitution of the State of
Missouri: and that I make this oath without any mental reservation
or evasion, and hold it to be binding on me.

8

A New Organization

*On his arrival at the counter, the man on the
opposited side drew a revolver and presented it at
Wm. Bird and demanded the money of the Bank.*
—Account of cashier Greenup Bird on the occasion
of the first daylight peacetime bank robbery, 1866

John and Bob Younger found that they enjoyed living in St. Clair
County very much. While the war had affected this county,
especially if one were to remember what had happened at Osceola,
the damage wasn't as evident as it was in Jackson and Cass
counties. St. Clair County wasn't as populated, and that made a
great difference. Frank Younger welcomed the boys to his home in
Appleton City but was not comfortable with the responsibility for
keeping them in line. They were, after all, two troubled young
men. Frank was twenty-seven years old, just a few months older
than their brother Dick would have been had he lived. Frank had
felt overwhelmed at having to deal with Henry's properties and
businesses. Although he felt obligated to help Bursheba with her
boys, Frank was most anxious to settle into his own life with his
own family now that the war was over. He thought it best that
John and Bob spend some time under the influence of their Uncle
Littleton Younger, Frank's half-brother, who also lived in St. Clair
County. After all, Littleton was fifty-three years old and had a
family of his own. He also owned a sizable farm, and the boys
could be put to work there. They could also enjoy the company of

their uncles T. J. and Bruce. T. J. was four years older than John, and the two would become great friends. Bruce was the same age as Bob. The boys reluctantly agreed to continue living away from their mother and younger sisters. They would develop relationships in St. Clair County and a love for this area of Missouri that would last a lifetime.

Meanwhile, Jim decided to stay near his mother as Bursheba attempted to straighten out Henry's affairs. They rented a pair of rooms in Harrisonville and enlisted the services of Squire William Allen, an old friend of Henry's, to help them with their financial problems. Jim realized that he had a talent for organization, and he was able to put to use some of the self-education he had enjoyed before he left home to fight with Quantrill.

Cole Younger found it difficult to adjust to civilian life. He was still a wanted man, and he felt that he would never be able to walk the streets of Missouri unless he surrendered and stood trial. The chances of taking his case all the way to trial were slim. Several of the guerrillas had been hung by the posses, and others were driven from Missouri by threats of violence against them or their families. Cole didn't think he would survive the process even if he were to be granted a trial. The position he had held with the Quantrill and Shelby organizations was well known. Cole knew that it was impossible for him to surrender. At the same time, his actions during the war had earned him the respect and gratitude of many. These farm families, along with the families of his comrades, were more than happy to provide Cole with shelter and companionship after the war. Cole enjoyed reliving his encounters and experiences as he spoke to the awed children of the friends he visited. The children were thrilled to hear of the adventures of the expatriot living within their midst, and Cole enjoyed the celebrity it brought him. Although he was not free to do what he wanted with his life, the recognition was welcomed. As Cole started to formulate plans for the future, he kept close contact with his guerrilla friends.

Jesse James had been gravely injured while attempting to surrender to the federal forces in the spring of 1865. While he recuperated in the various homes of his family, he began to think of an elaborate scheme to get revenge against those who had "won" the war. While it is most likely that Jesse was still too ill to participate in his carefully designed plan, it seems that Frank James approached Cole in the winter of 1865–66 to discuss his younger brother's idea. Cole was impressed and agreed to discuss the plan with those guerrillas with whom he was still in close contact, especially his mentor, brother-in-law John Jarrette. Frank would talk to others of his and Jesse's friends, and a tight-knit group would be formed. The result of this meeting would make history.[1]

On Tuesday, February 13, 1866, at about 2:00 in the afternoon, a band numbering between ten and fourteen men dressed in blue coats and other bits of Union Army apparel rode into the peaceful college town of Liberty, Missouri. The bank of the Clay County Savings Association was located across from the county courthouse, where the sheriff had his office. The "square" was the focal point of community activities, and much of the business conducted in the immediate area was done by the students of nearby William Jewell College. The group of riders stopped in the square and attempted to look uninterested in the events around them as two of them entered the bank. In his account of the event Cashier Greenup Bird wrote:

> Two men entered the bank dressed in Soldiers blue overcoats. They both came up to the stove. One of them turned and went to the place at which we receive and pay out money and he said he wanted a bill changed. Wm. Bird left his desk and went to the counter to change it. On his arrival at the counter, the man on the opposited side drew a revolver and presented it at Wm. Bird and demanded the money of the Bank.[2]

Thus began the first daylight, peacetime bank robbery in the history of the United States.

Jesse's idea to rob a bank and gain access to the thousands of "Yankee" dollars within it was exciting news to the men who were selected to join with Frank James and Cole Younger in carrying out the plan. They had been unable to raise any money on their own and the thought of instantaneous wealth was not only appealing but the illicit manner in which it was to be obtained thrilled their sense of adventure and revenge. These men were, for the most part, former guerrillas to whom taking risks and chances meant little or nothing. It has never been proven who was (or was not) at the robbery, but various accounts name several men as having been identified after the fact by the citizens of Liberty. Many were, after all, men who had lived in the Jackson/Clay County area. Among those "recognized" were Oliver Shepard, Bud and Donny Pence, Frank Greg, James Wilkerson, and Joab Perry. Additionally, James Wilkerson's brother Bill, Ben Cooper, and Red Monkus were said to have been present.[3] Younger family history relates that John Jarrette was happy to have been counted in the number of the group, and there have been suggestions that Allen Parmer, future brother-in-law of the James brothers, was along for the adventure as well. Together with Frank James and Cole Younger, this would bring the number of robbers present to thirteen.

Jesse James was most likely home at Kearney, some seven miles north of Liberty, at the time of the robbery. It was reported later that several of the men crossed the Missouri River by boat after the robbery but that Frank James returned home to Kearney. Some believe that the purpose of Frank's delayed departure from the county was to enable him to return home with the ill and weak Jesse who had, after all, planned the robbery. It is likely that although he planned the details of the robbery, Jesse remained bedridden at home where he waited for Frank to return to give him a detailed report of what had happened. Many accounts of the robbery suggest that Jim Younger was one of the men as well. This also is unlikely as Jim was in Cass County with his mother at that time tending to the affairs of his father's estate. It appears that warrants were issued for the arrest of three men who probably were not even present at the robbery: Aaron Book, James Couch, and William Easter. Couch was later arrested but was released when no case could be made against him.

The men who entered the bank were described as tall men. These two men were probably Frank James and Cole Younger. They demanded that Bird and his son William hand over the money in the bank, threatening them that if they made any noise they would be shot. The Birds were ordered to be "quick." Greenup Bird stated that his son hesitated and was struck in the back with one of the robber's pistols. Shoved against the vault door, the young Bird was forced inside and followed by the robber. A large cotton wheat sack was then produced. The young man was told to place all "coin" in the sack. Greenup Bird continued:

> The other robber had me in tow outside of the vault and demanded the Greenbacks. I pointed to a tin box on the table and told him they were in that box. He hoisted the lid of the box, took out Greenbacks 7/30 and UM Bonds and told the robber in the vault to put them in the sack and to be in a hurry.[4]

At this point both father and son were shoved back into the vault and the door was closed. The robbers quickly departed, running out the door to the street. Their horses and comrades were waiting for them. The Birds discovered that the door was not secured and fled the vault. They ran to the window, leaned out, and yelled that the bank had been robbed. At this point, the bank robbery had been a success. All that was needed to complete the adventure without negative incident was for the men to have mounted their horses and ridden out of town. As they attempted to do this, the call began to be heard outside the bank where two college students were walking along the sidewalk. One of them, George "Jolly" Wymore, had noticed that something out of the ordinary seemed to be taking place outside the bank. As the Birds' cries were heard, Wymore and his friend turned in the direction of the courthouse. One of the robbers was on the ground adjusting his saddle girth. It has never been determined which man this was. The robber yelled at the students not to move and then fired his revolver at them. The seventeen-year-old unarmed Jolly Wymore fell mortally wounded. The robbers raced out of the area screaming the once-familiar guerrilla yell.

It is hard to say who might have been Wymore's killer. Little is really known about the personalities of several of the men believed to have been present that day. It is hard to say which of them might have acted in such an impulsive and deadly manner. The guerrilla code of silence would hold and the boy's killer would never be named.

With the exception of the boy's tragic death, the experiment was successful. Approximately $60,000 worth of currency and bonds was taken by the handpicked group of Jesse and Frank James and

Cole Younger.[5] The men headed in the direction of nearby Missouri City, chased by a posse who eventually gave up trying to track them because of a snowstorm that had conveniently begun hours after the robbery. Gathering at a church on the other side of the river, Frank and Cole divided the money. The men were offered either hard cash or some of the government bonds. Nearly all of them preferred the cash, and the bonds were left to Cole and Frank. Over the next few years, Cole would cash these bonds as he roamed throughout the United States, sometimes traveling as far east as Cincinnati and New York City. Cole would, however, deny any involvement whatsoever in the robbery:

> At one point, I was happy to cash bonds given to me by friends who had not had the opportunity to cash them. I never knew where the bonds came from as I never asked it of the friends who had given them to me to cash.[6]

Cole would always claim that he was nowhere near Liberty at the time of the bank robbery.

Cole wrote that, in the summer of 1866, the governor of Kansas asked the governor of Missouri to hand over to him three hundred of the men who had been participants in the Lawrence raid, listing them by name. Cole claimed that a group of attorneys from Independence decided that they would defend, without charge, any of these men against any crime other than murder. Cole wrote that he and others brought together the "Jackson County boys" for a meeting, which was held in Blue Springs (near Independence and Strother). Cole wrote:

> It was while at this that I saw Jesse James for the first time in my life, so that sets at rest all of the wild stories that have been told about our meeting as boys and joining Quantrill. Frank James and I had seen service together, and Frank was a good soldier, too. Jesse, however, did not enter the service until after I had gone South in the fall of 1863, and when I saw him early in the summer of 1866 he was still suffering from the shot through the lung he had received in the last battle in Johnson County in May, 1865.[7]

Cole's statement is dubious. If such a meeting occurred, why did Jesse James attend? Jesse wasn't at Lawrence. It might have been that the attorneys felt able to defend the same men against other crimes committed in the state of Kansas. In that case, Jesse might very well have gone to Blue Springs to attend the meeting. It is likely, however, that while Cole did, indeed, meet Jesse for the first time in the summer of 1866, it was not at any Blue Springs meeting. After Cole returned from his first trip East to cash some of the bonds, he met with Frank James in Independence. The bonds that he had been able to cash thus far had netted quite a bit of money. This money needed to be divided among Cole, Frank, and Jesse. Cole traveled to the James farm in Kearney to meet briefly with the James brothers and deliver their portion of the booty.[8] This perhaps was Cole's first meeting with Jesse James. It certainly was not his last.

Whatever happened to both the "hit list" from the governor of Kansas and the defense of the guerrillas is not clear. It is not evident that such a demand even existed. It was at this time that Reason Judy allegedly started his campaign against Cole. Whether the Judy story is accurate or not, Cole began to feel additional pressure to leave Missouri for a while. With his money from the Liberty bank robbery, Cole felt that he might like to invest in a cattle business out of state. John Jarrette, who was now living in Jackson County with Josie and their children, told Cole that he would like to be involved in a business venture with him. Jarrette, after all, had his money from the robbery as well. Cole continued to look up to Jarrette and would always pay attention to anything that Jarrette had to offer. Jarrette first thought about becoming involved in farming, and he and Cole visited Lafayette County to put in a bid on a large farm that had come up for auction.[9] When Jarrette's answers to the banker's questions about his past aroused suspicion, Jarrette was denied the farm. Cole wanted to return to Texas to start up a cattle business, but Josie was not keen about Jarrette leaving their family nor was she interested in relocating out of state. Cole felt somewhat guilty about leaving his mother and brothers, even though they were scattered all over western Missouri. Also, if he left for Texas at this time, it would be hard to return without notice. Word spread fast, and his enemies would know very soon that he had left Missouri. To Cole, leaving the state might be misconstrued as admitting defeat, something he would never do. Bearing all this in mind, Cole and Jarrette decided that they would purchase some cattle and Cole would travel into Louisiana using an alias to sell them. So it was that Cole found himself in Louisiana and parts of southern Kansas throughout the remainder of the year. Cole said that he stayed in Carroll Parrish, Louisiana, until an illness drove him back to Missouri in 1867.[10]

In Independence, on New Year's Day, 1867, Sally Younger married Jephthah Duncan from Kentucky. Jep was considerably older than Sally and had been a private in Captain Harden's Company 4 of the Regiment of the Kentucky Volunteers during the Mexican War.[11]

The rest of the family would stay where they were until at least the spring of 1867. John and Bob were thriving in St. Clair County, the happiest they had been since the border troubles had begun. Jim continued to stay close to Bursheba, who was making little headway with the estate but attempting to move forward with its intricacies. Jim, too, was relatively content for the first time in many years. He was not bothered in Cass County, and the heat of Cole's presence was not constantly felt. The thing that bothered Jim most was observing his mother's unhappiness as she attempted to review all of Henry's business transactions and her constant dwelling on the life that would have been her family's had the war not come. Bursheba longed for her family to be reunited and for the happiness she had felt through her home with Henry.

On October 30, 1866, $2,011.50 was taken from the Alexander Mitchell and Company Bank in Lexington, Lafayette County, Missouri, by armed robbers. Two men entered the bank and asked to change a $50 bill. Cashier J. L. Thomas told them that the bank was not buying that kind of funds. Two other men entered the bank, guns drawn. The cash drawer was emptied, and the men demanded $100,000, claiming that they knew such an amount was in the vault. The cashier stated that he did not have a key to the vault and the man and the premises were searched without result. Calmly, the men gave up the search and left the bank. Within minutes Dave and John Poole, former Quantrill guerrillas, led a posse after the fleeing robbers.

After a very short chase, the posse was abandoned.[12] This robbery raises several questions. Had the Poole brothers been in on the robbery and had the "posse" been a ruse to dissuade others from chasing the robbers? Probably. Who participated in the robbery? If Jesse James had not been present at Liberty, perhaps he was anxious to experience the adventure of a bank robbery first-hand and had made plans to visit Lexington. Lexington, then, might have been Jesse's first bank robbery. If Jesse was present, it is likely that Frank was also. The Youngers were fairly well known around the area of Lexington, as some of the Fristoes had lived there for years and their brother Dick had attended college there. If Jesse had suggested their take might be $100,000, however, Cole might have been persuaded to attend the festivities. Cole had included John Jarrette once before, so if Cole was involved, it is likely that Jarrette would have been also.

A different theory altogether comes to mind. John Jarrette was very high in the Quantrill organization, serving right alongside Bill Anderson and George Todd. He was known to be a cunning and forceful leader. Might this have been the bank that turned Jarrette's farm proposal down? Perhaps Lexington had been Jarrette's idea passed on to Cole, who included Frank and Jesse. With Liberty having been the Jameses' idea and Lexington the Youngers', this may have been the basis for the formation of the equal billing within the ranks of the James-Younger Gang. Jim Younger may have been asked to accompany the group, but his disappearance from Harrisonville, where he had lived for nearly a year, would have been quite conspicuous. It is doubtful that Jim would have been persuaded to participate.

It has never been proven who made up the group of men who robbed Alexander Mitchell and Company that day. However, there remains one very interesting fact. Cole would claim often and would later write:

> I will take my oath solemnly that what I say is the truth. Notwithstanding all the accusations that have been made against me, I never, in all my life, had anything whatever to do with robbing any bank in the state of Missouri. [13]

Although he would continuously, and with conviction, deny his involvement in every other bank robbery of which he was accused, Cole never specifically denied being present at the Lexington bank that day in October, 1866.

Savannah, Missouri, was the site of the next robbery attempt. The private banking house of Judge John McClain was approached by five or six would-be robbers on March 2, 1867. McClain was shot and injured when he refused to deliver the key to his vault and the men left empty-handed. This may have been the first "copycat" robbery attempt without either the James brothers or Cole having been present. The Jameses have not been linked with this robbery, and it is unlikely at that time that Cole would have engaged in any robbery without them. They were, after all, "partners." Although it would have been difficult to drive cattle in the winter and Cole may have been looking for something to occupy his time, it is possible that he didn't know anything about the plans set for this robbery. On the other hand, perhaps he did know and chose not to be involved without his good friend Frank James. In any event, Cole would write that the five men who attempted the robbery were identified although he did not state who these men might have been. Further, he wrote, "There were no Younger boys in the party."[14] He did not mention John Jarrette.

The next robbery wrought terrible results for the men who participated. About twelve men rode into the town of Richmond, Missouri, on May 22, 1867. Four men entered the Hughes and Wasson Bank and robbed it of about $3,500. From there the robbers' luck evaporated. For the first time, the bandits were met with active resistance outside the bank. A gun battle ensued between the townspeople and the group of robbers, resulting in the killing of Richmond's mayor, John B. Shaw. A young man, Frank S. Griffin, attempted to thwart the robbers' escape and was shot. When Griffin's father, William Griffin, ran to help his son, he too was shot. Leaving three bodies in the street, the group managed to outride a posse who at one point exchanged fire with them.[15]

This doesn't appear to be a James and Younger endeavor. Cole, Frank, and Jesse had already learned that they could be fairly successful using only a handful of men and that the rewards were greater if so many were not involved. Second, to Cole and Jesse, unwarranted violence was undesirable. Cole had dissuaded it even as a soldier. At Richmond, there were simply too many men involved to ensure that the robbery would proceed smoothly and without problems. Who might have planned it is unknown. Though he was never named, John Jarrette was familiar enough with the basic plan that he might have attempted to lead a group of his own. After all, Cole, Frank, and Jesse had been making all the decisions thus far and Jarrette had been the senior soldier during the war. He had held the highest rank and had been the one to encourage Cole to join with Quantrill. Perhaps Jarrette wanted to regain some of the "position" he had formerly held as leader. In any event, several of the men who participated in the robbery would come to regret the day they agreed they would be involved.

Two days after the robbery, Felix Bradley, a horse thief imprisoned in the Richmond jail, was taken from the jail and hung. It was said that Bradley had talked about the robbery with a cell mate. Eight men were charged with the robbery: James and John White, Tom Little, Payne Jones, Dick Burns, Issac Flannery, Andy McGuire, and Allen Parmer. Allen Parmer provided an alibi that he was at work in Kansas City. He was not bothered by legal authorities again at this time, but he left soon after to live in Texas. Several years later he would be arrested in Texas for another robbery. Jones was found at his father's house by a posse several days later, but he escaped after killing a member of the posse and a little girl who had gotten in the way of the gunfire. Dick Burns managed to escape the posse, but a few months later both Burns and Jones were found and lynched. Tom Little was arrested, but before he could have a legal trial he was made to stand a mock trial at which point he was found guilty and hung. Andy McGuire was arrested in St. Louis. McGuire was returned to Richmond, where he was put in a cell with a fellow named Jim Devers who had also been arrested for alleged involvement in the robbery. Both were lynched within days. The Whites seemed to have been successful at eluding authorities at this time.[16] Cole's alibi this time seems to be true:

> I was living on the Bass Plantation, three miles below Lake Providence, in Louisiana. Capt. J. C. and Frank Lea of Rosewell, N. M. and Tom Lea, of Independence, Mo., were living in the same house with me, any one of whom will vouch for the truth of my statement that I was not anywhere near either of these towns [Richmond or

Savannah] at the time of the robberies in question, but was with
them at the plantation referred to above.[17]

Cole was probably investigating further cattle propositions in
Louisiana in anticipation of a meeting with his family. He would
discuss the possibility of the family moving to Texas to establish a
ranch of their own. It is doubtful that he was in Richmond that
day. The people of Missouri surely sent a message to any would-
be bank robbers who might engage in violent activities against
townspeople. Violence and killing would not be tolerated. Robbing the banks of "Yankee" money was one thing, but turning
against their own was something else. A grave lesson would be
taught at Richmond.

By Christmas of 1867, Bursheba decided to reunite her family.
It bothered her greatly to have them scattered hither and yon
throughout western Missouri. She decided to return to the farm in
Strother and retrieve the younger children from Pleasant Hill and
St. Clair County. Jim accompanied her to the farm near Greenwood and rode down to tell John and Bob that Bursheba wanted
them back with her. Although the boys were extremely reluctant
to leave St. Clair County, they did miss their mother. Jim had
made several trips down to check on them during the past year
and had become quite close to the boys. The young men were
always happy to see Jim and hear reports of the others of their
family. They were interested in returning to Jackson County, as
Jim had told them things had calmed down and it now appeared
safe for them to live there.

Little mention was given to Cole, who was still in the South.
Whether or not Cole had been present at the robberies was not
something that was discussed in Bursheba's presence. By the time
the daring exploits at Liberty had been made known down in St.
Clair County, John and Bob enjoyed assuming that Cole had been
involved. They could get neither a confirmation nor a denial from
Jim, however. Jim had little to say about Cole. Jim sent word to
Cole through friends that the family was now together in Jackson
County. Cole decided to leave the cattle with friends of Jarrette's,
and he traveled north to visit with the family he had barely seen
for the past few years.

The pull of family ties was felt by many of those who had been separated from their loved ones during and after the war. Frank James, who had been with Quantrill all those years, felt the need to attempt to locate the grave of his father. Rev. Robert James had died while ministering to goldminers in California. Frank went to California about the same time Cole was heading for his family in Jackson County. Unable to find Robert James's grave, Frank decided to spend some time with his father's brother, Drury James, in Paso Robles, California. Drury's ranch was near some wonderful hot springs, and by letter Frank encouraged Jesse to join him in California, as the springs might be of great help to Jesse's tenuous physical condition. It was a suggestion that would have to wait. Jesse wrote back to Frank that a business venture was needed to finance his plans for an extended stay in California. Frank understood and returned from California to join Jesse in Kentucky. Still bothered by his wartime lung wound, Jesse had been staying with his father's relatives in Champlin, Kentucky. Everyone seemed to know the extent of Jesse's difficulties, and they would later provide him with a very good alibi.

It is likely that Frank James contacted Cole through their mutual guerrilla friends and asked him to meet with Jesse and him in Kentucky. Cole arrived before Frank, and Jesse explained to him plans that he had developed for another robbery. The target was Russellville, Kentucky, some twenty-five miles from where the two men spoke. While he awaited Frank's return, Cole decided to check on the Nimrod Long Banking Company himself, posing as a cattle buyer, to see if Jesse's assessment was correct.[18] Of course, Jesse was unaware of Cole's actions and would have been angered to think that Cole questioned his abilities or authority. Jesse believed that he held the position of "leader" of the new enterprise and was quite taken with his own ideas and the eventual execution of his careful planning. Cole, on the other hand, was not really impressed with Jesse and usually thought of him only as Frank's brother. Cole did not see in Jesse what Jesse saw in Jesse. The partnership of the three men had so far proven successful, however, and so Cole felt little need to let his true feelings be known to either Jesse or Frank.

Frank eventually arrived, and on March 20, 1868, the Nimrod

Long Banking Company of Russellville, Kentucky, was robbed. At 2 p.m., while the clerk and the cashier were at dinner, three men entered the bank and asked Nimrod Long, the bank president, to cash a bond. (A Liberty bond?) Long looked at them dubiously and refused. At this point the men jumped the counter with their pistols drawn and demanded the funds of the bank. Long ran into a rear room and was met by a fourth man who had entered through the side door. As he ran, Long was shot, the bullet grazing the side of his head. While the men emptied the money of the bank into Cole's trusty wheat sack, Long attempted to get out of the bank. The robber at the door, possibly John Jarrette, shot him. At this point, the robbers scooped up what was left and exited the bank. Mounting their horses, they left the town, traveling in several directions. Their day's activity had netted them $14,000.

The following item appeared in the *Louisville Daily Journal* on March 28, 1868:

Description of men:

The Russellville Bank Robbers. All of the known information concerning the five ruffians who robbed the bank at Russellville on Friday has been imparted to our detective police and they are on the sharp lookout for the scoundrels. Four of them are thus described by the gentlemen who were in the bank at the time of the robbery:

One, riding a bay horse with Morgan saddle, 26 years old, black hair and whiskers, florid complexion. 5 feet 8 inches tall, weighs about 140 pounds, wore a felt-hat, sack coat, vest made of velvet, and silver spurs.

One, 5 feet 7 inches in height, short curly, sand hair, round bull-dog head, prominent eyes, red face, and weighs 160 pounds.

One, 5 feet 6 inches high, thin visage, 32 or 33 years old, shabbily dressed in light clothes, defect in one eye, light hair and whiskers, weighs 150 pounds, had on a white hat much worn.

One, 6 feet high, weighs 140 pounds, 33 or 34 years old, light hair, inclined to curl, thin whiskers, was shabbily dressed in dark clothes.

It is fairly certain that Frank, Jesse, and Cole were present that day. The others probably included John Jarrette and Oliver and George Shepard. A certain Arthur McCoy, who had ridden with

Quantrill, was at one point a suspect, but the number of men seen by the townspeople of Russellville seemed to number five or six.

The selection of the Nimrod Long Banking Company was an interesting one. The Jameses' father had been educated for the ministry at Georgetown College on a scholarship program funded by the bank's former owner, George Norton, and by Nimrod Long himself. Is it possible that Jesse didn't know this or simply chose to ignore it in view that the man was just another "Yankee banker"?

Immediately after the crime was committed, a posse was formed. Kentucky was a little more organized than Missouri had been, and a detective by the name of D. T. Bligh was called in from Louisville. It was Bligh who determined who had been involved in the robbery and who, for the first time, named Cole Younger and Frank and Jesse James as part of the robbery party. Cole, claiming that a certain "Colburn" was mentioned as one of the robbers, wrote that this name was confused with Coleman, and this was the manner in which he was identified as having been there. At any rate, Cole did not deny his participation but rather went to great lengths to provide his brother Jim with an alibi.[19] Jim, who was in Jackson County, had not been named as a participant in the first place!

A damaging article appeared in the June 3, 1868 edition of the Kansas City *Commercial Advertiser*. Belle Younger's husband, Richard Hall, told the newspaper a story of how his brother-in-law, John Jarrette, and Ol and George Shepard had planned the robbery. Hall claimed that this group went to the Younger farm in Jackson County and talked Cole into accompanying them. Hall would later say that this was Cole's first robbery and that he blamed Jarrette for leading him into a life of crime.[20] The truth was that Cole probably wasn't at the Younger farm previous to the Russellville robbery and Hall didn't realize that in his attempt to discredit Jarrette, whom he disliked, he was implicating Cole. Though warrants were never issued for the James brothers, Cole, or Jarrette due to lack of evidence, the Shepards did not fare as well. A posse found Oliver Shepard at his father's home in Missouri, and Shepard was killed when he attempted to escape. His brother George was arrested in Kentucky and taken to Russellville, where he was identified, tried, and found guilty. He was sentenced to three years in prison for his role in the robbery.

An unsubstantiated family story circulates that Josie and John Jarrette were the victims of an attack by John's political enemies sometime in 1867–68 when their house was set on fire. Their two children, Margaret and Jeptha, were burned, but rescued. Josie and John perished. The children were sent to live with Anne and Curg Jones, who temporarily served as their guardians. It is perhaps this final act of retribution against the Youngers and their associates that convinced Cole that his family could not live without duress in Missouri. While the fire is the story of Jarrette's death believed to be true by the Jarrette family, guerrilla Jim Cummins, in his autobiography, calls Jarrette one of the most "daring, desperate and shrewd" of Quantrill's men and claims that he died in the "Frisco Mountains" of California in 1891. Cummins further tells a story of Jarrette being arrested for stage robbery and his daughter having turned state's evidence against him. Cummins says that he was pardoned when he implicated others.[21] According to her granddaughter, Margaret Jarrette did not have recollections of her father past the burning of the house in St. Clair County.[22] Another story has Jarrette becoming the owner of a large sheep ranch in Arizona after the war. Neither of these last two stories mentioned what might have become of Josie.

After Bursheba decided to return to Jackson County and her youngest daughter was returned to her, Anne and Curg Jones decided to move to Texas. They were anxious to leave the war behind them and settle in a place where they might have adventures of a positive nature. They decided to go to Sherman, where they knew many families who had the same goal as they. They often spoke to Bursheba about the need to lead her family forward in life by starting over in a place that would not cause pain and discomfort to them all. Martha Anne was the third of the Younger children. She married Lycurgus Jones, a farmer, in 1852 while the Youngers were still living in Jackson County. Although he was considerably older, Anne's husband Curg and her brother Cole were close friends. Upon relocating to Texas, the Jones family established a fine furniture store. Anne and Curg had six children, one son being named Cole. Anne and Curg made Denison their permanent home.

When Cole appeared in Jackson County full of ideas and flush with the money from his share of the Russellville robbery, he did not face opposition to relocating as he once had from Bursheba. Bursheba decided that the time might be right to go to Texas. She had managed to extract some of Henry's money from the legal system, and Cole assured her that he had many contacts in Texas. He told his mother he had many friends who would be more than happy to help them get established. Available cash was not mentioned.

In the fall of 1868, Cole, Jim, John, Bob, and Retta accompanied their mother to their new home in Dallas County, Texas. Daughter Emilly, born in 1852, suffered the war with great difficulty. Emma was a quiet girl and devoted herself to the care of her mother after the death of her father in 1862. So attached was Emma to Missouri that she married Kitt P. Rose at the age of seventeen rather than relocate with her family to Texas. Emma and Kitt had several daughters. Kitt eventually became one of the managers of the Jackson County Poor Farm, which was built in Lee's Summit on land bought from Henry Younger. An unsubstantiated story circulates that Emma was killed in a train wreck in 1907. Regardless of the validity of that story, it is certain that she died at a fairly young age.

Bursheba's health was beginning to fail, and the warmer climate was welcomed. The town of Scyene was selected, as there were other Missouri families nearby and so that Bursheba would not have to adjust to a totally foreign environment. Cole continued to buy lots in cattle stock, and he soon convinced Jim that this might be a wonderful calling for him also. Jim was able-bodied, but he was not as fond of the lonesome work as Cole. John and Bob, on the other hand, abhorred anything whatsoever to do with the cattle business. John declared that he was meant to work in a shop or some other type of less strenuous environment. Bob insisted that he was meant to be a farmer, which was a far cry from cattle and the ranching business. The boys would, however, do anything to restore the spirits of their mother and settled into Cole's buying and selling endeavors while Retta attempted to nurse their mother to better health.

Back in Missouri, on December 7, 1868, the Daviess County Savings Bank at Gallatin was the scene of a robbery and cold-blooded murder. Two men entered the bank and asked for a bill to be changed. While the president, John W. Sheets, wrote a receipt, he was shot through the head and the heart without warning. William McDowell, the clerk, was shot several times while he attempted to escape. The two men rode off with several hundred dollars. The slaying of Sheets was controversial even at the time. The clerk said that the two men had whispered together prior to the shooting and had claimed to have shot Sheets in retribution for the killing of a brother, Bill Anderson. Some reports claimed that Sheets was really S. P. Cox, the man responsible for "Bloody Bill's" death, while others said he was only one of the men who had been with Cox at the time of Anderson's death. When the investigation of the robbery began, the horse that was seen at the robbery was identified as belonging to a "James of Clay County." The James-Samuel farm was raided shortly afterward and a running gun battle ensued involving the James brothers and Deputy Sheriff John S. Thomason of Clay County. Thomason's horse was shot out from under him. The pursuit ended with Thomason borrowing a horse from the Jameses' mother, Zerelda Samuel, so that he could return to town. Jesse had let it be known years before that he would avenge Anderson's death. Had he had this opportunity and taken it? The heat was beginning to rise for Frank and Jesse James.

The Youngers, on the other hand, were thriving. Although they missed the green grass of St. Clair County, John and Bob found they were able to make friends easily. They enjoyed spending time with contemporaries, something they had not been able to do in Missouri. Jim seemed to like Texas quite a bit. With his talent for organization, he decided to become employed as a census taker in Dallas County for the 1870 census. He was so enthusiastic about his job that he soon had Cole involved as well. Cole, with his gregarious nature, took to the job immediately. He enjoyed meeting the people of Dallas County and being paid to chat with them and learn their business. While Jim frowned on Cole's obvious taste for gossip, Cole decided that perhaps the experiment of relocating the family for happier times was working.

The Younger boys had many friends in Texas, and the Shirley family of Carthage, Missouri, were some of them. The Shirleys' daughter Belle, later to be known as Belle Starr, was fascinated by the Youngers. The story of Belle Starr is one of violence and intrigue. Belle was born Myra Maibelle Shirley in Carthage, Missouri, in 1848. Her father, John Shirley, owned a livery and tavern-hotel in Carthage, and the Shirley family was very popular. Belle attended "finishing school" as a young girl and was known for giving wonderful piano recitals. Then came the war. Belle had several brothers. Brother Bud was active with the guerrillas. Belle was also. Her great-great-granddaughter claims that Belle worked as a spy for the Confederacy at a young age, carrying messages by horseback to the men in the brush.[23] In 1864, Bud was killed during a skirmish with federal troops near Sarcoxie, Missouri. Preston later died in a Texas tavern shooting while Ed, a horse thief, was shot and killed before he was twenty-one years old.

Shortly after Bud's death, John Shirley moved his family to Dallas County, Texas, where his brother and son Preston had been living. Shirley opened another inn. As the guerrillas traveled south to Texas during and after the war, they often stopped and stayed with the Missouri family. It was during one such visit that Belle met Cole Younger. Belle said that she was a young girl when she met and fell in love with the dashing soldier. Cole claimed that Belle was fourteen when he first met her in Scyene in 1864. He wrote that he next saw her after she was married and six months pregnant with her first child. In 1868, Belle married former guerrilla Jim Reed. Their daughter Pearl was born in 1869. Reed and Belle first lived in Texas but soon left for California when Reed became wanted for the murder of two men. It was in California that their son Eddie was born. The Reeds eventually returned to Texas. Cole wrote that after the Reeds arrived from California they had no place to live. Because of John Shirley's kindness to the guerrillas during and after the war, Cole claimed to have helped the Reeds establish a ranch and to have given them several head of cattle from the Younger herd. Cole believed that gesture alone would have put Belle enough in his debt for her to later name her ranch Younger's Bend. He wrote that he had been warned of Belle's love for him but steered clear of any involvement with her as she was the wife of his former comrade.[24]

In 1874, after having been involved in several robberies, Jim Reed was killed by a U.S. Marshal near Paris, Texas. At some point between 1875 and 1880, Belle entered into a serious romance with Bruce Younger, uncle of the Younger boys. The two spent time together in Kansas and were married there in 1880.[25] Within weeks of their marriage, Bruce was out of the picture. Belle took her children to Indian Territory and settled along the Canadian River. Belle soon married an Indian named Sam Starr. What happened between Bruce and Belle is not known, nor is it known if Belle ever obtained a legal divorce from Bruce.

Belle lived with Sam Starr near Eufala, Oklahoma. Very soon after their association, Belle and Sam became involved in horse rustling. They were sentenced to a term in prison by Judge Isaac Parker for stealing a horse, but both got off for good behavior after serving a few months. Evidently, Belle was not monogamous during her time with Starr. Starr was said to have killed two of Belle's lovers: John Middleton, a horse thief, and Blue Duck, another outlaw. Sam Starr was killed during a dance in 1886 because of a family feud. After Starr's death, Belle associated with an Indian named Jimmy July.

Belle told her daughter Pearl of her great "love" for Cole Younger and intimated that Cole was Pearl's real father, something Cole would adamantly deny until his death. One of Cole's sisters told her daughters that Pearl was John Younger's daughter.[26] Other opinion is that perhaps Bruce had known Belle for many years previous to their marriage and Pearl was his daughter. The Starr descendants think that Ed Reed, Belle's legal husband at the time of Pearl's birth, was Pearl's father and that perhaps Belle wanted so badly for Cole to be the child's father that she simply "pretended" this was the case.[27] Regardless, Pearl sometimes went by the name of Younger. When Pearl was seventeen, she gave birth to her first daughter. Because Belle was opposed to the father of the child, the baby was put up for adoption. Pearl eventually ran several houses of prostitution in the Ft. Smith, Arkansas, area and became the mother of three more children.

On February 3, 1889, Belle was shot in the back. She had been involved in a dispute with a neighbor during this time, and the neighbor was tried for her murder. The man was acquitted. Belle's son Eddie, who did not get along with his mother, was considered to be a likely suspect in her murder, but he was never formally charged. Eddie was killed in a gunfight in Oklahoma in 1896. Belle was buried at Younger's Bend, her ranch near Eufala. Her restored tombstone carries the following inscription: "Shed not for her the bitter tear, nor give the heart to vain regret, 'tis but the casket that lies here, the gem that filled it sparkles yet."

Bob Younger turned sixteen that autumn in Texas. He had felt the weight of the war lift from his young shoulders, if only temporarily. It was his fervent hope that his mother would recover her health and that the family would find peace and happiness. Yet he didn't enjoy the Texas heat and the voluminous dust from the cattle. He longed for the fields and meadows of Missouri. The Younger family began attending church, something they hadn't done together in many years. Jim and Bob sang in the choir, and when Cole was around after having made one of his many "cattle trips," he would join them as well. His feeling of security higher than it had been in years, Bob allowed himself to fall in love with the daughter of the minister of the church the Youngers attended. Although he was still a teenager, Bob began to think of marriage even as his brother John taunted him about where the young couple might live, Missouri or Texas, if they were to be married. Bob's courtship of the young lady was at times vexing, as she was the only child of the minister and his wife and could act quite spoiled.[28] She evidently was very pretty though, and Bob liked the idea of being old enough to have a girlfriend and potential fiancée. The Younger boys began to think that they might have something of a life free from strife after all.

9

Discontent and Texas

He defied them and was strung up four times. . . . the
boy was unconscious.
—Cole Younger on the hanging of his brother John

Whatever tranquility the Younger family had felt was soon just
another memory. Bursheba's health was failing rapidly. Retta had
been unable to nurse her mother back to the strong woman she
had once been. Although Bursheba was happy to see her family
settling into a more peaceful life in Texas, she herself was unable
to put the past behind. She reminisced during the day and had
nightmares after she fell asleep. She relived the events of the past
ten years over and over. She grieved for her husband and for the
loss of the innocence of her daughters. She wondered if her sons
would ever be free from the effects of the war.

Bursheba found the strength to make her way through the
winter of 1869–70. When spring came, she asked to go home. She
knew her life was nearly over and she wished to die near Henry in
the land of their happiness, Missouri. Freely granting their mother's request, the family made plans to return Bursheba to Jackson
County.

Refusing to admit that his mother was dying, Cole decided that
it was not necessary for him to return with her to Missouri. Cole
claimed the cattle business needed his attention and that a drive of
several hundred head was scheduled to be made through Louisiana
into Oklahoma and possibly Arkansas. Missouri was still an unsafe

place for Cole. Interestingly, while the Youngers owned hundreds of head of cattle at various times from 1868 to 1872, the records indicate that they owned little land, at least under their real names. The Youngers may have leased their land or simply availed themselves of the "open range" policy of Texas, as hundreds of others were doing at that time. The presence of the Younger family in Scyene and Sherman was hardly a secret. The Youngers moved about the area quite freely and, as noted, even registered for fairly high-profile county jobs.

Jim's heart sank when he thought about returning to Missouri. He loved his birth state, but the memories of Jackson County at times seemed too much for him to bear. His sensitive nature caused him to be uncomfortable with all the old memories. He thought of his sister Caroline, who had found it necessary to leave Missouri to live in Illinois because she had been unable to deal with the war and the effects it had on her family. Jim's love for his family was great, but he saw little need to dwell on the family's turbulent past. He decided he would go to Missouri with Bursheba, Retta, and the boys just long enough to get them settled and then would return to Texas, where he could keep records for Cole.

John and Bob insisted on accompanying Bursheba. Although they were not happy about leaving their friends, they had grown very close to their mother over the years and knew, instinctively, that she would die very shortly. Bob said good-bye to his girlfriend, telling her that he would be back. Including Retta and their faithful companion Suze, the family returned to Jackson County, arriving about April of 1870.

It wasn't long before the Youngers' presence in Jackson County was noted by friends and enemies alike. Within a week, a small posse appeared at the Younger farm looking for Cole and Jim. When John explained that Jim had already served time in the federal prison at Alton, the men of the posse claimed they wanted to talk to Jim himself and would be back. When Jim returned home after being away from the farm for the day, John confronted him with the news of the posse. Jim said that he had no desire to stir up old trouble and prepared to leave for Sherman the following morning. He asked his brothers to let him know if things got worse with their mother, but he was not going to wait for a posse to appear to give him more of the grief that he had been subjected to his previous years in Jackson County. Bursheba agreed with Jim's decision. Bidding his mother farewell, Jim returned to Texas the first part of May.

Within days of Jim's departure, the posse returned. They told John and Bob that Jim had been spotted in the area and that they knew he was in Jackson County. When the boys told them Jim was not in the county, they were called liars. The posse further reasoned that if Jim, Bob, John, and even their mother were in Jackson County, it would stand to reason that Cole was around as well. Cole was, after all, the one they were really looking for. John stated that the family hadn't seen Cole in years. The posse scoffed at John's denial and ordered him outside to continue the conversation. When Bob started forward to join his brother, he was pushed roughly to the floor. His head hit the side of a table and he was knocked unconscious. With Retta at her side, the broken mother attempted to help her youngest son while her other boy was half dragged out the back of the farmhouse into the yard. Within his mother's sight, the sturdy young man was wrestled to the ground and a rope was placed around his neck. Fighting for all he was worth, the nineteen-year-old John was unable to overpower the posse, which numbered about six grown men. Recovering from his fall, Bob ran out into the yard to help his brother. Two of the men knocked Bob to the ground, where they held him fast while the others of the posse dragged John to the barn. They threw the rope over a beam and hoisted him. According to Cole, the house was searched for the former guerrillas and John was repeatedly questioned as to their whereabouts as he hung from the rope. Cole wrote: "He defied them and was strung up four times. The fourth time the rope cut deeply into the flesh. The boy was unconscious."[1]

Realizing that there would be no report forthcoming from either of the Younger boys, the posse left, vowing to keep a close eye on the family home. They swore that if Cole Younger stepped foot back into Jackson County he would soon be a dead man.

Bursheba was inconsolable. For her this was the last straw. As John lay recuperating in a bed next to her, Bursheba became nearly comatose. Bob and Retta attempted to nurse both Bursheba and John, and eventually Belle Hall was called upon to help. On June 6, her fifty-fourth birthday, Bursheba Younger died. Her trials were now at an end. Strother had incorporated into the Town of Lee's Summit while the Youngers had been in Texas. It was in the cemetery of the new town that Bursheba was laid to rest. The Halls had remained in the area over the years and had needed to purchase a plot in the cemetery to bury their young son Richard. The family placed Bursheba close to young Richard and were thankful that she was not to be given the unmarked grave that had been the necessary fate of Henry Younger.

After their mother's funeral, John, Bob, and Retta left for St. Clair County, where they met Jim. Jim felt guilty that he had not stayed with Bursheba until her death and had decided it was unsafe to attend her funeral. The boys assured their brother that he had had no choice. John and Bob thought that they could best support Jim by returning with him to Texas and attempting to pick up the life that they had left behind there. They would go back to Sherman. Retta would stay with their sister Anne Jones in nearby Denison.

Cole continued to travel throughout the South for the next year, at least. Without the presence of his mother, Cole felt uncomfortable about staying at home. He knew that his brothers hadn't really severed ties with Missouri and embraced Texas as wholeheartedly as he had. Cole felt scorned by his brothers because he thought they felt that his reputation had "run" them out of Missouri. He even entertained the thought that his family held him responsible for their mother's ill-health and eventual death. This was not the case, but Cole would grapple with his guilt for a very long time.

Shortly after the death of Bursheba, Cole was involved in a gunfight in Louisiana. The fight concerned a rigged horse race. Cole, however, was not the culprit. According to Cole, Capt. Jim White, who years before had insulted one of Cole's friends, swindled another of his friends out of some money during this horse race. The two men "dueled," and although Cole claims to have shot White, the injury was not fatal. News of this incident made its way back to Texas.

In the wake of the news, other rumors about Cole's past were discussed. Cole's alleged involvement in the Russellville robbery was mentioned. The Youngers had become regarded as upright citizens around Dallas and Grayson counties and word of this possible aspect of Cole's activities came as a shock to Bob Younger's young fiancée. With minimal explanation, the girl broke off her relationship with Bob. Cole claimed that he had been in Mississippi driving cattle at the time of the robbery and evidently offered to show the girl receipts from his "business trip." Cole said that her father, the minister, accepted his explanation but the girl wanted nothing to do with a family associated in any way with robbing banks, whether the rumors were true or not.

Bob was furious at the turn of events and the fact that his brother's reputation continued to haunt him. He decided to leave the area immediately and went to live with his sister Anne in Denison. Although Bob lived in Denison only briefly, his quiet manner and intelligent personality would earn the Youngers a positive reputation in that area.

Cole Younger evidently employed others as well as his brothers to help with the cattle while in Texas. Young "Johnnie George" was eleven years old when he went to work for Cole and was paid $1 a day. According to George, this incident occurred as a herd was being driven from Lancaster to Five Mile Creek in Texas:

"Another boy was also working for Younger," said George. "He was a year or two older and from Dallas. One day he broke out in a nasty oath. Younger said, 'Look here. I can stand a man saying that, but I don't like it. But I can't stand a boy saying it. Don't ever say that again in my presence.' A couple of days later the boy busted out again. Younger just reached in his pocket, pulled out his money bag, counted out the boy's wages and said, 'Now get on your horse and go home.' When sixteen-year-old Johnnie George read about the Youngers' robbery in Northfield in 1876, he couldn't believe it. Said George: "Cole Younger was the favorite of mine of all the men I worked for."[2]

Cole had taken John with him on a cattle drive to Louisiana the previous year, and the trip had served to instill in John a great dislike of anything having to do with cattle. John decided to leave the family and take a job as a clerk at a dry goods store in the city of Dallas. The city was newly established and already had a reputation as a boomtown. There was lots to do and see as the character of the town began to take shape. John made friends quickly, although the character of his friends was not all that sterling. That didn't matter to John. He vowed to make up for lost time and engage in some of the fun that he had seen others having but which had been denied him for so many years. John Younger, at least, was happy again.

With the family unit splintered, Jim felt at loose ends. He had gladly assisted his family throughout their many troubles. Now without Bursheba, they no longer seemed to need him. Even his baby sister Retta was happy to stay in Denison after her brother Bob had arrived. Bob and Retta had become very close throughout the years, and Retta was anxious to help her brother nurse his broken heart. Nursing was, after all, what Retta had learned to do best. Jim felt the ties to his father pulling him back to Missouri. He didn't understand why he had shied away from Missouri when his mother needed him most just a few months ago. Jim had heard John and Bob talk a great deal about the peace and good times they had experieinced while in St. Clair County. In an effort to regain his closeness to his brothers, Jim decided to talk to the younger boys to see if they would like to return to that area for a visit. John might not be able to go because of his new job, but Bob might like to leave Texas while he recovered from his personal troubles. To Jim's surprise, both said they would like to go with him. Bob was ready to leave immediately, and John would take a leave from his clerking job. John felt that if his job was not available on his return, with Dallas growing so fast there would be other, better jobs for him. Cole was informed of his brothers' decision, and the three set off for Missouri. The young men had previously written to Theodrick Snuffer, a friend of their family's for many years. Snuffer informed them he would be happy to put them up. The boys thought that between staying with the Snuffers and the time they would probably spend at the hotel in Monagaw Springs, they might be in for a relaxing respite. They arrived in Roscoe, St. Clair County, in the fall of 1870.

John enjoyed the nightlife surrounding the hotel in Monagaw Springs, a popular spot noted for its mineral springs, which were said to have healing powers for nearly every affliction. Families would often travel into Monagaw to vacation while various of their members enjoyed the medicinal treatment offered there. John, with his curiosity and love of adventure, enjoyed determining if the town's transient visitors were friend or foe. If there seemed no reason to question their motives, he would enjoy card games and other passive activities with them. Continuing the lifestyle he had begun to develop in Texas, John yearned to have fun and just enjoy life for a change.

Jim, on the other hand, passed his time taking long walks in the countryside of Monagaw and nearby Roscoe. He reflected on the past and wondered about the future. Jim felt ill at ease just passing his time without purpose, as he had felt so much responsibility over the years. Jim often climbed the cliffs alongside the beautiful Osage River, which passed through Monagaw. There was one spot in particular that Jim found himself returning to more and more. If he stood on the top of one of the river cliffs, he could see for miles in every direction. Beneath him as he stood in his special spot was a large cave. Whenever he felt threatened, Jim retreated to the cave until whoever was passing had gone. Jim told Bob and John about his find, and the three of them would sometimes sit for hours looking out over the river and the foothills of the Ozarks. John made it be known very quickly among their friends that this cave and plateau now existed for the exclusive use of the Younger boys. Others were discouraged from presenting themselves anywhere around the cave unless by specific invitation of one of the boys.

Bob Younger enjoyed the tranquility of the area but felt a certain stirring, as most boys of seventeen do, to do more than just sit around visiting with friends or passing the time playing cards. Bob had received several letters from Retta in the short time he was in St. Clair County. Retta proclaimed that in light of the recent death of their mother and the other activities of their brothers, she viewed Bob's absence from her life as desertion. Wouldn't he please return to Texas so that she could enjoy the company of at least one of her brothers? Bob felt guilty and decided to return to Texas briefly to visit Retta and let her know that, although he loved her a great deal, he had a life of his own that he needed to start living.

D. C. McNeill was one of the most popular and respected doctors in St. Clair County. A resident of Osceola, Dr. McNeill had served as a surgeon for the Confederacy during the war. Dr. McNeill was the father of a lovely daughter named Cora. On one of his visits to Osceola, Jim became acquainted with the young girl. Dr. McNeill and Cora were apparently quite friendly with Littleton Younger. During the time John and Bob lived in St. Clair County, John often visited Osceola with his uncle T. J. It was at that time that John first met Cora at Dr. McNeill's drugstore. It is probable that John introduced Jim to Cora. At any rate, when Jim ran into Cora in 1870, he decided that he wanted to pursue a relationship with the doctor's daughter. Apparently, the feeling was mutual, as Jim and Cora began to be seen in each other's company often, taking walks amidst the fields and meadows surrounding Osceola. Jim was frequently invited to supper with Cora's family, and he found himself in love for the first time. Jim asked Cora to marry him, and although she claimed she was in love with Jim, Cora felt that perhaps the proposal was premature. Jim said that he would wait for her, as she had made him the happiest he had ever been. John and Bob were delighted with this turn of events, as they had always felt Jim was lonely in spite of the fact that he had thirteen siblings. Perhaps Cora was just what Jim needed.

The story of Jesse James and "The Widow" is a very popular tale in James folklore. Younger folklore may have a "widow" story of its own. Cora McNeill related the following incident in an 1897 interview with the Kansas City *Star*:

> I saw Cole Younger do a thing once I shall never forget. A woman went into a store to buy some groceries. She asked for credit and was refused by the proprietor. "You owe me a bill now," said the groceryman. "My husband is sick" replied the woman. "And as soon as he is able to work, we will pay you." "Can't credit you," said the merchant. Cole Younger stood near. Neither the merchant nor the woman knew him. Stepping closer to her, he asked, "Will you accept assistance from a stranger?" The woman demurred but he insisted and thrust $50 in her hand. "Can I wait on you?" the

merchant asked Younger. The big rough rider drew himself up to his full height, looked the storekeeper squarely in the eye and said gruffly, "No, there's nothing in your store I'd have."

John decided to return to Scyene where there was more action. He arrived back in Texas during the winter of 1870–71 and was able to get another clerking position. His heart wasn't really in his job. John enjoyed visiting with his friends more than working. Once again, he associated with the "rowdies" his brothers Cole and Jim had warned him against. One of his friends at this time was the brother of a wartime friend of Cole's from Missouri, Tom McDaniels. McDaniels was using the name Tom Porter in Texas.

On the night of January 15, 1871, John was with his friends passing the time in a saloon in Scyene. All of the "boys" had been drinking quite a bit and soon became involved in harassing a slow-witted man named Russell. John told the man to stand still while he attempted to shoot a pipe out of his mouth. Russell was too frightened to protest, and John fired several shots near him. Eventually John tired of the game and realized that he was scaring the man to death. John's friends encouraged him to keep the game up, but John's better sense prevailed and he refused. At this point, the boys in the saloon laughingly told Russell that John had been trying to kill him and suggested Russell go to the sheriff at once to seek a warrant for John's arrest. Little did they realize that Russell would do just that. Russell went to the office of Dallas County sheriff Jeremiah Brown and had a warrant sworn for the arrest of John. The Youngers were well known in the town, but what John had done to the old man was not acceptable. It was likely that John would be arrested and fined, at the very least.

Sheriff Brown assigned one of his deputies, Charles H. Nichols, to arrest John. Nichols had served under Shelby during the war. He was friendly with the Youngers and would make the confrontation with John go more smoothly. The following morning Nichols and his friend James McMahon looked for John. They found him eating his breakfast at the hotel. Nichols told John that he was going to arrest him, and John asked if he could finish his breakfast first. Cole later claimed that John had even invited the two men to join him. Nichols said he would allow him to finish and told John to report to him at the dry goods store, where he and McMahon could be found warming themselves by the stove.

At this point, the story becomes legend. There are at least three different scenarios, any one of which may have been the actual story of what happened after the agreement was made. One story is told that John and Tom McDaniels thought better about turning themselves into the law and instead went to the livery. Once there, they found that Nichols had placed a guard on their horses. At this point, sharing a drink of whiskey, they decided to confront the deputy. John and McDaniels entered the store where the two men were waiting for John and began shooting. McMahon was shot at first fire and was killed instantly. Nichols and John exchanged simultaneous fire and both were shot. John was hit in the arm while Nichols was more seriously wounded. John and Tom took Nichols's horse and fled Scyene.[3]

Another version has John entering the store and confronting the deputy about the guard placed on his horse. John was annoyed that the deputy, a friend, had not had more faith in John and had felt it necessary to go to such lengths. When John complained about the guard, McMahon drew his pistol. John, further irritated, drew his gun at the same time, and the two exchanged fire. McMahon was killed, and Nichols immediately shot John. John returned the fire, and Nichols went down.[4]

Cole wrote that John confronted Nichols with the fact that the guard had been placed on his horse and that Nichols denied having done any such thing. Cole said that a brother of Russell's shot John in the arm, causing the scene to explode in gunfire. Tom McDaniels shot Nichols while John shot McMahon. Cole claimed that it was Russell who had placed the guard on the horses, evidently believing that Deputy Nichols was too friendly with John to arrest him. Nichols was unaware that this had taken place and when he denied such action to John he was telling the truth.[5]

While any one of these accounts could be true, it is unlikely that John Younger would walk into a store in the town of his residence and simply open fire. John's anger could be easily ignited, but when one considers that his family was well known and well liked in the area, it is unlikely that he would jeopardize this new security by such a wanton and foolish act. It is certainly acceptable to believe that Nichols had every good reason to place a guard over the young men's horses as that would have been a natural act in the course of the execution of his job. If John had broken the law, which he all but admitted by calmly agreeing to surrender himself, then he should have been treated like a lawbreaker. He had already imposed on his friendship with Nichols by asking the deputy to allow him to finish his meal. No matter how foolhardy he had acted the night before or what amount of liquor he had been able to consume that morning, John Younger would not have been likely to kill a deputy sheriff with whom he had been friendly without provocation or a misunderstanding of some sort. It is likely, therefore, that the second version of the story is correct and that the confrontation by John encouraged Nichols to draw his gun in the first place. Regardless of what happened, Charles Nichols died from his wounds four days later and became the first lawman to be killed in Dallas County. John Younger and "Tom Porter" were indicted for murder but were never arrested. By the time Nichols died, John was back in St. Clair County seeking the counsel of his brother Jim.

Jim suggested that it wasn't wise for John to stay in Missouri because, if someone were looking for him, that would be the first place they would look. Additionally, his presence would place a burden on their friends and family in the area. Both John and Jim knew what a hardship such an imposition could be. John decided that he would go down to Little Rock, Arkansas, for a while. He had never spent any time there, and no one would know him. Upon arriving in Little Rock, John once again took a job in a dry goods store. He was quite surprised when he found out that the store was owned by former Missourian Wade Blayne, who had once managed Henry Younger's livery in Harrisonville.[6] Perhaps for that reason, John left Arkansas and was back in Missouri by April of 1871. He visited his sisters Sally and Laura in Kansas City that spring. Whether or not they knew of John's trouble, they were happy to see their brother. John made plans to spend the summer with his sisters.

10

United in Crime

I yield to the man on horseback.
—Henry Clay Dean to Jesse James, Corydon, Iowa, 1871

The night of June 2, 1871, four men stayed in the barn at the Alcorn farm in southern Iowa. When the strangers left the following morning, one of them gave young Miles Alcorn a silk handkerchief that the boy had admired.[1] On June 3, the Iowa town of Corydon was celebrating a visit by noted orator Henry Clay Dean. The townspeople gathered at the courthouse square to listen to Dean talk about the possibility of a new railroad in the area. After the festivities were well under way and while the town listened spellbound to Dean's oratory, the four men entered the bank and "withdrew" funds. Leaving the bank with between $6,000 and $10,000, the men paused to tie up the cashier so that he was unable to alert anyone. The robbers are believed to have been Cole Younger, Frank and Jesse James, and a new member of their organization, Clell Miller. As the gang quietly left town, they heard the impassioned speech of Henry Clay Dean. One of them, assumed to be Jesse, couldn't pass up the opportunity to become a part of the excitement and asked to be recognized by Dean. The orator said in reply, "I yield to the man on horseback." At this point Jesse informed Dean and the gathered crowd of townspeople that the bank had been robbed and that the clerk was tied up. The robber suggested that someone in the crowd might like to set the clerk free. With that, the robbers went on their way. Believing that the interruption had been made to disrupt the meeting, Dean continued with his speech and the bound cashier was not found until some time later.[2]

A posse was formed, but by that time the robbers had fled south to Missouri. Tom Stevens, a farmer who lived halfway between Corydon and the Missouri border, had left a horse and colt tied to a hayrack near his road. He later found both gone and a heated horse left in their place. The mare was never seen again. During the search for any tracks that the robbers may have left, posse members stumbled upon several pennies scattered under a tree in a grove close to Woodland. Resident B. C. Bay suggested that the grove had been where the robbers divided the money. While the excitement was still in the air at Corydon, a young man named Adam Ripper came forward to tell a story of how he had been thrown a coin by one of the robbers shortly after the robbery and told to "alert the town." Ripper's story was discounted, however, as the town had been alerted by the robbers themselves.[3]

In subsequent interviews, William A. Pinkerton of the Pinkerton Detective Agency would claim that the Corydon bank robbery was the first time that his agency was called in to help with the detective work of any robbery having to do with the James and Younger boys. Robert Pinkerton was sent to Corydon, where he followed the trail of the robbers into Missouri. One of Pinkerton's operatives, a detective named Westfall from Chicago, eventually arrested Clell Miller in Clay County. Authorities claimed that Miller had been "caught" when he agreed to participate in another robbery and he was brought to trial in Wayne County, Iowa. Clell Miller was acquitted after a lengthy trial when he was able to produce several witnesses who swore he was elsewhere at the time of the robbery in Corydon.[4]

Concerning his part in the robbery, Jesse James wrote to the Kansas City *Times*:

> As to Frank and I robbing a bank in Iowa or any where else, it is as base a falsehood as ever was uttered from human lips. I can prove, by some of the best citizens in Missouri, my whereabouts on the third day of June, the day the bank was robbed, but it is useless for me to prove an alibi.[5]

When John heard about the robbery, he decided that it was no longer safe for him to stay in Kansas City. He immediately set off for St. Clair County. He thought that he could catch up with Cole to see what he was going to do next and get advice from Jim as to where a safe retreat might be. Unbeknownst to John, Bob had decided to visit Jim at this time also. All four brothers were together in St. Clair County for the first time in years. While Jim openly scorned Cole's alliance with the James brothers, Cole jokingly encouraged his brothers to join him the next time. When Bob questioned Cole as to how he could be so bold as to rob banks, Cole laughed and responded, "We are rough men used to rough ways." This would not be the last time that statement was heard.

Thomas Jefferson Wilson was the son of Charles Lee Younger and Parmelia Wilson. As were his brothers and sisters, Thomas Jefferson was permitted to change his name to Younger by a stipulation in his father's will. He was known as Jeff throughout St. Clair County, where he was born in Osceola on November 20, 1847. His family, Younger nephews included, called him "T. J." T. J. was a student in the Agricultural and Mechanical College of Kentucky University during the 1866–67 term.[6] On August 16, 1871, he married Emma C. Barmour in St. Clair County. The couple had two children, a girl named Jessie and a boy named Charles. Jessie died at a young age.

T. J. had previously visited California, and in 1871 he and Emma made a return trip there for their honeymoon. T. J. told John that the couple was planning to return to Los Angeles where a friend of his, Philip Ruiz, was a merchant in hardware and saddles.[7] Suggesting that John had already proven himself adept at being a clerk, T. J. invited John to join them. He said he would see to it that his friend gave John a job. John took his uncle up on the offer and left with the couple for Los Angeles.[8]

While Cole encouraged John and Jim to join him in his adventures with the Jameses, he could not in good conscience invite Bob to do so. Bob was the "baby brother." While Cole had not made any consistent efforts to act as a positive example to Bob or John in the past, he felt that his mother would have expected him to at least try to encourage Bob to seek the finer things in life through respectable means. Cole told Bob that he was going to send him to William and Mary College in Virginia. When Bob protested, feeling that his lack of education thus far would prove to be a handicap, Cole insisted. Cole told Bob that although he would give Bob the money to pay the college himself, Cole would personally escort Bob to the institution. After much argument, Bob suddenly agreed. After dropping his brother off at William and Mary, Cole planned to visit Florida to see what that state had to offer.

Jim felt that Cora and his relatives and friends in St. Clair County needed a break from the presence of the Younger boys and decided to brave the climate and return to Texas. This was a very courageous move on Jim's part, as he had no idea what type of reception he would get. The Youngers had not been seen near Dallas County since John's trouble with the law. The Joneses in Grayson County had not suffered any ill effects from John's indictment. Jim felt that perhaps his sterling reputation would hold and he would be welcomed back to the area without any serious problems. He was mostly right. Cole and Bob left shortly after the first of the year for the Southeast, while Jim attempted to find employment in Dallas. Cole wrote later that Jim found work with the Dallas County Sheriff, but if that were true, the work was only of a part-time nature.[9] Jim's main occupation was working with the horses on a ranch managed by J. D. Prichart. Jim had always loved horses and found his new job to be enjoyable and relaxing even though he worked long and hard hours.

Bob had allowed Cole to deposit him at William and Mary, realizing several months before their trip that Cole had made no effort to "apply" for Bob's enrollment.[10] Cole had assumed that all Bob needed to do was simply show up with the money. Bob, guessing otherwise, had gone along with his brother's plan, knowing full well that after Cole had given him the money for the college Cole would leave for Florida. Bob also had traveling in mind. He felt totally unqualified for college due to his lack of schooling once the war had begun. He decided that it would be interesting to use the money that Cole would give him, since the means of its procurement was questionable anyway, to see some of the South himself. For a short time Bob traveled about Virginia

and the Carolinas. He eventually sensed that his lack of sophisti-
cation put him at a disadvantage when it came to socializing with
the people with whom he came in contact. Also, Bob was very
shy and had never been without the company of at least one
member of his family. With his cover story intact, Bob found his
way down to Florida, where he located Cole. Telling his brother
that he had been ostracized by his classmates at William and Mary
because of his Younger name, Bob said that he had little option
but to leave the college. Cole bought Bob's explanation without
question and suggested that Bob spend some time with him while
he got over the humiliation he had suffered at the hands of the
Easterners. Bob agreed. With Cole's typical egotism he would
write:

> I sent Bob to school at William and Mary college, but the same
> proud spirit that caused him to leave Dallas in 1872 impelled him to
> leave college when his fellow students began to connect his uncom-
> mon name with that of the notorious Missouri outlaw, Cole
> Younger.[11]

Many errors appear in Cole's autobiography. Bob did not leave
Dallas in 1872 but rather in 1870. Regardless, it is unlikely that
many of the students at William and Mary knew Cole's name.
Younger was a common name in the area even if they had known
who Cole was. Neither Cole nor Jim would ever be told the true
story by Bob.

As Bob spent time with Cole, he realized that they actually had
little in common. Bob grew agitated when Cole talked about the
war years, which Cole did with great frequency. Bob loved his
brother but found little satisfaction or comfort in rehashing the
past. Bob had long enjoyed the friendship of Dru Garrett, whom
he had known since he was a young boy in Jackson County.
During his exile to St. Clair County, Bob had suggested that Dru
stay with Bob and his relatives for a while. Dru accepted the offer,
and the two boys, along with Bob's uncle Bruce, became great
friends. Dru had left Missouri in 1871 bound for Louisiana. He
wrote to Bob that he had obtained a very good job on the docks
at the Mississippi River in New Orleans. He encouraged Bob to
join him. Bob decided that Dru's company would be preferable to

Cole's and told Cole that he would like to try his own luck in New Orleans. Reminding Bob that he had a tendency to become homesick and miss his family, Cole questioned Bob's decision. Bob assured him that Dru's companionship would be sufficient.

Bob arrived in New Orleans and began working for one of the large shipping companies that based itself in the port. Both Jim and Cole later wrote that the name of the company Bob worked for was Gulf Shipping. However, a careful check of the directories, logs and newspapers of the time failed to turn up a company with such a name at the time Bob was in New Orleans. In 1866 an advertisement appeared in the New Orleans newspaper *The Crescent* concerning the Gulf Shipping Line.[12] While it is difficult to trace the further existence of this line, this may have been the company for which Bob worked. Bob stayed in Louisiana that year, enjoying the steady income but perhaps not enjoying the hard work of lifting and loading goods onto the seagoing vessels that frequented the docks of New Orleans.

Four men entered the town of Columbia, Kentucky, on April 29, 1872. It is fairly certain that three of those men were Frank and Jesse James and Cole Younger. It is likely that the fourth man was Clell Miller. Miller had been on his first robbery with the gang the month before at Corydon. He had not yet been arrested at the time of the Columbia robbery and would not go on trial until June 3, 1872. John, Bob, and Jim Younger have been suggested as having participated at Columbia. John Younger was in California at this time, and Bob was at work in New Orleans. Neither of them had ever participated in a robbery. Neither had Jim Younger, who was very happy working in Dallas at the ranch. Two of the men in the party entered the Bank of Columbia, where they met with the immediate suspicion of the cashier, R.A.C. Martin. Bank robberies were, after all, grave possibilities at this time. Watching the strangers closely as they approached, Martin possibly saw one of them handling a gun. Martin immediately shouted, "Bank robbers!" The cashier was instantly shot dead. Two of the customers in the bank jumped out the window while a third ran through the door, meeting and pushing aside yet another robber who had been guarding the entrance. The two in the bank realized that the robbery was not going well, scooped up the money that was easily accessible, and left the bank. The "haul" at Columbia was a mere $600. While Cole would later claim that he was at Neosho Falls, Kansas, with a herd of cattle, it is suspected that Cole, Frank, and possibly Jesse had been in the area at least a week while they posed as cattle buyers. This ploy would be used often to enable the gang to get a feel for an area and the business of a bank before they committed a robbery. Detective "Yankee" Bligh of Louisville was called in to see what he could do to turn up evidence against the robbers. Based on descriptions from the people that had seen them, Bligh named Frank, Jesse and Cole as three of the robbers who looted the Bank of Columbia and murdered cashier Martin.

John Jarrette has sometimes been suggested as not only having participated in the robbery at Columbia but as having been the man responsible for shooting the cashier. Again, it is doubtful that Jarrette was still alive at this time. In a letter written to the Missouri newspapers on September 21, 1875, Jesse James claimed that neither Jarrette nor the Youngers had anything to do with a robbery that occurred in Huntington, West Virginia, on September 5, 1875. Jesse may have been throwing the officials off the track by mentioning Jarrette as if he were still alive, or it is possible that Jesse did not know that Jarrette was dead. This is hard to believe, however, as Jarrette had been a part of the James-Younger Gang from the beginning, and his absence from any further robberies would naturally have been explained to Jesse. It has been written that Jarrette went west at some point to start a sheep ranch in Mesa, Arizona. There is a slight possibility that Jarrette may have taken the money from his participation in some of the robberies to do so, which would explain his not being present at either Corydon or Columbia. He may have returned to Missouri shortly before he was burned to death in the fire in St. Clair County. Not knowing the exact date of the fire and the death of the Jarrettes makes it difficult to speculate on what Jarrette's position in the gang might have been from 1869 to 1875.

Jim Younger says that his brother John wrote to him in April, 1873, from California. While it most likely that the letter came for Jim in April of 1872, Jim's account is very interesting. John wrote that Uncle T. J.'s friend Philip Ruiz had offered John a partnership in his saddle business because John had been doing well working there and Ruiz had no son.

John suggested that Jim travel out to California to see how things were for himself. Besides, John was very homesick for his family. Jim, for John's sake, agreed. Jim arrived in Los Angeles, where T. J. was living near the Merced Theater at the Pico House. Inquiring about his brother, Jim was told by T. J. that he should stay with John in the "house on the hill." The house was evidently quite a grand one consisting of three stories with six rooms on each floor. Jim found his brother more than just a little homesick. John told his brother that Ruiz would be happy to make John a partner in his business. In return Ruiz expected John to marry his daughter, Carmelita. John was aghast. Such a marriage was certainly not in his plans. John asked Jim to help him leave Los Angeles without offending anyone. Jim agreed to stay with John while they developed a plan.

Jim was put to work handling the fine horses that belonged to the customers of the saddle shop. After a short time, however, Jim found that he, too, was quite homesick. Although he liked working with the horses, he found that he couldn't speak Spanish very well. Jim decided the time was right to talk to his brother about his "long cherished dream."[13] Jim told John that it was his greatest desire to live near Dallas on a ranch where he could raise and train cavalry mounts for the U. S. government. John, in an attempt to cheer his brother, agreed. John said that it was a good idea and halfheartedly suggested that they "make it a foursome" with Bob and Cole. It is unlikely that John was really committed to the idea, as he was still wanted for murder back in Texas. John was probably so anxious to leave California that he would have agreed to anything. Perhaps without John's knowledge, Jim wrote about his plan to Cole. Cole wired back that he and Bob were quite interested and that the four of them should meet in Missouri as soon as possible. It is doubtful that Bob Younger ever knew of the plan, for he had sworn years before to stay out of Texas. Nevertheless, Jim and John made their plans to return to Missouri. Uncle T. J. stayed behind for the time being.[14]

Jim visited the San Gabriel Valley to pick up horses for himself and John from Carlos Ruiz. He returned to Los Angeles to pick up John, and the two headed north up the El Camino Real to San Francisco, which they reached in twelve days. From San Francisco they boarded a train and traveled into the Black Hills of the Dakotas. They experienced some adventures with mule skinners and Indians during their trip and eventually made their way to St. Clair County. Cole was waiting for them. Residing still in Louisiana, Bob was nowhere to be found. Jim and John decided to stay in St. Clair County to visit with their friends and family. They also enjoyed the time with Cole, although Jim's plans for the ranch in Texas seemed to be forgotten by his two brothers.

The Kansas City Exposition was a highly anticipated and financially successful event held yearly at the Kansas City fairgrounds. On September 26, 1872, an event occurred that put the newspapers in an uproar. Accounts would greatly differ as the story was retold many times throughout the years. What appears to have happened is that three men rode up to the "ticket office" on the fairgrounds. One of the men got off his horse, grabbed the money box from cashier Benjamin F. Wallace, and emptied the contents into his pocket. Then he threw the box to the ground and began to mount his horse. At this moment, Wallace left his booth and attempted to get the money away from the bandit. One of the men with the robber shot at Wallace, missing him but seriously injuring a little girl who had been standing nearby with her mother. Over 10,000 people attended the fair that day, and thousands of dollars had been collected by the time the robbers appeared. However, only $978 was in the box when it was snatched.

Reports at the time said that before the box was taken from Wallace, the robber had identified himself as Jesse James. Whether or not this was indeed the real Jesse James, and who was with him if it was, became the basis for wild speculation among the people of Kansas City. The newspapers soon got into the act. Maj. John Newman Edwards, who had long been Jesse's champion, wrote that the act, committed in broad daylight in front of so many people, was so daring that "we are bound to admire it."[15] Jesse himself wrote to the paper that a Mr. James Chiles of Independence said (although Jesse does not say to whom) that Jesse and Cole and John Younger were the ones who robbed the gate. Jesse continued on to say that Mr. Chiles said he saw the three men on the road prior to the robbery. Jesse claimed that it was impossible, as Jesse had not seen the man for at least three months.[16] Jesse asked that Mr. Chiles write a letter himself backing up Jesse's story, which Chiles evidently did. Cole was greatly irritated that Jesse had provided the Younger brothers with an alibi, as neither he nor John had been mentioned as suspects before Jesse's letter appeared in the newspaper. Cole wrote a letter to his brother-in-law, Curg Jones, who was then involved with the Pleasant Hill *Review*. Cole wrote that it was true that he and John were in Jackson County visiting their sister Emma and other friends and relatives. He admitted being in Kansas City on business and claimed that he and John were seen by many friends while in the area. Cole claimed that neither he nor John had anything at all to do with the robbery at the fairgrounds. Cole wrote:

> Neither John nor myself was accused of the crime until several days after. My name would never have been used in connection with the affair had not Jesse W. James for some cause best known to himself, published in the Kansas City *Times* a letter stating that John, he and myself were accused of the robbery. Where he got his authority I don't know but one thing I do know, he had none from me. We were not on good terms at the time, nor have we been for several years. From that time on mine and John's names have been connected with the James Brothers.[17]

It is interesting to imagine what may have caused Jesse and Cole to be on bad terms since the Columbia Robbery five months before. There may not have been any truth to that part of Cole's statement in the first place. It does seem apparent that Cole and John were not involved in the fairground robbery. Cole would have easily been recognized in that part of the state and it doesn't seem in character that any members of the James-Younger Gang would overtly announce themselves and then, with total disregard for the safety of bystanders, fire a gun into a crowd. Additionally, this type of robbery would be in total contradiction to the credo of the gang, which was still at this point to get revenge on the Union sympathizers. With so many people in attendance at a social function, it is ridiculous to imagine that many of them would not be friends and families of Confederate supporters.

While carrying on about Jesse's lack of discretion and the stupidity of what had happened at the fair, Cole began to talk to John and Jim about another plan. Assuming that he would patch things up with Jesse, if such a rift truly did exist, Cole outlined an idea that had been discussed by him, Jesse, and Frank in regard to a bank in eastern Missouri. Jim confronted Cole about his plans for the Texas ranch. Cole vaguely dismissed the idea as something they could think about in the future. Disgusted, Jim made plans to return to Texas by himself.

Jim arrived in Texas in the winter of 1872–73. He sought employment while he determined whether or not he would be able to put together the ranch idea on his own. Jim joined the Dallas Police Department and became one of the nine policemen under Marshal Tom Flynn.

It appears that the Younger name and reputation, while still sterling among certain of their ex-Confederate friends, was beginning to be questioned by others. Whereas Jim's family name did not prevent him from being hired by Marshal Flynn, an event occurred with which Jim Younger's name was negatively linked. A robbery took place in February, 1873. Jim and another of the Dallas policeman, J.J.L. Hollander, were indicted.[18] Involvement in a robbery doesn't fit either Jim's character or his plans at that time. The Younger name itself may have turned suspicion against Jim. Possibly Hollander, who may have been guilty, named Younger as his accomplice because of the Younger name and to protect whoever it was who really was involved with him. Jim thought that he was not likely to be given a fair trial and left Texas before he could be arrested. Hollander was found guilty and sentenced to five years in prison. He later was granted a new trial. For Jim Younger, the dream of a Texas horse ranch was over. He returned to St. Clair County, where he knew he was safe.

Cole had talked John into participating in the Missouri adventure. John didn't need much encouragement and was pleased to have Cole think enough of him to want to include him. John knew that each participant in the James-Younger Gang had to be intelligent, alert, and trustworthy. John would become the youngest man to ride with the gang and he was quite honored. He also looked forward to the adventure. Cole had already discussed the idea of bringing his brothers into the gang with the Jameses. With the gang's reputation growing, it was very important to seriously consider each person who wanted to ride with them. They needed to be very careful about including only those whom they could trust with their lives. If not their brothers, then who? Jim, however, would have nothing to do with Cole and his friends the James boys. He chose to make his living by honest work, regardless of the fact that his family's name made such a proposition very difficult and, sometimes, nearly impossible. Cole, knowing Jim's sensitive yet headstrong personality, didn't push him. He was happy to have John along for the ride.

May 27, 1873 was the date selected for the robbery of the Ste. Genevieve Savings Bank. Two men entered the bank and relieved the cashier of about $4,000. A young man who had been in the bank at the time the robbers entered darted from the building and alerted the town that the bank was being robbed. The robbers grabbed the cashier, O. D. Harris, and used him as a shield while they made their way outside to where two others of their gang held four horses. The cashier was let go, and the four rode out of the town yelling "Hurrah for Hildebrand!" Hildebrand was a popular Bushwhacker who lived not too far from Ste. Genevieve. The bandits sought to align themselves with Hildebrand to gain the sympathies of the ex-Confederates in the area. Sam Hildebrand was born at Bog River, St. Francois County, Missouri, on January 6, 1836. He is reported to have been commissioned a major in the Confederate Army by Gen. Jeff Thompson. Hildebrand was ruthless in his wartime activities and continued the war long after Lee surrendered. He is said to have been indicted for at least twenty murders in Missouri. On March 21, 1872, Hildebrand attempted to kill a man in Pinckneyville, Illinois. Hildebrand was arrested and tried to kill the arresting marshals. Officer Ragland shot Hildebrand in the head after he was gouged by Hildebrand's knife.

Three of the robbers of the Ste. Genevieve Bank are believed to have been Frank, Jesse, and Cole. The fourth was probably John Younger, participating in his first robbery and the latest member of the James-Younger Gang.

John apparently enjoyed the robbery and was very happy to have his share of the money. He didn't have great plans as to how the money would be spent, but he was anxious to participate the next time something was planned. Cole undoubtedly told him to sit tight. Bob Younger had returned from Louisiana about the same time that Cole and John returned to St. Clair County from Ste. Genevieve. Bob was unhappy, as a life of manual labor while in the employ of someone else was not what he had in mind for his life's work. He continued to voice his desire for a farm similar to the ones on which he had grown up. Bob verbalized his greatest dream: to have a farm of which his Pa would have been proud. While Cole merely scoffed at the idea that any one of the Youngers could live openly, as a farmer would need to, John was quick to tell Bob of his involvement at Ste. Genevieve. He talked about the money that was available just for the taking. Bob, who had never been involved in anything outside the law, had seen the results of Cole's involvement with Frank and Jesse James. John and Bob had enjoyed visiting with Jesse a few years before while they were living in Sherman, Texas. Bob liked Jesse and thought he was both clever and trustworthy. While John talked incessantly about what Bob would gain if he were to become involved also, Bob began to listen. He started to think that his dream of a farm like his father's might be obtainable through such funds. Bob had no idea that Cole, Frank, and Jesse had already talked about making James-Younger history once again.

Cole and the James brothers enjoyed the travel time involved in their interstate robberies for the opportunity it gave them to have long talks about themselves, their personal goals, the state of Missouri and the country. The men realized that the Union forces of Missouri were still hard at work building on their plan to run out those with anti-Union interests and retain the power that they had been enjoying since the end of the war. Carpetbaggers were now well ensconced in the banking community. They tightly controlled the purchase of new farms and the money needed for the maintenance of older enterprises. The James-Younger Gang enjoyed the favorable regard of the average citizen of western Missouri as they continued to "get even" with the "Yankees" in their midst. Right or wrong, many people felt that the gang was making a statement that spoke for a lot of them. The boys were befriended and alibis were freely given.

The railroads were ever expanding into Missouri, and much of the same lack of sensitivity demonstrated by the banks was evident during the development and construction of the railroads. Many considered those who held the power within this relatively new enterprise to be the same type of "Yankees" that they opposed in government and banking. While this was the belief of the Jameses and Youngers as well, what they primarily saw in the railroads was an additional source of income. Given the large amounts of money the railroad freely transported all over the country, the opportunity for greater profits seemed likely. Cole, Frank, and Jesse came to an obvious conclusion: why not rob a train? Careful planning would be required, but the rewards could be overwhelming.

Train robberies had been accomplished before in the East. In September, 1866, the Ohio and Mississippi Railroad was robbed of $12,000 seventy-five miles west of Cincinnati. Frank, Jessie, Sim and Jack Reno were said to be the bandits. Not a shot was fired as the express car was detached from the train. A copycat robbery was attempted by two teenagers shortly after, and the Reno brothers successfully robbed a second train. The brothers were eventually captured in connection with the second robbery.[19] However, no one had ever attempted to rob a train in the "West." The James-Younger Gang would be the first.

While Frank and Jesse studied the intricacies of intercepting a train on the Chicago, Rock Island and Pacific Railroad, Cole informed both John and Bob that they would be allowed to participate. John was delighted and found the prospect of robbing a train thrilling. Bob, only twenty years old, was much more cautious. He asked that he be told the details of the plan before he would commit. Cole, irritated at Bob's attitude, accused him of not being honored to have been asked along in the first place and suggested that maybe Bob should not be included after all. Bob, with John's urging, backed off and agreed. For his first robbery, Bob would accompany Cole, John, Frank and Jesse James, Clell Miller, and two other new members of the gang. Charlie Pitts was a friend of Cole's from Jackson County, and Bill Chadwell was someone Jesse knew. With this expanded James-Younger Gang, what could go wrong? Regaling his brothers with stories of reputations being made, Cole urged Jim to set aside his stubborn

Younger pride and join his brothers in what might be the adventure of their lives. While Jim protested to Cole, stating that he was completely uninterested in committing any crime, he admitted to Bob that the idea did intrigue him. Bob suggested that Jim "go along for the ride."[20] Cole told Jim that, if nothing else, he could hold the horses. This most likely was the first and only time that all four Younger brothers participated in a robbery. July 21, 1873 was a day that went down in the history of the United States as well as the family history of the Youngers.

11

Trains, Banks, and Pinkertons

Their evidence would be taken in a court of heaven.
—Cole Younger's remark on those who would give
him an alibi

In early July, Frank James and Cole Younger traveled to Omaha to
determine the date a shipment of gold worth approximately
$75,000 would be sent by rail from the Cheyenne region. Frank
and Cole had somehow heard that the shipment would be sent via
the recently built rails of the Chicago, Rock Island and Pacific
Railroad. On July 21, 1873, two travelers bought some pies as
their noonday meal from Mrs. Robert Grant, the foreman's wife
at the section house near Adair, Iowa. At about the same time,
several other strangers to the area broke into the handcar house. A
spike-bar and hammer were stolen. A short time later, as the
farmers of Adair ate their suppers, a group of men met at the
tracks about one and a half miles from the town. They used the
tools that had been procured earlier to pry off a fish-plate that
connected two of the rails. They then pulled out the spikes. A
rope was tied on the west end of the disconnected north rail. A
rope was then passed under the south rail to where the men hid
along a cut they had made in a nearby bank.[1]
  Early that evening the men heard the approach of the train as
they waited by a curve in the tracks west of Adair at a place called
Turkey Creek. When the train approached the disconnected rail,
the remaining rail was jerked, causing the engine to slam into a

ditch and topple on its side. Engineer John Rafferty of Des Moines was killed instantly. Fireman Dennis Foley received serious injuries. As passengers and employees reacted to the derailment, two of the men jumped into the express car. They forced guard John Burgess to open the safe. To the robbers' dismay, the gold shipment had been delayed and the safe held only $2,000 in currency. The group was so disappointed about the absence of the gold that they passed through the train and collected an additional $1,000 from the frightened passengers. After they had taken what they could from the passengers, the robbers rode off into the night.

An employee of the railroad, Levi Clay, walked to the town of Casey, where the alarm was sent by telegraph to Des Moines and Omaha. A second train carrying armed men was dispatched from Council Bluffs.[2] As the train headed for Adair, it dropped small detachments of men along the route where saddled horses waited for them. A posse was formed. The trail of the robbers was followed to Missouri, where the horses and riders split up. The trail was lost. Jim Younger had allowed his brothers to talk him into attending this history-making event. It was a decision he would regret for the rest of his life. Killing and harming innocent people was never part of the plan in any of the gang's robberies, but Jim had to reason as to what could be expected when tons of steel and great speed were involved. Had he taken the opportunity to learn the plan, he would not have participated. The others of the gang argued that while the death of the engineer and the injury of the fireman were indeed most unfortunate, their fate had been an error in judgment not planned or anticipated. Such results were part of the risks involved with untried methods and new ventures. Jim told his brothers that he wanted nothing further to do with robbing trains and declined his share of the money when it was offered to him. Jim remembered how his father had been killed without regard, and the death of Rafferty upset him greatly. Bob, flush with the excitement of the event, began to realize the seriousness of the affair as he listened to Jim. This was not, after all, the war. The robbers knew nothing at all about Rafferty and Foley other than that they worked for the railroad. Jesse argued that fact alone made them fair game, and Bob halfheartedly accepted this viewpoint. All the members of the gang used Jesse's way of looking at the accident as a way to ease their conscience.

Jesse mentioned the Adair robbery in a letter he wrote in December, 1873. Addressed as being from Deer Lodge, Montana Territory, it was another of Jesse's famous letters to the editor. Jesse denied that he or Frank had had anything to do with the train robbery. Cole had been so disturbed about the deaths that had occurred in Iowa that he later wrote a lengthy denial of his participation, complete with named witnesses:

> As to the Iowa train robbery, I have forgotten the day, I was also in St. Clair County, Mo., at that time, and had the pleasure of attending preaching the evening previous to the robbery at Monagaw Springs. There were fifty or a hundred persons there who will testify in any court that John and I were there. I will give you the names of some of them: Simeon C. Bruce, John S. Wilson, James Van Allen, Rev. Mr. Smith and lady. Helvin Fickle and wife of Greenton Valley were attending the springs at that time, and either of them will testify to the above, for John and I sat in front of Mr. Smith while he was preaching and was in his company for a few moments, together with his wife and Mr. and Mrs Fickle, after service. They live at Greenton Valley, Lafayette county, Mo. and their evidence would be taken in a court of heaven.[3]

This alibi was contained in a letter that Cole wrote to Curg Jones on November 15, 1874. All the Younger boys attended services while at Monagaw Springs and came to know the others of the congregation quite well. It was not uncommon for the Youngers to be at services, and members of the congregation would have thought nothing about saying that they were in attendance, if any were asked. By the time Cole wrote his letter and named the names of those who might make good witnesses, it is unlikely that those named would have remembered exactly just what night he was talking about. It is also unlikely that by the time the letter was published in the Pleasant Hill *Review* such upstanding citizens (a preacher and ladies included!) would have been asked. Life at the Springs was so transient by nature that by the time anyone could have arrived in Monagaw from Iowa or Chicago, the people that were being sought for questioning would most likely have departed. Cole's written alibi, in any event, made it seem as though he were innocent. Bob and Jim were not mentioned because they had never participated in a robbery and had never been named as suspects. There was no need for them to offer alibis.

Cole was telling the truth when he wrote Curg Jones that he had been in St. Clair County "around" the time of the robbery. After fleeing Iowa, the Youngers headed for Monagaw and the safety of their friends and family. Jim's retreat on the river was a welcome sight, and the boys stayed in and about the cave for a month or so while the events at Iowa seemed to blow over in Missouri. All four of them decided to settle into St. Clair County for the summer and fall, albeit for different reasons. Cole and John, with their funds from the previous two robberies, found it unnecessary to work. They decided to relax with their friends and enjoy themselves. They didn't worry much about a posse finding them, as the people of the towns of Monagaw and Roscoe were well aware of their desire to stay secluded. The Youngers felt safe. Jim, feeling remorseful about having participated in the Adair robbery, consoled himself in the arms of his beloved Cora Mc-Neill. Bob, although saddened by the deaths of the two men in Iowa, made plans for the money he had received. His spoils were small compared to what members of the gang had collected at other times, but to Bob they provided a hope that he would be able to somehow start up his farm. He hadn't thought far enough ahead to determine the particulars of his plan but felt that there was no time like the present to begin thinking about it. He questioned his uncles and friends about farm crops and what equipment would be needed to get the operation started. Humoring Bob, those whom he questioned provided him with more than enough knowledge to actually allow him to believe his dream was a possibility. Bob knew he had to raise much more money somehow, but that was for the future. For the summer, he would be content simply gathering information and formulating his plan.

There exists a tale in Younger folklore that has been repeated so often it likely has basis in fact. The story takes place in St. Clair County. Sometime during the summer (perhaps after the Iowa train robbery?) Marshall Cobb of Appleton City led a posse of ten local men after the Younger boys. The posse came upon one of the springs near Monagaw and tied their horses to avail themselves of the water. Out stepped the four Younger brothers. "Hands over your heads," they commanded. Once this was accomplished, Cole Younger said to the eleven men, "How would you boys like some coffee and a bite to eat?" The astonished posse was marched up the hill to the Monagaw Springs Hotel where they all were served breakfast, joined by the four Youngers. When they were through with their meal, Cole and his brothers lined the men up outside. The inexperienced posse believed they were goners. Instead of killing them, Cole delivered a stern lecture reminding them that the war was over. Cole advised them that they should not be hunting their neighbors for the purpose of collecting Pinkerton reward money. He told them that they should be ashamed of themselves and continued that it was very important they remember what had happened at Monagaw that day. Cole closed with, "That's all, men. You can go. And go down on your marrow bones and ask your God to forgive you because the Younger boys, they do."[4] However bold an undertaking this capture of a posse might have been, it is typical of Cole and John's humor and might just be true.

Summer turned into fall and then winter as the Younger boys enjoyed each other's company and the carefree atmosphere of Monagaw Springs. They often had long talks together but mostly spent time in the company of others. Jim spent his time with Cora, and Cole visited with former war buddies while he managed to maintain a low profile. John continued to spend most of his time enjoying himself at the Monagaw Hotel, and Bob visited with his many friends in the area. Bob spent a lot of time with his Uncle Bruce that winter. The boys visited often with Hannah McFerrin, who was the sister of Suze. The boys liked to visit and enjoy made-to-order meals. "Aunt" Hannah was very good to them as were most of the others in the area. Bob and John also spent quite a bit of time at the Snuffers: they liked Theodrick, and Mrs. Snuffer reminded them of their own mother. All four boys spent the Christmas of 1873 at dinner with the Snuffers. Shortly after Christmas, they received a visit from Jesse James. Jesse said that he had come to enjoy the springs but also to discuss another idea. He asked the Youngers if they were interested in being involved in another train "job." Jim was horrified and adamantly refused to be involved. He steered clear of Jesse and had nothing whatsoever to say to his brothers when they attempted to broach the subject with him. Jim clearly did not wish to participate. That left Cole, John, and Bob. Cole and John readily agreed, but Bob had second thoughts. He still felt quite remorseful at what had happened to the engineer and fireman in Iowa. Jesse told him these plans did not include derailing a train but rather stopping it outside a station. Assured that the possibility of an innocent man getting hurt was minimal, Bob agreed. He hoped to "earn" additional money for his farm. Clell Miller would once again join the James and Younger brothers. This time they hoped to be more successful.

Although both the Jameses and the Youngers had heard that the Pinkertons had been hired by the railroad after the Iowa robbery, they felt little concern about the detectives. Cole, John, and Bob reasoned that since the Chicago detectives had failed to show up in St. Clair County, they obviously had little knowledge of the habits of the Youngers. Frank and Jesse had been home to Kearney for Christmas, and nothing out of the ordinary had been detected by them, either. It was to the gang's advantage that few people other than their friends and relatives knew what they looked like. No photographs were circulated.

Jesse showed the Youngers a special supplement to the St. Louis *Dispatch* that had been published on November 22, 1873. It was a lengthy article entitled "A Terrible Quintette" and was written by Maj. John Newman Edwards, who was now working for the paper. The article was said by Edwards to be based on interviews with Frank and Jesse James and Arthur McCoy. McCoy had been named by Detective Bligh as having been involved in the Russellville robbery. Edwards also claimed that information regarding the Youngers had been supplied to him by their friends and acquaintances. Edwards defended the James and Younger brothers, detailing alibis for every robbery in which they were said to have been involved. He began with Russellville and continued up to the most recent, the train robbery in Iowa. Edwards scoffed at the detectives and sheriffs who had not been able to find the James and Younger boys following the incident at Adair.

More important, for the very first time in print, Edwards

provided biographical information on both sets of brothers. His central theme was that these men had gallantly served the Confederacy, a cause which they had been driven to support by the constant and complete harassment of their families. Edwards portrayed both the James brothers and Cole as ferocious soldiers retaliating against the onslaught of the Union forces which had made life hell for themselves and their loved ones. Their wrath knew no bounds as they sought to fight for the common man, and now look, they were being accused of robbing banks and trains. The war was, after all, over. Edwards reasoned that if the James and Younger boys were to be left alone they might have something worthwhile to offer the great state of Missouri. Instead, they were being hounded and every crime committed laid at their innocent feet.[5] Edwards wrote several lines about John Younger as well as Cole. Cole assumed that this was in response to Jesse's defense of the boy in regard to the Kansas City Fairground robbery. Taking up the mantle of defense, Augustus C. Appler began a series of articles defending the Youngers in the Osceola *Democrat*. Aided by Owen Snuffer, Appler further detailed the Younger story and later published it in book form.

John Newman Edwards was born on January 4, 1839, at Front Royal, Virginia. He relocated to Lexington, Lafayette County, Missouri, sometime in the mid-1850s. He shortly found work on the Lexington *Expositor* as a printer and eventually became the editor of that paper.

While living in Lexington, Edwards met the future Confederate general Joseph O. Shelby and the two became great friends. Edwards joined Shelby in military service, enlisting in the Confederate Army from Lafayette County in 1862. He served as Shelby's adjutant. A born journalist, Edwards documented his experiences during the war.

For over twenty years after the war, Edwards was considered one of Missouri's premier newspapermen. He held positions at the Kansas City *Times*, St. Louis *Dispatch*, Sedalia *Dispatch* and St. Joseph *Gazette*. Edwards became the foremost champion of the James and Younger brothers and published the article explaining their lifestyle in 1873. "A Terrible Quintette" appeared in the St. Louis *Dispatch*.

Cole and the Jameses were pleased with Edwards's work. How much was truth and what was fiction mattered little. Their story was being told, and a major figure in publishing had chosen to defend them. John Younger was delighted to have been included in the dissertation. Bob was relieved to have been left out. The idea of leaving well enough alone when public sentiment seemed to be in their favor is an idea that apparently never crossed the minds of the James and Younger brothers. It certainly hadn't by January, 1874. The new year would bring pain, horror, and regret to the men so eloquently portrayed in the novelette by Major Edwards.

History was made by the James-Younger Gang once again when they committed the first train robbery in the state of Missouri on January 31, 1874. The gang selected the Iron Mountain Railroad. The location they picked to accomplish their deed was the station at Gad's Hill, one hundred miles south of St. Louis. Gad's Hill was the flag station on the downgrade into the piedmont. It served as a center for the cordwood and charcoal business of the Pekin Coal Company.

About 5:30 in the evening, five men walked into the station with their guns drawn. Most of the men of the small town were in the station socializing, as men of that time were apt to do. The ticket agent and the other men were put under guard and left in the company of one of the robbers. The other robbers went outside and placed a signal flag on the track which would signal the train to stop for passengers when it arrived at the station. The plan worked. As the train stopped, the conductor, C. A. Alford, stepped down. He was placed under guard by yet another robber, and the remaining members of the gang boarded the train. Baggage Master Louis Constant stood by as the express safe was looted of an undetermined amount of money. The robbers continued through the train to where the passengers watched the excitement. Examining the hands of the men and telling the passengers that they did not wish to take the hard-earned money of "working men" or ladies, the robbers took the money and jewelry of their more affluent victims.[6]

There were various reports stating that an interesting incident took place during the robbery. One newspaper story claimed that a man thought to have been a Pinkerton was taken to a private compartment in the train, where he was stripped in the attempt to determine if he was indeed a detective.[7] Exactly what the robbers were looking for remains a mystery. Another report told of a man being forced outside the train, where he was stripped down to his underclothing. Why this may have occurred was not addressed. Perhaps the robbers thought this entertaining punishment for someone who may have "talked back" to them or perhaps for someone they suspected or even knew to be affiliated with the trains or banks of the East or North. As was proven later, John F. Lincoln, superintendent of the St. Paul & Sioux City Railroad, and John L. Merriam, founder of a shipping and express business, the Merchant's Bank of St. Paul, and a member of the Minnesota legislature, were aboard the train that day. Lincoln was robbed of $200, and Merriam, who was identified as "Merryman," was robbed of his watch and $75. Could one of these men have had the misfortune to have been so publicly humiliated?

Their business completed, the robbers prepared to leave. As they mounted their horses, one of them handed engineer William Wetton a written account of the robbery. All that needed to be done to complete a fairly accurate description of what had just happened was to fill in the amount of money taken in the space provided by the author of the press release. Such an audacious act is representative of Jesse's humor. As the robbers disappeared into the dense woods surrounding the station, the train started toward Piedmont, seven miles down the line. Once there, the engineer telegraphed the news of the robbery. A posse was formed the following morning but had little chance of catching the robbers, who by then had traveled many miles into central Missouri.

The railroads had hoped what had happened in Iowa was an isolated incident and that the death of Rafferty would serve as a deterrent to anyone thinking of robbing another train. They hoped that the men involved would return to robbing banks, as that most likely was where the scalawags had come from. With the second robbery, the railroads realized that a new phenomenon was being born. This time they did not rely on local posses to catch their defilers but immediately called on the services of the Pinkerton Detective Agency. Although they silently entered the state of

Missouri after their prey, the James and Younger brothers, the presence of the Pinkertons would be felt and exposed very quickly.

The Youngers parted company with the Jameses and returned to St. Clair County. Cole encouraged Bob to look over property in Arkansas if Bob was still interested in farming. Assuring his brother that he was, Bob told Cole that he was interested in farming only in Missouri. Cole thought the idea preposterous especially in light of recent events and told Bob so. Bob finally agreed to accompany Cole to Arkansas if only to enjoy the atmosphere of Hot Springs and get away from St. Clair for a while. Although Cole had spent time there during the war, the two felt anonymous in Arkansas. They decided they could engage in some travel and entertainment, which would be financed by their new-found wealth. John planned to accompany them, but Jim decided to stay right where he was. He was not pleased with his brothers' activities and would not "celebrate" with any ill-gotten money. Shortly before they left for Hot Springs, John became ill. Saying it was nothing serious, John encouraged Bob and Cole to stick to their original plan to leave for the Hot Springs and made plans to join them when he felt better. Cole and Bob left for Arkansas, arriving there within days of their departure from Missouri in February, 1874.

One of the Pinkerton detectives sent to Missouri to find and hopefully capture any or all members of the James-Younger Gang was a man named John W. Whicher. On March 10, Whicher arrived in Clay County. He told the former sheriff of the county, O. P. Moss, and the president of the Commercial Bank of Liberty, D. J. Adkins, that he planned to capture the James brothers. He outlined his plan. He stated that he would present himself at the James farm as a hand for hire, would gain the confidence of the James family, and when that was accomplished, arrest the James brothers. The two Liberty men were aghast at the naive plan and told Whicher that the Jameses would kill him if they were even to suspect that he was not who he claimed to be. Whicher ignored their warnings and set out in the evening for the James farm in Kearney. He never returned. His body was found along the road near Independence in Jackson County the next morning with bullets through his head and heart. A story was told by the ferry operator at Blue Mills that four men had crossed the river at three o'clock the previous morning and that one of them had been bound and gagged. Three of the men told the operator that the fourth man was a horse thief that they were delivering to the authorities while they looked for his accomplice.[8] The story has been told that the Jameses confronted Whicher on the road leading into Kearney, and he inquired about work in the area. The Jameses questioned the detective and when his answers did not satisfy them as to his intent, they shot him. Whicher would not be the only Pinkerton operative to die that month in western Missouri.

12

Black Day in Roscoe

Just rambling around.
—Pinkerton Detective Louis J. Lull's response to
John Younger's question of "What are you doing in
St. Clair?" March 17, 1874

John Younger's illness was likely an ailment having to do with little sleep and too much nightlife. In addition to spending most of his time at the hotel in Monagaw, John also liked to visit a little town in Kansas. La Cygne was called "The Toughest Town in Eastern Kansas." The town "boasted" five saloons, and John, Cole, and sometimes Bob would ride over to amuse themselves watching the various types of people that frequented the town. While Cole and Bob rarely drank, John had little compunction when it came to having a good time. One account of the town stated that the "Younger Boys were there several times, well-dressed, smooth, sleek fellows who looked like successful professional men."[1]

John tried to get Jim to accompany him in the absence of Cole and Bob, but Jim declined. He didn't drink and was quite happy being monogamous in his relationship with Cora. Jim urged his brother to cut back on his nightlife so that he might feel better and join his brothers in Arkansas.

On the night of March 16, 1874, John asked Jim to accompany him to a dance that was being held at the Monagaw Hotel. Jim agreed and once there found that he enjoyed himself quite a bit. He and John stayed at the dance until late in the evening. Leaving

Monagaw, they spent the night at the large cabin of Aunt Hannah McFerrin and her husband John. The cabin was located three miles southeast of Monagaw.

Sometime earlier that week, two men checked into the Commercial Hotel in Osceola as cattle buyers. Louis J. Lull and James Wright (who was also known as Boyle) worked for the Pinkerton Detective Agency out of Chicago. Both men had been in the group of Pinkertons that had been sent to Missouri to investigate the Gad's Hill robbery. While the search for the Younger and James brothers had begun in Wayne County, it soon became clear that the gang was nowhere in the area. The Pinkertons looking for the Youngers continued their search into St. Clair County but had no luck finding them. Ironically, the Youngers were holed up in their cave at the time the detectives were in Monagaw. The Pinkertons left to look throughout western Missouri, but Lull and Wright eventually returned to St. Clair County.

Louis J. Lull, twenty-nine, had served with the Union Army. He had attended Annapolis as a member of the class of 1866 but did not graduate.[2] At the time he took the Younger assignment from the Pinkertons, he was a captain on the Chicago police force. James Wright was from St. Louis. Some reports claim that he was in the Confederate Army and had served with some of the men from St. Clair County. If this were true, it would help to explain some of his actions in the confrontation to come. Fearing that his name might be known, Lull checked into the Commercial Hotel under the name of W. J. Allen.

The detectives determined that the Youngers usually were around the McFerrin and Snuffer places or in Monagaw when they were in St. Clair County. They enlisted the help of an Osceola man, Edwin B. Daniels. Daniels had been working part-time as a deputy to Osceola sheriff James R. Johnson. Daniels had lived in the county several years and was no doubt very familiar with the Younger boys.

Ed Daniels was born on August 5, 1843, in Boston, Massachusetts, the son of Edwin T. Daniels of Massachusetts and Christina Blandford of England. The Daniels family moved from Boston to Sedalia, Missouri, in 1864 at the height of the Civil War. Edwin B., however, served the Union in the First Regiment of the

Massachusetts Volunteer Cavalry. The Daniels family moved to Osceola in 1866, and it appears that Edwin B. was with his mother and father at this time. His father was employed as a bookkeeper. Edwin T. sat on the committee to incorporate the City of Osceola. He later resigned his position, and his son Edwin B. took his place. Edwin B. was elected a constable of Osceola Township.

On March 16, as Jim and John were enjoying the dance at the Monagaw Hotel, the two detectives and their scout checked into the Roscoe House, a hotel in the small town of Roscoe. They heard that a Widow Sims, who lived nearby, had some cattle for sale. If questioned, this knowledge would give the men an alibi for being in the area.[3]

About 1:30 the afternoon of March 17, John and Jim rode over to the Snuffers' for lunch. The Youngers frequently stayed at the Snuffers' home in St. Clair County. John, Bob, and Jim had become very close to the Snuffers at the time the boys first went to live in St. Clair County.

Theodrick Snuffer's father, George, was killed in action during the War of 1812. Theodrick's first wife was the daughter of Col. Josiah Baker, who was an officer during the Revolutionary War. Theodrick married Sallie Patton in 1793 and settled in St. Clair County near Roscoe in 1838. The Snuffers had five sons and one daughter. Josiah Snuffer was their eldest son and a close friend of Cole's. He was killed in 1863 at Little Rock, where he was serving under Sterling Price. In addition to Josiah, the sons included Cyrus, who was murdered by a band of outlaws while in the Choctaw Nation, and Owen, who was an officer in the Confederate Army. Owen was closest to the Youngers after the death of Josiah and became known around the area as a journalist and writer. He wrote articles for the newspapers about the early settlers of the area and about the burning of Osceola. He was also the author of "The Battle of Lone Jack," a contemporary history of the encounter. Owen later assisted A. C. Appler in writing his account of the lives of the Younger brothers.

Jim and John had just sat down at the table when they heard horses outside the Snuffer house. Lull and Daniels approached the house. Wright hung back, out of sight. The two Youngers went up into the attic, where they could see the "cattle buyers." Theodrick

Snuffer answered the detectives' inquiries about directions to the Widow Sims house. After the two rode off, John and Jim came down from the attic.[4] Snuffer told them the cattle buyers rode off in the opposite direction from that which he told them. John wanted to follow the two, but Jim declined. Jim wasn't looking for trouble. John insisted, stating that the younger of the men (Daniels) looked nervous and that both had been too well armed to have been simply cattle buyers. Finally, Jim agreed to investigate with John. They mounted the two horses they had hidden in the Snuffers' barn and rode in the direction the two men had taken.

Lull and Daniels were joined by Wright three-quarters of a mile up the road from the Snuffer farm. While Wright rode in front of them, Lull and Daniels walked their horses along, discussing the objects of their search. Suddenly they heard horses behind them and turned to see John and Jim Younger. Wright had seen the Youngers as they approached and fled the scene altogether, riding his horse at a breakneck speed through the fields. Jim yelled at Wright, ordering him to stop. When he didn't, Jim shot at him with the pistol he held in his hand. The bullet missed Wright but took off his hat.[5]

John and Jim ordered Lull and Daniels to stop and drop their guns. They did, and Jim got off his horse to pick up the guns. Jim admired Lull's English-made .43 caliber Trantor and thanked him for the present. When the Youngers asked Lull and Daniels who they were and where they were from, Lull answered. Saying they were from Osceola and could prove it, the men were asked what they were doing in the Roscoe area. "Just rambling around," was the reply. By this time there were several witnesses to the scene on the road. Two farmers, Ol Davis and Speed McDonald, a friend and sometime cook for the Youngers, looked up from their chores curious as to what was happening.

Pointing his double-barreled shotgun in the direction of his captives, John asked the two men if they were detectives. They said they were not. John then asked them why they were so heavily armed. Lull responded that they had the right. John lowered his shotgun at Daniels's chest as Daniels made an additional comment. With the Youngers' attention on Daniels, John and Jim did not see

Louis Lull reach under his coat to withdraw a small No. 2 Smith & Wesson pistol. Lull removed the gun with one swift motion and shot John through the neck. As Lull's horse lurched forward, John fired at Lull, hitting him in the shoulder and arm. Jim fired at Lull as well but missed. Lull remained on his horse and took off down the road. Daniels attempted to follow Lull, but Jim stopped his escape by shooting him through the neck. Daniels fell, mortally wounded.

As Lull's horse ran through a grove of trees, he was knocked from his saddle by a low-hanging branch. John, his fury holding him on his horse, rode up to where Lull lay on the ground and fired his pistol twice. One round missed while the other hit Lull squarely in the chest. John started to ride back to Jim but found it difficult to stay in the saddle. Jim rolled Daniels over and saw that he was dead. He looked up and saw John nearly falling from his horse. Jim called John's name and John looked at his brother. Then John fell, his body landing on the other side of a fence. John Younger was dead.

Jim ran over to John and saw that he was dead. Speed McDonald reached John at about the same time as Jim. Speed watched Jim remove John's pistols, watch, and personal effects. Jim threw one of John's pistols to Speed and told him to take his horse and ride down to tell Snuffer what had happened. But first, he asked McDonald to take care of John. In shock and with anger, Jim mounted John's horse. He believed Lull was also dead and rode in the direction in which Wright had fled.[6]

Ol Davis had reported the incident to his father. John Davis examined the body of Daniels and determined he was dead. He saw that John Younger was dead also. As he walked around the site of the confrontation, he came upon Lull, who had propped himself up against a tree. Expressing the thought that he hoped he had fallen into good hands, Lull looked up at the farmer. Assuring him that he had, Davis attempted to help Lull.[7] McDonald had placed himself near John's body until he could get help to move him. By this time, people from the area had begun to arrive, and they helped Davis move Lull to the front porch of Aunt Hannah's cabin. John's body was in the meantime taken inside along with Daniel's body. Later that evening, Lull was placed in a spring wagon and taken to the Roscoe House. Drs. A. C. Marquis and L. Lewis were called to care for Lull. Upon examining his wounds, the doctors decided the detective would live. The exact method of medical treatment would later elicit questions and accusations from Lull's wife.

Pinkerton Agent Wright had made a report to Sheriff Johnson back in Osceola by this time. After he left the Chalk Level road upon sighting the Youngers, he rode northwest. Obtaining a hat from a farmer so he wouldn't be recognized easily by the Youngers, who he thought were in close pursuit, Wright eventually wound around to Osceola. Wright told Johnson about the "capture" of Lull and Daniels and reported that he heard gunshots as he rode away. Johnson organized a group of men led by Deputy Simpson Beckley. He instructed them to ride to Roscoe to determine what had happened and to make sure further violence did not occur. As the group was being organized, Wright disappeared, apparently never to be seen in St. Clair County again. The Lee's Summit *Ledger*, reporting on the death of John Younger on March 25, 1874, claimed that "the St. Louis detective who escaped, was not named Wright, but Duckworth, who resigned from the detective force of St. Louis some weeks ago, but who is believed to have been in Pinkerton's service."[8]

Ed Daniels' body was later returned to Osceola where he was buried. The citizens of St. Clair County would always debate whether Daniels was a hero or a traitor.

David Crowder, a young man who lived in Roscoe, was asked to guard John's body as it lay in Aunt Hannah's cabin that night. John's friends wanted to be sure the "law" did not remove it before they had a chance to bury it. They did not want any of the anti-Younger contingent from Osceola desecrating John's body in any way. The next morning John was buried in a shallow grave on the Snuffers' property, where his body could be guarded. Jim had returned after he failed to locate Wright. He asked Theodrick to see to it that John was buried and that his body was not disturbed. Jim then left for Arkansas to tell Cole and Bob the tragic news. That night Speed and Snuffer put John's body into a wagon and took him to the Yeater Cemetery a few miles southeast of Snuffer's farm. Knowing full well they could not "mark" John's burial site,

Snuffer and Speed laid John at an angle with his head to the northwest and his feet to the southeast. In this way the grave could be recognized by those who knew it was there.

A coroner's jury was called the next day. Reading testimony from those involved, John Davis, G. W. Cox, W. Holmes, R. C. Dill, H. Greason, and A. Ray found that John Younger had been killed by a pistol "supposed" to be in the hands of W. J. Allen (Lull) and that Daniels had been killed by a pistol "supposed" to have been fired by James Younger.[9]

According to the Pinkertons and other law officials in Osceola, Lull's condition worsened and he died after several days. A Mr. Linden of the agency accompanied Marian B. Lull to her husband's bedside. Lull's mother also joined him. This is where the controversy begins. Many of the people of St. Clair County believed that Lull did not die in Missouri and that his death was a hoax. Claiming Lull was dead, the Pinkertons took his body by train from Clinton to Illinois. He was buried at Rose Hill Cemetery in Chicago. Many thought the transportation of Lull's "body" was fictitious. They reasoned that the body was said to be that of the dead Lull in order to protect Lull from the wrath of the surviving Younger boys, who would certainly avenge the death of their beloved brother. The doctor who attended Lull once he was moved to Osceola was Dr. D. C. McNeill, Cora's father. Never in the years to come would Dr. McNeill either confirm or deny that Lull died in Osceola. However, many years later, his daughter Cora intimated that the hoax may have been a reality. She claimed that whenever her father was questioned about it his response was the same: "You must learn to keep the game in your lead."[10] Evidently, in order to keep from incriminating himself, Dr. McNeill felt the only thing he could do was keep quiet. While the truth of the matter is unknown, it is possible that Lull did not die in Missouri. It is also possible that Lull did indeed take a turn for the worse and died either while en route to Illinois or shortly after his arrival in Chicago. An impressive funeral was held for the former police captain with hundreds of policemen attending. Lull was laid to rest in a spacious Chicago cemetery.

The death of Louis J. Lull, a captain with the Chicago police department and a detective for the Pinkerton Detective Agency, brought great controversy. Even the manner of his death and the naming of the man who shot him were subject to varying opinions. The following is the account of Lull's wife, Marian. The piece appeared in the Chicago *Tribune* shortly after Lull's death.

LULL'S DEATH.—The Body Of The Detective Killed In Missouri Arrives In Chicago - His Wife's Story

The remains of Captain Louis J. Lull arrive in the city this morning, accompanied by his widow, his mother, and Mr. Linden of Pinkerton's Agency, who have been with him since the encounter with the Younger brothers in the Missouri wilds. In conversation with The Journal reporter subsequently, Mrs. Lull said that her husband's death was caused by the coward Wright, in the first place, and by the ignorance and blundering of Dr. Marcus in the second. Upon Wright fell the heaviest blame. Had he not fled from his companions without the least regard for anything but his own life, she believes Captain Lull would be alive and well today, and to him, also, is attributed that a doctor was procured who knew nothing of his profession.

Mrs. Lull gave a most interesting account of the battle, hot and hand-to-hand, which resulted in the death of three men and the wounding of a fourth. The country was the wildest and most difficult to cross she had ever seen, and the road full of turns and twists. According to her husband's relation, the Younger brothers were on the party before they had any intimation. The first word Captain Lull heard was "Halt" and he looked around only to see himself covered by a shotgun. What followed has been so fully told in these columns that it will be readily recalled. Wright sped away, Daniels and John Younger fell dead, and James Younger and Captain Lull, both with plunging, racing steeds, fired back and forth at each other from their saddles. Of four shots Lull sent one through his antagonist's body, as was afterwards proved. In return he received two bullets. One struck his left wrist, shattering the bones and grazing his body after passing through the heavy clothing, the other entered the left breast, two inches below the lung and passed entirely through him. Unable to control his horse he was knocked from the saddle by the brush and lay under the bushes until discovered. Mrs. Lull charges on Wright that he not only ran away when he might have shot James Younger and saved her husband, but that he went to Osceola, found Daniels brother, a coward like himself, got drunk with him, never telling a soul what occurred till next morning. Then when Captain Lull had been found and housed, Wright discouraged the idea of sending for Doctor McNeil, an able surgeon, because he charged too much and insisted that Marcus would do all right. When Mrs. Lull reached her husband she found him rapidly growing worse. The physician had plugged up the wound in the breast without washing it out and she was sure it was bleeding internally causing violent hemorrhage. The doctor told her it was the proper treatment but she would not believe it, and took out the plug herself, washing the wound as well as she could. It was then in a terrible condition. The doctor bandaged the patient again, when she discharged him, removing his blundering work and had Dr. McNeil brought at once. He confirmed her entirely and feared the effects of the false treatment could not be counteracted. The wound had not been probed and the gathering of poisonous materials had passed into the lung, beyond his reach. Everything possible was done for the wounded man. Mrs. Lull said that they did not expect that he would ever be strong again but his constitution was so fine that it was thought he would live some years. The attention bestowed upon them at Roscoe was all that the people could possibly bestow. Delicacies were brought from St. Louis and Captain Lull was kept alive by his will and excessive stimulus. He grew weaker daily, however and it became evident that his whole system was poisoned by the stoppage of the wound in its first stages. He was determined not to give up and confident he should return to Chicago. "When I do," he said to his wife, "I will tell the people how you saved my life." Congestive chills set in a few days before his death and the doctor gave up all hope. On Wednesday morning last, he was seized with more violent congestion and then his own hopes failed.

His mother said to him, "You will rest soon," and he replied, "Yes, I will rest soon in heaven." His mind was clear and bright. At 7: o'clock in the evening, after bidding them all farewell, he died without a struggle. Mrs. Lull, the mother, said the death scene was beautiful. Her son was perfectly resigned when he knew he was to die and passed away as he had lived, like a brave and faithful man.

The funeral will take place tomorrow morning, the Masonic Order of which the deceased was a member, conducting them. The procession will take the train for Rosehill at 10: o'clock. As large a number of the police force as can be absent will pay their respects to their former captain, whose record was untarnished.

For some unexplained reason, Jim Younger failed to arrive in Arkansas to tell his brothers what had happened to John. Whether he wasn't able to locate them or had stopped somewhere along the way to recover from his own personal shock has never been determined. About two weeks after the incident at Roscoe, Cole and Bob were having their breakfast at a hotel in Hot Springs, Arkansas. Cole casually picked up a newspaper to read as he drank his coffee. Suddenly Bob saw Cole's face turn white. Bob asked him what was the matter, and Cole could only hand the newspaper to him. Bob read that his brother John had been killed by Pinkerton detectives in St. Clair County. Jim Younger's whereabouts were unknown. The two brothers were rendered speechless as they looked at each other. Cole finally stood and without looking at Bob said that they must go to Missouri and find Jim. Bob didn't move. He could not believe the brother with whom he had survived the war and who had become his greatest confidant was dead. The pain was great in Bob's broken heart. Cole repeated that Jim must be found and ordered his brother to accompany him. Bob managed to find his voice and wondered if Jim might be looking for them in Arkansas. Bob said that he couldn't go to Missouri. It was an ordeal he couldn't yet face.[11] He said he would look for Jim in Arkansas while Cole returned to Missouri. Cole agreed, and the two brothers parted company.

Halfway to the Missouri border, Cole met up with the dejected Jim. The only explanation that was offered in regard to Jim's whereabouts was that Jim had been "around" Arkansas, looking for his brothers. Cole and Jim returned to Hot Springs, where Jim related to his brothers the terrible encounter with the Pinkertons and the events that led up to the death of John. Bob could barely stand to hear Jim's words but forced himself to listen. After Jim completed his story, the brothers sat in silence. Eventually, Cole broke the silence by asking his brothers what they planned to do. Cole himself had decided on returning to Lake City, Florida, where he would attempt to get involved in some type of business venture, preferably more cattle.

Jim informed his brothers that he could not and would not return to Missouri. He wondered how this event would affect his relationship with Cora. Jim had decided somewhere in between St. Clair County and Hot Springs, Arkansas, that he would go to California. He did not want to return to Los Angeles but rather go somewhere else where he could once again become involved in ranching. Cole suggested that Jim contact two people: their Uncle Coleman, head of the San Jose Horticulture Society, and perhaps the Jameses' uncle, Drury. Drury James had a fair-size ranch in the middle part of California in San Luis Obispo County. Jim agreed that he would contact someone he knew to get himself set up in California and prepared for his journey west. Cole vowed to himself that he would find a way for Jim to return home to be with his family after the shock of John's death lessened.

Bob remained silent as he realized that Cole was heading in one direction and Jim in another. Without John, there was no middle for him. He knew that he would be welcomed by either brother if he were to ask to accompany him but he also recognized his own need to take time for himself to mourn the loss of his closest brother. Telling his brothers that he would be visiting his sisters in Sherman, Bob made plans to return to Missouri. He knew that Cole would not support his desire to go back to St. Clair County to commune with the spirit of his dead brother. The area was now unsafe. By mentioning any such plans to Cole, Bob knew that he would have to listen to advice he would rather not hear.

The three brothers parted company that spring, with Jim heading for California, Cole traveling to Florida, and Bob returning to Missouri. Each of their hearts must have been heavy with grief over the loss of John, and each of the brothers chose to experience his pain by being alone. The public's fascination with the events of the Roscoe Gun Battle continued for years to come. Dreat Younger, a cousin to the Younger boys, related the following incident:

There was a carnival in town, Berryville, Arkansas, and with the show was a side show extolling the fact that they had John Younger's body inside on display. This was about 1921–22 This was doing a good business until my dad [Arthur S. Younger] and my Uncle Melburn went inside to view the body. When they came out, they informed the carnival barker that the body was not that of John Younger and warned him to shut the show down and git the hell out of town. As they [Arthur and Melburn] weighed around two hundred pounds each, they convinced the fellow quickly as to what course to take. He left. He also left the body he had on display. The town authorities in the little town explained to Uncle Melburn and Dad that they had created the problem by running the fellow off, so it was up to them to take care of it. They buried the body themselves under the watchful eye of the authorities. Never learned who he was.[12]

13

A Look to the Future

. . . a bit small . . .
   —Mattie Hamlet on the Lexington robberies

Bob Younger decided to take a circuitous route back to Missouri
so that he could keep the upper hand on who might recognize him
along the way. He and Cole had read of the murder of Whicher
previous to John's death. The boys had discussed the fact that the
Pinkertons appeared to be out on a full-force hunt for the James
and Younger brothers. Cole warned Bob to be careful in Texas, as
the Chicago detectives seemed to appear out of nowhere. Deciding
to visit his mother's grave before confronting John's death in St.
Clair County, Bob approached Jackson County from the east.
Sometime on that trip, the vulnerable Bob met and fell in love
with a beautiful widow from New England named "Maggie" who
lived on a farm east of Jackson County. Although new to the area
from the North, Bob's new love had not been affiliated with the
federal army in any way, and evidently Bob felt no "Yankee"
threat as far as she was concerned. A kind, beautiful woman could
help ease Bob through his loneliness in a way that his staunch,
loner, surviving brothers could not.

Jim had been welcomed at Uncle Coleman's ranch in San Jose
but soon sensed that his uncle was uncomfortable with his presence. Jim realized that when Cole had visited San Jose it had been
wartime and Cole had not been an outlaw. Jim told his uncle of
the death of John and the Pinkerton confrontation. Even though

145

the world knew nothing of his involvement with the train robbery in Iowa, Jim did, and he felt his association with Uncle Coleman and his family was improper. Jim decided to seek employment elsewhere in California. Coleman Younger was quite active with the various cattle associations, and his special breed of short-horn cattle was known throughout the world.

Drury James, uncle of the James boys, was nearly as noted a cattleman as Coleman. He was a very interesting man who had accomplished much in the previous couple of decades. Living in Oldham County, Kentucky, where he was involved in the mercantile business, Drury volunteered for service at the onset of what has come to be known as the Mexican War. After the war, Drury and his nephew, Robert Mimms, joined a company for the overland trip to the gold mines of California. Drury was in the same area as Robert James, the James boys' father, when Robert died there sometime in 1850.

Drury soon became involved in buying and selling cattle. He sold beef to the miners in "Hangtown" at a substantial profit. In 1851, he extended his cattle drives as far south as Los Angeles with stops and buys in San Luis Obispo, Monterey, and Santa Clara counties. One time he drove 1,500 head of cattle from Los Angeles to northern California. It is likely that he met Coleman Younger sometime around then. In 1860, Drury purchased 10,000 acres of government land at a place called La Panza outside Paso Robles in San Luis Obispo County. In 1869 Drury purchased half-interest in the Paso de Robles Hot Springs and the surrounding land for $11,000. He was also director of the Bank of San Luis Obispo and half-owner of the Eagle Stream Flouring Mill.[1]

It is fairly certain that living in the same state, Drury James and Coleman Younger would have been quite familiar with each other and probably would have done business together at some point. Perhaps it was Coleman who suggested that Jim ask Drury James if he knew of employment in San Luis Obispo. Perhaps Jim remembered that Cole had suggested he look up the Jameses' uncle. Either way, Jim showed up in San Luis Obispo County and soon had a job on one of Drury James's ranches at La Panza.[2] The closest town was the sleepy village of Santa Margarita. Jim enjoyed the rugged work of the cowboy and the quiet and beautiful surroundings of the California mountains. Jim began to think of earning enough to start up his own enterprise and asking Cora to live with him in California as his wife.

Bob was still in deep pain over the death of John and even his newfound love could not comfort him. He traveled to Jackson County, where he visited the grave of his mother. From there he finally ventured into St. Clair County, where Snuffer showed him where John had been buried. Unable to stay but a very short time, Bob thanked Theodrick for all he had done. The anguish Bob felt at being in St. Clair County, knowing that John would never be with him there again, was great. Bob decided to leave immediately for Texas before Cole learned of his absence and caused him more upset. Bob arrived at his sisters' home in Denison at the end of April.

On April 24, 1874, Jesse James married his longtime sweetheart, Zee Mimms. The wedding was performed at the home of Zee's sister near Kearney. There were many reports as to where the couple honeymooned, including Mexico and Vera Cruz. Whether these destinations were reached or not, it is fairly certain that the Jameses spent at least part, if not all, of their honeymoon in Sherman, Texas. Jesse's sister Susan and her husband Allen Parmer lived close by at Wichita Falls, and both the Jameses and the Youngers had many friends in the area.

Allen Parmer was born in Clay County and is said to have joined with Quantrill when he was very young. His Confederate pension application, under the name of Allen Palmer, a name that he is said to have often used, states that he served with Company D, Shanks Regiment of Shelby's Brigade. As did his future brother-in-law Frank James, Parmer surrendered at Samuel's Depot, Kentucky, in 1865. Parmer returned to Clay County after the war and soon married Susan Lavinia James. Stories have circulated over the years that Jesse and Parmer were enemies originally, but no conclusive evidence has substantiated that idea. In fact, Parmer was very likely included in the group that was present at the first bank robbery at Liberty and was possibly involved in other robberies by former guerrillas. Susan and Allen relocated to an area near Sherman, Texas, where a lot of Confederate soldiers had gone after the war. Jesse and Frank visited their sister, as well as the Youngers' ranch, which was just miles outside Sherman.[3]

When Bob heard that Jesse James was in Sherman, he decided to visit and perhaps get to know Jesse a little better. A close friendship would culminate in the greatest mistake in Bob Younger's life.

On Sunday afternoon, August 30, 1874, two omnibuses were robbed in Lafayette County, Missouri. The first robbery occurred along the banks of the Missouri River at Lexington. The second took place sometime later between Waverly and Carrollton. The Lexington bus held passengers who had just returned from a train trip. The path of the omnibus was clearly visible from the riverbank as it made its way through the town. Anyone along the bank, and there were several strollers that day, could have witnessed what happened. Three men came out from behind a house to hold up the nine passengers of the bus at gunpoint. Mollie Newbold, who was walking in the area, ran to alert others that a robbery was in progress. Several people watched from the bank as the robbers casually collected valuables from the stunned passengers. Later Mattie Hamlet of Lexington would tell newspapers that she recognized the robbers as Frank and Jesse James and Will Younger. Miss Hamlet went on to say that she had known the James and Younger families for years and had asked the robbers during the robbery why they were resorting to stealing from travelers. The robbers, she claimed, admitted the act was, indeed, "a bit small" for them. Mattie Hamlet would later refuse to sign a formal affidavit stating that she knew who the men responsible for the robbery were. The James boys and Cole were never indicted for the Lexington robbery.[4]

It seems doubtful that the James-Younger Gang would take such a risk as to rob civilians in broad daylight in the presence of several witnesses. Any among those watching the robbery as it progressed might have been lawmen. The robbery could have erupted into gunfire at any point. Again, this was hardly desirable for the gang. It also seems unlikely that the Jameses and Cole would rob people that they knew, and they knew a lot of people in the Lexington area. They were not above the cruel act of taking people's belongings, as witnessed in the Iowa train robbery, yet it is unlikely that they would have resorted to robbing people with whom they were friendly. They had no way of knowing who was on the omnibus that day. What is more likely is that these robbers were not Frank, Jesse, and Cole but rather impostors who may have gone along with the charade when Miss Hamlet appeared to have recognized them. Committing robberies in the names of the James-Younger Gang was beginning to be popular sport among other outlaws, and this may very well have been one such incident.

After the robbery in Lexington, the newspapers once again began to do battle over the issue of the James-Younger Gang. Some newspapers continued to defend their actions while others accused the state government of doing little to stop the lawlessness that the activities of the gang encouraged. On behalf of Missouri governor Woodson, acting governor Charles P. Johnson asked the St. Louis police department for help in bringing indictments against the men believed to have been responsible for the Lexington and Waverly robberies. Flourney Yancey was assigned but was unable to bring in either hard evidence or any of the members of the James-Younger Gang.

The "copycat" robberies apparently continued when, on December 7, the Tishimingo Savings Bank of Corinth, Mississippi, was robbed of $5,000. Four men seem to have been involved, two having entered the bank and stolen the money under the threat of knives. Again, this was not the usual operation of the James-Younger Gang, and it is unlikely that any of them were in the area at the time. Cole had returned to Texas shortly after Bob arrived. It is likely that he, too, spent some time with Jesse. Cole, Jesse and Bob may have discussed another "business transaction."

Bob visited Maggie when he returned from Texas. He asked her if she would help him establish a farm in Jackson County. If everything went well, they would marry. As to the subject of outlawry, Bob was undecided. He didn't wholeheartedly support the outlaw business but still believed that robbery was one means to support his quest for a decent farm in Missouri. Bob certainly was unable to take a job. He also felt that John's death had demonstrated that the Youngers would be hunted whether or not Bob himself participated in any robberies. He felt that he had little to lose and much to gain. As he prepared to move to Jackson County, Bob was able to locate a suitable farm. He made plans to visit Muncie, Kansas, with Cole and his newfound best friend, Jesse James.

14

A Plea for Amnesty

They are of necessity made desperate.
            —Excerpt from the 1875 Amnesty Bill

On December 8, 1874, the day after the robbery in Corinth, the Kansas Pacific Railroad was robbed of $30,000 by five men at Muncie, Kansas. Although similar to the robbery at Gad's Hill, this one was slightly different. The men approached the depot and forced the section hands to load the tracks with ties. After this was accomplished, the hands were secured in a shed while the approaching train was flagged down. Once the train stopped, the crewmen were directed by the armed bandits to uncouple the baggage and express cars from the passenger cars.[1] The robbery was a success. The smoothness with which the robbery was carried out indicates that this was the work of the real James-Younger Gang, probably consisting of Cole, Jesse, Bob, Frank, and Clell Miller. Some members of the James family have subsequently indicated that it is their belief that the gang interrupted a robbery already in progress by Bud McDaniels and Bill Ryan, former associates of members of the gang. It is also their belief that the original group of robbers was Frank, Jesse, Clell Miller and his brother Ed, Jim Cummins, and Billy Judson, a young man whom they say Jesse had befriended.[2]

That the robberies were continuing, and continuing with success, angered the train and express companies. The Kansas Pacific Railroad offered a reward of $5,000 and encouraged the governor

151

of Kansas to match it with a reward of his own. The express company involved in the Muncie robbery offered its own $5,000, plus $1,000 for any of the robbers, dead or alive. The public position of the Pinkertons at this point was one of involvement, but involvement to what extent was unclear. The Pinkertons had been acting as advisers to the railroads but had, thus far, been unable to really help them with their greatest problem: train robberies. The Pinkerton detectives, known throughout the world as the best of the lot, looked incompetent and ineffectual as their search for the James-Younger Gang continued to come up empty. The Pinkertons were embarrassed and met to decide on a more forceful demonstration of their abilities that would produce some definitive results.

Bob Younger used his profits from the Muncie robbery to lease several acres of land and a farmhouse near Greenwood in Jackson County. Although he had needed to use an alias to do it, he was proud. By the end of the month Bob, Maggie and Maggie's son Jeremy were enjoying their first Christmas together. Bob couldn't believe that he had acquired a companion, a family, and a farm, all of which he could call his own. With the optimism of a man in love, Bob looked forward instead of back for the first time in his adult life.

Not to be denied, the Pinkertons set a plan into action that would have grave consequences for the James family and discredit the Pinkerton organization itself. On the night of January 26, 1875, Pinkerton detectives and operatives surrounded the James-Samuel farmhouse looking for Frank and Jesse. The detectives' presence was made known, and in the confusion that followed, a deadly act was committed. Under the guise of flushing the outlaw brothers out of the sleeping farmhouse, a "torch" was thrown into the house. The small cabin was illuminated and the Jameses' mother, step-father, and their children were made clearly visible. Mrs. Samuel pushed the "torch" into the fireplace before it could catch the house on fire. A second object was thrown into the house. Believing it to be another torch, Mrs. Samuel attempted to push it, as well, into the fireplace. Suddenly the object, which was revealed to be a bomb, exploded with great force. The Jameses' step-brother, eight-year-old Archie Samuel, received the brunt of the explosion, and a large hole was ripped into the small boy's side. Zerelda Samuel's arm was blown away at the elbow. Others of the family were injured, and the house turned into chaos. Archie Samuel died that night as the Pinkertons fled over a fence before their identity could be revealed.

It is not really known whether or not the James brothers were at their mother's house that night, and what the Pinkertons had hoped to accomplish by such a murderous act can only be speculated upon. It was suggested later that the man throwing the bomb had thought it was just another torch. Also suggested was the fact that the Pinkertons were desperate and perhaps hoped to flush the James boys out of hiding as they sought to revenge the attack on their home. In 1991, James historian Ted Yeatman would uncover letters from Pinkerton which would indicate that the purpose of the bombing was to annihilate the James brothers. Whatever the reasons, excuses, or explanations, the bombing of the Samuel home was waved like a red banner in front of the eyes of the pro-James contingent and would further incite those who had defended and excused the crimes of the James-Younger Gang. The old adage of "they was drove to it" became a renewed, even more bitter cry.

Shortly after the bombing at the James-Samuel farm, a resolution was introduced into the Missouri State General Assembly by Stilson Hutchins, owner of the St. Louis *Dispatch*. The resolution asked Gov. Charles Henry Hardin to formally investigate the incident that had taken place on January 26. Hardin sent Adj. Gen. George Caleb Bingham to Clay County in February. Nothing really new or conclusive was contained in Bingham's report. In March, a grand jury held in Clay County found indictments for the murder of Archie Samuel against Robert J. King, Allen K. Pinkerton, Jack Ladd, and five others, unknown.[3] No one was ever arrested, however. Either not enough evidence was presented to extradite Pinkerton from Illinois or his powerful friends and political contacts simply made the issue disappear. On September 13, 1877, the court ordered the case "continued," which put the issue on hold indefinitely. The case simply died.

Jesse James was a great supporter of Bob's idea to get his own farm and make his home once again in Jackson County. Jesse believed in the sanctity of family and knew the comfort of always having a refuge. He had often returned home to the James-Samuel farm in Kearney. In spite of the amount of harassment his family had to endure, Jesse knew that there would always be some place that would welcome him with open arms oblivious to what his activities might have been. It angered Cole greatly that Jesse encouraged young Bob to live out his dream. Cole had always felt the need to urge his own family to shy away from confrontation and, if need be, move to places where they would be bothered as little as possible. He could not understand Bob's attempting to live in a community of farmers, no matter how warmly such a community might feel toward him or what degree of shelter they might offer. It simply wouldn't work, and Cole thought Bob a young fool for even entertaining such an idea. As Cole witnessed Bob's alignment with Jesse over this issue, he felt any influence he might have over his brother deteriorate. Cole had always been at odds with Bob and John, and now Jesse was driving a further wedge between Cole and his younger brother.

Cole seriously resented Jesse, starting with his influence over Bob and not exclusive of Jesse's need to always take credit for every success the gang enjoyed. Cole listened to Jesse's plans first out of respect for Frank and second because the younger man was a careful and innovative thinker. Cole did not support any ideas that Jesse may have had about Jesse being the "leader" of the gang. Cole felt that all the senior members were equal and discouraged any beliefs to the contrary. Jesse's encouragement of Bob left Cole finally fed up with Jesse and feeling that perhaps the days of the James-Younger Gang were numbered, if not over completely. Cole decided to take his money from the Muncie robbery and return to Florida, where he might enjoy a side trip to Cuba. Leaving Bob to enjoy his new farm and hoping his ignorance of its consequences would not cause Bob great harm, Cole left for Florida.[4]

In February and March, editorials began to appear in such papers as the Chicago *Tribune* and the St. Louis *Dispatch* suggesting amnesty for the James and Younger brothers. The general and usual argument was based on the fact that the Drake Constitution had not allowed the men to pursue normal lives after the war. On March 17, 1875, a year to the day after the death of John Younger, Jefferson Jones of Callaway County introduced into the Missouri

House a resolution to grant complete amnesty and a full pardon to Jesse, Frank, Cole, Jim, and Bob. The pardon would cover acts charged to them during the war and full protection and a fair trial for any crimes that they had been charged with since. Because the issue was due to be voted on March 20, there was little time for public debate. A short but heated discussion took place in the press. The main themes, pro and con, were that, on the one side, the Jameses and the Youngers had been driven to their actions. On the other hand, others had been subjected to the same laws and treatment by the federal and Missouri governments and had been able to lead perfectly peaceful lives since the war.

The 1875 Amnesty Bill presented to the Missouri State Legislature on March 17 by Legislator Jones of Callaway County read:

Whereas, by the 4th section of the 11th article of the Constitution of Missouri, all persons in the military service of the United States or who acted under the authority thereof in this state, are relieved from all civil liability and all criminal punishment for all acts done by them since the 1st day of January, A.D. 1861; and

Whereas, by the 12th section of the said 11th article of said Constitution provision is made by which, under certain circumstances, may be seized, transported to, indicted, tried and punished in distant counties, any Confederate under ban of despotic displeasure, thereby contravening the Constitution of the United States and every principle of enlightened humanity; and

Whereas, Such discrimination evinces a want of manly generosity and statesmanship on the part of the party imposing, and of courage and manhood on the part of the party submitting tamely thereto; and

Whereas, Under the outlawry pronounced against Jesse W. James, Frank James, Coleman Younger, James Younger and others, who gallantly periled their lives and their all in defense of their principles, they are of necessity made desperate, driven as they are from the fields of honest industry, from their friends, their families, their homes and their country, they can know no law but the law of self-preservation, nor can have no respect for and feel no allegiance to a government which forces them to the very acts it professes to deprecate, and then offers a bounty for their apprehension, and arms foreign mercenaries with power to capture and kill them; and

Whereas, Believing these men too brave to be mean, too generous to be revengeful, and too gallant and honorable to betray a friend or break a promise; and believing further that most, if not all of the offenses with which they have been charged have been committed by others, and perhaps by those pretending to hunt them, or by their confederates; that their names are and have been used to divert suspicion from and thereby relieve the actual perpetrators; that the return of these men to their homes and friends would have the effect of greatly lessening crime in our state by turning public attention to the real criminals, and that common justice, sound policy and true statesmanship alike demand that amnesty should be extended to all alike of both parties for all acts done or charged to have been done during the war; therefore, be it

Resolved by the House of Representatives, the Senate concurring therein, that the Governor of the state be, and he is thereby requested to issue his proclamation notifying the said Jesse W. James, Frank James, Coleman Younger, and James Younger and others, that full and complete amnesty and pardon will be granted them for all acts charged or committed by them during the late civil war, and inviting them peacefully to return to their respective homes in this state and there quietly to remain, submitting themselves to such proceedings as may be instituted against them by the courts for all offenses charged to have been committed since said war, promising and guaranteeing to each of them full protection and a fair trial therein, and that full protection shall be given them from the time of their entrance into the state and his notice thereof under said proclamation and invitation.

Perhaps Jefferson Jones helped with the legal wording of the document, but the manner and wording of the resolution itself reflects the active involvement of John Newman Edwards.

On March 20, General James Shields, representing the Commission on Federal Relations, presented an alternative measure suggesting that all the James and Younger brothers were entitled to was a fair trial and to be protected against harm should they cooperate and stand trial. The measure failed to pass because, although the vote was 58 in favor and 39 against, a two-thirds margin was required to pass. No further action was attempted.

On April 12, 1875, Daniel Askew, a neighbor of the Jameses in Kearney, was killed. Jack Ladd, one of the men indicted as having participated in the James farm bombing, had been a hired hand on

Askew's farm. It looked as though while the legislators were trying to absolve the Jameses of acts said not to be of their doing or fault, the Jameses' penchant for revenge had caused the death of Daniel Askew.

On May 13, in the evening, a store owned by D. B. Lambert in Clinton, Missouri, was robbed of some $300. While eight young people played croquet on an adjacent lawn, four well-dressed men rode up and entered the store. Pistols were drawn, and the croquet players were "invited" to join the others inside. According to one witness:

> In the meantime a little over $300 in greenbacks were taken, also a very favorite silver watch, a fine shotgun, two revolvers, and a lot of other goods from the store. They turned up every box in the house, and searched every comer. They came in from the west and when they left started in the direction of Clinton. They were all well dressed, well armed and mounted on the finest of horses. No uncouth language was used by any of the robbers. Lambert had his money in his pocket, also his watch, which they made him shell out.[5]

The description of these robbers certainly fits that of Jesse, Frank, Cole, and Bob. What the four of them would be doing robbing a community store in a small town in western Missouri is curious. Such a robbery certainly does not fit the style of the James-Younger Gang, and one can't help but wonder if this was not another carefully executed copycat robbery. Matthew Dorman, one of the farmers of Clinton, later stated that he had conversed with two of the Younger brothers and two others two days previous to the robbery of the store. No efforts were made either to find the bandits or recover Mr. Lambert's money and goods.

While Cole was not anxious to do business with Jesse again at this time, it is possible that Cole and Frank made plans of their own that included Tom McDaniels and a man known alternately as Tom Webb or Jack Keene. Bob was busy working on his farm and Jesse was living in Nashville, Tennessee, where his wife Zee had just given birth to their first son, Jesse Edwards James. Cole and Frank had not seen much of each other in the recent past and perhaps chose to renew their friendship and have an adventure at the same time.

On September 1, 1875, $10,000 was taken from a bank in Huntington, West Virginia. Four men entered the town, and while two presented themselves inside the bank, the other two watched from across the street. One stationed himself near the horses and the other in Sanburn's Blacksmith shop. Cashier Robert T. Oney was asked at gunpoint to open the safe, which he claimed was already open. The robbers stated that they were more interested in the inner compartment of the safe and asked for the key. Oney denied knowledge of its whereabouts, but one of the robbers soon found it in a drawer; $9,000 was taken from the inner vault, and an additional $1,000 was found on the counter. Oney was asked if any of the money in the bank was his own personal funds. When he replied that his balance was about $7, the robbers gave him that amount, explaining that it was not necessary for the encounter to cost him money.[6]

A messenger named Jim entered the bank, and he and Oney were used as shields as the two robbers crossed the street to where the horses stood. Once there, they were joined by the man in the blacksmith's shop. As the robbers left town, the bank president attempted to arm himself and chase them but discovered that one of the robbers had taken his gun from inside the bank.

The following descriptions appeared in the Louisville *Courier-Journal* on September 15, 1875, after the Huntington, West Virginia, robbery:

No. 1. Heavy-set man, at least six feet high, weight two hundred pounds, tolerably dark hair, with reddish whiskers and moustache, red complexion, black hat, long linen duster and blue overalls, gold ring on left little finger.

No. 2. Tall, slim man, in height about six feet, one hundred and fifty pounds, delicate looking, light hair and sandy whiskers, high forehead, long nose, gold buttons in shirt, left little finger had a ring, long duster and blue overalls.

No. 3. Tall, slim man, about six feet high, weight one hundred and sixty five pounds, short, black whiskers and black hair, slim face, black hat, long duster, blue overalls, suit of black twilled cloth with stripes, fine boots, two gold rings on little left finger, had two collars washed with 'London' printed on the bands.

No. 4. Heavy-set man, about five feet ten inches high, weight one hundred and eighty pounds, very stout, square-looking man, brown hair, round red face, patches of red whiskers on his chin, light colored hat, linen duster, gray striped coat and vest, pants similar, but not like coat and vest, red drilling overalls, fine boots, broad gold ring with flowers cut in it on his left little finger.[7]

No. 3 matches the description of Thompson McDaniels, wounded and captured after the robbery. No. 4 is likely the description of Tom Webb, also captured. No. 1 and No. 2 closely resemble the descriptions of Cole Younger and Frank James.

A posse was formed, and the four robbers were chased quite a distance. Several miles outside Huntington, a Mr. Barbour was taken at gunpoint by the robbers to use as a scout. He traveled with the band about an hour. The posse finally came upon the group near Pine Hill in Kentucky.

This settlement was only a few miles from Crab Orchard, birthplace of Henry Washington Younger. As the group approached the farm of William Dillon, the farmer called out to the strangers, asking them what they wanted. A gun was fired, and Dillon returned the fire, wounding one of the group outside. The group attempted to hide the wounded man in a cornfield and rode off.[8]

The James-Younger Gang's nemesis, Detective Bligh of Louisville, was already on the case by the time the outlaw was wounded and captured. Bligh interviewed the robber, who claimed he was Charley Chance. The outlaw refused to divulge any information about his accomplices. An identification made through items found in the fallen man's pockets indicated that he was Thompson McDaniels. McDaniels was soon dead from his wounds. Before he died, while in the midst of his delirium, McDaniels muttered, "Did they get Bud?"[9] Bud McDaniels, Tom's brother, had been killed in a cornfield after he escaped from the jail he had been confined to since having been convicted of the Muncie robbery. Perhaps Tom McDaniels was referring to his brother or perhaps he was referring to Cole, who was sometimes called Bud by his friends.

While McDaniels was dying, the other three robbers were racing toward Tennessee. One of the horses threw a shoe, and the rider was forced to dismount. Before any of his comrades could come to his aid, a posse surrounded and arrested him. There was some confusion at first as to who the man was, and Detective Bligh believed that he might have Cole Younger in his possession. Eventually it was determined that the captured robber was, in fact, Thomas J. Webb. Tom Webb had $4,500 in his possession when captured. He was returned to West Virginia, where he was tried and convicted for his part in the Huntington robbery. He was sentenced to twelve years in prison. The other two robbers, probably Cole and Frank, continued their retreat without incident. A close call but a successful venture for those who had been fortunate enough to find their way home.

Back in St. Clair County, Uncle Frank Younger had been elected Constable of Monagaw and Uncle T. J. Younger appointed Judge of St. Clair County.[10] The year ended with Cole and Frank visiting Jesse in Tennessee, Jim happy on La Panza ranch in California, and Bob at home in Jackson County on his new farm. No one could have been prepared for what the new year would bring.

15

Bob Takes a Stand

Come home. Bob needs you.
— Cole's wire to Jim, 1876

Bob Younger's life was happy despite the fact he had overextended himself financially in order to get his farm off the ground. The farm he had chosen needed quite a bit of work to become operational, and the farmhouse needed certain amenities to make it safe for someone of Bob's reputation. Bob had created a "hideaway" where he could enjoy family life while at the same time work freely to develop the farmland. The people of the area were old friends of the Youngers and while Bob's presence was not secret, it was not publicized. Bob further ingratiated himself with his neighbors by always being available when there was hard work to be done or some special favor needed. Bob was well liked. He was trying to determine where he could get the money he needed to plant and realize his first large crop when he was visited by Jesse James.

Jesse had a very specific plan in mind when he visited Bob that spring. It involved particulars that might not have been well received by the others in the gang. Jesse knew that he had a strong ally in Bob, and he knew that Bob more than likely needed additional funds for his new farm operation. Jesse decided to visit Bob's farm to see how the younger man was getting along and to see if he might be interested in his intricate plan. Bob was happy to see Jesse, as the two had continued to develop the relationship they had begun in Texas. Jesse knew that Bob was somewhat in awe of him, and he enjoyed Bob's deference. At the same time, Jesse knew that Bob was not stupid, and the men enjoyed each other's intellect and ambition although their life's goals seemed much different.

Jesse asked Bob if he was interested in being involved in another undertaking having to do with a bank, and Bob responded that he might be if the results were very favorable. Bob further stated that if he were to become involved in another robbery and his share was enough for the farm's requirements, he would retire from the "business" and devote his total efforts to farming. Jesse agreed that Bob's idea would best suit him. After Jesse visited with Bob, the two men agreed to meet in a few weeks to discuss the details of the plan. Bob was very honored to have been asked by Jesse to participate in the planning of the upcoming venture. Jesse advised Bob to keep their conversation to himself until after they had the opportunity to plan in detail, at which point they would inform the others of the gang.[1]

Eventually Jesse sent word to Bob to meet him at a hotel in Kansas City, a point halfway between Bob's farm and the James-Samuel farm. There Jesse unfolded his elaborate idea to rob a bank in Minnesota. He mentioned the town of Mankato. Mankato was noted for its rich farming community and was sure to be full of "Yankee" dollars. The gang would dress as businessmen and after conducting their "business" would leave the state as quickly as possible. When Bob questioned their ability to navigate the unknown area and terrain of Minnesota, Jesse informed him that Bill Chadwell was a native of Minnesota and knew the state like the back of his hand. Jesse's enthusiasm convinced Bob that robbing a bank in Minnesota would finance his farm plans and allow him to put his life of outlawry behind him. Bob informed Jesse that he would talk the plan over with Cole. Jesse and Bob made plans to meet at Monagaw the following week, and Jesse said he would bring Clell Miller along as well.

Clelland D. Miller was born in Holt, Missouri, on January 9, 1850. He was one of the six sons of Moses and Emilene Miller. When Clell was fourteen, he joined the ranks of "Bloody Bill" Anderson. It is presumably at this time that he became friendly with Jesse James, a Clay County neighbor. Miller's "enlistment" with Anderson is given as October 23, 1864. Miller was captured by Union forces on October 26, 1864, in Ray County during the encounter that took the life of Bill Anderson. Miller was held in the Jefferson Barracks in St. Louis until April, 1865, when he was released and returned home to Clay County.[2]

When the men met at Monagaw the next week, Bob had been unable to talk to Cole about the plan. Cole had been in Texas, and Bob had written to him there, asking that he come up to Missouri to talk over a business proposition. Cole had not arrived in Monagaw by the time of Bob's meeting with Jesse, and Bob wasn't even sure that Cole had received his letter. Jesse asked Bob to contact him after he had spoken with Cole. In the meantime, Jesse, Bob, and Clell enjoyed a couple of days at the springs. While it was still difficult for Bob to be in Monagaw without John, he enjoyed being in Jesse's company and felt more at ease there than he had at any time since the death of John.

Less than a week after Bob arrived back home in Jackson County, he heard from a friend that Cole was in Monagaw. Bob returned to the springs to find that Cole had not received his letter. Bob explained Jesse's plan and waited for Cole's response. Cole's reply was not long in coming. Cole thought the plan foolhardy and was particularly irritated that Jesse had chosen to present the plan to Bob rather than to him. Bob defended his position in the gang, citing Cole's position that all members of the gang were equal. That statement did little to bring Cole over to Bob's side. Cole thought the idea of going to Minnesota, territory unknown to the gang, extremely risky. He was not encouraged when Bob told him that Bill Chadwell, someone he had not known long and who had been brought into the gang by Jesse, would be the guide. The gang had planned robberies far from home before, but at least the general area had been known and they had not had to rely on one man to be their guide. More important than the argument against uncharted destinations was the fact that Cole was extremely rankled by Jesse's having brought Bob to the forefront of the gang. It was another test of his family authority, as far as Cole was concerned. The more Cole objected to the entire plan, the more determined Bob became. Now his authority was being questioned. He was a man, after all, with a farm and a family. Bob thought there was no reason except pride that made Cole question Bob's ability to plan a robbery. Cole wondered about Bob's resolution to become a farmer. Bob informed him that the intended robbery would put to rest his monetary concerns for his farm and that this would be the last time he would feel compelled to participate. Cole continued to scoff at Bob's intention of farming in Missouri and offered to finance a ranching venture in Texas for Bob. Bob told Cole, again, that he had no wish to return to Texas. That had been Jim's dream.

Cole asked Bob to delay talking to Jesse about Minnesota. Bob refused, saying that whether or not Cole decided to participate, if Jesse was going, so was he. Bob was, after all, over twenty-one and free to do as he pleased. Cole threatened to hurt Jesse if Bob did not tell Jesse that he would wait two weeks before committing himself to the plan. Bob reiterated that he was going, and that time was of no consequence to his decision.

Finally, Cole agreed to meet with Bob and Jesse in Kansas City at the end of the month as long as Frank James was included. In the meantime, without Bob's knowledge, Cole sent a wire to Jim in California. "Come home," the wire read. "Bob needs you."[3] Believing Cole's wire to indicate that Bob was in serious trouble, Jim immediately left La Panza for Missouri. Jim would always be with his brothers at their time of need and the nature of Bob's problem was unrevealed in Cole's wire. Without thinking twice, the loyal and loving Jim found himself in Kansas City.

Cole had decided that if he were to accompany Bob to Minnesota with the James boys, Jim needed to go as well. Jim didn't understand the reasoning behind Cole's decision and questioned Bob as to whether or not he felt it necessary to his safety. Bob repeatedly told Jim that he did not want Jim to go and suggested he return to his peaceful life in California immediately. Bob was furious with Cole for having involved Jim in the first place. When Jim heard Bob and Jesse's plan, he became alarmed. He didn't find the idea sound, either. He later wrote that he hated the idea and held Jesse responsible for influencing Bob to make such a decision.[4] Feeling under siege by both of his brothers now, Bob became more adamant and insisted that he was going to Minnesota with or without either of them. What Cole said to Jim can only be speculated upon because Jim never divulged exactly what was said to cause him to throw his tranquil life in California away. Jim agreed with Cole that the only way Bob should go to Minnesota with the James brothers was in the company of both of his own. Resignedly, Jim agreed to go.

The three Younger brothers met with the two James boys and made the commitment to travel north. All for one, one for all, they were united. After the agreement had been made, Bob apologized to Jim for hurting him but reiterated his commitment to the plan.[5] It was a prideful decision that Bob Younger would forever regret.

Jesse and Bob had decided to finance the trip to Minnesota with a robbery close to home. At first Bob rejected Jesse's idea that this be done, but as the plan progressed and Bob realized that business suits, transportation, lodging, and fine horses needed to be procured, he decided that Jesse's idea was a sound one. Jim once again refused to participate, much to the chagrin of Cole. Cole thought Jim's decision might be misconstrued as a lack of unity, since it had been decided that the robbery group would consist of those going to Minnesota. Jesse suggested that Hobbs Kerry, someone he had evidently known for some time, be included to take the place of Jim. Cole and Bob agreed, as Kerry had become known to them through his previous association with their Uncle Bruce. This association was, presumably, having to do with horses.

The target was selected. A bridge was being constructed over the Lamine River near Otterville in nearby Cooper County. The Missouri Pacific Railroad would pass through the banks at a spot known as Rocky Cut while it slowed for the construction. On the night of July 7, 1876, the watchman was seized at the bridge and his red lantern was used to flag the train as it slowed for the bridge at Rocky Cut. While the crew and passengers were held at gunpoint, two safes containing over $15,000 were emptied. A minister who was a passenger on board prayed aloud for the souls of those passengers who would be killed should there be a mass annihilation. He soon had the passengers singing hymns. The passengers were not robbed, and the entire affair was over in minutes.[6] A small posse was formed during the night but proved futile. The

Jameses, three Younger brothers, Miller, Pitts, and Chadwell, with their new associate Hobbs Kerry, had successfully gained the funds to finance their larger Minnesota venture.

Governor Hardin offered a $300 reward for any of the robbers of the Missouri Pacific Railroad. While such a reward had failed to entice citizens in the past, it may have been different that July. After the robbery and split-up of the gang, Hobbs Kerry passed through Granby, his old stomping grounds, where he made little effort to conceal a large amount of money. He wrote to Bruce Younger, probably inquiring about a horse. The chief of the St. Louis police department, James McDonough, had been called into the case prior to this time. One of his informants had somehow learned of Kerry's actions at Granby and of the correspondence between Kerry and Bruce Younger. McDonough sent detectives into southern Missouri to investigate. Their inquiries resulted in the arrest of both Hobbs Kerry and Bruce Younger.[7] Kerry had been identified by a Sedalia farmer and his wife as having been one of a group of men who had stopped at their house prior to the robbery. Before long, Kerry confessed that, yes, he had been one of the robbers at Otterville. Furthermore, Kerry volunteered that Jesse and Frank James, Cole and Bob Younger, Miller, and Chadwell were there with him.

Bruce Younger was the half-brother of Henry Washington Younger. He was born in Osceola, Missouri, in 1853. His mother was Charles Lee Younger's mistress, Parmelia Wilson. His father died when Bruce was less than a year old and he was primarily raised by his sister, Sophia Ragan. By the time he was seventeen, Bruce followed the example of his brothers Henry and Frank and bought some fine horses to become one of the area's more reliable and honest horse traders. He eventually became partners with his cousin Bob's friend Dru Garrett of Jackson County, and business boomed. Bruce and Dru became co-venturers in breeding and selling horses throughout some of the southern states, as well as Missouri. Bruce remained close to his cousins Bob, John, and Jim Younger and would often help them secure horses when they lived in Grayson County, Texas.

Although he was arrested for participation in the Rocky Cut train robbery in 1876, Bruce was not known to have ever participated in any of the robberies of the James-Younger Gang. He was released from custody when no evidence could be found that tied him to the train robbery at Otterville.[8]

Jesse wrote to the Kansas City *Times* on August 18, denying his part in the robbery. Going one step further, Jesse suggested that Bacon Montgomery, leader of the posse out of Sedalia, was instead the culprit. Montgomery responded to Jesse's accusation by also writing to the paper, offering to allow himself to be investigated for the crime if Jesse would go to Sedalia to be investigated as well. Jesse never responded. Cole would later use Kerry's confession and implication of the Younger and James brothers in a most convenient way. Cole wrote:

> Every daylight robbery in any part of the country, from the Alleghanies to the Rockies, was laid at our doors; we could not go out without a pair of pistols to protect ourselves from the attack of we knew not whom; and, finally, after one of the young ruffians who had helped in the robbery of the Missouri Pacific express car at Otterville "confessed" that we were with the robbers we decided to make one haul, and with our share of the proceeds start life anew in Cuba, South America or Australia.[9]

The plans were finalized, the financing had been accomplished, and the James and Younger brothers gathered to head north for Minnesota.

16

Northfield, Minnesota

If he betrayed not, death was sure;
Before him stood the murderous thief.
He did not flinch.
Of one life fewer.
The angels turned the blood-sealed leaf
That night, and said "This page is pure."
—"On a Faithful Bank Cashier" by George Parsons
Lathrop, 1892

Perry Samuel threw back the doors of the barn at the command from the voice inside and Frank and Jesse James began their trip north to Minnesota.[1] Hiding under a tarp in the bed of a wagon probably driven by Charlie Pitts or Bill Chadwell, the Jameses met up with the rest of the James-Younger Gang somewhere north of Clay County. Fast horses were being held, and the eight men proceeded to Council Bluffs, Iowa, where one of them was able to somehow sell the horses. It is likely that no one ever came forward to detail this transaction, as the new owner may have assumed the horses had been stolen and had no desire to claim knowledge of buying them. Or perhaps he had no desire to be connected to the James-Younger Gang in any way.

Little is known about Bill Chadwell. He was born William Stiles in Monticello, Minnesota. While living in St. Paul, Stiles was arrested as a horse thief and served time in jail. Sometime after his release, he relocated to Missouri, using the name Chadwell. It is not known when or under what circumstances he might have met and become friendly with Jesse James. It does seem likely that

Jesse was the one who brought him into the James-Younger Gang and who suggested he participate in several of their robberies. Chadwell was quite personable and well liked. It appears that he was also trusted by the gang enough to become a welcome addition after the demise of John Jarrette.

The men boarded a train and arrived in Minneapolis, Minnesota the third week of August. Cole gave several accounts of the Northfield robbery over the years, each one with variations sometimes contradicting the others. In his autobiography written in 1903, he stated that the group traveled to Minnesota by rail. In an account given to Harry Hoffman several years later, Cole told an elaborate story of how the men rode all of the way to Northfield on horses from home. Since there are witnesses who saw the men buy horses in different parts of Minnesota and who later recognized them as being the Northfield robbers, it is safe to assume that they did not have their own horses when they arrived in Minnesota.

The first destination of the gang has also been questioned. In Bob's account, Jesse suggested Mankato to him at their second meeting. It is possible that Jesse had ideas for additional robberies while the gang was in the area, as Jesse and Frank visited Northfield before the September 7 robbery. Cole wrote that Mankato had been ruled out previous to the gang's arrival in Minnesota because the area was having its own problems at the time. He wrote:

> That we talked about the banks in that part of the state is true, but we came to the conclusion that they had enough to do to care for the farmers who had already suffered too much from the grasshoppers to be troubled by us; therefore we went to Northfield in expectation of getting the $75,000 belonging to ex-Governor Ames and General Butler.[2]

In other interviews Cole would state that they had been scared away from Mankato when someone in their party was recognized. The first theme is the one Cole returned to whenever he addressed the topic of the Northfield robbery in his later years. Taking funds from the questionable resources of two former carpetbaggers would certainly seem more acceptable than stealing the hard-earned money of farmers in Mankato. The fact that the entire gang rendezvoused in Mankato after roaming around the Minnesota countryside for a couple of weeks further weakens Cole's claim.

Retracing their steps from the beginning, it is hard to determine whether or not all members of the gang rode the same train from Council Bluffs to Minneapolis. It is evident that they all arrived about August 15 or 16 whether or not they did travel together from Iowa to Minnesota. While they encountered each other in and around the city, the members of the gang split, traveling in smaller groups. Bob Younger and Charlie Pitts decided to engage in some poker playing the night they arrived but they ended up losing almost $200.[3] This might have been a warning of the lack of luck the state held for the two men, but it was a warning unheeded. Several people said later that they had seen two men who looked very much like Pitts and Younger, well-dressed and good-looking, asleep on the bank near Sibley and Fifth streets.[4] It may be that Bob and Charlie were unable to obtain lodging for the night, or they may have lost in poker the money allocated for a hotel that evening. It is also very possible that the two men seen were not Bob and Charlie at all.

The next day, all the men left for the neighboring city of St. Paul. Cole and Bill Chadwell stayed at the Merchant Hotel on 3rd and Jackson streets. They also decided to take to the gaming tables and frequented a gaming parlor on East 3rd owned by Guy Salisbury. They, unlike their counterparts, were very successful. However, when Bob and Charlie appeared at the establishment ready to join the game, Cole refused to play with them. He later said he would never play in a game with Bob.[5]

Frank and Jesse James, Jim Younger, and Clell Miller took a buggy out to an establishment called the Nicolette House. The Nicolette House was located outside St. Paul and was run by Miss Mollie Ellsworth, a well-liked and well-known madam. They were soon to be joined by Bill Chadwell, who had left Cole, Bob, and Charlie in the city. Perhaps the five men decided to stay at the Nicolette House, as they would blend into the transient ambiance of the establishment and would not seem out of place or suspicious. Chadwell was evidently quite familiar with the women at the house and conversed with Kitty Traverse, who worked there.

The men gambled and relaxed while visiting the hostelry and had a great opportunity to meet others and gather information about the area, its people, and its banks. Kitty Traverse later stated that those living in the house noted that one of the men was said to be ill and never left his room.[6] This was likely Jim, who was not happy to be along on the trip in the first place and who probably retreated to his books and other forms of self-entertainment. Given that Jim disliked Jesse and that at this point neither Jim nor Cole really trusted him, it is possible that Jim was sent along to keep his eye on Jesse.

Sometime toward the end of their visit to St. Paul, the five men were joined at the Nicolette House by Cole. There the six amused themselves at one point by sitting on the balcony and throwing down $8 worth of coins, one at a time, to a little girl in the street below.[7]

On August 20, Charlie and Bob visited the Hall and McKinney Livery but were unable to find horses they liked. While at the livery, however, they bought two McClellan saddles and a bridle. They then went to a store on Robert Street, Nortons & Ware, where they bought a bit. They were finally able to obtain horses from William A. Judd on 4th Street. A black and a bay horse were purchased.[8]

The six men who had been staying at the Nicolette House ventured back to the city of St. Paul. A man later said to have resembled Jesse was seen at a bookstore purchasing a map. Around this time, Bill Chadwell encountered Patrick Kenny of the St. Paul police department. Kenny recognized Chadwell, having been involved in his arrest as a horse thief several years before. Kenny asked Chadwell how he was and what he was up to. Chadwell informed the police officer that he was doing well and was planning a trip to the Black Hills in the near future.[9]

On August 26, Frank, Jesse, Jim, and Clell took the train to Red Wing. They registered at the National Hotel as J. C. Hortor of Nashville, A. L. West of Nashville, Chas. Wetherby of Indiana, and Ed Everhard of Indiana. They used their old ploy of posing as cattle buyers. After dinner on that evening, they purchased three horses. A. Seebeek provided two sorrels and a dun was obtained from J. A. Anderberg's livery.[10]

Cole and Charlie took the train in the opposite direction to St. Peter. They stayed in a hotel called the American House and registered under the names of J. C. King and J. Ward. Here the two men bought a bay horse and a horse characterized by white socks from a man named Hodge. They bought their gear at Moll & Sons. It was while visiting St. Peter and breaking in their new horses there that Cole met Horace Greeley Perry, a small girl with big ambitions.[11] Bob and Bill Chadwell remained in St. Paul.

Frank and Jesse immediately separated from Jim and Clell and were at Brush Prairie outside Northfield by August 28. There the two outlaws pretended to "buy" the farmland of John Mulligan. After reaching an agreement about the purchase price, the two buyers claimed that their money was in a bank at Red Wing.[12] While negotiating the purchase, Frank and Jesse had been able to learn a great deal about what type of community nearby Northfield was and what the fair city had to offer in the way of both opportunities and services, such as milling establishments and banks.

The city of Northfield, Minnesota, was named after John W. North, an attorney with a great interest in development, women's suffrage, the antislavery movement, and the temperance issue. North purchased over three hundred acres of land along the Cannon River in 1855, where he built a mill. New Englanders moved into the area and established the town of Northfield. Hiram Scriver built the first store and North the first hotel. North wrote the charter for the University of Minnesota and was also head of the Minnesota delegation to the Republican Convention at which Lincoln was nominated. North was appointed surveyor general of the Nevada Territory by Lincoln in 1861. After the war, North joined with other entrepreneurs moving into the war-ravaged state of Tennessee, where government and business positions became available to supporters of the federal government for the asking.

Meanwhile, Northfield thrived as milling and lumber concerns became big business in the area. The city became quite prosperous, and Carleton College and St. Olaf College drew their own communities.

On August 29, Cole and Charlie decided to investigate the area further. They had been waiting for Bob and Chadwell to join them in St. Peter, but the two had failed to show. It was later learned that they had missed their train. The two men passed through the very small community of Hanska and stopped at the house of Mads and Grenhild Ouren. Grenhild was alone at the farmhouse, and she spoke only Norwegian. Mads was in the fields haying. Cole and Charlie asked if they could spend the night and waited patiently for Mads to return home to hear their request. Mads spoke English and was happy to have the two men as overnight visitors. One of the men admired Mads's fine gun which hung over the kitchen door.[13]

Frank and Jesse visited Northfield for the first time on August 29. They left their horses near a restaurant and had a talk with a merchant possibly named Trussel about the roads in the area. They represented themselves as the potential buyers of Mulligan's place and possible new residents of Northfield.[14] The bank having been checked out firsthand from the outside, Frank and Jesse rode back toward St. Peter.

On August 30, Cole and Charlie rode to Madelia where they stayed at the Flanders Hotel, which was owned by Thomas L. Vought. Cole and Vought became very friendly and talked at length about driving cattle.[15] Bob and Chadwell finally made it to St. Peter where they registered at the hotel under the names of B. T. Cooper and G. H. King, both from Illinois.

On September 1, all eight men reunited in the city of Mankato. John Jay Lemon wrote in 1876 that two of the men stopped at the Clifton House while two stayed at the Gates House. He claimed that two others spent time in a notorious saloon on the other side of town owned by Jack O'Neil.[16] Where the last two stayed is unknown.

The area around Mankato, Minnesota, was first sighted by a group of Frenchmen who passed the winter of 1700 at the junction of the Blue Earth and Le Sueur rivers. The city of Mankato was laid out in 1852 when settlers moved west up the river from St. Paul. In 1862 there were several Indian encounters in the area around Mankato in places such as New Ulm and Wood Lake. In the summer of that year, the Indians surrendered at Camp Release near Montevideo. Three hundred Indians were taken to Mankato, where they were tried and sentenced to death. Thirty-eight were hanged on the levee at Front Street before the executive order of Abraham Lincoln caused the release of the rest of the Indian prisoners.

The Omaha Railroad reached Mankato in 1868. The arrival of the Northwestern Line was in 1870. Most of the rich farmland was destroyed by the grasshopper blight that began in 1873 and continued until 1877. Blue Earth County offered 10 cents a quart for grasshoppers. Over 15,000 bushels were brought in before the country had paid out $31,000 and withdrew the offer.

On September 2, two men, likely Jesse and Bob, visited the First National Bank of Mankato, where one of them asked to have a $50 bill changed. Having cased the inside of the bank, the two went back outside. The streets were anything but quiet that afternoon, as both a meeting of the board of trade and construction on a building located next to the bank brought many people to the immediate area. At this point, it has been reported, Jesse was either recognized or thought he was recognized by a man named Charles Robinson.[17] If the police were alerted by Robinson, they obviously didn't believe him, as nothing further happened. It is likely, however, that Jesse thought he had been recognized and decided to call off the Mankato bank caper.

The men split into groups and left the town as quickly and as inconspicuously as possible. Once outside Mankato safely, the men met to decide what to do. Should they return home to Missouri or select another Minnesota location? Frank and Jesse told the group about their findings in Northfield and suggested that they make that their next target. Bill Chadwell embellished the James boys' information when he told the gang of the involvement in the city of two carpetbagging chiefs, Adelbert Ames and Benjamin Butler. State Parole Agent F. A. Whittier later wrote that Cole told him "repeatedly" that the reason that the Northfield Bank was decided on was that the gang "hoped to meet Butler on one of his visits to Minnesota and if not [they] were to get even with him in a measure by raiding this bank which [they] did."[18]

Adelbert Ames was born at Rockland, Maine, on October 31, 1835. He graduated from West Point in 1861. He served as a general in the Union Army and was present at Gettysburg. Ames received a Congressional Medal of Honor for remaining on the field at Bull Run after being severely wounded. He was appointed provisional governor of Mississippi by President Grant at the close of the war. Ames served as a U.S. Senator from that state from 1870 to 1873 and was then elected governor, serving until 1876. Involved in the continuing politics of North vs. South, Ames was impeached by the Mississippi legislature. Although he was cleared of all charges, Ames decided to leave the South and relocate to Northfield, Minnesota, where his father and brother lived.

Ames bought a part of the Northfield Mills and became a noted citizen of that community. It was said that he funded his investment with money obtained through carpetbagging in the South. Ames's father-in-law, Gen. Benjamin F. Butler, had also served in Mississippi. He was also a big investor in the mills of Northfield, and his funds as well were said to have been derived from carpetbagging activities in Mississippi and Louisiana. Both Ames and Butler were believed to have kept their considerable wealth locked up in the First National Bank of Northfield.[19]

After Northfield was decided on, the gang once more split in two. On September 4, Bob, Jesse, Charlie, and Frank arrived in Janesville. Cole was perturbed with Jesse once again, claiming that Jesse's vanity was at fault for their having to forego the Mankato plan. He and Frank decided on their own that Frank would travel with Jesse and Bob so that he could keep an eye on them lest they try to cook up something other than the agreed-upon plan to go to Northfield. The four men stayed at the Johnson House registered under the names of George Pryor, Dave Smith, Jno. Jones, and James Johnson. The men said that they were railroad engineers.

Cole later wrote that his group traveled to Le Sueur Center, where they spent the night of September 4.[20] He went into great detail about how their sleep was disturbed because court was in session and the town was completely packed with people. If his recollections of the reason as to why his accommodations were uncomfortable is correct, he was in the wrong town. It is likely that the group stayed at the Adams Hotel in Cleveland. Cleveland was the county seat of Le Sueur County, and the commissioners' reports show that court was in session there several times in 1876.[21]

On the night of September 5, Bob and Jesse's group found themselves in Waterville. It was later said that a man answering

Henry Washington Younger
(Courtesy State Historical Society)

Bathsheba Leighton Fristoe
(Courtesy Jackson County Historical Society)

Charles Richard
"Dick" Younger
(Courtesy the Hall family)

Young Frank James
(Courtesy Ethelrose
James Owens)

H. W. YOUNGER

ON HAND ONCE MORE!

H. W. YOUNGER would announce to the citizens of HARRISON-VILLE and surrounding country that he has just returned from New York with an entire New Stock of

SPRING & SUMMER GOODS!

PARTICULARLY ADAPTED TO THIS SECTION OF THE COUNTRY.

HIS STOCK CONSISTS OF

DRY GOODS

BOOTS, SHOES,

HATS & CAPS,

HARDWARE, NOTIONS, &c.

HIS OLD FRIENDS AND THE PUBLIC ARE INVITED TO CALL AND EXAMINE HIS STOCK.

HARRISONVILLE, Mo., MAY, 1862.

H. W. YOUNGER.

MAKER & GODWIN, PRINTERS, PRINTINGHOUSE SQUARE, OPPOSITE CITY HALL, N. Y.

Flyer from Henry Younger's livery
(Courtesy Cass County Historical Society)

John Jarrette and Jim Younger
(Courtesy Armond De Gregoris Collection)

Bob Younger
(Courtesy Armand De
Gregoris Collection)

Cole Younger, Frank James (seated), possibly Jim Younger (standing left), and unknown friend (standing)
(Courtesy Armand De Gregoris Collection)

John Younger
(Courtesy the Younger family)

Cole Younger
(Courtesy State Historical Society of Missouri, Columbia)

Richard Marshall Fristoe
(Courtesy the Hall family)

Cole and John Younger
(Courtesy State Historical
Society of Missouri, Columbia)

Monagaw Springs Hotel
(Courtesy Wilbur Zink)

Club House, Monegaw Springs, Mo.

Site of Cole's death with members of Hall family in front.
(Courtesy the Hall family)

Jim Younger
(Courtesy Jackson County
Historical Society)

John Newman Edwards
(Courtesy State Historical Society
of Missouri, Columbia)

Clell Miller
(Courtesy State Historical
Society of Missouri, Columbia)

Bob Younger
*(Courtesy State Historical
Society of Missouri, Columbia)*

*Jesse James
(Courtesy Armand De Gregoris Collection)*

Joseph Lee Heywood
(Courtesy Northfield Historical Society)

Interior of the First National Bank, 1876
(Courtesy Northfield Historical Society)

*First National Bank,
Northfield 1876
(Courtesy Northfield
Historical Society)*

The Younger's house in Strother (Lee's Summit)
(Courtesy Jackson County Historical Society)

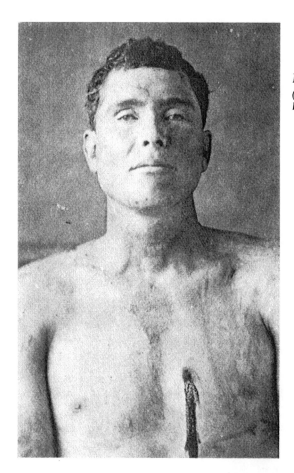

Bill Chadwell in death
(Courtesy Northfield
Historical Society)

Charlie Pitts in death
(Courtesy Northfield
Historical Society)

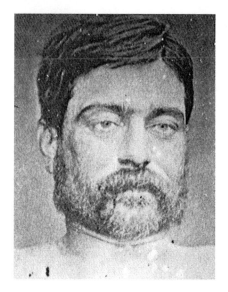

Cole Younger upon surrender
(Courtesy the Younger family)

Jim Younger upon surrender
(Courtesy the Younger family)

*Jesse James
in death*
(Courtesy State
Historical Society of
Missouri, Columbia)

Bob Younger
(Courtesy State Historical
Society of Missouri, Columbia)

Cole Younger in prison
(Courtesy State Historical Society of Missouri, Columbia)

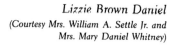

Lizzie Brown Daniel
(Courtesy Mrs. William A. Settle Jr. and
Mrs. Mary Daniel Whitney)

Jim Younger
(Courtesy Brookings Public Library)

Cole in Texas, 1906
(Courtesy Western Historical Collection,
University of Oklahoma Library)

Alix Muller
(Courtesy Brookings
Public Library)

Cole Younger
(Courtesy
Mrs. William A. Settle, Jr.)

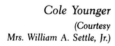

THE GREAT
COLE YOUNGER
AND
FRANK JAMES
HISTORICAL WILD WEST

Plunket and West End Avenue
NASHVILLE, MONDAY, JUNE 1

A Proudly Pre-Eminent Exhibition of
Universal Interest
THE MOUNTED WARRIORS OF THE
WORLD IN MARTIAL ARRAY

RUGGED ROUGH RIDERS

A Gathering of Extraordinary Consequence to fittingly illustrate all
that Muscular, Heroic Manhood has and can endure.

Cow Boys, American Indians, Mexican Ruralies, Bedouin Arabs.
Hungarian Cavalry, Russian Cossacks, American Cavalry, Roosevelt
Rough Riders, Western Cow Girls, and all the features that make
this GREAT EXHIBITION FAMOUS. The two famous men,

COLE YOUNGER and FRANK JAMES

Who will Review the Rough Riders in a Gorgeous
Military Tournament.

TWO PERFORMANCES DAILY—2 and 8 P. M., Rain or Shine

Watch for the Big Free Street Parade at 10 a. m., Monday, June 1

EXCURSION RATES ON ALL RAILROADS.

Flyer from the Wild West Show   (Courtesy Ted P. Yeatman)

Harry Hoffman
(Courtesy Naohm Hoffman Coop)

Frank James with his half-brother
John Samuel
(Courtesy Armand De Gregoris Collection)

Jesse Edwards James and Harry Hoffman at Quantrill reunion
(Courtesy Ethelrose James Owens)

LECTURE:
"What Life Has Taught Me."

BY

Who is Cole Younger

The Letters Printed Here Will Tell You

COLE YOUNGER
(Last of the Famous Younger Brothers.)

Instructive to Every Man, Woman and Child.

President Taft, in a recent address at the University Club dinner, held in Washington, D. C., speaking of Cole Younger, said:

"I am impressed with the fact that the University of Missouri is a great institution of learning. I am informed that three men great in the public life of the country for many years were graduated there. I mean Steve Elkins, Bill Stone and Cole Younger."

Opera House, 8:15 p. m.

Tuesday, December 6, 1910

"What Life Has Taught Me"
(Courtesy Carolyn Hall)

Jesse's description became involved in a confrontation with someone who thought Jesse was somebody else. The man was said to have told Jesse to leave town, which Jesse resisted. The situation was diffused when it was realized that Jesse was not who the man thought he was.

Cole's group made their way to Cordova the night of the 5th. They stayed at the Dampier House. W. W. Barlow of Wisconsin shared a room with them that night, as the hotel was full. Barlow later said that he recognized Bill Chadwell as having been one of the men with whom he shared the room. He said that all the men were polite and he was pleased to have been in their company.[22]

On September 6, Bob, Jesse, Frank, and Charlie stayed overnight at the farm of C. C. Stetson on the old Faribault Road five miles outside Northfield. Cole, Jim, Chadwell, and Miller put up at the Cushman Hotel in Millersburgh. Here, again, later reports would state that one of the men appeared to be sick and stayed in his room through dinner. Jim was not anxious to arrive in Northfield the next day.

On the morning of September 7, 1876, all eight men once again united in the woods outside Dundas, several miles west of Northfield. They made their last-minute plans. It was decided that Bob and Jesse would go into the bank, as they were the nominal leaders of the expedition. Frank James offered to accompany them. The three would enter the bank, providing the street was not too crowded, after they saw Cole and Clell cross the bridge that led to the center of town. A quarter-mile behind Cole and Clell, Jim, Charlie, and Chadwell would wait on the bridge. After the men entered the bank, Cole and Clell would ride up to hold stations near the door of the bank and be near should anything go wrong or any kind of trouble start. Cole would signal the others if this should happen and they would come in from the bridge to help. Their assignment was to fire their pistols in the air and deliver rebel yells should any shooting begin.[23]

Bob, Jesse, and Frank entered the town about 1:00 p.m. and ate their lunch at a restaurant across from the bank on the corner. They tied their horses near the bank before going in. About 1:50, they walked over to some dry goods boxes that were stacked in front of Lee & Hitchcock's store. They sat on the boxes and chatted casually. At 2:00 p.m., the three men entered the First National Bank of Northfield.

Cole later contended that the plan was not carried out according to agreement from the beginning. He wrote:

> When Miller and myself crossed over the bridge I saw a crowd of citizens about the corners, also our boys sitting there on some boxes. I remarked to Miller about the crowd and said, "Surely the boys will not go into the bank with so many people about. I wonder why they did not ride straight through the town." We were half way across the square when we saw the three men rise and walk up the sidewalk toward the bank. Miller said, "They are going in," and I replied, "If they do the alarm will be given as sure as there's a hell, so you had better take that pipe out of your mouth." The latter part of my remark was called out because Miller was so sure that there would be no trouble that he had lit his pipe just before we crossed the bridge, saying as he did so that he was going to smoke through the entire proceedings. As we rode into Division Street the three men ahead entered the bank, and I looked back and saw the other three men crossing the bridge.[24]

When Cole and Clell crossed the bridge into the town of Northfield, one of the first people they saw was Adelbert Ames walking with his father and his son. Cole said quietly, "Look, it's the governor himself." Ames overheard the remark and said to his son, "Those are Southerners. Nobody up here calls me Governor." The trio watched the men ride over the bridge and continued on their walk.

As Cole and Clell neared the bank door, they noticed that it had been left ajar. While Cole got down from his horse, pretending to adjust his saddle girth, he told Clell to close the door. Clell walked over to do so. Just after he turned from shutting the door, Clell was approached by J. S. Allen, a hardware merchant, who was attempting to enter the bank. Miller put his hand out to stop Allen. Allen jerked away from Clell and ran around the corner shouting, "Get your guns, they're robbing the bank!"

Henry M. Wheeler, a medical student home on vacation from the University of Michigan, watched Cole and Clell from the wooden sidewalk in front of his father's drugstore. Wheeler was born June 23, 1854, in North Newport, New Hampshire. He moved to Northfield with his family in 1856. Wheeler first studied at Carleton College in Northfield, graduated from the University of Michigan Medical School in 1877, and from the College of Physicians and Surgeons in New York in 1880. Eventually, Wheeler practiced medicine in Grand Forks, North Dakota, from 1881 until his death. When Wheeler saw Miller grab Allen's arm, he shouted, "Robbery!"

Clell and Cole mounted their horses immediately. Joined by Jim, Charlie and Chadwell, the five men rode their horses in circles, firing their guns into the air to create confusion. Cole rode over to the door of the bank and called inside, "Hurry up! They've given the alarm." Townspeople were kept at bay by the action of the horses and the firing of guns while the gang ordered everyone out of the street and away from the bank.

Bob, Jesse, and Frank had entered the bank after having agreed that Jesse would "oversee" and give directions as he saw fit. Jesse stepped up to the cashier's window with his gun drawn. The first bank employee he encountered was Alonzo E. Bunker, the teller. As Bunker was told to throw up his hands, Bob and Frank trained their guns on Joseph Heywood and Frank J. Wilcox. Jesse told them, "We're robbing this bank. Don't any of you holler. We've got forty men outside." Then Bob, Jesse, and Frank climbed up and over the counter. Heywood, who had been sitting at the cashier's desk, was asked if he was the cashier. "I am not," he replied. In actuality, Heywood was acting cashier as his boss, G. M. Phillips, was in Philadelphia attending the Centennial Exposition. Jesse said to Heywood, "I know you're the cashier, now open the door damn quick or I'll blow your head off."[25] Heywood replied that he could not open the safe. The "request" was made of the other employees as they were asked if they knew the combination. Each said he did not.

Frank James stepped over to the door of the vault to inspect the safe more closely. Heywood ran up behind him and attempted to push Frank into the vault. As Frank resisted, his arm and hand were nearly smashed in the closing door. Bob leaped forward and grabbed Heywood, throwing him to the floor. Jesse ran up to the cashier and put a knife to his throat. Jesse whispered, "Open the safe or I'll cut your damn throat from ear to ear." Bravely, Heywood replied, "You'll have to cut it then for I can't open it. It

has a chronometer lock."[26] The robbers looked at each other.
They were unfamiliar with the use of the new "timelock." What
Heywood was failing to tell them was that the timelock was not
engaged and the safe could have been opened at any time. "What's
that?" one of the robbers asked Heywood. "It can only be opened
at a certain time of the day" was the reply.

Bob had been guarding Bunker while stuffing his coat pockets
with some of the cash and coin that lay about the counter. When
the incident with Heywood began, his attention shifted away from
Bunker. Bunker suddenly made a dash for the back door of the
bank. Bob shot at the fleeing assistant bookkeeper, hitting him in
the shoulder. Bunker stumbled but was able to throw himself out
the door and then run up the street to the doctor's office yelling
"They're robbing the bank! Help!"

A veritable battle was occurring outside. Once alerted, the
citizens in the streets had run back to where they knew they could
obtain weapons and were now firing at the robbers in the street
with whatever weapons they had been able to produce: pistols,
rifles, and shotguns. Even rocks were being thrown. The city of
Northfield was not about to be so ravaged without a fight.

While trying to deflect any gunfire coming his way, Cole
continued to fire into the air, warning the citizens to retreat from
the street. He called to Nicholas Gustavson, a man wandering in
the street apparently without purpose, to "Get off the damn
street!" Gustavson continued to ignore Cole's warnings. Suddenly, in the cross fire, Gustavson was hit by a bullet and went
down. Mortally wounded, the Swedish Gustavson had not been
able to understand the warnings, which were issued in English. He
died four days later. It is not known who fired the bullet that took
the life of Gustavson. "Credit" has always been given to the
bandits, but it is also very likely that the man could simply have
been caught in the cross fire and the bullet that found him could
have been fired from either side.

The following letter was written from Northfield on November
14, 1876:

Geo. N. Baxter Esq.
Faribault

Dear Sir:
    In reply your postal of the 11th which only arrived the 13th

would say. Have found out by the Norwegian Priest who buried him that his name was Nicholas Gustavson. Will write it again so there will be no mistake Nicholas Gustavson.

I think you will find Dr. D.J. Whitney [?] good evidence as to what was said on the street. I am told that Dant Bow [?] saw the sweed killed and recognize the one who did it.

There is good evidence here but some people are timid. You had better send [help] to sift it.

Yours respectfully,
John T. Ames

If anyone saw who it was that fired the bullet that killed Nicholas Gustavson, he did not come forward.

Wheeler had stationed himself at a second-story window of the Dampier Hotel, across the street from the bank. Here he armed himself with an old army carbine and began to make his move against the robbers. As Clell Miller attempted to go back to the bank to see why the men inside had not yet left, he decided that it was too dangerous to be off his horse. As Clell attempted to remount, he was shot in the face with a small-caliber fowling piece by Elias Stacy. Stacy had been given the firearm by J. S. Allen, who was by then back at his store handing out guns and ammunition to anyone who would take them.[27]

Anselm Manning came running closer to the scene armed with a breech-loading rifle. Manning was born in Canada and moved to Northfield in 1856. He was an able man who at times worked as a blacksmith, carpenter, and surveyor. When the railroad arrived in Northfield, Manning was one of those who helped survey. He eventually established a hardware store on Bridge Street. From his place on the corner, Manning could see the robbers and the horses that had been left to wait for the men inside the bank. Manning carefully lowered his gun and shot Bob Younger's horse. Manning backed up, reloaded, and faced the street again. Cole ran to the door to see why the men had not yet left the bank. Manning shot at him but missed. Cole remounted his horse in haste. Manning reloaded again, and this time his aim was fatal. From seventy yards, Manning shot Bill Chadwell right from his horse, the bullet piercing Chadwell's heart. Wheeler, in the meantime, was shooting at whoever passed his window and hit Jim in the shoulder. His next target was Clell Miller, and his aim was successful. Clell's subclavian artery was severed, and Clell fell from his horse. Cole ran over to Clell only to see that he was dead. Manning fired again, hitting Cole in the thigh.

Inside the bank, Jesse dragged Heywood over to the vault, demanding that he somehow open it. He pointed a gun away from Heywood's ear and fired a shot into the floor. Bob heard the commotion and shooting in the street. When Cole came up to the bank door the last time, he shouted, "They're killing our men! Get out here!" Seeing that the scene in the bank was going nowhere, Bob ran out to help with the battle in the street. Jesse, disgusted at the turn of events, was shortly behind him scooping up change from the counter. Only Frank James remained in the bank, still angry over Heywood's attempt to shut him in the vault and his resulting injury. Clerk Wilcox, who had stayed out of the fray by moving to the side and doing only what he was told, was an eyewitness to what happened next. He later stated:

> He [the last robber] mounted a desk at the front and as he turned to go fired a shot at Heywood, which I do not think is the one that took effect. Heywood dodged behind his desk, or sank into his chair. Heywood's desk stands at right angles to the bank desk, and he sat sideways to the opening at the front with his back next to the wall and as the robber made over the desk railing he turned and placing his revolver to Heywood's head, fired.[28]

A contemporary account details the gory aspects of Heywood's death, describing the blood and brains covering the fallen cashier's desk.[29] With this last action, Frank James left the bank and entered the war zone out front in the street.

When Bob exited the bank to mount his horse and help those outside in their struggle to stay alive, he found that his horse had been shot and killed. He ran down the street, under fire, attempting to catch one of the dead men's horses. At this point he was not sure which of his comrades, or even his brothers, the three men lying in the street might have been. Bob ran down the sidewalk and confronted Manning. The two men shot at each other, both missing. Bob ducked behind a staircase where he could see Manning, and the two exchanged fire again. Wheeler, still at his post in the second-story window, didn't have a good line of vision to

Bob but fired anyway. His bullet struck Bob's elbow, breaking his arm. Bob calmly shifted his revolver to his left hand, he being the only one of the Younger brothers to be ambidextrous, and resumed firing. While Manning and Wheeler reloaded, Cole became aware of the tight spot Bob was in. According to Harry Hoffman:

> Almost at the same instant [Bob was spotted] one of Cole's bridle reins was clipped by a bullet; he quickly reached for his knife and cut the other rein close to the bit. Guiding his horse with knee and hand, he whirled and returned to the spot where Bob staggered in the street, trying to regain his feet. Cole's horse now reflected the training he had received; he performed perfectly, responding to every pressure of the knee; he whirled at the precise second, putting Cole in position to reach down and grab Bob by the belt and pull him onto the horse behind him. Bullets screamed and spat with a thud on the pavement; guns flamed and roared; Cole felt a sting in his side, another high on his shoulder; his hat was shot away, the horn of his saddle was ripped loose and hung there—swaying in the wind. Through it all, man and horse worked swift as light, every move as accurate as if rehearsed many times. The moment Bob landed behind Cole, the horse, carrying his double burden, was gone like a streak in the direction taken by the others.[30]

Frank and Jesse had been able to mount their horses easily and were quickly out of town. Jim waited for Cole just before the bridge while Cole rescued Bob from the ground. Charlie covered Cole, and the six outlaws fled the town of Northfield, most of them unaware of the fourth body, Gustavson's, left behind. The eight-minute gun battle had taken its toll, and $26.70 had been removed from the First National Bank of Northfield.

Three major controversies continue to haunt the story of the Northfield bank robbery. The question of who the actual men in the bank were is always first. Eyewitnesses were very vague with their descriptions until after Charlie Pitts's body was available for identification. Bob Younger readily admitted that he was one of the men in the bank and immediately claimed that neither of his brothers was with him. Pitts may or may not have been accurately identified. It would have been far less complicated to pin the murder on someone who was already dead and at hand, and this seems to be what the law authorities chose to do. It saved face for them and quelled the public's questions about Heywood's murderer. The Youngers were unable to support this theory, however, and only Cole, years later, named Charlie as having been in the bank. It would have saved the Youngers many years in prison to simply say that the man who had been killed with them when they surrendered to the posse at Hanska Slough had been the murderer of the cashier. This they did not do, causing us to believe that the cashier's murderer was still at large. This leaves either Jesse or Frank as suspects. The killer was likely Frank, as it was Frank who had his hand and arm slammed in the vault door by Heywood. This could not have made him happy, and perhaps that action was Frank's motivation for the killing of Heywood. There have been stories of how Frank believed Heywood to be going for a gun when he shot him. Along with Wilcox's statement of events, this seems unlikely as Heywood was hardly in a position to complete such an act with the desperados still within eyesight and their already having demonstrated they were prepared to deal with any such folly. In his autobiography, Cole claimed that the killer was Pitts. On his deathbed, Cole told Jesse E. James and Harry Hoffman who it was who shot Cashier Heywood but swore them both to secrecy. He also told them they were not to reveal who it was who rode the dun horse into Northfield that fateful day. Hoffman was able to get around his vow not to name names by not denying that Frank James purchased a dun horse for use in the Minnesota robbery. The James family itself accepts the fact that Frank James murdered Joseph Lee Heywood, although they believe his action was in self-defense.[31]

Another myth, this one perpetrated by Cole Younger, surrounds the robbery. Cole claimed in later years, after the death of Bob, that the robbery plans fell apart because the men who entered the bank had been drinking. Cole later wrote to Dr. A. E. Hedback:

> The fact is that all of the trouble was caused by a quart of whiskey which I learned afterward one of the three men had concealed and between when they left us in the woods and town drank most of it and were drunk. That accounts for them not shutting the door of the bank and not coming out according to our agreement when I called to them that the alarm was given. Had it not been for the

whiskey there would not, in all probability, have been a man killed, and I can truthfully say that had I known they had whiskey I would never had gone into the town; for with all my faults, and I am sorry to say there are many, whiskey drinking was not one of them and I never had confidence in a man who drank.

It is unlikely that Frank James, cut from the same military stock as Cole, would have had confidence in a man who drank, either, especially during a robbery. Since Frank was one of the men who entered the bank, he would have known if one of the others had been drinking. It is possible that it was Frank who had been drinking, but this is highly unlikely given his experience at bank robbery and his knowledge that he could be placed in a life-threatening situation at any moment. Jesse James did not drink, except for an occasional glass of wine, and was never known to have been drunk. Bob Younger may have drunk socially on occasion but certainly was not of a mindset to jeopardize himself, his brothers, or his comrades by appearing at a bank robbery the slightest bit under the influence of alcohol. Cole is correct when he stated that he was too savvy to participate in a robbery where he knew any of the others had been drinking. However, in an account he gave to Harry Hoffman, Cole stated that the plan was to have Bob stay at the door of the Northfield bank while Cole was to go inside. But due to the fact that Bob was drinking heavily, Cole deemed it wise to change the plans, realizing that Bob was too quick on the trigger when drinking. This was why Cole sent him into the bank. This is an extremely contradictory presentation of Cole's account of the bank robbery and his earlier statement that he did not know any of the men had been drinking and would have stopped the entire proceedings then and there if he had. The idea of proceeding with a robbery when even one of the participants was drunk, regardless of whether he was placed inside or outside the bank, is preposterous. It would seem that the statements about the men having been involved with whiskey that day were completely fabricated to cover the embarrassment Cole felt at the progression of events at Northfield and the subsequent "capture" of the Younger half of the great James-Younger Gang. It obviously was far easier for Cole to lay the blame on his dead brother and unnamed accomplices than to admit that things had simply not gone according to plan on September 7, 1876.

Joseph Lee Heywood was born August 12, 1837, in Fitzwilliam, New Hampshire. His father was a farmer with political interests, anti-slavery and pro-Whig. Heywood left home in 1857 at the age of twenty and began a somewhat transient life on his own. He seems to have had a hard time deciding where he wanted to establish a home for himself. Over the next five years he lived in Concord, Massachusetts, Fitchburg, Massachusetts, New Baltimore, Michigan (where he worked as a drugstore clerk), Moline, Illinois, and eventually settled in Chicago.

In August, 1862, he became a member of the 127th Illinois Regiment of the Union Army. While a member of this unit he served at the Battle of Vicksburg. Shortly after, he became ill and was removed from service and hospitalized. When he was able, he was sent to his brother's home in Illinois to recuperate. Eventually, recovered, he was sent to the Union Army Dispensary at Nashville to serve as a druggist. He was discharged at the close of the war in 1865 and returned to his brother's home in Illinois.

In the next year Heywood again looked for a suitable home, first living in Faribault, Minnesota, then Minneapolis, and eventually settled in Northfield in 1867. After his arrival in Northfield he became employed as a bookkeeper at the lumber yard of S. P. Stewart. In 1872 he accepted a job as bookkeeper at the First National Bank of Northfield. Heywood was married twice. His first wife was Mattie Buffum of Massachusetts. Mattie and Heywood had a daughter in 1871. Mattie died shortly thereafter. Heywood's second wife was Lizzie Adams, also from Massachusetts.

Heywood found acceptance in the community of Northfield and served as treasurer of both the city of Northfield and Carleton College. After his murder, over $12,000 was received from banks all over the United States and Canada for his family. His daughter was sent to Carleton College on a scholarship, where she received a degree from the School of Music and eventually became a music teacher. Many tributes were paid to Heywood in and around the city of Northfield after his death, including a Joseph Lee Heywood Library Fund and a window bearing his name in the Congregational Church of Northfield.

17

End of the Line

Captain, I can die as game as you can. Let's get it done.
—Charlie Pitts to Cole Younger at Hanska Slough

As the gang fled from the streets of Northfield, little did they know that the small posse forming to chase them would be the nucleus of the largest manhunt in the history of the United States at that time. Eventually, over a thousand men would attempt to apprehend the Northfield robbers: some lawmen, some townspeople, some simply curious sightseers. Some knew what they were doing, others did not. Some didn't care. The excitement was fierce, and everyone wanted to be involved in bringing down the gang of desperados. It was only toward the end of the search that the robbers were mentioned as possibly being the James-Younger Gang. The telegraph wires had not been cut by the gang on the way out of town. This allowed the message to go through immediately that the bank had been robbed and four people were dead including two of the robbers. The other six outlaws were last seen riding west out of Northfield.

It has been said that Jesse sustained a thigh wound on his way out of town as he was hit by one of the last bullets. Other stories claim that Frank and Jesse were riding double out of town and that a bullet passed through both their legs. Regardless, it does seem that one of the Jameses, probably Jesse, was wounded on the retreat. As Charlie waited for Cole and Bob, he also was shot.

The gang rode hard and fast southwest through Dundas. They stopped briefly at the Cannon River, where they cleansed their wounds and began to make preliminary plans for their retreat. While they talked, Philip Empey appeared on the road next to where they hid, hauling rails with a horse. The horse was soon procured for Bob.

Because of the swiftness of their retreat, even without the telegraph wires having been cut the robbers traveled well ahead of the news of the robbery for some time. They passed through Dundas and Millersburgh without incident. Immediately after the robbery, J. T. Ames, son of Adelbert, called for a volunteer posse and telegraphed the state capital for aid. The response by the various law enforcement agents in the immediate area was great. Soon an organized and able posse was under way out of Northfield and cities nearby to catch the robbers.

The first sighting of the gang was by two scouts who saw them take the horse from Empey on the Dundas Road. The odds not being in their favor, the two scouts trailed the robbers rather than confront them. After taking the horse from Empey, the group stopped at the farm of Robert Donaldson for a pail of water to cleanse Bob's wound. Donaldson asked the group how the man had been hurt, and they replied that they had been in a fight with a "blackleg" at Northfield. Bob had been shot and the "blackleg" was killed. Donaldson asked the name of the man killed and the answer was "Stiles."[1]

At least two different versions have been told about the next time the gang was spotted. One account claims that in the evening the group stopped outside a saloon near Shieldsville to use a water pump. Very discreetly, as they drank they pumped water onto rags to use later to tend to their wounds. Coats were thrown about them so that their injuries could not be detected. An old man in front of the saloon watched them with curiosity. Suddenly Bob, who had been fighting consciousness, fell off his horse into the dirt. Noticing the old man's reaction, Jesse thought quickly and dragged Bob back up on his horse saying, "We're going to hang that damn cuss." When the man lifted his eyebrows, Jesse explained that Bob was a captured horse thief. The old man walked back into the saloon, where he relayed his story. As the outlaws mounted their horses, four men appeared in the doorway of the saloon. Holding them at gunpoint, the gang told them to stay where they were and retreated out of town and into the woods. The four men at the saloon were joined by fourteen others of the town. They eventually caught up with the gang and surrounded them in a ravine. Shots were exchanged. Pitts was thrown by his horse but was able to climb back up. As he remounted, the saddle girth broke, throwing him once again to the ground. Charlie jumped up on the back of Bob's horse.[2]

Cole related this encounter differently:

> Here (at Shieldsville) a squad of men, who we afterwards learned, were from Faribault, had left their guns outside a house. We did not permit them to get their weapons until we had watered our horses and got a fresh start. They overtook us about four miles west of Shieldsville, and shots were exchanged without effect on either side. A spent bullet did hit me on the "Crazy Bone," and as I was leading Bob's horse it caused a little excitement for a minute but that was all.[3]

As the gang escaped this first encounter, the skies opened up and torrential rains began. The rain would continue on and off for the next two weeks. The outlaws disappeared into the "Big Woods" where they would be shielded for a while and could assess their situation while resting. Bob was bleeding profusely from his arm and had started to develop a fever as infection began to grow in his elbow. Jim's shoulder injury was quite serious and had started to infect as well. Cole's thigh was bleeding freely. He wrapped it tightly to enable him to walk using a stick cane he had fashioned. The others were holding their own.

By the time of the Shieldsville incident, there were over 200 men in the field. By Friday, September 8, there were over 500, with the number growing by the minute. If the apprehension of the robbers had been left to the professionals, the job may have been accomplished much quicker. The mainstay of the posse was law enforcement agents and veteran soldiers who knew what they were doing and were able to follow orders. Even many of those who had no real experience with such a venture were smart enough and committed enough to follow both the lead and the orders of those who did know what they were doing. However, once the inexperienced thrill-seekers began to join the hunt, the organized effort was weakened. George Huntington of Northfield wrote:

> There were also, of course, in so large and hastily-mustered a force, very many who had no fitness for the service, either in personal qualities or in equipment and no conception of the requirements of such a campaign. They came armed with small pistols and old fowling pieces of various degrees of uselessness, and utterly without either judgment or courage. Their presence was a source of weakness to the force. Their foolish indiscretions embarrassed and defeated the best-laid plans; and their failure at critical moments and places to do what they had been depended upon to do made them more than useless, worse than enemies.[4]

Many of the amateurs who joined the posse did so because of the large rewards that had been offered by the governor and the Northfield bank. On September 9, 1876, the governor of Minnesota issued the following proclamation:

> A reward of $1,500 will be paid by the state for the capture, dead or alive of the men who committed the raid, and afterwards escaped, on the bank of Northfield on September 7, 1876, or a proportionate amount for any one of them captured. (signed) J. S. Pillsbury, Governor.

As the professional posse dealt with the elusive Northfield robbers, the citizen posse, and those incompetents who called themselves posse, the organized efforts of the law enforcement agencies struggled to keep track of all the activity. They continued massive efforts just to do their job. The most professional posse to be organized was that of Sheriff Ara Barton out of Faribault, the county seat of Rice County. Picket lines were laid well in advance of the robbers and covered routes, roads, bridges, and fords. Unfortunately for the law, the Big Woods completely engulfed the outlaws, and the horrible weather made tracking them difficult, if not impossible. Since there were so many men in the field, many of the posse members had no idea who the others of their group were. This allowed the James-Younger Gang oftentimes to pose as posse members and cross picket lines or secure horses and food. Information was being telegraphed all over the state, and sometimes the whereabouts of the gang was erroneously reported, causing greater confusion. Then, again, sometimes the reports were accurate.

On September 8, two of the group, probably Frank and Jesse, appeared at the farm of George James near Waterville. The men were riding two horses and leading a third. The two men asked Mrs. James if she had seen two black mules. They wondered if there was any marshy area up ahead by the river where the mules might have bogged down. Mrs. James told them that there was. The men thanked her and went on their way.[5]

The Cannon River was high from the rain. As the gang attempted to cross it, they realized that it was probably unsafe to do so. Instead, they traveled down the Cordova Road, where they saw a few men in a shelter. The men had been working on the road and had stopped because of the rain. Casually, the outlaws asked the men how they might reach the other bank of the river, as they were looking for the robbers who had been involved at Northfield. The road crew told them that there was a bridge farther down the road. As the gang approached the bridge, they saw part of the posse that had been formed by a Captain Rodgers. The outlaws passed the bridge. The group went around Tetonka Lake and on the other side came face to face with the entire Rodgers posse. Shooting began, and the gang spurred their horses into the lake, crossed to the other side, and were swallowed up into the surrounding woods.

Later that afternoon, the outlaws crossed a cornfield and headed for Janesville. Along the way they were able to steal four fresh mounts: two from farmer John Laney and two others from Ludwig Rosenau. Rosenau's son Wilhelm was "requested" to lead the group across the river, which he did.

In Le Sueur County, the men stopped at the Rosenhall farm and forced two boys to unhitch their plowing horses and guide them to the Elysian Road. The spent horses were left at the Kohn farm near Waterville, where a couple of the outlaws who had not been seriously injured were able to secure a meal.[6]

On September 10, after the entire group reunited, they found themselves surrounded by over 200 posse members at Lake Elysian. That night the gang stayed on an island where the posse was unable to locate them. They released the stolen horses and tied three of the others to a tree. They continued on foot in the morning. The horses were found several days later. The posse had been operating under the assumption that the outlaws would not give up their horses. They felt fairly certain that the horses had not passed through their picket lines. The men continued to look in the area in which the robbers had last been seen. When they found the horses they knew that the outlaws had a good three-day lead on them. Many of the posse simply gave up and went home, believing the robbers to be long gone in who knew what direction.

The next day the gang camped one mile west of the lake where they were able to redress their wounds. Bloody rags and clothing were later found at their campsite. They decided to hole up a day or so to regroup and spent the next day and a half at a deserted farm ten miles northeast of Mankato.

On September 12, after leaving the safety of the farm, the group came upon a farmhand named Thomas "Jeff" Dunning. Since Dunning would be able to identify the gang and could reveal their whereabouts, his release was debated. Dunning could lead a posse directly to the gang if he was allowed to go free. Dunning, of course, swore he would tell no one. Eventually it was decided that the man should not be killed in cold blood and Dunning was released. Cole later stated that they thought of tying the man to a tree but were concerned that he might not be found in the denseness of the woods and would die. The gang released Dunning and took their chances. L. M. Demarary, a farmer from whom chickens would be stolen by the outlaws the next day, relayed the following:

> His [Dunning's] feelings when tied to the tree could better be imagined than described. His nerves were considerably shaken and after reaching home he acted so strangely that the Shaubuts [the people for whom he worked] noticed it, but as Mr. Dunning had some trouble with his heart they attributed it somewhat to this condition. However, as his demeanor did not change they commenced to question him and after a period of approximately three hours he finally admitted the real cause. Of course by that time the Gang was several miles away.[7]

The outlaws continued on their way, crossing the Blue Earth River at a railroad bridge. They followed the tracks around the city of Mankato without incident. Now that the robbers' general whereabouts had become known, the posse realized that the outlaws had traveled only fifty miles since the robbery and felt encouraged. A local posse was formed by General Pope of Mankato.

On September 14, outside Mankato, another discussion occurred among the gang. Jesse and Frank believed that Dunning's release would renew interest with the posses. All the men knew that Bob and Jim were impeding the escape. Even though their injuries continued to improve, their movements were slow, for they had to stop for rest periodically. Bob suggested that he be left to enable the others to escape. Cole and Jim would not allow it. Jesse and Frank, however, thought it a good idea that the group at least split up. Those who could travel faster would stand a good chance of moving out of the area. This would serve two purposes. The faster group would be better able to escape. The posse would probably follow them, allowing the men left behind to continue on unmolested for a while.

This plan was agreed upon.[8] At no time did Jesse suggest shooting Bob so that the Jameses could escape. That story, perhaps one of the biggest folklore tales of the James-Younger Gang, is totally fictitious. Cole Younger told the following account to Jesse E. James and Harry Hoffman on his deathbed in 1916:

> No, Jesse James nor any person ever made that request or suggestion [that Bob be killed]: this is what happened when the James Boys left us at that last camp near Madelia, and made their escape; About the third day we were hiding there, Frank and Jesse went out one night and searched the neighborhood trying to find horses, so that we could all try once more to escape on horseback. Along toward morning they returned and informed us they could find but two horses. Jesse suggested that I and Bob take the two horses and ride away, that he and Frank and the others would try to escape on foot. But during this night Bob's arm had taken a turn for the worse and he was suffering great pain and I told Jesse and Frank to take the horses and go. And this they did. Their acts and treatment of us were honorable and loyal.[9]

The Jameses followed the Blue Earth River, and that night they approached Lake Crystal, where they spied a group of several men asleep on a bridge. One guard, Richard Roberts, saw the two men and shot at them. His bullet removed the hat from one of the mysterious riders. Jesse and Frank, however, escaped into the night. They stole two grays which they rode bareback. Riding hard, due west, in forty-eight hours they crossed the Minnesota border into South Dakota. On September 17, they exchanged their horses for two black steeds, but they soon found out that one horse was blind in one eye while the other was blind in both. They quickly obtained other horses. The James boys rode through Sioux Falls to continue their retreat from the Minnesota posse.

After the Jameses and Youngers split up, the posse chased the Jameses, thinking it was the entire gang, as the Jameses had suggested they might. Others of the posse didn't believe this was the case and spent much time ousting men from saloons and gaming houses in the area. They managed to turn up two horse thieves but none of the Northfield robbers.

Not far from the Sioux City Railroad near Linden, the Youngers and Charlie gathered watermelon, chickens, a small turkey, and corn. They began to prepare a much-desired breakfast. Several voices were heard up on the Crystal Road. Before the boys determined whether or not it was a posse, they abandoned their meal and scrambled up the banks and into the woods. This was a smart move, as it was a posse that they heard. The group pursued the gang through the woods to the top of Pigeon Hill, where the outlaws disappeared. Examination of their camp revealed interesting items left along with their still-cooking breakfast: a ripped, backless shirt; a fairly new shirt with the initials G.S.O.; a blood-soaked handkerchief; a blue gossamer coat; a new brown linen duster; two leather bridles, and a piece of five-foot-square three-ply carpet. Bob Younger later claimed that the two coats were his.

The next day found the Youngers and Pitts seven miles outside Madelia. The swamps were thick, swollen from the rain. Progress was slow, and the boys were not sure where they were. Although they knew they were continuing westward, the swamps and forests confused them and they spent much time turning in circles.

Near sunrise the morning of September 21, the four outlaws

began moving again. Expecting few people to be up and about at that time of the day, they followed the road along Lake Linden in Brown County. As they passed a farm, they saw a young man milking cows, but they remained calm. They bid the boy good morning and continued walking, disappearing into the woods. The boy, Oscar Sorbel, seventeen, sought out his father Ole, who was working on the other side of the barn. Oscar told of the men he had just seen and suggested to his father they might be the Northfield robbers, about whom they had all been reading. His father scoffed at the idea and told Oscar to return to work. In about an hour, two of the men, dressed heavily in long dusters, returned to the Sorbel farm. They asked to buy some bread, which they did. Then they disappeared once again. Oscar was convinced the men were the robbers, and this time his father agreed with him. Oscar mounted his horse and rode to Madelia, seven miles away, just as quickly as his horse could travel.

In Madelia, Oscar came upon Sheriff James Glispin in the company of Col. T. L. Vought. When Oscar told the sheriff of the sighting of the men, Vought remembered his conversation with Cole when Cole had stayed in Vought's hotel the month before. Cole had asked about the roads and terrain of the area. Vought had already become suspicious that the man with whom he had talked about cattle in August may have been one of the Northfield robbers, as the descriptions matched. Glispin and Vought left immediately for the Sorbel farm while Civil War veteran Captain W. W. Murphy formed a posse. The posse was not hard to gather. Stores were closed and nearly the entire male population of the small town joined the group heading out to Sorbel's farm.

An hour after Oscar had reported the sighting of the outlaws, Glispin and Vought spotted them as they attempted to cross a slough south of Hanska Lake. The slough was so boggy that horses were not able to walk through. Glispin ordered the four men to halt. At this point they broke into a run and disappeared into the wooded area just above the Watawon River. Glispin and Vought were joined by four others. Splitting in two, they walked their horses around the slough. By this time the outlaws had disappeared. Glispin and the five men again spotted the outlaws about a quarter of a mile from the river, deep in the brush. Glispin called to them to surrender, but the men continued running. The small posse fired, and the outlaws returned the fire as they ran.

By this time, the larger group of men from the town had come upon the scene. The robbers hid in a thicket, where they loaded their guns and prepared to fight. They could see that there was little chance of their escaping so large a group of men from where they had been trapped in the thicket. Charlie suggested to Cole that they surrender. Cole wasn't ready to admit defeat and looked back at Charlie with determination, saying, "Charlie, this is where Cole Younger dies." Cole said later that he was most impressed with Charlie's loyalty and courage when Charlie responded, "All right, Captain, I can die as game as you can. Let's get it done."[10] Bob reloaded guns for his brothers and Charlie as they waited for the posse's next move.

Murphy and Benjamin Rice approached George Bradford near the bank of the river and suggested that a group of men go into the thicket to face off with the outlaws. Glispin agreed, and the four men were joined by Charles A. Pomeroy, S. James Severson, and Vought. Although Glispin was technically in charge, Murphy, calling on his military experience, took command. Murphy told the assembled men to shoot low. He also ordered that they not shoot first, as it had been agreed by Murphy and Glispin that the robbers would be commanded to surrender and the posse would attempt to take them alive.

The seven men proceeded down to the river while another group of at least nine watched them from a short distance away. Bradford later said that he thought the entire group was going to participate but noticed the others remaining some distance back when the time came to go into the brush to face the outlaws. The brush was so thick that in places it was difficult to follow the line of the river, but the seven men slowly advanced on the Youngers and Charlie. George Bradford wrote of what happened next:

> I became convinced that we were getting away from the river and leaned down to look under the brush and told Mr. Glispin that I thought he was getting away from the river, when something drew my attention to the front and glancing that way saw some of the men we were after and just then one of them [Pitts] jumped up and fired. Almost simultaneously with his shot two men at least fired

and Pitts dropped. I had raised my gun to shoot, when a bullet struck, or rather grazed, my wrist and disturbed my aim, so it was a second or so before I fired. Several shots were fired from both sides and a volley from across the river by parties there. They could not see us from there but fired, the bullets cutting the twigs over our heads. Murphy called to cease firing and ordered a surrender.[11]

Even as Charlie Pitts fell dead with a bullet close to his heart and several more having found their mark besides, the Youngers were reluctant to give up the fight. Cole's gun was shot from his hand. He picked up Charlie's and resumed firing. A rifle ball hit Jim in the jaw, taking out several of his teeth and lodging somewhere in his mouth. Almost at the same time, a bullet hit Cole's face, somehow lodging over his right eye. He, too, fell. Bob looked at his brothers lying on the ground along with the dead Charlie and yelled at the posse to stop their firing. As first Cole and then Jim stirred, Bob called out, "I surrender, they're all down but me." Glispin ordered the posse to hold their fire.

After a moment, Bob staggered up from the thicket holding a handkerchief in his upheld left hand. From the bank, a shot was fired, hitting Bob in the chest. One of the men who had been cautious about confronting the outlaws face-to-face now sought to make his contribution to their capture by shooting an unarmed man who had been called to surrender. Bob fell to the ground, astonished. "I was surrendering," he called weakly. "Somebody shot me while I was surrendering." Glispin yelled at the men on the bank to hold their fire and told them in no uncertain terms that he would shoot the next man who fired.

The posse of seven slowly advanced on the group of outlaws who lay on the ground. Bob was helped to his feet. Charlie Pitts lay dead. Jim Younger slowly rose. Cole, awakening in the belief that he was still in the throes of battle, offered to fight the posse hand to hand. Bob put his uninjured arm around his brother and told him, "Cole, it's all over. Give it up or they will hang us for sure."[12]

While the posse helped the Youngers walk out of Hanksa Slough, as it was called, Bob asked for a plug of tobacco to chew to ease his pain. He was given one, and as he chewed he watched the body of his friend and comrade Charlie Pitts being carried out by the men who had waited on the bank.

Charlie Pitts was born one of twelve children near Commerce, Oklahoma, in 1844. At the age of sixteen, Charlie was hired as one of the hands of affluent farmer Washington Wells. Charlie was accompanying Mrs. Wells on errands in the neighborhood of Westport on July 20, 1862, when they happened upon the body of Henry Washington Younger. Charlie stayed with Henry's body while Mrs. Wells returned to town for help. Cole met Charlie sometime later and thanked him for helping his father. Thus began a relationship that continued through the next decade.

It is not clear what role Charlie played in the war. It has been said that he aided the guerrilla movement, although he doesn't appear to have been a "formal" member. After the war, Charlie spent time with the Cherokee Indians and also in the Ozark Mountains. Charlie applied the medical knowledge he had obtained from the Indians and became known as the Ozarks Medicine Man.

It is possible that Charlie married Emma Henderson at Columbus, Kansas in 1874. Charlie became friendly with Bob Younger after having participated in a couple of the James-Younger Gang's robberies and visited Bob and Maggie after they had established their farm.

The only "injury" of any of the posse members was that of Murphy. Believing himself to have been shot, Murphy later discovered a bullet had pierced his vest and bounced off his brierwood pipe.[13]

The three wounded Youngers were helped into a wagon and escorted back to town by the posse. As the wagon entered Madelia, the people of the town cheered. With eleven wounds in his body, Cole Younger struggled to his feet and tipped his hat in salute to the crowd. The James-Younger Gang's trip to Minnesota had been unsuccessful to say the least, but the Youngers' stay in Minnesota was just beginning.

The seven men who made up the small but brave posse to whom the Youngers surrendered received only $240 of the reward money offered for the capture of the Northfield bank robbers. The state received claims from hundreds of men who believed they were entitled to some of the reward because they had encountered the outlaws at various points along their routes of retreat. The rewards were issued on January 15 (ironically Cole and Jim's birthday), 1878.

Axle Oscar Sorbel was born of Norwegian parents in the United States. He became a veterinarian and practiced his profession in Webster, South Dakota. Oscar received $56.25 for his participation.

John Glispin was born in Linn, Massachusetts. He worked as a wool inspector before relocating to Madelia, Minnesota, where he first sold farm implements. He was elected sheriff of Watawon County, a position in which he served three terms. He eventually moved to Santa Rosa, California, where he became involved in the mercantile business. He relocated to Spokane Falls, Washington, and was elected chief of police. He later became sheriff of Spokane County. He retired from law enforcement and went into real estate, his profession until his death in 1890 at the age of forty-six.

George A. Bradford was born near Patriot, Indiana, on June 28, 1847. He arrived in Minnesota when he was twenty. He became a farmer and schoolteacher. He soon went into business as the owner of a dry goods store. He eventually retired from business to return to farming.

William W. Murphy was born in Liginier, Pennsylvania, on July 27, 1837. In 1854, Murphy decided to seek his fortune in the California gold fields and remained there until 1861. He then returned to Pennsylvania. He volunteered into the 14th Pennsylvania Regiment and served first as a second lieutenant and then as a first lieutenant. Eventually, he was appointed captain for "gallantry on the field" at the battle at Piedmont, Virginia. During his first years of service, Murphy served under General Sheridan. In 1866, Murphy relocated to Minnesota where he raised stock and farmed. In 1871, he was elected to the Minnesota legislature.

Charles A. Pomeroy was born in Rutledge, New York. His father was one of the earliest settlers in Madelia, arriving in 1865. His father was a justice of the peace. Pomeroy lived in Madelia quite a while and eventually relocated to Cleveland, South Dakota.

Thomas Lent Vought was born in Walcott, Minnesota, on April 29, 1833. He grew up on Lake Ontario until his family moved to

Rock County, Wisconsin. When he was nineteen, Vought moved to La Crosse, where he became employed as a lumberman. He eventually served as a clerk in a hotel there. Vought and his new bride, Hester Green, moved to Bryce Prairie, where they operated a farm until the war. Vought enlisted in the 14th Wisconsin Regiment. He moved to Madelia in 1866 where he operated a line of mail and passenger stages. With the arrival of the railroad, Vought purchased the Flanders Hotel. After the Northfield robbery, Vought moved several times from Madelia to New York to South Dakota and eventually back to La Crosse, Wisconsin. He was employed as a farmer, a merchant, and a landlord.

S. James Severson was born in Wisconsin in 1885. After his arrival in Minnesota he spent time as a farmhand. He eventually became a clerk in a store, which is what his profession was at the time of his encounter with the Youngers. He relocated to Brookings, South Dakota.

Benjamin M. Rice was born in Green County, Alabama, on February 8, 1851. He attended the Christian Brothers College in St. Louis. In 1869 his family moved to Minnesota. Rice was appointed an engrossing clerk in the state legislature. Following the surrender of the Youngers, Rice moved to Murfreesboro, Tennessee. He eventually relocated to Lake Weir, Florida, where he died on August 14, 1889, at the age of thirty-eight.

There seems to have been little respect for the body of a dead robber in Minnesota at the time of the Northfield robbery. None of the bodies of the three men killed there was properly buried.

After his death in Northfield, Clell Miller's body was photographed and held in that city. Somehow, a promoter gained possession of Miller's body, had it embalmed, put it in preservative alcohol, and then proceeded to display it throughout the Northwest. Eventually, Miller's family obtained a court order and were able to retrieve his body for burial at the Muddy Fork Cemetery in Clay County.

After Bill Stiles was killed in Northfield, his body was to have been buried. However, Henry Wheeler told the authorities that cadavers that could be used for dissection purposes at medical schools were scarce and suggested Stiles's be used. To not offend, Wheeler suggested that a pine casket filled with rocks be "shipped" somewhere while the body was turned over to Wheeler, who had it placed in a pickling box.[14]

Charlie Pitts's body was sold to a Dr. Murphy of the practice of Murphy and Quinn for use as a skeleton. The body was put into a weighted box and lowered into Lake Como outside St. Paul. Later in the winter, the box could be seen through the ice near the farm of Joshua Robertson. The St. Paul police were called to investigate and the embarrassed doctors explained what they had done. Charlie's body, still in the box, was moved to the field of a Mr. Hoyt where the bones could bleach.[15]

18

Abiding the Consequences

*We tried a desperate game and lost. But we are rough
men used to rough ways and we will abide by the
consequences.*
>   —Bob Younger to St. Paul *Pioneer Press*

The three wounded outlaws were escorted up to the top of the
bank. One of the men who had waited there was sent to get a
wagon. After the wagon arrived, Cole, Jim, and Bob were helped
into it. As Colonel Vought assisted Bob, Cole recognized him,
calling him "landlord."[1] The group proceeded slowly to Madelia.
Jim, bleeding profusely from his chin, placed his face over the side
of the wagon. At one point in the journey, the family of George
Thompson passed by in a buggy. Mrs. Thompson gave Jim a
handkerchief to hold over his chin. Cole and Charlie had visited
Thompson's store in St. James, and Cole acknowledged meeting
Thompson there.[2]

The flight finally ended, the three men were in bad shape. Cole
had eleven bullet wounds and Jim had five. Bob had the serious
elbow wound from Northfield and the hole in his chest from the
posse member. The three men suffered most from exposure,
however. They had wrapped pieces of their clothing around their
feet. When he removed his boots, Cole's toenails fell off.

The sorry group was taken to Vought's hotel, the Flanders
House. They were carried up to the second floor, where Cole and
Jim were placed in a bed at one end of the floor while Bob was

203

taken to the other end. The townspeople donated fresh, dry clothing for them. Drs. Overholt and Cooley were called to examine the three outlaws. As the men were transported upstairs, Mads Ouren greeted Cole. Cole remarked that he had recognized Ouren's fine gun, the one that hung over Ouren's kitchen door observed by Cole when he had visited. Cole also noted, "But you didn't shoot it." Cole was right. Ouren had loaned his gun to the posse but had not participated himself.[3]

Guards were posted in and around the hotel to keep watch for any escape efforts, although the men were in no shape to even try. The guards also watched for rescue efforts and for vigilante attacks from the outside. Soon people entered Madelia by the hundreds. Local townsfolk, sightseers from neighboring communities, reporters, photographers, and detectives gathered outside the hotel.

Charlie Pitts' body was placed in the small Madelia jail, where he was covered by a sheet. His fatal chest wound was left exposed. The sightseers were allowed to pass by the jail and observe the fallen outlaw.

The Youngers had decided on their way into town that they would reveal their own true identities but not those of their comrades, dead or alive. There was no need for them to name the two men killed at Northfield, as Police Chief McDonough of St. Louis had already identified them as Clell Miller and William Stiles. From descriptions, he also concluded that the James brothers had been present and that the robbery had been the work of the James-Younger Gang. It was also McDonough who later identified Pitts. Bob and Cole freely admitted who they were but would not tell of the others, including Jim, who was unable to talk. This added fuel to the fire that had been burning in the papers that one of the outlaws was the infamous Cal Carter of Texas. Jim was said to be Carter. When he was able, Jim denied being Carter and identified himself, to no avail. When asked if the James brothers were involved in the Northfield robbery, the Youngers unequivocally stated that they were not.

A rumor arose concerning the injury of Jim. Some of the men present stated that after the surrender of the Youngers, one of the outlaws was shot. The man who fired the shot was not viewed as a hero. While it was Bob who had been shot in the chest when he surrendered, the story grew that a man named Willis Bundy had shot Jim in the chin while Jim lay helplessly on the ground. Jim had, in fact, been shot by B. G. Yates. Whether or not Bundy was the one who shot Bob was never made clear. Cole was later quoted as having expressed his admiration for the bravery of the posse at Madelia save for Willis Bundy. Cole was said to have vowed, "If I live to be a free man I will hunt that man down and kill him."[4]

The Youngers were allowed to sleep that night while hundreds more people poured into Madelia to see the outlaws. Posse member George Bradford guarded Bob Younger through the night but noted that Bob had little to say.[5] In the morning, both Cole and Bob would be ready to make their statements.

The two doctors worked diligently to treat the three men. Bullets were removed and wounds were dressed. Jim continued to bleed quite a bit, and his mouth wounds were repeatedly cauterized. The outlaws had little in their possession when they surrendered. Cole claimed that they had given their money, watches, and rings to their escaping comrades.[6]

Cole and Bob each had $5 in their billfolds. Jim had $150.[7] Evidently, Jim had not trusted the Jameses with his money. The fact that Cole and Bob had given the Jameses their possessions further indicates that the parting was on amicable terms and that the Jameses and Youngers hoped to reunite someday in the future.

As soon as the doctors decided that the outlaws were up to it, the press was allowed in to talk to the Youngers. Jim, of course, was unable to say anything but watched Cole with interest as Cole began to retell the events contained in Edwards's "A Terrible Quintette." Cole solicited compassion as he told of the murder of Henry and the burning of his mother's house. Cole maintained that the circumstances of the war were what had brought the Youngers to Minnesota and the attempted robbery of the Northfield Bank. Cole, as well as Bob, expressed gratitude and relief at the way the three brothers had been treated by the posse and the people of Madelia. They had expected to be lynched.

A reporter from the St. Paul *Pioneer Press* met with Bob and described him in the following way:

> He is a man fully six feet high, well built, sandy complexion, and has a pleasant face. We should pick him out of any crowd as a kind-

hearted man whom we should expect would grant a favor readily. He conversed freely and answered most of the questions put to him without apparent reserve.[8]

Bob called on better days when he quoted Cole in response to the reporter's question as to why they had robbed the Northfield Bank: "We tried a desperate game and lost. But we are rough men used to rough ways and we will abide by the consequences."[9]

Of course the question of who shot the cashier at Northfield was on everyone's lips. The Youngers wouldn't say. Bob admitted that he was inside the bank. He further stated that the killing of the cashier was an "act of impulse" on the part of the man who had done it and was something all of the group had regretted. He would not divulge who it was that had fired the fateful shot, however, even when asked if it had been the man who had been killed in Hanska Slough.

On a lighter note, Bob was asked if he liked baseball, a sport that was beginning to attract the attention of the country. Bob smiled and said that he did. He recalled seeing the local St. Paul team, the "Red Caps," as they left the Merchant Hotel, traveling to play a game somewhere in the state. The reporter gave Bob a copy of the *Pioneer Press* which proclaimed the capture of the Northfield robbers. Bob smirked and said he had heard hundreds of papers had been printed and that he was glad somebody was making money off the botched affair. He claimed that he was "out $500."[10]

In the meantime, Glispin met with Cole to determine exactly who the robbers were who had been able to escape. McDonough had conveyed that he believed them to be the James boys, but Cole refused to tell. Finally, Cole said that he would have a statement on the matter in the morning. When morning came, Cole handed the sheriff the following note: "Stay by your friends even if heaven falls." Neither Cole Younger nor his brothers would reveal that most-desired information.

The Youngers were to have been taken to Faribault on Friday, but Jim's injury had not started to heal to the satisfaction of his doctors and they advised against it. However, on Saturday morning, September 23, the Youngers were placed in the custody of

Sheriff Ara Barton of Faribault. They were escorted on board the St. Paul and Sioux City Railroad and began their trip east. Charlie Pitts's body was loaded on the train to be taken to St. Paul, which was the first stop. The transport had been broadcasted by word of mouth, and people knew the train would stop in St. Paul on Friday. Hundreds of people gathered to met the train and view the outlaws. They were very disappointed when they heard that the Friday train transport had been canceled. The following day the train was met by fewer people when it finally did stop briefly in St. Paul. Pitts's body was removed and turned over to the officials.

The train arrived in Faribault about noon on September 23. By that time, hundreds of people had already gathered to await their opportunity to see the notorious outlaws. The Youngers were taken to the Faribault Jail. The jail itself was a sterile building of 30 by 20 feet. The three men were placed in separate cells which measured 7 feet high and 3½ feet wide. Jim was in so much pain that he didn't really care that his quarters were so small as he lay on the cot that had been provided him. Bob, who was over 6 foot 2, had to place his feet on the grate in order to be comfortable, and this action caused people to think that he was acting "bold." Bob sat quietly in his cell with two other prisoners who were pleased to have the "celebrity robber" in their company. He was offered cigars, which he accepted. Cole, for some reason, was allowed to sit on a cot near the doorway of the prisoners' portion of the jail. He was also allowed to wander through the corridor at will. This was probably because Cole was the prisoner most likely to offer interesting conversation to those allowed in to talk with the Youngers. Eventually Cole was confined to his own cell as visitors began to arrive and sightseers lined up to go inside the jail and "view" the outlaws. By September 26, over 4,000 people had been through the small jail.[11] The lines were long as people from all over the state gathered to await their opportunity to see the Younger brothers face-to-face. Bob later stated that he developed a serious case of claustrophobia which haunted him for years.

Cole talked freely with his visitors, oftentimes returning to his dissertations on the early life of the Youngers. His mournful stories told of how the boys had been driven to a life of crime through the most unfortunate of circumstances. The local papers began seriously to oppose this obvious play for sympathy. Accounts of Cole's stories were not favorably reported in the Minnesota papers. The validity of Cole's claims was overlooked because of the overblown manner in which Cole dramatically recounted even the most personal family incidents. While claiming to dispute tales written and told about the Youngers, Cole might as well have been dictating a novel of his own. His brothers were disgusted at Cole's blatant plays for sympathy. Bob gained the respect of the newspapermen as a straightforward man who offered no excuses while expressing regret for the series of events that brought him to the Faribault Jail. Jim, in horrible pain and discomfort, was able to say little and did not talk to the papers at this time.

During the first days of the Youngers' stay at the jail, letters began to appear said to be from the members of the "Younger Gang" and others of the outlaws' friends. Threats were made to the men who had killed the robbers at Northfield. The town itself was said to have received more than a few notices that the deaths of the outlaws and "capture" of the Youngers would be avenged. The law enforcement officials at Faribault began to worry that members of the James-Younger Gang would appear to liberate the Youngers. Plans were set into motion to increase the guard to prevent anything from happening.

Within days of the arrival of the Youngers, James McDonough of the St. Louis police department and C. B. Hunn, the superintendent of the United States Express Company arrived in Faribault to identify them. The two men had traveled to Minnesota with over seventy-five others, including women, who were anxious to be a part of the official party and see the captured outlaws. They had first gone to St. Paul to look at the dead Pitts. With information they had obtained from Hobbs Kerry after his confession of the Rocky Cut robbery, the men were able to absolutely identify Charlie. Using Kerry's detailed descriptions, they were further able to substantiate Cole and Bob's claims that they were who they said they were. However, since Jim had not participated in the Otterville train robbery, Kerry did not have a description to offer to the officials in regard to Jim. McDonough continued to state that Jim was Cal Carter of Texas. Although Jim shook his head in denial, the law continued to advance that theory. Bob and

Cole told McDonough that Jim was their brother, but the police chief refused to believe them. At one point, Cole offered to bet him $500 that he was in error.

The surgeon general of the state of Minnesota, Dr. Murphy, arrived to examine the prisoners and found Jim in dreadful condition. Dr. Murphy found the bullet that had entered Jim's jaw was still embedded in front of his left ear. Jim was miserable, in acute pain and suffering from severe depression. Bob's wounds were healing, yet Bob had decided that he had said all he wanted to the press in Madelia. While he was polite, he now declined to answer most questions. The *Pioneer Press* called him "The Knight of the Bush."

It was at this time that Mayor Ames of Northfield arrived in Faribault. He told the Youngers of the death of Gustavson. Ames accused Cole of having fired the shot that caused the man's death. Cole adamantly denied having done so. An argument ensued between Ames and Cole, and eventually Cole asked that Ames be removed from his cell. Sheriff Barton agreed, as he was most anxious not to have additional trouble with so many people in and about the jail. A coroner's jury in Northfield had already found that the death of Nicholas Gustavson was caused by "a stray bullet which had been fired by an unknown party."[12]

Several other interested parties visited the Youngers in addition to the sightseers. Detective Bligh attempted to get Cole to admit to the Huntington, West Virginia, robbery but had no success. State legislator John L. Merriam and John F. Lincoln, the superintendent of the St. Paul and Sioux City Railroad, wanted to talk to the prisoners about the Gad's Hill robbery. Both men had been passengers on the train that had been robbed there in January, 1874. Without being told who Merriam was, Cole asked the man if they had not met before. Merriam smiled and told Cole that he had been a passenger on the Gad's Hill train. Cole denied he was present at that robbery and said that he and Bob had been in St. Clair County. By prearrangement, Lincoln was at that same time accusing Bob of being one of the robbers at Gad's Hill. Bob denied his participation also, claiming that he and Cole had been in Arkansas at the time of the robbery.[13]

By Monday, the streets of Faribault were packed with people.

The sheriff began to become extremely uncomfortable and a larger guard was posted. Barton also began to fear that a rescue attempt might be made, as any strangers could blend in perfectly with the throngs of people gathered around the jailhouse. The law enforcement of the city and county was on the alert.

That day the Youngers were photographed in their cells. Although their wounds were starting to heal, they were quite sore. Jim continued to become more depressed, and although he did not discuss his feelings with anyone, he lay on his cot staring at the ceiling, discouraging any form of communication.

On September 26, Justice John B. Quinn arrived at the jail to formally deliver warrants to the Youngers. He was accompanied by Judge Samuel Lord. Cole, in the presence of attorney Thomas Rutledge from Madelia, waived the preliminary hearing.

The crowd gathered outside the jail became even more excitable, and Barton decided that the Youngers should be placed in irons. Although they accepted Barton's decision without protest, the prisoners were discouraged by this development.

On October 2, an unfortunate incident occurred. Deputy Henry Kapanick was bet $5 by his friends that he would have no problem gaining entry to the jail through the heavy guard that had been placed there. Frank Glaser, one of the guards on duty that night, gave his account of what happened:

> I was on guard at the east end of the jail and had just been down to the corner of the building and was going back; heard footsteps beyond the engine house. As I heard them I stepped behind the bushes near the pump. As he came up I kept watch of him. Just as he stepped from the sidewalk to the ground I ordered him to halt. He didn't stop; said something I cannot remember; think now he took me for another guard with whom he was acquainted. It was the first time I had been on guard. I spoke to him again and asked, "Who are you" and as I did so I stepped back a couple of paces. He was coming right towards me. When I spoke he appeared to be trying to get between me and the jail. He said, "Don't you know I'm a policeman" Still kept coming towards me; thought he must be a robber; thought he intended to finish me with a knife and had accomplices nearby. He then put his hand up to his breast and then brought it out, as a man would do if he were drawing a revolver or

knife. I stepped back a step or two and he took a few steps forward. Then I fired[14]

Henry Kapanick was killed. An inquest found that Glaser had acted in self-defense.

On October 5, Retta Younger and her brother-in-law Richard Hall arrived in Faribault. Retta and her sisters wanted to be sure that the robbers who were being held prisoner and who had been accused of the Northfield robbery were indeed Cole, Jim, and Bob. Retta first encountered Jim as she entered the jail. She broke into tears and put her arms around her brother. Now the authorities could be sure that Jim Younger was who he claimed to be and not the infamous outlaw Cal Carter. Retta visited with her brothers, and she and Richard Hall left Faribault after two days, promising to return.

Henrietta was the youngest and most adored of the Younger family. Retta, as she was known, was totally devoted to her family after having experienced the agony of war at home with her mother, sister, and two brothers. Retta was particularly close to her brother Bob. Retta was educated in the county schools of Dallas, Texas, after the war. At the time of the Northfield robbery, Retta said, she was attending the Baptist School in St. Joseph, Missouri, with her education being financed by her brother Bob.

The Youngers remained in the Faribault Jail for over a month before they went to court. In that time, they became quite friendly with Sheriff Ara Barton, whom they grew to respect a great deal. They were still subjected to frequent and undesirable visits from people they did not know but caused no problems for the police. Jim's wound began to heal somewhat, but his disposition was quite gloomy. Although the lights of the jail burned all day and night, allowing the prisoners little privacy, many of their visitors continued to treat them well and offer some comfort. Bob was often sent nuts and candy by young ladies who were too shy to give them to him themselves.

On November 9, Retta and Richard Hall returned. Bob, Cole, and Jim met with their family to decide what course of action should be pursued. Rutledge advised them that should they be indicted for the murder of Heywood, Minnesota law had a saving clause. If they pleaded guilty, they could not be hung. The sentence would be life imprisonment and they would no doubt be out on parole after ten years or so.

On November 18, the Younger brothers finally had their day in court. The courthouse was packed. The Youngers were moved through the throng shackled together at the wrists. Many in the crowd jeered, yet the men walked along without emotion. At times they tried to amuse each other and whispered quiet remarks about several of those in the crowd.

The Rice County District Court was called to order, and Sheriff Barton demanded that those lucky enough to have obtained a place in the courtroom to view the proceedings take their seats. G. N. Baxter, the prosecuting attorney, called for the indictments. The Youngers were charged with the following crimes: accessory to the murder of J. L. Heywood, attacking A. E. Bunker with intent to do bodily harm, and the robbery of the First National Bank of Northfield, Minnesota. Finally, Coleman Younger, as principal, and Robert and James Younger as accessories, were indicted for the murder of Nicholas Gustavson while participating in the robbery of the bank.

Thomas Rutledge, along with local attorneys Bachelder and Buckham, represented the Youngers and said that they were in the courtroom ready to participate. Baxter remarked that their irons should be removed and a discussion regarding this took place, resulting in the removal of the wrist irons. One by one the Younger brothers were called before the judge, where they were charged and asked their pleas. Each one quietly pleaded guilty. Observers noted that each man appeared calm and almost relieved at finally being called upon to deliver his plea. Bob was said to have acted almost indifferent, but this was likely Bob's way of accepting the inevitable result of the actions he had instigated nearly five months before. Bob was overwhelmed with guilt and regret and was nearly numb with emotion. After their pleas, argument as to the degree of their guilt was postponed.

Upon resumption of the proceedings, each man was asked if he had anything to say in regard to either the charges or the anticipated sentencing. The three replied as a group, no. At that point, Judge Samuel Lord addressed each man, announcing that they were to be "confined to the state prison to the end of your natural life." Jim turned to his sister, who was standing behind him, and put his free arm around her. Then the three brothers were once again placed in wrist irons. Holding their heads high, they were led back to the Faribault jail to await removal to the Minnesota State Penitentiary at Stillwater.

On November 20, 1876, the Youngers boarded a train accompanied by Sheriff Ara Barton and guards John Passon, Thomas Lord, W. H. Dill and Phineas Barton. The group traveled to St. Paul. After their arrival there, the prisoners were transferred to a wagon to begin the ride to Stillwater. Crowds were present at various places along their route. The Youngers were very surprised to hear many of the people they encountered cheer them or offer words of encouragement. Others shouted epithets and applauded the fact that the robbers were now facing their just rewards. The Youngers were confused by the reception along the route to the Stillwater gates, but the sterile institution looming in front of them offered a very distinct message. Cole, Jim, and Bob Younger would be confined within its walls to become a part of its environment for a very long time.

19

A New Life in Stillwater

*The first month or two are the most severe upon the
new arrival. His environments force him to dwell
continually upon the depths of degradation to which
he has sunken, and he suffers the keenest possible
mental torture; but after passing this period he begins
to readjust his viewpoint and adapt himself to his
surroundings and then calmly awaits the termination
of his sentence.*
    —Convict Life at the Minnesota State Prison, 1909

As the Younger brothers entered the Stillwater Penitentiary they
realized immediately that they would not be treated with the
celebrity they had enjoyed at Faribault. They would quickly be
forced to integrate into the prison society as Convicts #899, #900,
and #901. Cole wrote: "When the iron doors shut behind us at
the Stillwater Prison we all submitted to the prison discipline with
the same unquestioning obedience that I had exacted during my
military service."[1]
    Upon their arrival, Cole, Jim, and Bob were put through the
procedures involved with becoming residents of the prison. They
were registered and searched. All their personal belongings were
given to the captain of the cellhouse to be held until their parole
or death. They bathed and put on the uniform of the third-grade
prisoner, a black-and-white striped suit. Their hair was clipped,
and they were weighed and read the rules. They endured being
measured according to the Bertillon system. This included mea-

215

surements of the head, ears, fingers, trunk, arms, and feet for permanent identification purposes. They were then fingerprinted and given complete physicals.[2]

Each of the men was led to a separate cell, away from his brothers. The 5 by 7 foot cells contained each prisoner's furnishings: a Bible, two cups, a mirror, a spoon, two towels, soap, a comb, a water jar, a bed, and appropriate linen.[3]

The "Rules of the Dining Hall" were given to them:

1. On entering the dining hall take your seat promptly, position erect arms folded, with eyes to the front until the signal is given to commence eating.

2. Strict silence must be observed during the meal. Staring at visitors, talking or laughing, fooling or gazing about the room is strictly forbidden.

3. Eating or drinking before or after the gong sounds, using vinegar in your drinking water, or putting meat on the table is prohibited.

4. Should you desire additional food make your wants known to the waiters in the following manner: If you want bread hold up your right hand. Coffee or water, hold up your cup. Meat, your fork. Soup, hold up your spoon. Vegetables, hold up your knife. If you desire to speak to an officer about food or service in dining hall, hold up your left hand.

5. Wasting food in any form will not be tolerated. You must not ask for or allow waiter to place on your plate more food than you can eat. When through with meal leave pieces of bread unmussed on left side of plate. Crusts and small pieces of bread must not be left on your plate.

6. After finishing your meal place knife, fork and spoon on right side of plate. Sit erect with arms folded. When the signal is given to arise drop hands to your side. At the second signal of the gong march out and to your respective places in line in a prompt, quiet and orderly manner.

7. In passing to and from the dining hall you must not gaze into cells or loiter on the gallery. Walk erect with your eyes to the front. It is strictly against the rules to carry out any of the dining hall furnishings or to carry food to or from the dining hall at any time except on Sundays and holidays, when you will be allowed to carry lunch to your cell for the evening meal.

One can only imagine the emotions of those free Missouri spirits that night as they began to comprehend their new lifestyle. As the Youngers would begin to adjust to their new home, they would realize that the experience of prison life was even more difficult than they imagined. These restrictions would be particularly hard on the gregarious Cole. Jim, still feeling ill and depressed, would find the solitutude a welcome relief. Bob reacted typically and simply accepted his fate as he waited to see what would happen next.

The following morning the Youngers met with Warden J. A. Reed to receive their work assignments. Until he decided otherwise, Warden Reed thought it best to put the brothers together at one station where guards could keep an eye on them. They were assigned the detail of making tubs and buckets in the basement. Although the prison authorities believed there was little chance of success, there remained a caution that members of the James-Younger Gang might appear at any time to try to liberate the boys.

Within a short time, Warden Reed realized that the Youngers were a cut above the average Stillwater prisoner in both demeanor and intelligence and elevated them to second-grade prisoners. Now they wore black-and-gray checked suits and caps. They were allowed to let their hair grow to a length that could be combed. They could write two letters a month, draw a ration of tobacco weekly, and see visitors once a month. They were allowed to eat in a dining room with other second-grade prisoners. Since interaction between prisoners was not allowed, regardless of the fact that they were brothers, the Youngers were permitted to visit with each other only once a month. That schedule of visitation would continue until 1884.

When the boys were made second-grade, they were assigned to other jobs. Their next place of employment was in the thresher factory. Cole made sieves while Jim made belts. Bob's injured right elbow continued to bother him, and he was unable to straighten out his arm or fully use the fingers of his right hand. He was put to work painting walls as the prison doctors believed that the motion of such work would provide Bob with a form of physical therapy. Bob endured the pain of such motion for several weeks before he asked that his job be changed. The doctors, not having realized the extent of Bob's discomfort, readily agreed. Bob was put to work making straw elevators in the thresher factory with his brothers.[4]

Second-grade prisoners were allowed to read, and the three Youngers took advantage of the library and its books. Jim became a voracious reader and favored books having to do with theology, metaphysics, and literature. Bob, having been influenced by Maggie, enjoyed studying medical books and periodicals. Cole indulged his love of history and read historical biographies and classics.

Although their wounds continued to heal, each of the men was bothered by the lingering effects of his injuries. Cole had chronic headaches for several years after the surrender at Hanska. Bob found that the dampness of the prison environment caused him to catch frequent colds. The wound he had received while surrendering added to his susceptibility to become ill from the dampness of his prison cell. Jim was unable to overcome the results of his Minnesota wound. He never again was able to manage solid food and was forced to "eat" his meals through a straw. He suffered from severe headaches and tremendous bouts of melancholy and depression.

The Youngers continued to make the best of their situation and never complained or made demands. They were considered model prisoners by the prison authorities. They became respected by other prisoners because of their willingness to accept their fate and act as they were expected.

After the James brothers escaped from Minnesota, they headed for Tennessee. Jesse and his wife Zee had moved to the Nashville area sometime early in 1875. Using the name John Davis Howard, Jesse posed as a grain speculator. He and Zee were living at 606 Boscobel Street in Edgefield when their son Jesse Edwards (named after John Newman Edwards, of course) was born there on August 31. By the summer of 1877, Jesse had rented a cabin on the W. H. Link farm near Waverly, Tennessee. Frank took up residence in Nashville, farming on the Josiah Walton place near the Clarkesville Pike and using the name Ben J. Woodson.[5]

In February 1878, both of the James brothers became fathers,

Jesse for the second time. Zee gave birth to twins, which the couple named Gould and Montgomery. Unfortunately, both babies died as infants. Frank James's wife Annie gave birth to Robert Franklin, the couple's only child.

During the spring of 1878, Jesse developed malaria. Also that year, Steve Johnson of Nashville sued "Dave Howard" for his failure to repay on a bad check he had written Johnson to cover a loan of $1,000. Jesse purchased some cattle which he sold to pay off Johnson. The case was settled out of court. In the winter of 1878–79, Jesse joined Frank and his family in Nashville, where they lived together on the Felix Smith farm. Jesse's daughter Mary was born there in July. Jesse had become involved in race horses, had not been lucky, and had managed to incur many debts. For whatever reasons, Jesse's efforts to farm were not successful. He needed money badly, and by the fall of 1879, Jesse had moved back to Missouri, where he made plans to develop avenues of revenue for the care of his family.

With Jesse's reputation for having been the half of the gang that had escaped the diligent posse in Minnesota, many would-be robbers were anxious to affiliate with him. When word got out in guerrilla circles that Jesse might be starting a new gang, several men approached Jesse to apply for the open positions. The new James Gang was made up primarily of petty robbers and horse thieves. They included Dick Liddil, Bill Ryan, and Tucker Bassham. Ed Miller, Clell's brother, and Wood Hite, Jesse's cousin, completed the group.

On October 8, 1879, the Chicago and Alton Railroad was robbed of $6,000 at Blue Cut, Missouri, near the Glendale Station. The robbery caused great distress to the railroads and the law enforcement agencies. The James-Younger Gang had not been active since the surrender of the Youngers three years previously. While the law would have preferred to think that Jesse and Frank James had retired from robbing trains and banks, the manner of the Glendale robbery was too reminiscent of the style of the James-Younger Gang to be ignored.

About this time a story spread that Jesse had been killed by former guerrilla George Shepard. While the truth is that Jesse was back in Nashville, where he had returned with Ed Miller to race horses, the death hoax caused a lot of excitement. When asked if he believed the story that Jesse had been killed, Cole commented, "I believe it is true if George Shepard says it is true."[6] George Shepard's account was ambiguous, however, and nobody really believed that Jesse was dead.

In the winter of 1879–80, Frank James moved to the Jeff Hyde farm in Nashville and went to work for the Indiana Lumber Company. Frank continued using his Ben J. Woodson alias and became a member of the Nashville community. He made many friends and was probably the most comfortable he had been in years.

In 1880, Jesse briefly returned to Missouri with Ed Miller. Tucker Bassham had been arrested and had confessed to having participated in the Glendale robbery. What Jesse and Miller hoped to accomplish in Missouri is not known. Ed Miller disappeared on that trip. Accounts of his disappearance vary. Some say that Jesse believed that Miller could not be trusted and that if he were arrested he would implicate Jesse in the Glendale robbery. Another account claims that Miller and Jesse had an argument and Miller foolishly fired a shot at Jesse, missing him.[7] Jesse is said to have killed Miller and buried his body alongside the road.

In July, 1880, Jesse returned to Nashville with Dick Liddil and Bill Ryan. Frank was very upset that Jesse had brought the two outlaws to Nashville, as Frank felt that their presence jeopardized the James brothers' newfound security. He called the two robbers what they were: small-time thieves. He particularly objected to Bill Ryan's known drinking habits.

On September 3, 1880, Jesse and Bill Ryan robbed a stage near Mammoth Cave, Kentucky. Frank was upset that Jesse wanted to return to robbing as a way of life. While Frank was likely present at Glendale to support his brother, there exists the possibility that he was not. He was enjoying the peaceful life he had built for himself and his family in Tennessee. Frank did not want to endanger his assimilation into the Nashville community by becoming involved in another robbery. In November, Jesse and Dick Liddil returned to Missouri. However, Jesse was soon back in Nashville, this time in the company of Jim Cummins, a fellow guerrilla.

Upon hearing of Miller's disappearance, Cummins became suspicious and asked Jesse questions Jesse preferred not to hear. By now Jesse knew that the new outfit he had pulled together did not have the properties of the James-Younger Gang. Trust did not come as easily and several of the men seemed to have loose tongues. The more Cummins questioned Jesse and the others of the gang about the disappearance of Miller, the more uncomfortable Jesse became. Finally, Jesse felt compelled to discuss Cummins "removal" from the gang with Dick Liddil. Immediately upon hearing that Jesse was considering killing him, Cummins left the Nashville area. Frank and Jesse were very ill at ease with this development. They did not know if Cummins could be trusted or if he would go to any of the law authorities. Frank and Jesse both decided that the best thing to do was leave Tennessee while they waited to hear about Cummins's next move. Although Cummins did not talk to anyone at that time, Frank and Jesse waited in Alabama for the coast to clear for their return home to Tennessee. On March 11, 1881, over $5,000 was taken from the paymaster at the Muscle Shoals, Alabama, Canal Project. Jesse and Frank's time in Alabama had not been wasted.

Back in Tennessee, Bill Ryan's actions would further necessitate the Jameses' relocation from Tennessee. Drinking heavily one night at Earthman's Store in Nashville, Ryan boasted about his involvement in several robberies and was arrested. Jesse and Frank knew that they must now leave Tennessee for good. Frank and Jesse rode up to Adairville while their wives and children were sent to relatives in Nelson County, Kentucky. Ryan was sent back to Missouri, where he was tried and convicted of the Glendale robbery. He was sentenced to twenty-five years in prison.

It is likely that the James brothers returned home to the James-Samuel farm sometime in the summer of 1881. It is probable that one or the other of them heard that William Westfall was serving as conductor on one of the trains that ran through Missouri. It is believed that Westfall was in charge of the train on which the Pinkertons had arrived and departed that fateful night in 1874 when the James farmhouse was bombed and Archie Samuel was killed. On July 15, 1881, the Chicago, Rock Island and Pacific Railroad was stopped outside Winston, Missouri. Five robbers boarded the passenger cars and the express car was subsequently robbed. As Westfall attempted to determine what was going on, he was shot in the back. While he lay on the floor of the car, he was shot again at close range. At some point a passenger named Frank McMillan was also killed. The robbers were said to have been Frank and Jesse James, Dick Liddil, and Clarence and Wood Hite. The death of Westfall was said to have not been an accident. Later Liddil would testify that Jesse James had killed the conductor and Frank James the passenger.[8] The Jameses' need for revenge seems not to have been sated.

While Jesse was returning to his life of robbery, the Youngers continued to maintain a low profile up at Stillwater. By 1881, they had served five years of their life sentences. They were well respected as prisoners, and they gave no trouble as they waited for time to pass so that they could begin their parole appeal. Their uncle, Littleton Younger, now of Oregon, visited St. Paul in 1881. He was granted a personal audience with Gov. John S. Pillsbury. He asked for his nephews to be pardoned or paroled. Littleton claimed that circumstances had driven the Youngers to their crime, presenting the theory that Northfield had been their only robbery. He suggested to the governor that the three men had paid their debt to society and should be allowed to leave Stillwater and return to Missouri.

In July of that year, a small pamphlet, not unlike "A Terrible Quintette," was published. However, it was reported that some obvious errors were contained in "A Brief History of the Younger Brothers and the Reasons Why They Should Be Pardoned."[9] In October, 1881, Littleton returned to talk with the governor a second time. This time he was armed with affidavits from various influential persons in Missouri.[10] Littleton's efforts, however, were unsuccessful. The boys realized that their stay in Stillwater was not about to come to an end any time soon.

Jesse eventually returned to Missouri with his family. They lived for a short while in Kansas City and in the fall of 1881 moved to St. Joseph. Using the name Tom Howard, Jesse rented a house high on a hill in that city for $14 a month from a city councilman.

Early in 1882, Clarence Hite had been arrested in connection with the Winston robbery. Rather than face trial, Hite pleaded guilty and was sentenced to twenty-five years in prison. Dick Liddil began to believe that Jesse suspected him of disloyalty. The specter of Ed Miller haunted members of the new gang as they realized that Jesse was becoming increasingly paranoid about the trustworthiness of his recruits. Continued references to the outstanding qualities of the Youngers were made by Jesse. The gang began to think that each of them would be better off if he could think of a way to terminate his association with Jesse. This would not be an easy task, as the men felt that Jesse would, understandably, be suspicious of their future actions and they thought their lives might be in danger.

Liddil took his problems to Martha Bolton, sister of Charlie and Bob Ford. Several of the outlaws were "sweet" on Martha, and they were always welcome at her house. During Liddil's visit, Wood Hite appeared. Hite was also interested in the Widow Bolton, and an argument ensued. Liddil killed Hite. Liddil realized that when Jesse heard of the death of his cousin Wood at the hands of Liddil, his fate would be sealed. Liddil decided to surrender to any robbery charges made against him. On March 31, 1882, Dick Liddil turned state's witness.

Gov. Thomas Crittenden was determined to use Liddil's testimony to bring down the James gang. He enlisted the help of Sheriff James Timberlake of Clay County and Kansas City police commissioner Henry H. Craig. The Ford brothers had approached the governor, offering to bring Jesse in, and Crittenden felt that the time was right. He didn't think that Jesse would submit to a trial, however, and he did not know Frank James's whereabouts. The actual "deal" cut between the Fords and Crittenden isn't really clear. However, by the end of the month of April, Jesse James would be dead.

Jesse had taken his new gang members, Bob and Charlie Ford, with him on a visit to his mother's at the end of March, 1882. Mrs. Samuel warned Jesse that she thought the Ford brothers were suspicious characters, but Jesse scoffed at her remarks. However, when the time came for Jesse to leave in the company of the Fords, Jesse said to his mother, "Ma, if we don't meet again, we'll meet in heaven."[11]

While they discussed plans to rob a bank at Platte City, Missouri, the Fords stayed with Jesse and his family. Jesse remarked that the upcoming robbery would be his last. He would take the money obtained at Platte City and retire with his family to a farm in Nebraska.

On April 3, 1882, Jesse James was shot from behind by a Smith & Wesson .45 Model 3 held in the hand of Bob Ford. Jesse James was dead. The Fords' reward for the murder of Jesse was said to have been $10,000, but this was not the case. The Fords immediately surrendered to the sheriff. A grand jury in St. Joseph indicted them for murder in the first degree. The Fords pleaded guilty and were sentenced to hang. Immediately upon hearing the sentence later that day, Governor Crittenden granted Bob and Charlie Ford a full and unconditional pardon. The Fords received only about $500 for expenses, but their place in American history was secured.

Jesse's body was returned to Kearney for burial on the James-Samuel farm. Most of his belongings were auctioned off in St. Joseph to help Zee with expenses. The total money brought in from the auction was $117. Jesse's dog Boo was sold for $5.00, bringing in the highest bid of the day.

Bob Ford wrote the following letter to the editor of the Missouri *Republican* on February 12, 1884, from St. Louis:

dear sir, if you think these lines are worth publishing you will oblige me very much by so doing.

I wish to answer the dirty lieing remarks made by a member of the post Dispatch. In wich he accuses Govener Critenden of a dishonorable act in hiring Thugs to assassinate Jess James in presents of his wife & children. In the first place I don't know who the Pup has reference to.

I am the one who removed the lamented Jess & am freed of it but I was not hired by Gov. Critenden or any one else or did I act under any bodys instruction.

I had the proper authority to bring Mr. James to Justice which I did but did it in no ones presence but my Brother Chas. & I did it with my own Revolver which I payed for but had no assurance of any pardon in case I did it. but the would be smart news paper man seems to know more abut the mater than either the Governer or my self. I only did what thousands of others were trying to do but failed & did not to rob any body or steal any horses to get the chance to do it. & the man that calls me an assassin is a CONTMPT-ABLE SNEAK & if he wishes to resent it he will find me at the St James Hotel in this city.

hoping you will oblige by publishing these lines I remain Very Respectfully, BOB FORD

The Youngers' reaction to the death of Jesse was not expressed in public in light of their statements that they had not been involved with the James brothers and had not seen them since the close of the war. While Jim may have been relieved that Jesse's influence on his brother Bob was indeed over once and for all, Bob was greatly dismayed at the death of his friend. Cole believed that the reported death of Jesse might have been another hoax to enable the authorities to get the Youngers to say, at last, that the James brothers had participated in the Northfield robbery. Cole enlisted the help of his sister Retta to check on the body said to be that of Jesse and let him know if the story was true. Retta traveled to St. Joseph, where she was able to determine that Jesse had, indeed, been killed by Bob Ford. It is said that Retta personally viewed the body of Jesse for her report to Cole, but time may not have allowed her to do that. Regardless, Cole believed that Jesse was dead and made statements to the effect that he accepted the fact. He said little more in regard to this newsworthy event. Had they not been confined to the Stillwater Prison, the Youngers may have felt the loss of Jesse more. As it was, he was just the latest in a series of friends and family that had been lost to them.

With the death of Jesse and the Youngers in jail, the James-Younger Gang came to an end. The success of the Pinkertons and their supporters would really not be apparent until many years later when the demise of the gang could be studied objectively. At first glance it appears that the Pinkertons were not the ones ultimately responsible for the defeat of the gang, and while this is true, fallout from the pursuit of the Pinkertons did cause serious, fatal repercussions to the internal structure of the gang.

There are several reasons why the gang was allowed to operate and enjoy such popular support in the state of Missouri. The people of the state were attempting to put the war and its consequences behind them while they built back their farms and business during Reconstruction, yet they were still quite angry at the government. At the end of the war, the general public realized that the war had not been fought for the people but rather for the power elite. They were unhappy about the carpetbagging that was going on and the increased strength of the railroads and the banking institutions. Support for the activities of the gang was an extension of their support for the guerrilla element during the war. The gang wasn't bothering the average person but was rather pestering the institutions that most of the people of Missouri were bothered by. Besides, with so much popular support, opposing the gang might get you killed.

Why it took the Pinkertons so long to make their influence felt is a good question. At the base of the problem is that fact that oftentimes their operatives were either lacking courage, as in the case of Wright, or lacking sense, as in the case of Whicher. The James-Younger Gang was very mobile and traveled all over to commit its crimes. The Pinkertons could never tell where they were going to turn up next. They were able to leave the scene of the crime quickly, and due to the fact that their photographs had never been published, they had no problem riding the trains. The gang had its own operatives and supporters in high places who had no compunction about telling them the movements of the Pinkertons. This was no more than an offshoot of the guerrillas' informal network. The people who felt that the gang was serving their interests would tell them anything, do anything for them. Yet, in the end, it was the gang itself that let the Pinkertons defeat it by instilling distrust and confusion and splitting the gang apart internally. They were driven out of Missouri to various areas of the country where they were not able to draw strength and support from each other. Once the gang members left the comfortable nest of their local support, they allowed their own personal ambitions to destroy their once successful unity. The damage had been done whether Jesse lived or died. This knowledge must have been a bitter pill for the remaining members of the gang to swallow.

On January 8, 1884, a fire burned in the woodworking shop and two storage buildings at Stillwater Prison. The cause of the fire was believed to have been by arson. On the 25th of that same month, a much more serious event occurred at the prison. About 11:30 at night, the entire prison erupted in flames. Several fires burned simultaneously, and the prisoners, behind their locked cell doors, panicked. The guards and administration acted quickly. Fire alarms were sounded by both bells and telegraph, and soon every piece of fire-fighting equipment within thirty miles was at the prison. The St. Paul equipment was sent by railroad and arrived in a record thirty-five minutes from the capital, twenty-three miles away. Over 350 prisoners were chained together and forced to stand in the subzero weather while nearly all the prison buildings burned.

The Minnesota National Guard had been called in to stand watch over the prisoners as they exited the burning buildings. Acting with Warden Reed, head guard George F. Dodd was placed in charge of helping the prisoners out of the buildings to safety. Some of the trustees were put in charge of other prisoners, an act that was risky but necessary. The Youngers were led with the others to a vacant room to await their removal from the premises. They were standing together when Dodd hurried past. Cole asked the guard if there was any way the Youngers might be of help. Dodd, realizing that his decision would be controversial, said yes. Although the Youngers were life prisoners and the possibility of their escape continued to be the talk of the Stillwater community, Dodd asked Cole, Jim, and Bob to help him. They would relocate the female prisoners and Dodd's wife, the women's matron. The prisoners would be taken to the deputy warden's house outside the prison walls. He handed Cole a revolver and Jim and Bob were given an ax and an iron bar. The Youngers calmly and quickly led the women to safety. After this was accomplished, they surrendered their weapons.[12] In the reports of the fire, the press wondered if the Youngers had attempted to break out of the prison at any point during the disaster. The warden and the prison administration were quick to tell of Dodd's decision and the Youngers' cooperation. Cole wrote:

> Had it been in our minds to do so, we could have escaped from the prison that night, but we had determined to pay the penalty that had been exacted, and if we were ever to return to liberty it would be with the consent and approval of the authorities and public.[13]

It was suggested that the prison fire had been set by an arsonist(s). It had started in the basement of one of the buildings that housed a railroad car manufacturing operation. It's possible that the fire was an "insurance fire" set by someone on behalf of that company. The prisoners were all locked up at that time of the night, and the only people with access to the basement were the guards and the maintenance employees of the railroad car company. Warden Reed declared that the fire had not been the work of an arsonist but rather had been caused by overheated steam pipes.[14] Most of the prison buildings were destroyed, including the hospital, library, and cellblocks. The prisoners' clothing and personal possessions were gone, and there was no place on the premises to lodge the prisoners. They were sent to other facilities at St. Paul, Winona, Hastings, and Minneapolis.

The Youngers were held in custody at the prison while it was decided where they might be placed. The discussion was concerned more with ensuring their safety than in preventing them from attempting escape. Eventually they were sent to the Washington County Jail, where they stayed for the following month while the prison set up temporary quarters for all the prisoners and attempted to reestablish the facility.[15]

As the prison began to return to normal, new positions opened up for the Youngers. Jim was put in charge of the mail, and Bob was put to work binding medical books. Cole worked in the library.

As 1885 drew to a close, the Youngers had been residents of the Stillwater Prison for nine years. They felt they would be eligible for parole at this point. With great anticipation they awaited the decision of the parole board to begin proceedings that would enable them to leave Minnesota and return home to Missouri.

20

Broken Hearts

... the life which he has lived has been so entirely
different from the lives of most of us.
—Rev. A. B. Francisco of Bob Younger, 1889

One of the foremost reasons the Youngers were able to adjust to the rigid procedures and life at Stillwater Prison was that they had been led to believe by their supporters, and continued to have faith themselves, that they would be eligible for parole after ten years. Waiting until the ten-year milestone to begin the attempt to move public sentiment in their favor was difficult. The Younger family began thinking of its strategy sometime before the tenth anniversary of the Northfield robbery.

Jim enjoyed his work as a postal clerk. Cole was pleased to be working in the library. Eventually, after Cole became a hospital trustee, his position at the library would be awarded to Jim. Before long, Jim would become head librarian. Jim had little interaction with prisoners other than his brothers. He read everything he could and began to study current events. He soon wrote on the subject as well. Continuing to be outgoing, Cole enjoyed his interaction with the prisoners. Bob, although always friendly and polite, kept mostly to himself. He, too, liked to read and favored medical journals. Although their lives were far from what the boys wanted them to be, they realized that at this point things could be worse.

Things were going fairly well with Frank James on the outside.

On October 4, 1882, he had surrendered to Gov. Thomas Critten-den of Missouri. Frank James would be acquitted of all charges after four years of legal wrangling.

The issue of Frank James being allowed to go free after so public a life of crime is still hotly contested today. The Gilded Age, in which Frank was brought to trial was one of excessive corruption in the country's various government levels. James's surrender and all that entailed had been engineered by John Newman Edwards. Edwards used every personal political connection, favor, and influence at his disposal to see that Frank James went free. Those who were selected to represent Frank, most of them without fee, later went on to become members of congress and to hold various judicial offices. A Democratic jury was permitted, and people such as Gen. JO Shelby and the maimed Zerelda James Samuel were allowed to witness, characterizing Frank as a Southern hero and Jesse James as one who was methodically hunted down and mur-dered by the state of Missouri for little cause other than the fact that he was a former Confederate. The surrender and terms of trial were so well planned that there was never really any doubt as to their favorable (to Frank) outcome.

A most important aspect of the terms of surrender was Ed-wards's influence on Governor Marmaduke of Missouri to agree to refuse to hand Frank James over to the state of Minnesota to stand trial for any charges having to do with Minnesota. Frank was no doubt very concerned that at some point in time he would be charged with robbery or murder or even some lesser offense arising out of his participation at Northfield, especially in light of the media circus that surrounded his trials at home. Minnesota would certainly be less forgiving than Missouri, and Edwards's insistence on the guarantee of the governor that Frank not be extradited was probably well founded. Ironically, whether because it did not think it had a strong enough case or because it knew that the Democratic faction of the Missouri government would not cooperate, the state of Minnesota never charged Frank James or asked that he be returned to them for trial.

In 1883, Bob became an accounting clerk, working with the prison steward. This work was more enjoyable for Bob, as he had begun to have bouts of illness that he seemed unable to overcome.

He developed a chronic cough, which at times depleted his physical energy.

The brothers' aunt, Frances Twyman, decided to become involved in her nephews' attempt for parole. Frances Twyman was born on April 20, 1829, in Independence, Missouri. She was the youngest of the seven children of Judge Richard and Mary Fristoe. She married a prominent Independence physician, Lydall Twyman, and was quite active in the civic affairs of Jackson County. Mrs. Twyman thought that the most effective thing she could do was to introduce certain prominent people to those who would be involved in the parole drive. Perhaps they would unite to begin some kind of formalized attempt to approach the parole board. Her husband, Dr. Lydall Twyman, was well respected. The Twymans were considered society in Jackson County.

Different plans were brought forward to the brothers. The hope was that some of the Minnesotans who had expressed kindness toward them in the past would help them obtain whatever favor was necessary to instigate parole or pardon procedures. Cole had suggested that Sheriff Ara Barton might be willing to speak on their behalf. However, Barton felt that his knowledge of the Youngers and his involvement in their lives had ended upon their arrival at Stillwater. Barton would later change his mind. In the meantime, Bob wrote a letter addressed to "Aunt," claiming that he thought that any approach to Barton was really futile. Bob felt that Barton had done all he was going to by extending courtesies to the brothers while they were held in his jail at Faribault. In his letter, Bob shows his straightforward and honest approach to life. He claimed that the recipient of his letter should not assume that Cole speaks for Bob or that Bob is not capable of "holding forth" with his own opinion.[1]

In the fall of 1885, the Youngers had a visitor from Missouri. Former Confederate soldier Warren Carter Bronaugh of Clinton decided to visit Stillwater Prison on his honeymoon. "Wal" Bronaugh obtained a letter of introduction to Warden Reed from Captain Allen of the St. Paul Merchants Hotel. He further requested an interview with the three brothers. Bronaugh said later that he did not realize that he was personally acquainted with any of the Youngers but simply wanted to see if there was anything he

could do to help the cause of his fellow Confederates. Bronaugh
was a bit put off when his letter was greeted tenuously by Warden
Reed. Informing Bronaugh that "we look upon Missourians here
with a great deal of suspicion," Reed nonetheless allowed Bronaugh to meet with the Youngers.[2] The condition of this introduction was that Bronaugh bear his arms to the elbow and stay within
close range of the deputy warden, who would listen closely to
every word exchanged. Bronaugh agreed and was shown to the
cells of the three prisoners.

Upon introducing himself to Cole, Bronaugh said he realized
that the two men had met before. Bronaugh had enlisted in the
Confederate Army in 1861. He was with the troops of Col. Vard
Cockrell in the Battle of Lone Jack. The day after the battle,
Bronaugh and a friend rode out of their camp in an attempt to
obtain breakfast. On their way back, they became separated from
the Cockrell command. They were stopped by a guerrilla picket
outside Lone Jack and told that Cockrell and his men were in full
retreat. General Blunt was now in Lone Jack with 1,500 troops.
Had they not met the picket, Bronaugh and his companion would
have ridden into the enemy camp. Their fate would have been
obvious. The picket they met on the road and with whom they
talked for over an hour that day was the young Cole Younger.

Twenty-four years later, Cole and Wal Bronaugh met again at
Stillwater. Although this is the story that Bronaugh put forth and
which has been accepted all along, a letter found in 1992 raises
some questions. In the letter, which is addressed to Frank James,
Bronaugh writes of having seen the Youngers and tells James of
their physical condition and the high level of their spirits. He does
not mention being surprised that he recognized Cole Younger as
being the man whom he met during the Lone Jack encounter. In
this letter, Bronaugh almost appears to be making a report to
Frank James. In his official account of his involvement in the
Younger parole drive, *The Youngers Fight For Freedom*, Bronaugh
does not mention even knowing Frank James let alone being
friends with him prior to his involvement in the Youngers' cause.
Although it is certainly plausible that, while both were Confederates, the two may have met sometime during the war, a reader of
the letter has to wonder if Frank James was possibly behind the

meeting that had occurred in Stillwater. Bronaugh does tell James that he had much to talk to him about that he did not want to write in a letter and that he was most anxious to visit with James when James came to Clinton to see him.[3] Regardless of whether or not Frank James was involved, after he spoke with the Youngers, Bronaugh left the prison determined to do everything within his power to help with their parole.

Warren Carter Bronaugh was born in Buffalo, West Virginia, in 1841. His father, C. C. Bronaugh, served during the War of 1812. His grandfather, Col. William B. Bronaugh, served in the Revolutionary War and was a member of Washington's council. The family moved to Henry County, Missouri, when Wal, as he was called, was an infant.

When he was twenty years old, Bronaugh followed in the footsteps of the Bronaugh men and enlisted in Company B of the Confederate Army at Springfield serving under General Price. After the war, Wal and his brothers Frank and Samuel moved to Texas, where they raised cattle for feed lots. That venture went broke in the 1880s during a Texas drought. The brothers then started a similar venture south of Nevada, Missouri. The town where they raised their cattle was named Bronaugh.[4]

Cole, Jim, and Bob continued to deny that the James brothers had participated in the Northfield robbery. Cole gave an interview to the Cincinnati *Enquirer* stating that everyone except the Youngers who had been involved in the gang that attempted to rob the bank was dead. This story, of course, was primarily to alibi Cole's friend Frank James, as Jesse was already dead.

Cole and Jim became involved in woodcraft. Over the course of their time spent in Stillwater, the two managed to produce several fine pieces of wood sculpture, which they gave to various people as gifts. Cole made beautiful wood and leather walking canes. Both Cole and Jim created outstanding wooden boxes and chests of all sizes. Another of their specialties was delicate wooden picture frames which delighted their recipients. Bob, still unable to use several fingers of his right hand, could not share his brothers' hobby.

By late 1885, Bob and Maggie's relationship began to weaken. Bob's guilt over his part in the planning of the Minnesota robbery and his decision to go with Jesse regardless of his brothers' advice to the contrary caused him to experience great periods of despair. His pride enabled him to keep the depth of his regret to himself in the presence of his brothers. While Bob continued to write to Maggie, he discouraged her from visiting him. He said that the visits would make him feel even more helpless, and he was fearful that her identity would become known. He was afraid her life would be ruined by the questions and exposure of the press. Bob wanted to separate himself from Maggie until the day he was paroled from Stillwater and could return to Missouri to live with her as a free man.[5]

By 1885, Mrs. Twyman had many letters of support from prominent men in Missouri government. She had even managed a letter from former governor William R. Marshall of Minnesota. Marshall was originally from Missouri but had moved to Minnesota with his family before the war.

Wal Bronaugh wrote to Mrs. Twyman on Cole's suggestion and was invited to dinner at her house in late 1885. He was met in Independence by John H. Taylor, brother of Fletcher Taylor. Fletcher Taylor had been one of Quantrill's leaders and, in fact, had been Jesse James's sponsor into the ranks of Anderson's group. While Bronaugh enjoyed the hospitality of the Twyman household, he and Frances agreed that he was capable of leading a major parole campaign. Frances decided to share her contacts with him in this great effort. By letter Frances introduced Bronaugh to Governor Marshall. Marshall invited Bronaugh to meet with him when he next visited the Missouri capitol at Jefferson City in June, 1886. Marshall again expressed his support for the Youngers' release and introduced Bronaugh to ex-governor Thomas Crittenden, who supported the action as well.[6] The endorsement by Crittenden was a surprise, as he was, of course, the Missouri governor who had worked so hard to break up the James-Younger Gang and who was so instrumental in the death of Jesse and the later surrender of Frank James in 1882. Crittenden said that he felt the Youngers had served enough time and would no longer be a threat to the state of Missouri. He saw no reason why they should not return home.

While the majority of people in Missouri agreed with Crittenden, Marshall was criticized up in Minnesota for his pro-Younger sentiments. Such criticism did not dissuade Marshall from continued involvement, however. Marshall wrote a long and detailed letter expressing his views on a potential Younger parole which was published in the St. Paul *Pioneer Press* on July 26, 1886. Marshall, whose writing was in the explosive style of John Newman Edwards, wrote of Cole's outstanding military record. He devoted full paragraphs to the fact that Cole had not been engaged in the war in Missouri from the fall of 1863 until the close of the war. Marshall detailed some of the heroic events that Cole was said to have participated in while he served with the "regular" army. He stated that none of the Youngers had been connected with the killing of Heywood and told of an incident that involved the Youngers' flight from Northfield. According to Marshall, Cole had given their last gold coin to a widow who had shared what little she had with them for a meal. Marshall told how these men were of the finest breeding, which could be proved by the fact that they had chosen not to leave their wounded brother to ensure their escape. He claimed that they had become involved in outlawry in the first place only because of the murder of their prominent father, the burning of their homes, and the harassment of their family. Marshall explained the support of the most respected men in Missouri. He told of the views of those involved when the Youngers surrendered who now believed that the time had come to allow the Youngers to return to Missouri, where they might finally live as productive members of society. Marshall's effusive letter contained classical allusions as well: "Like Byron's Greece," he wrote, "it were long to tell and sad to trace, their fall from splendor to disgrace." Wal Bronaugh was so encouraged by this supportive piece of writing that he had 25,000 copies of the letter printed at his own expense to be circulated throughout the midwest and south.[7] Marshall wrote a second, similar letter to the *Pioneer Press* on August 13, 1886, naming various of the Youngers' "friends."

To sustain the momentum of Marshall's first letter, Cole wrote to the *Pioneer Press* himself on August 1, further extolling his virtues as a soldier and a gentleman. He adamantly denied previously printed stories about his having tested the Enfield rifle by shooting fifteen men. He humbly explained that he had always tried to show mercy to his enemies and was, in fact, well known for the gracious acts he had committed during the war.

In 1887, Andrew R. McGill became governor of Minnesota. Halvur G. Stordock was appointed warden of Stillwater Prison because of his political friendship with McGill. Former warden Reed was accused of vague improprieties. Reed counterattacked with suspicions about the actions of the new administration. An investigation was conducted, and both wardens were exonerated. In August of 1889 the Minnesota legislature attempted to remove political favoritism by creating a five-member board of managers for the prison system. John J. Randall was appointed to replace Stordock as the Stillwater warden.

Jim continued to turn inward more and more. On the other hand, he became more opinionated than he had ever been in his life. This was probably out of frustration for not having articulated his opinions in his earlier years and having been forced to suffer the consequences of following others' beliefs and viewpoints. Jim began putting his ideas down on paper during this time. Together with illustrations, he created an amusing and political "newsletter." Those who were able to share Jim's writings encouraged him to write more. They suggested that he form a newspaper which could be distributed throughout the prison so that all the Stillwater inmates might enjoy his writings and observations. This idea was completely rejected by Jim. He did not wish to share his opinions with strangers. He made clear that his writings were for his own amusement and nothing more.

Jim did, however, express interest in the formation of a newspaper and suggested that someone else follow through with the idea. He and Cole initiated a newspaper fund that would provide start-up money for such a venture. Eventually, fifteen other prisoners contributed, and $200 was raised. Bob, who wished to support the newspaper if for no other reason than Jim's interest, contributed $10.[8] What money he received from friends, relatives, and supporters that was not freely given to the Youngers' defense fund was sent home to Missouri. In this way Bob was able to feel that he was somehow contributing even if in such a small way.

Lew Schoonmaker was appointed the first editor of *The Prison*

Mirror. The masthead of the first edition included the name of Cole Younger as "printer's devil." Cole's position was described at that time: "Cole Younger, our genial prison librarian, has received new honors at the hands of *The Mirror* by being appointed to the honorable position of 'printer's devil,' in which he will in the future keep flies off the gifts of 'wedding cake,' and other editorial favors of like nature which may find lodgement in our sanctum sanctorum."[9]

The Prison Mirror was a great success and to this day enjoys the reputation as the oldest most continuously published prison newspaper in the United States. Jim enjoyed the newspaper immensely yet continued to write his private newsletters for some time to come.

In 1888, the Youngers' fiercest enemy to date took office as Governor of Minnesota: William R. Merriam. In the spring of that year, John Newman Edwards composed a petition which was to be signed by the members of the General Assembly of the state of Missouri and sent to the new Minnesota governor. The petition was signed by twenty-eight members of the General Assembly of Missouri and sent to Minnesota governor William R. Merriam. It read:

> We, the undersigned members of the General Assembly of Missouri, most respectfully ask at your hand the pardon of Cole, James and Bob Younger, now confined in the Stillwater Prison, and for the following reasons:
>
> Because they have been in prison for more than thirteen years.
>
> Because during this entire period their behavior has been so excellent as to win not alone the respect, but perfect confidence of the prison authorities.
>
> Every intention of the law has been fulfilled, in this, that the punishment for the violation of it has been ample and complete.
>
> If restored again to freedom, almost the entire population of this state would stand security as a mass to their becoming law-abiding, peaceful, upright and worthy citizens.
>
> Because their downfall and departure from the path of rectitude was unquestionably the direct result of the unfavorable conditions surrounding them during and following the late Civil War.

Whatever may have been said to the contrary, the men were brave and honorable soldiers in battle, and merciful in victory.

Because these men have served twice the length of time allotted the life prisoners committed to prison on life sentences, less than ten years being the average time.

Because we are informed that every warden under whom they have served has learned from close contact with them to trust them and to place them in positions of responsibility, and have advised that, if liberated, they would become good, honorable and useful citizens.

Because they are now old men, and we believe the spirit of Christian charity and mercy suggests that they should be permitted to spend their few remaining days among their friends and relatives, many of whom are ready and willing to furnish them constant employment, by reason of which they may and will be self-supporting and independent.

Because it is a recognized principle of penology that the object of all punishment is to reform the punished, and when this reformation has been accomplished, to longer continue the punishment is of no benefit, but is turning the arm of the law into an instrument of torture to satiate revenge.

Your petitioners are of all political faiths, and are of either military service. We simply come to you as one united whole, asking this pardon in the name of mercy and humanity, ever praying your help, happiness, and long continued prosperity.

Waller Young, a representative from St. Joseph, began the process of asking the members of the legislature for their support and signatures. Shortly into the project, Young became ill. Bronaugh stepped in to complete the process and was able to obtain the support of twenty-eight of the thirty-four senators. While he was elated at this support, Bronaugh was disappointed that Missouri governor D. R. Francis would not favor the movement with his own letter of commitment.

Bronaugh's campaign scored another victory when the first governor of Minnesota, Henry H. Sibley, added his voice to the Youngers' cause. On July 8, 1889, Sibley wrote a letter, which ended: "Minnesota has shown her power to punish malefactors, let her now manifest her magnanimity, by opening the prison

doors to the men who have so long suffered for a violation of her laws, and bid them 'go and sin no more.' "[10]

Over the past year, Bob had continued to be plagued by health problems. He fought off such nuisances as best he could and refused to discuss his ailments with anyone. Bob, as well as his brothers, had become quite good friends with deputy warden Jacob Westby. Deputy Westby spent some of his free time with Bob, as he enjoyed Bob's intelligence and wit and his somewhat humorous approach to his predicament. Although Bob shared many of his thoughts and memories with Westby, he didn't allow the friendship to become so close that Westby would feel free to discuss Bob's great guilt for the incarceration of his brothers.

Westby became good friends with Bob sometime in late 1888. The two men often passed their free time in each other's company. Jacob Andrew Westby was born on October 19, 1848, in Christiania, Norway. He was a sailor in the Norwegian Navy who relocated to the United States about 1867. Westby lived in Red Wing, Minnesota, where he married and became a member of that city's police force. He was recruited as deputy warden of the Stillwater Prison under Warden Halvur Stordock in 1888. The Westby family lived in the deputy warden's residence just outside the gate of the prison.[11]

Because he spent so much time with Bob, Westby began to notice that Bob frequently fought fatigue and often looked pale. When Westby questioned Bob, the prisoner would tell him that he was fighting off a chill or make some other excuse. Under Westby's repeated questioning, Bob finally admitted that he had not felt well for some time. Bob asked that his brothers not be told. Westby insisted that Bob talk to the prison doctors, and Bob reluctantly agreed. Bob informed the doctors that he had been prone to lung congestion ever since he had received the chest wound during his Hanska surrender.

The doctors' examinations did not relieve Westby's concern. Bob was diagnosed as suffering from phthisis, which was better known at the time as consumption and would be described in layman's medical terms as pulmonary tuberculosis. Bob was told quite frankly that he would not live much longer. Bob received this information calmly, almost as if he had already guessed his fate. Bob told his brothers of his illness but asked that they not discuss it in his presence. He pledged that he would continue to work toward their parole and expressed his desire that such an event would come in time for him to enjoy his remaining time at home in Missouri. Following Bob's brave lead, Cole and Jim allowed Bob to joke about his illness and his need to return to the clean, fresh air of Jackson County. Whenever they returned from a visit with Bob, however, Cole and Jim would sit quietly in their cells reflecting on the fate of their youngest brother. Jim and Cole knew that Bob played down his condition and strived to maintain his sense of humor. The two brothers were told often that the prison doctors were doing all that they could for Bob.

During his wedding trip to Minnesota, long before he had become actively involved in the Youngers' cause, Wal Bronaugh had canvassed the citizens of St. Paul to determine their sentiments in regard to the release of the Youngers. Most of the people Bronaugh talked to claimed that they didn't believe he would get far with a campaign to help the Youngers out of Stillwater. Many advised him to go home and forget about the idea. However, when Bronaugh conducted the same survey in Missouri, he was met with overwhelming support. Respected and powerful men continued to come forward to aid Bronaugh in this difficult endeavor.

Support came from an unexpected faction of the state of Missouri: a respected former officer of the Union Army. Col. E. F. Rogers had been in the same room with Major Foster after the Battle of Lone Jack when Cole had intervened on Foster's behalf. Rogers admired Cole for his involvement and offered to help the Youngers in their bid for parole. Stephen C. Reagan was a former officer in the Confederate Army and a friend of the Younger family. Reagan and Bronaugh met with former governor Marshall in St. Paul and then proceeded to Stillwater for a meeting with the Youngers. Marshall suggested that the group meet with Judge Mott of Faribault. Mott arranged for the three men to meet with twenty-five of Faribault's most esteemed citizens. The men were able to obtain twenty-three letters of support.

Rogers, Reagan, and Bronaugh decided to canvas southern Minnesota to determine the views of the citizenry of that area. The men were able to obtain 163 letters stating that the Youngers had served enough time and should be freed from the state prison. Bronaugh decided to take his letter campaign to an unlikely source: members of the posse to whom the Youngers had surrendered. Even here the parole movement found favor as Capt. W. W. Murphy, B. G. Yates, and George Bradford wrote letters of support to Governor Merriam. Liberty Hall, a newspaperman, was introduced to Bronaugh by Major Edwards to do "honest, earnest and effective work" in the Minnesota press. Bronaugh credits him with having done so although exactly what he accomplished is not clear.[12]

Not all the approaches by Bronaugh and his colleagues were met with favor. Philanthropist George A. Pillsbury refused to write any letter of support, as did Senator Washburn of Minnesota. However, U. S. Senator Cushman K. Davis readily agreed to lend his name to the cause.

The following are some of the prestigious personalities who, according to W. C. Bronaugh, supported "The Youngers Fight For Freedom":

William R. Marshall, former governor of Minnesota

John Marmaduke, governor of Missouri

T. T. Crittenden, former governor of Missouri

L. H. Waters, Union Army

Maj. John Newman Edwards, Confederate Army officer and newspaperman

Cap. Stephen C. Reagan, Confederate Army officer

Hon. Waller Young, Missouri legislator

Gen. Henry H. Sibley, first governor of Minnesota

John C. Wise, editor of the *Mankato Press*

David Day, Democratic postmaster at St. Paul

William Lee, Republican postmaster at St. Paul

Hon. D. M. Sabin, U. S. Senator from Minnesota

Hon. Horace W. Pratt, former president of the Minnesota State
Agriculture Society

B. G. Yates, member of the posse

Capt. W. W. Murphy, member of the posse

George A. Bradford, member of the posse

Col. E. F. Rogers, Union Army officer

Judge Mott, Faribault

Judge Cushman K. Davis, U. S. Senator

J. A. Reed, former warden of Stillwater Prison

Ara Barton, former sheriff of Rice County

Maj. William Warner, former commander-in-chief of the Grand Army of the Republic

Judge Ray of Minnesota

Webster Davis, Assistant Secretary of the Interior under McKinley

Hon. James O'Brian, Minnesota state senator

Hon. Lon V. Stephens, Missouri state treasurer

Hon. S. B. Elkins, U. S. Senator from Virginia

R. C. Dunn, Minnesota state auditor

Henry Wolfer, warden of Stillwater Prison

James R. Waddell, Missouri superintendent of insurance

F. M. Cockrell, U. S. Senator

John F. Phillips, U.S. District Court Judge

George G. Vest, U. S. Senator

Maj. James Bannerman, president of the Ex-Confederate Association

Hon. John J. Crittenden

Champ Clark, Congressman from Minnesota

Hon. Shepard Barclay, Judge of the Missouri Supreme Court

Hon. J. L. Bittinger, U. S. Consul to Montreal

Hon. W. S. Cowherd, Missouri congressman

Hon. M. E. Benton, Missouri congressman

W. J. Stone, U. S. Senator from Missouri

Col. Norrish, Board of Parole, Minnesota

George P. Wilson, Minnesota state senator

The time had arrived. Having worked hard and diligently for several years, Bronaugh prepared the letters, affidavits, and statements of support to be presented to the governor of Minnesota. With so many powerful and influential men involved with the movement, it was hard for Bronaugh and the Younger family not to be overwhelmingly encouraged. Cole did not see how the presentation could fail. Jim remained skeptical, however, that any movement supported by the Youngers could be successful. Bob's desire to spend his last days at home in Missouri was so great that he was unable to verbalize his feelings as to whether or not the appeal to the governor would succeed.

In the spring of 1889, representatives of the Younger parole movement met with Minnesota governor William R. Merriam in the executive mansion in St. Paul. Ex-Governor Marshall, ex-Warden Reed, Sheriff Ara Barton, Colonel Rogers, Colonel Reagan, Aunt Frances Twyman, Retta Younger, and Wal Bronaugh presented their material, made their speeches, and awaited the governor's decision. Bronaugh wrote of what happened next:

> Our suspense was not of exceedingly short duration. Cool, calm, cold and collected, the chief executive of the great commonwealth of Minnesota, with the power of liberty or confinement, death or life at his command, arose and said: "I cannot pardon these men. My duty to the state and my personal prejudice against them make it impossible.[13]

Bronaugh never explained what Merriam's "personal prejudice" against the Youngers might have been. It is likely that he didn't know. It is likely that the Youngers never realized what it was either. The facts reveal that Gov. William R. Merriam's father, John L. Merriam, was the same John L. Merriam who had been robbed on the train at Gad's Hill. It is possible that John Merriam might have been the man who had been forced down to his underwear and humiliated during that robbery. John Merriam had visited the Youngers while they were in jail at Faribault and was convinced that they were the Gad's Hill robbers.

Since the name of the man who had been stripped that evening was apparently held in confidence, it does seem possible that he may have been the state legislator. It is likely that whoever the victim was, he would have kept publication of the event at a minimum and may not have revealed his identity to more than his family or a very few close friends. Having made the comment that his prejudice was of a "personal nature," this may have been a "secret" that Gov. William R. Merriam was continuing to hold. Governor Merriam would be unforgiving. The Youngers were, then, not being punished as bank robbers but as the perpetrators of a ill-fated practical joke. If John L. Merriam was the victim of an act of folly on the evening of the Gad's Hill robbery, it was a joke that the Youngers paid for with over fifteen years of their life and liberty.

Refusing to discuss the issue further, the governor dismissed the group and escorted the devastated supporters from the governor's office. Bronaugh and Retta vowed to the others that they would not give up the fight and would continue to attempt to obtain a pardon for Bob at the very least.

Having lost none of their support regardless of Merriam's decision, Bronaugh, Retta and Aunt Frances Twyman continued their battle. Bronaugh began to change the focus of his drive to center on the terminally ill Bob. Many of the anti-Younger contingent expressed the thought that Bob's illness was a hoax and that his problems had been exaggerated to gain sympathy for the Youngers. One of these people was G. M. Phillips, who had been president of the First National Bank of Northfield in 1876. With the Youngers' approval, Phillips sent a Dr. Ogden from Northfield to confer with the prison physician, Dr. Pratt. Upon their examination of Bob, which Bob grudgingly allowed, Ogden became convinced that Bob was indeed very ill and likely to die shortly. Dr. Ogden returned to Northfield, where he recommended that Bob Younger be pardoned.

In July, 1889, Bronaugh and Marshall once again sat in the chambers of Governor Merriam. They presented him with additional letters centering on the desire of the Younger supporters to allow, at the very least, the pardon of Bob Younger. Merriam, his attitude unchanged since the two men's previous visit, replied: "I would not pardon the Youngers even if Mrs. Heywood should come to life again and make the request."[14] Bronaugh and Marshall could not believe that even Mrs. Heywood, who had died since her husband's murder at the hands of Frank James, would deny Bob Younger the peace of living out his last days in Missouri. Merriam had replied to the request and dismissed the matter once again. Bronaugh wrote: "Merriam was as merciless as an avenging Nemesis. Every resource at our command had been exhausted to mollify him."[15]

Before Merriam once again ushered the two men out of his office, Bronaugh grasped at one last straw. He offered to take

Cole's place at Stillwater as a "hostage" if the Youngers could be allowed to visit their home in Jackson County for thirty days. Additionally, Bronaugh suggested that he was willing to raise a bond of $100,000 or even $1 million as a guarantee of their "good citizenship" if they would be pardoned. When Bronaugh's offer was refused by Merriam, former governor Marshall himself offered to serve as the "hostage." Merriam asked the two men to leave. As far as Merriam was concerned, the matter was closed.

Ironically, Governor Merriam chose to parole another prisoner during this time. The Stillwater "resident" in question had been convicted of murdering his wife, stuffing her body under the floor, and holding a party in their home over her body the evening of her murder.[16]

At the end of May, 1889, Bob finally agreed to stay in the prison hospital rather than in his cell at the men's residence building. Cole was now a hospital trustee and was able to spend time with Bob. When he first arrived, Bob was uncomfortable with Cole's attentions. He preferred to be left alone most of the time, claiming that was what was needed if he was to get better. Dr. S. S. Kilvington visited with Bob and proclaimed that Bob did not have much longer to live. Kilvington stated that even if he were allowed to return to Missouri, Bob would not live more than eighteen months. If he stayed in the prison, Kilvington predicted, Bob's time would more likely be less than four months.[17]

On June 12, in recognition of the gravity of Bob's condition, the following item appeared in the Butler, Missouri *Times*:

> His [Bob Younger's] former florid complexion has faded to an ashy paleness. His cheek bones stand out prominently and his whole face is that of an invalid. He has lost much flesh, his arms and limbs are narrowed down almost to bones and his hands are thin and shallow. He is but a shadow of what he was up to a year ago. As he speaks his voice is husky and he once in awhile coughs. His steel blue eye is yet bright and restless. He knows he is far from well, but his iron will, so the attendants say, does not for an instant weaken and he says he is sure he will be better.[18]

During the summer the newspapers conducted a deathwatch. Bob's family and friends continued to appeal to the governor through the press to allow Bob the opportunity to die at home in

Missouri. Bob's cause may have been weakened somewhat by this statement of Cole's to the newspapers in August: "It is specially desirable now to secure Bob's release, yet in all except the matter of health, Jim and I have the same and just grounds upon which to base an appeal for release."[19]

Cole's statement only served to downplay Bob's health consideration, which was the strong point of the appeal on Bob's behalf in the first place. Bronaugh requested that Cole consider his statements more closely.

Retta arrived at Stillwater in September to stay by her brother's bedside during his last days. Jim and Cole were taken off their jobs so that they, too, could spend time with Bob. This was further evidence of the prison authorities' respect for the Youngers. Nearly every time he saw either of his brothers, Bob would ask if they forgave him for his stubbornness in refusing to accept their advice regarding the Minnesota robbery trip. While they reassured him that they did, Bob continued to be guilt ridden and remorseful.

At 6:00 p.m. on September 16, 1889, Bob asked his brothers and sister to stay with him. Calling on his vast medical knowledge, Bob knew that he would not live more than a few hours and said so. Bob also insisted that Deputy Warden Westby stay. He held Westby's hand as he told his friend that he was a "good man" and that he was liked by all the men. As Bob's life began to slip from him, he heard a bird calling outside his window. He reminded Cole of the birds back home in Missouri. He asked to be raised so that he might see the sky again and remarked that when he died he thought his soul might rest a moment on the hill outside his cell window.[20]

All in all, the evening was very emotional. Cole, Jim and Retta could not help but be moved to tears as their young brother began to die. Retta started to cry, and Bob asked her not to cry for him. At 10:30, Cole drew closer as Bob whispered in his ear. With thoughts of Maggie, Bob said, "Tell her I died thinking of her."[21] At the age of thirty-four, after thirteen years in the Stillwater Prison, Bob Younger closed his eyes and died.

Bob's body was placed in a black-broadcloth-covered casket with silver mountings. On the top of the casket was a small plaque bearing the inscription "At Rest." A short service was held in the chapel of the prison, and those prisoners who attended were visibly moved. Afterward, accompanied by Retta, Bob's casket was placed on the train. Upon arrival back in Missouri, Bob's body was taken by wagon to his sister Belle Hall's house in Lee's Summit.

The members of the family gathered, and the scene was reported by the local newspapers as being very emotional. Suze, who was now working with Emma and Kitt Rose at the Poor Farm, stood at the foot of the casket softly crying, "Bobby." This was not the reunion the Younger family had prayed for and for which they had hoped. On September 20, over 800 people packed the Baptist Church in Lee's Summit for the funeral of Robert Ewing Younger.[22]

Retta Younger had expressed her wishes for her brother's funeral service. Together with her sister Belle, Kitt Rose, and undertaker Joseph Martin, Retta made the final arrangements. At 11 a.m., with Mabel Campbell playing Webster's "Funeral March," his pallbearers brought Bob's casket forward in the church followed by his grieving family. The men who were chosen to carry Bob to his grave were, for the most part, childhood friends of his from Jackson County: Buford Lewis, William Anderson, Frank Gattrell, A. Flannery, J. S. Whitsett and J. W. McBride. H. C. Lesher led the choir in singing "Rest Weary Heart." A prayer by Rev. C. A. Buchanan of the Baptist Church followed, and Rev. A. B. Francisco of the Cumberland Presbyterian Church read the Twenty-first Psalm. While the congregation sang "We Shall Know Each Other There," Bob's sister Anne became hysterical. Reverend Francisco, who was the pastor at Belle Hall's church, gave the funeral address from the text "I Am Like A Broken Vessel, Psalms 22:12." The pastor said of Bob:

Friends, and friends of the deceased for this is a time when only friends should be present, he has been in the hands of enemies long enough, let us bury all prejudices in this hour of sad affliction and manifest our sympathy to these broken-hearted sisters and friends. This is an ordinary and yet extraordinary occasion; ordinary inasmuch as we have the living before the dead; extraordinary because the life which he has lived has been so entirely different from the lives of most of us.[23]

Reverend Francisco spoke of Bob's capacity for love and his willingness to do everything for a friend, statements that were met with much agreement from the members of the Lee's Summit community of which Bob had been a part. The pastor spoke the now familiar sentiments of how, if he had been born at any other time, Bob would have been an honored citizen. Reverend Francisco told of Bob's repentance and contrition and stated that Bob had discussed such matters only with his sister and pastor, for he did not wish to be considered hypocritical. Rev. W. B. Cobb of the Southern M.E. Church said a prayer following these remarks and the choir sang "Peace Be Still." Reverend Buchanan spoke of Christian charity, ending with the words "Let him that is himself without sin cast the first stone." The service closed with the choir's rendition of "Home of the Soul."

Over a hundred carriages and a large group of people on foot followed the casket to its resting place at the Lee's Summit Cemetery. Bob was placed next to his mother. Retta, hysterical, cried, "Oh, Bob" as several tube roses fell from her hand into the grave.

Along with Bob's many friends and relatives, noted members of Jackson County society attended the service. Among them in attendance were Lee's Summit mayor Joseph Stinson, William B. Howard, Tom Lea, and Dr. W. S. Strother.[24]

After the death of Jesse, Frank James decided to surrender to the law and attempt to clear the slate of accusations against him. John Newman Edwards worked with Frank. The two thought that if they proceeded cautiously they would be able to have Frank acquitted of any charges that might be brought against him. Edwards at first attempted to have Governor Crittenden pardon Frank, but the governor refused. He did, however, promise James a fair trial. On October 4, 1882, placing his revolver in the governor's hand, Frank James surrendered to Crittenden with these words: "I want to hand over to you that which no living man except myself has been permitted to touch since 1861, and to say that I am your prisoner."

Frank James knew that the statute of limitations and the difficulty of obtaining witnesses to crimes that might be charged to him prior to 1879 would be factors to be considered by those involved in the legal system. The witnesses after that date, in Frank's opinion, would be less than credible if his lawyers questioned them carefully.

Frank James was charged with the murder of Detective Whicher and the robbery of a bank in Independence in 1867. The charges were soon dropped because of lack of evidence.

On August 21, 1883, Frank James went on trial in Daviess County, Missouri, for the robbery at Gallatin and the murder of Cashier Sheets. He was also tried for the robbery at Winston and the murder of Frank McMillan. A dramatic trial ensued, which included the testimony of former James Gang member Dick Liddil on one side and character testimony, together with pieces of "evidence" from James's witnesses Zerelda Samuel, Susan James Parmer, Gen. JO Shelby, and even Governor Crittenden himself, on the other. Frank James was acquitted by the young, all-Democrat jury. He was then returned to Jackson County, where he was brought up on charges for his participation in the Blue Cut robbery. However, a Missouri Supreme Court ruling came down that Dick Liddil could not serve as a witness unless he obtained a pardon from the governor. Crittenden refused the pardon.

Frank was removed to Alabama, where he went on trial for the Muscle Shoals robbery. He was again acquitted when no one was able to absolutely identify him as being at the scene of the robbery. Crittenden had previously informed the authorities in Minnesota that James could not be taken to that state to stand trial for the Northfield robbery while the charges were still pending against him in Missouri. Alabama had been lucky in being able to seize James in order to try him for the Muscle Shoals incident. Missouri took possession of Frank James upon completion of his Alabama trial and returned him to Cooper County, where he was to stand trial for the Otterville robbery. James was released on bond, but before the trail could be organized, all charges were dropped. Crittenden had failed to be reelected, and John Marmaduke, a former general in the Confederate Army who had served with Shelby and Price, was the new governor of Missouri. It was likely Marmaduke's influence that caused the dropping of the charges.

By this time, the state of Minnesota could see that convicting Frank James was a difficult task. For whatever reasons, it gave up trying to bring him to trial. Frank James was a free man.

Cole and Jim Younger, on the other hand, longed for home more than ever. Cole was moved to write the following poem:

Twenty Years Ago

Tis twenty years and more, Jim,
Since we breathed the air of home,
Or gazed upon the hills and vales
We loved so oft to roam.
How oft we climbed the rugged hills
To view the landscape fair,
And bared our head to the gentle breeze—
Our own dear native air.

Methinks the flowers bloom more fair,
The birds have songs more sweet,
Where climbs the jasmin o'er the door,
Once trailing at our feet.
The anuabine falls on the hills, Jim,
With the glad light of yore—
Twenty years I have dreamed of it, Jim,
Shall we see its sun no more?

One grim old cliff I have in mind,
That stands majestic grand,
While far below the fair Osage
Sweeps o'er her silver sand.
There countless names are carved with ours,
Where we have stood with awe,
And gazed upon its marble face
Near dear old Monegaw!

The light of home gleams bright, Jim,
Through the mist of twenty years;
Is that what dims our eyes, Jim,
Or can it be our tears?
Nay, do not turn aside, Jim,
I do not deem you weak;
Full well I know that dauntless heart,
Though tears be on thy cheek.

Among those bonny hills of home
There's many a friend today
Would joyful give us welcome sweet—
Will faithful wait away;
But there's a better land than this,
Where shadows never fall,
Where gates of pearl inviting stand,
God's sunlight over all!

The question of whether or not Jim and Cole would ever again see those "hills and vales" remained.

21

A Long, Hard Campaign

As I stand here today, I ain't got a grudge against
any human being alive or dead. Men, I'm happy.
                                            —Cole Younger, 1901

Jim Younger became even more depressed after the death of Bob.
He figured if the authorities would not let Bob out of prison even
if only to die, any chances of Cole and himself leaving the
institution could be forgotten. Cole continued to believe that high-
level sentiments against him and his brother would eventually
change, and he decided to continue to make the best out of his
situation at Stillwater. To keep himself busy, Jim accepted the
warden's offer to have him handle the mail while he continued to
work in the library. In an account published in the Kansas City
World, ex-state senator John Ryder remarked:

> Cole had the preferable place as far as light, air and roominess were
> concerned. Jim's workroom was cramped; but he communed daily,
> hourly with the illuminated minds of the world, dead and alive. The
> older, stronger man [Cole] was ever in contact with acute suffering
> or patient misery, living in the drug store atmosphere, relieved only
> by the duty of ministering to pain or chiding petulance. The man
> with the bullets in his body [Jim], causing many an unseen twinge,
> found among the bookcases and their contents work to keep his
> brooding mind occupied to the point of contentment almost.[1]

When Governor Merriam came up for reelection, Cole sum-
moned Bronaugh from Missouri to discuss strategy that might be

employed should Merriam not be elected. Cole requested that Bronaugh meet with both Republicans and Democrats to determine the political climate. Such planning was in vain, however, as Merriam was reelected governor for two more years. Since Merriam had made clear to Bronaugh that he would never change his mind, this governor was not approached again by anyone in the Younger parole movement.

In February, 1891, Albert Garvin had been appointed warden of Stillwater. Garvin was the first professional penalist to head the Minnesota State Prison. He began to make positive changes in the institution but after a year and a half, Garvin left Stillwater to become St. Paul's chief of police. In June, 1892, Henry Wolfer was appointed as the new warden. Wolfer had twenty years' experience and had received his training at the Illinois State Prison at Joliet, a progressive penal institution. Wolfer would serve as warden until 1914.

Prior to Wolfer's arrival, Cole had been working in the laundry. A new hospital was being constructed. When the building was completed, Cole was appointed head nurse. During a visit to the prison at this time, Ben West from Harrisonville described Jim:

> Jim seems discouraged and has evidently given up hope. He plainly shows the effect of his wounds and close confinement. Large rings under his eyes and his nervous movements show him to be in bad physical condition.[2]

Knute Nelson was elected governor of Minnesota in 1893 but served only one term. Bronaugh claimed that he had heard that Nelson was not in favor of a Younger parole or pardon and so did not even approach the new governor.[3] One cannot help but wonder if Bronaugh was tiring of the effort, having been defeated so many times in the past. Retta Younger, in fact, had written a letter to Bronaugh claiming that she hadn't heard from him in some time and wondering why her letters to him had gone unanswered. Arrangements had been made for a photograph to be taken of Retta and all three of her brothers shortly before Bob's death. Bronaugh had said he would "sell" the photograph to raise money for the parole drive.[4] Evidently Bronaugh paid the photographer, a man named Kuhn, himself. There is mention of this transaction in a letter to Retta from the Youngers' friend Peter Freligh. The letter contains the information that Bronaugh sent $75 to Freligh for Kuhn's expenses and that Kuhn was then paid by Peter. Also mentioned is Cole's balance on his account with Kuhn, which Cole said Retta would settle when she received the proceeds from Bronaugh's sale of the photos.[5] Perhaps Bronaugh was simply enjoying a well deserved "time-out."

In 1895, Knute Nelson was elected to the U. S. Senate. Nelson's lieutenant governor, David M. Clough, became governor. At this time, Bronaugh reappeared and managed to collect another, updated group of letters addressed to the new governor. Included were the urgings of Maj. William Warner, the U. S. Attorney for the Western District of Missouri; orator Webster Davis; and Missouri state treasurer Lon Davis. Additionally, the Edwards petition was resigned by the current General Assembly of Missouri.[6] Former governor McGill was interested in supporting the Youngers, and Cole asked Bronaugh to bring that matter up with ex-governor Marshall. McGill had not been governor long, and his interest in the Youngers appears to have been somewhat personal in nature.

Cole wrote the following to Bronaugh on January 15, 1893: "I am forty-nine years old to-day and have not long for this life at best, and after serving sixteen years in here if I start down I will go fast."[7]

In 1896, U. S. Senator Stephen B. Elkins from West Virginia joined the movement. Elkins had been Cole and Jim's school-teacher before the war. Cole had managed to convince Quantrill not to kill Elkins when he was held by the guerrillas as a spy in 1862. Ben West claimed that Jim told him that he was the one who had saved Elkins's life, having rescued him on horseback. Also in 1896, Harry Jones, son of Anne and Curg, pledged his efforts to help secure his uncles' freedom. By that time, young Jones was an attorney living in Pleasant Hill, Missouri.

It was time once again for the governor of Minnesota to be approached. In October, 1896, state senator James O'Brian, state auditor R. C. Dunn, warden Wolfer, Harry Jones, and Bronaugh met with Clough in his office in St. Paul. O'Brien, Dunn, and Wolfer gave eloquent, detailed pleas on behalf of the Youngers.

Clough was visibly affected and began to pace around his office in indecision. Finally, unable to contain himself any longer, Dunn said to his friend:

> Dave Clough, sit down there and write that pardon out for the Youngers. There will be only nine days' howl over it by a lot of sore-heads and politicians. You know that I have been an outspoken advocate and champion of the Youngers and everybody in Minnesota knows how I stood and how I still stand. I have been elected Auditor three times and you know that in the last election I ran two thousand votes ahead of you.[8]

Though appreciative of his friend's bluntness, Clough still could not make up his mind. After continued thought, he finally announced that the Board of Pardons, which had been created by an amendment to the Minnesota constitution passed in the general election of 1896, should make the final decision. His parting words to the discouraged group were "Go home to Missouri, get another petition and have it addressed to the Pardoning Board."[9]

Jim's former sweetheart, Cora McNeill, continued to do everything she could for Jim. The two exchanged many letters throughout Jim's period of confinement. In 1897 Cora managed to have a book published. *Mizzoura*, a fictional work, was said by Cora to have been a thinly-veiled account of the Younger brothers and the women they loved as young men back in Missouri. Cora hoped that her book would show the Youngers to be the outstanding personalities she believed them to be. Although she remained friends with Jim, Cora married Minnesota legislator C. P. Deming.[10] After Deming's death, Cora married another man influential in the Younger parole movement, George M. Bennett.

Cole wrote Bronaugh on January 3, 1897: "While I have nothing new or interesting to communicate, I will write you all the same, to let you know we are well, and in good spirits. Had a jolly good Xmas and New Years. Music, speaking and reading by a very good looking lady."[11]

Bronaugh acted on Clough's suggestion and was able to collect a third petition from the General Assembly of Missouri. He also obtained letters from T. T. Crittenden; James Waddell, superintendent of insurance for Missouri; U. S. Senator F. M. Cockrell;

U. S. Senator George C. Vest; Shepard Barclay, Judge of the Missouri Supreme Court; and W. J. Stone, U. S. Senator from Missouri. These documents were filed with the Board of Pardons on July 8, 1897. At that time, the board consisted of Clough, Attorney General Childs, and Chief Justice Charles M. Start. Cole doubted that anything could come of such an appeal because of what he had heard of Start. Cole wrote:

> It was at first proposed that the board should consist of the governor, attorney general and the warden of the prison, but before the bill passed, Senator Allen J. Greer secured the substitution of the chief justice for the warden, boasting, when the amendment was made, "That ties the Youngers up for as long as Chief Justice Start lives."[12]

A public meeting of the Board of Pardons was held on July 12. Northfield sent a large, vocal opposition group. At the beginning of the meeting, appeals for the pardon were made by Judge James McCafferty, Colonel Norrish, who had been a member of the Board of Prison Officials, and Mayor Smith of St. Paul. Mayor A. D. Keyes of Faribault and Rice County Attorney A. L. Keyes pleaded against the pardon. Mayor Keyes stated that Jim and Cole should answer three questions: First, was Frank James in the bank during the Northfield robbery; second, who was the last man who left the bank, and third, who was the man on the buckskin (dun) horse? Governor Clough told the representatives from Rice County that the questions were of no consequence to the matter at hand and that the James boys were not on trial. Keyes countered with the following speech:

> These men come here and ask for a pardon on the grounds that they have reformed in mind and morals as well as in heart, and they are prepared to become good citizens, if they are released. We claim that it is not too much to ask that they shall remain where they are until they disclose the name of the man who killed Heywood. It is not an element of good citizenship to conceal a murderer. Good faith on their part demands that they disclose the name of the man who killed Cashier Heywood, that the man may be brought back to Minnesota and punished. If the murderer was Frank James, as we are led to believe, then he has never suffered anything for his crime. He has never even been imprisoned, and it is no more than right

that he should suffer the penalty in some measure at least. If the Youngers are now the good citizens they claim to be, they would go on the stand and by telling the truth would assist the authorities of this state in bringing the Northfield murderer to justice.[13]

After the county attorney's speech, affidavits of so-called "eye-witnesses" to the shooting of Gustavson were presented by C. P. Carpenter. All claimed that Cole was Gustavson's killer regardless of the fact that prosecuting attorney George Baxter had been unable to find any witnesses to the actual shooting of the man when he had questioned the Northfield community at length the day following the robbery. It was Baxter's investigation that influenced the coroner's opinion that Gustavson had been killed by a stray bullet fired by an unknown party.

Bronaugh spoke at length, and the presentations ended. The deliberations were not expected to last long, as the only way a pardon could be rendered was by unanimous vote. Judge Start, as expected, voted against the proposal. Making the decision unanimous, Clough and Childs reluctantly agreed with him.

The Board of Pardons was not required to give explanations for its decisions, but it released a statement regarding the Younger appeal. The board remarked that the Youngers had pleaded guilty to murder and that the board of pardons did not have the right to interfere with a sentence unless there were extenuating circumstances. The "character of this crime renders it one absolutely without extenuating circumstances," the document read. The Youngers had not become good citizens, as had "the men at Appomattox," according to the Board, and had instead chosen to live their lives as "a notorious band of outlaws." The board reasoned that if the Youngers were allowed to be paroled because they had reformed after twenty-one years of imprisonment, everyone convicted of murder should have the same opportunity. That was not a policy the Board of Pardons wished to set.

The desire of the Rice County Attorney to have the Youngers name Frank James as the killer of Heywood is an interesting one. Most of the people of Northfield had long accepted that Charlie Pitts had been the man in the bank and the last to exit. This was not a fact but rather a theory that had been presented to the citizens of Northfield by local authorities upon the return of Charlie's lifeless body to St. Paul. Claiming that Pitts had killed Heywood may have been one way for the Northfield posse to "save face" for not having captured the murderer although the Northfield community had nothing to be embarrassed about in regard to their performance during the robbery. Perhaps the theory was presented because Pitts's death allowed the community to go forward rather than become involved in the intricacies of deciding who the killer was, tracking him down, and attempting to bring him to justice. Minnesota had, at one point, tried to bring Frank James to trial for the Northfield robbery but had given up when James had been acquitted in several other states' courts. In a letter he wrote to the *Pioneer Press* on July 14, Bronaugh expressed his sentiments on the subject:

> I do not understand why the people of Northfield should make this claim, inasmuch as it has been frequently asserted that they are fully aware who these parties were, and that, acting upon reliable information, a requisition has been made by the Governor of this state upon the Governor of Missouri, over twelve years ago, for the body of the prisoner who it was claimed was the only living person, aside from the Youngers, who participated in the bank robbery. The Youngers feel, as I would feel under similar circumstances, that it would not redound to their credit as men to put themselves in the position of turning informants for the purpose of securing clemency for themselves. They feel, as I would feel, that they are responsible for their part in the crime committed and should suffer the penalty without attempting to save themselves by turning state's evidence. I honor the Youngers for this position, and I believe that every fair-minded man will do the same.[14]

The Northfield *News* reflected satisfaction with the board's decision later that week. The *News* read: "We are very glad to know that the Youngers behaved themselves while in prison—it is something they did not do out of it, and besides, what is there in state's prison to do but behave?"[15] The *News* editorial ended with the statement "Let life sentence mean what it says." Such editorials, of course, started another media debate, with both sides firing some rather interesting, if not formidable, shots.

Jim was so discouraged by the decision of the Board of Pardons that he decided he wasn't going to talk to the press any more. In effect, he was giving up his participation in the parole drive. Cole didn't force his optimism on Jim but rather allowed his brother to work through his frustration and disappointment. The resident doctor for whom Cole worked in the prison hospital was Dr. Morrill E. Withrow. Withrow described the Youngers at that time in an interview several years later. He said that Cole was a "friendly sort of person" who had a strong personality. Withrow observed:

> Jim, however, had the most astounding fund of knowledge that I ever knew in one person . . . he also possessed a most retentive memory and could give the most intimate details of any and all historic events. He once gave a most lucid description of the debates over the adoption of the Constitution, and of every major piece of legislation that had been adopted since the beginning of the history of our country. I used to attempt to dig up some question to ask him to see if it were not possible to puzzle him but I never succeeded in finding one, no matter how abstruse, to which he did not have a ready, offhand explanation.[16]

After the board's decision, Harry Jones and Bronaugh decided to visit Governor Clough. Clough told Bronaugh: "It was a great mistake that I did not sign the pardon of Cole and Jim when I was urged to do so by yourself, Dunn and the others. I have but one time to regret my action, and that will be all my life."[17]

In 1899, a bill was introduced to the Minnesota General Assembly which was written by George M. Bennett and championed by Sen. George P. Wilson, who had served as attorney general. The bill called for the parole of life prisoners who had served such a period as would have entitled them to release if they had been sentenced to a thirty-five-year confinement. The bill passed in the senate by a 48 to 5 vote but was defeated in the house.

About this time, Bronaugh once again disappeared from the scene in Minnesota. He later claimed that he was working on the effort in his own state.[18]

In 1901, an extraordinary event occurred in the life of Jim Younger. Alix J. Muller, a free-lance writer from St. Paul, managed to get Jim to agree to an interview. Perhaps the fact that Jim had begun to champion women's rights and Alix was a woman in a predominantly male profession encouraged Jim to let Alix talk with him. In any case, Alix kept in touch with Jim after the two met and they began to exchange letters on a regular basis. Jim began to fall in love with the lady writer, and his sentiments were returned by Alix.

In 1901, an amended bill similar in tone to the Bennett Bill was introduced in the Minnesota legislature by C. P. Deming, Cora McNeill's husband. The bill provided that life prisoners might be paroled by the Board of Control with the unanimous consent of the Board of Pardons after the prisoners served a thirty-five-year sentence, less good time, or a period of at least twenty-four years. The Deming Bill was passed by both houses, much to the surprise of Bronaugh and Cole. However, the bill needed to be approved by the five members of the Board of Prison Officials. On June 6, 1901, a meeting was held by that board. The result was that the Deming Bill was approved without dissent.

While the bill had been introduced as a tool to secure the pardon of the Youngers, over forty prisoners would be affected by its passage. The board was to meet on July 8 to decide, case by case, who would or would not be allowed parole from the Stillwater Prison. State senator Wilson suggested to Bronaugh, who had returned to Minnesota, that he obtain letters from the highest officials in Missouri written to the highest officials in Minnesota. Bronaugh returned to Missouri and accomplished this task.

Bronaugh wrote that he was in St. Paul on July 10, 1901, when the Youngers' names finally reached the agenda of the Board of Pardons. He desired to remain incognito and registered at the Merchant's Hotel as W. C. Carter from Texas. Bronaugh did not attend the board's meeting but rather received a moment-to-moment account by state auditor Dunn. Bronaugh never stated why he felt the need to remain unrecognized or why he did not attend the meeting. His remarks on the subject claim that his absence was for "obvious reasons."[19] Perhaps Bronaugh felt his presence would be detrimental to the proceedings, as he might be seen as a thorn in the side of those who had fought against the parole for so many years. He was, after all, a former Confederate soldier representing ex-Confederate guerrillas through a petition written by Missouri's foremost anti-Union representative, John

Newman Edwards. Perhaps Bronaugh's involvement of Edwards in the first place was a mistake as evidenced by the reference to Appomattox in the statement by the Board of Pardons when it had knocked down the Youngers' appeal. With so much public sentiment in their favor, much of it from prestigious political leaders, it is hard to understand why the Youngers were made to serve such a lengthy, severe sentence for a robbery committed when they were young men. Perhaps Bronaugh felt unnecessarily defensive about having had little to do with the Deming Bill or its passing in the legislature.

On July 10, while Bronaugh was eating his dinner, Dunn came up behind him in the restaurant. Slapping Bronaugh's back, Dunn announced the news that the Youngers had been paroled. Bronaugh had worked tirelessly for years to convince the highest officials that, in spirit, the Youngers had been punished to the full extent of the law. Their parole had always been denied by the whim of one or two of the men in power. It finally took the men of the legislature to step in and around such vindictive personalities and call for an end to a political war that evidently had not come to a close at Appomattox. Looking at the Youngers, who by now were fifty-seven and fifty-three, the representatives of the state of Minnesota decided that twenty-five years behind bars was enough punishment for a bank robbery. The current governor S. R. Van Sant, while having been swayed to the opinion that the Youngers should be released, became hesitant toward the end. He finally agreed to sign the parole documents when he was assured by State Agent Whittier and Warden Wolfer that newspaper involvement during the actual moments of release would be kept at a minimum.

Bronaugh was speechless. Before he made the trip to Stillwater to talk with Cole and Jim, he sent twenty-five telegrams to the Youngers' family and friends. The people back home in Missouri were ecstatic. Even more ecstatic were Cole and Jim, who were unable to accept the fact that they would be free men for the first time in twenty-five years.

The following document was signed, allowing a personal parole to Cole and Jim Younger:

> Know All Men by These Present: that the Board of Managers of the Minnesota State Prison, desiring to test the ability of (T. C.

Younger/James H. Younger), an inmate of said prison, to refrain from crime and lead an honorable life, do, by virtue of the authority conferred upon them by law, hereby parole the said (T. C. Younger/James H. Younger) and allow him to go on parole outside the buildings and enclosure of said prison, but not outside the State of Minnesota, subject, however, to the following rules, regulations and conditions, as made and provided by the law, and by the rules governing the conduct of life prisoners while on parole:

First. He shall not exhibit himself in any dime museum, circus, theater, opera-house, or any other place of public amusement or assembly, where a charge is made for admission.

Second. He shall proceed at once to the place of employment provided for him, and there remain until further orders.

Third. In case he finds it desirable to change his place of employment or residence, he shall first obtain a written consent of the said Board of Managers, through the Warden of said prison.

Fourth. He shall, on the twentieth day of each month, write the Warden of said prison, a report of himself stating whether he had been constantly at work during the last month, and, if not, why not; how much he has earned, and how much he has expended, together with a general statement as to his surroundings and prospects, which must be endorsed by his employer.

Fifth. He shall in all respects conduct himself honestly, avoid evil associations, obey the law, and abstain from the use of intoxicating liquors.

Sixth. As soon as possible after reaching his destination, he shall report to F. A. Whittier, state agent, show him his parole, and at once enter upon the employment provided for him.

Seventh. He shall while on parole remain in the legal custody and under the control of said Board of Managers.

Eighth. He shall be liable to be retaken and again confined within the enclosure of said State Prison for any reason that shall be satisfactory to the Board of Managers, and at their sole discretion.

Ninth. This parole is to take effect and be in force only upon the unanimous consent and approval of the members of the State Board of Pardons, expressed in writing.

The management of said State Prison has a lively interest in the subject of this parole, and he need not fear or hesitate to freely communicate with the Warden, in case he loses his situation, or becomes unable to labor by reason of sickness or other disability.

Given in duplicate this 6th day of June, 1901, by the managers of the Minnesota State Prison.

(signed) F. W. Temple
B. F. Nelson/A. C. Weiss
E. W. Wing/R. H. Bronson
Countersigned: Henry Wolfer, Warden

We hereby severally consent to this parole on the conditions therein named. Dated July 10, 1901

S. R. Van Sant, Governor
Charles M. Start, Chief Justice Supreme Court
Wallace N. Douglass, Attorney General

Within an hour after the Youngers were informed of their parole by Warden Wolfer, Bronaugh appeared at the prison in the company of a small group of reporters. The party was escorted to Deputy Warden Jack Glennon's office, where Cole soon appeared pale and out of breath. He looked from face to face as if he was not sure that the news he had received was not some kind of sick joke. As he observed the grinning faces before him, Cole finally realized that what he had been told was indeed true, and the large man bolted forward to shake Bronaugh's hand. Jim had been so overcome with emotion that he was unable to accompany Cole to the deputy warden's office. He had asked warden Wolfer if he might return to his cell to absorb the news. Jim joined the group a short time later.

The scene in Deputy Warden Glennon's office was touching as Cole and Bronaugh attempted to make conversation while regaining their emotions. After asking various questions as to who knew about the parole, Cole stated, "I feel like shaking hands with the whole world. As I stand here today, I ain't got a grudge against any human being alive or dead. Men, I'm happy."[20]

The Youngers did not know just when their moment of release would come. The following morning, July 11, they attended chapel services and then took up their posts in the library and the hospital. About 10 a.m. they were told they were wanted in the deputy warden's office. Not expecting to be released so soon, Cole and Jim assumed that they were to be briefed on their timetable for such an event. Instead, much to their astonishment. they were handed civilian clothes, told to put them on, and informed they did not have to return to their jobs. They would be free men within the hour.

The press awaited the two brothers as they cautiously walked through the gate of the prison. Breathing the "free" air, Cole and Jim paused outside the prison walls and looked at each other. Words were not needed for the two brothers to communicate their feelings to each other. Not allowing them much time to become accustomed to their new status, the newspapermen descended upon the two men and asked them question after question as the two began to stroll down the main street of the community of Stillwater.

The previous day, when Cole had met with Bronaugh and the reporters in the deputy warden's office he had stated that he didn't want to grant in-depth interviews to the press. According to Cole: "The past is dead to me. When I go out of prison walls, I go out a changed man. No, get all you[r] interviews now, for when I go out my lips are sealed."[21]

It was unlikely that Cole Younger's lips would forever be sealed, but the reporters respected the former prisoner's first day of freedom. The questions he and Jim were asked by the reporters who accompanied them related to their observations of how things had changed since they had last seen the city of Stillwater. The two men stopped at one point to examine an electric streetcar. They asked questions about its operation and continued a discussion about electricity as they walked on. They also remarked on the architecture of the city's buildings and the elaborate window displays. Jim, having vowed not to talk to reporters several years previously, with the exception, of course, of his new friend Alix Muller, had little to say. Jim told the *Pioneer Press* later: "I don't know what I thought. I've been keeping my feelings in check so long, ready to meet anything, that I'm afraid I didn't let myself out. But it didn't hurt me a bit."[22]

After walking around the town for about an hour, Cole and Jim returned to the prison. It had been prearranged that they would have lunch in Wolfer's office with Wolfer and Minneapolis representative J. W. Phillips. After lunch, the Youngers, Wolfer, Deputy Warden Glennon, and Superintendent Kilbourne of the Rochester Hospital for the Insane took a steamboat cruise on the St. Croix River. This outing had been arranged by R. H. Brunson, who was president of the First National Bank of Stillwater and who served as a member of the Prison Board. The cruise, which lasted over three hours, was enjoyed very much by Cole and Jim. Cole stated, "It was the finest outing I ever had in my life."[23] The Youngers dined again with Wolfer and spent their first night of freedom, ironically, as guests of the warden in his residence. Since final arrangements were being made for their employment, the Youngers spent the next couple of nights at the prison, although in the warden's residence rather than in their former cells.

At some point, Cole sent a telegram to Lizzie Daniels telling her of his good fortune. Lizzie had written to Cole earlier in the year renewing a relationship that had been dormant for at least twenty-five years. Cole wrote back to Lizzie on March 1, and the two continued to correspond.[24]

Perhaps because things had moved so quickly or maybe because of other reasons unknown, Cole and Jim's faithful sister Retta was not present at the time of their release. Retta lived in the Lancaster-Hutchins area of Texas, where she taught school. Her subjects were music and art. On April 2, 1894, Retta Younger married A. Bledsoe Rawlins, a prominent citizen and wealthy furniture dealer in the Lancaster area. Rawlins had previously been married to Ida Virginia Fisher, who died in 1892. The couple had seven children: Earl, Sam, Philip, Mary, Ruth, Roderick, and Fisher Younger Rawlins. This last child was only six months old when his mother died. While Retta raised all the children as her own after her marriage to Rawlins, she was especially close to Fisher. Why he was named Fisher Younger has always been a question of the Rawlins and Younger families. Fisher died at the age of twenty-one from meningitis while attending Texas A&M College.[25] It may have been the needs of her new family that kept Retta from traveling once again to Minnesota.[26]

On Monday, July 12, Cole accompanied Dr. Morrill Withrow

to a home-cooked meal at Withrow's mother's house a few miles outside of Stillwater.[27] Morrill E. Withrow was born on August 21, 1870, in Withrow, Minnesota. He was educated in Stillwater and received his doctor's degree from Hemline University in 1897. He became a resident physician at the Stillwater Prison in 1899. Cole served as prison nurse under Dr. Withrow, and the two men, as well as Jim Younger, became very good friends.[28] Dr. Withrow recalled:

> It was in the evening and as we drove out to the farm, we came upon a rise of land which overlooks a valley. The sun was just setting and the scene was grand. Cole suddenly asked me to stop. When I complied he sat silent for a moment, then slowly said, "This is the first time I've seen the sun set in twenty-five years." The pathos of that remark and its effect on me I will never forget.[29]

On July 16, a small reception was held in honor of the Younger brothers in the home of J. H. Schurmeier of St. Paul. Posse member B. G. Yates attended this affair, and Yates and Jim recalled, without bitterness, their encounter at Hanska Slough. Yates had been the one who shot Jim in the mouth. Yates asked Jim if he remembered how he (Yates) had tried to help Jim after the surrender. Jim replied that he did.[30]

By the 17th, Jim had become completely overwhelmed by the events of the past several days and chose to remain back at the prison while Cole and Bronaugh made several visits. The two men stopped by the *Pioneer Press* offices, where they thanked the editors for the courtesies extended them throughout the years. They also visited the offices of various state officials to convey their appreciation to them as well.

Even before the parole had been granted, offers of various types of employment began to pour into the warden's office for his consideration. Positions such as clerks at the James Elwin Cigar Store or the Andrew Schoch Grocery Company were offered. There was a request for one of the Youngers to start the races at the Winchester Fair. J. H. Schurmeier, the host of the July 16 reception, had relayed to the warden that he wished to open a cigar store in partnership with the Youngers.[31] Warden Wolfer received the following offers of employment for Cole and Jim

Younger when it began to seem probable that they would be paroled: Edgar W. Porter Co. (selling Mark Twain books); Dr. Frank Powell (Dr. Powell offered to pay Cole's tuition to nursing school); Harris Machinery Co. (shipping clerks or salesmen); Mains Circus attractions; The Frost Record (staff of newspaper, Frost, Minnesota); Union Shoe & Leather Co. (salesmen); Charles W. Kaddatz (salesmen of bakery goods); Abe Rohrbach (clerk in gentlemen's furnishings), and Minnesota Club (shoe-shine concession).

For some reason, a curious decision was made by Warden Wolfer and the members of the Parole Board. The Youngers were to be employed by the P. N. Peterson Granite Company of Stillwater and St. Paul. The primary business of this company was the production of tombstones. Jim was to work in the office and sell the grave markers in the Stillwater area. Cole would travel about the county performing the same job. Each salesman would receive $60 a month.

On July 18, 1901, Cole and Jim Younger left Stillwater Prison for the last time to begin life anew as Minnesota tombstone salesmen. Once again trying to make the best of their fate, the two brothers masked their true feelings, set their resolve, and attempted to assimilate into free society. The thought of complete pardon and their return to their home in Missouri, however, never left their minds.

22

Jim Surrenders

Good-by, sweet lassie.
   —Letter of Jim Younger, October 18, 1902

Cole and Jim started their jobs with the Peterson Granite Company on July 29, 1901. Jim, organized and efficient, enjoyed the paperwork which was part of his job in the office. His personality, however, was not suited to that of a salesman after twenty-five years of having spoken to very few people. Cole, on the other hand, was a traveling salesman for the company. Visiting with potential clients as he canvassed the countryside suited him. He was happy to be in the fresh air and always enjoyed meeting new people.

George M. Bennett, sponsor of one of the earlier parole bills, had written Warden Wolfer on July 15. He was surprised that neither Cole nor Jim had stopped by to pay his respects to him. He assumed that Deming, and others important to their final release, had not received a visit either. Bennett was concerned that some people, although he didn't say who, might be saying negative things about him to the Youngers. Bennett remarked in his letter: "They are so pleased to be at liberty, they haven't had time to think. There are probably 100 persons who can show them that they owe their liberty to them exclusively, and it takes time for them to hear it all."[1]

On July 22, Bennett again wrote to Wolfer. This time he stated that Cole had been to visit him. A full pardon had been discussed,

269

and Bennett was most anxious to work toward that end. He claimed that Cole was the greatest asset to any pardon drive, as "Cole simply captures all he talks to, and they in turn capture all of their friends for him." Bennett observed that Cole seemed to be adjusting quite well to life outside prison.[2]

The Youngers' ability to adapt to their freedom was quite different. Cole was very anxious to enjoy the pleasures he had so long been denied. In August, he went to see a stage production of *Uncle Tom's Cabin* and observed a few hotel dances. According to his parole report, he went to church and enjoyed reading the daily newspapers, Shakespeare, and a sketch of the life of Sen. C. K. Davis. Cole experienced a minor mishap when he was shaken up in a caboose while changing trains one day, but his report reveals his general state of mind to be quite positive. He wrote that he had been "treated kindly and with courtesy" since he had been paroled.[3]

Jim, however, found it difficult to change the habits he had formulated over the last quarter century. He worked for Peterson during the day and spent his nights either canvassing potential customers or reading the daily newspapers.[4] Jim was always in bed by 8:00 p.m. and did not go anywhere the first month. His friend Alix had gone to Boise, Idaho, to regain her health after a severe bout with a tubercular condition, but the two exchanged letters on a regular basis. Jim wrote in a letter to Lizzie Daniels that he corresponded only with "one dear soul." Earlier references in that same letter to Lizzie mention Jim's "best Girl . . . an intelligent, Liberal minded Lassie."[5]

Alix J. Muller, the daughter of John R. Muller, was born in St. Paul. She moved with her father and sister to Grand Rapids when she was a young girl. Alix suffered from consumption, and the move was said to have been related to her care for this condition. Alix attended college and eventually became a writer. She returned to St. Paul and in 1899 compiled a history of the St. Paul police and fire departments. In 1900 she worked as a freelance writer for several papers, including the Salt Lake *Herald*. It was at this time that she met and fell in love with Jim Younger.

Jim seemed unable to break his ties with the prison and kept in constant communication with Warden Wolfer. He wrote to Wolfer that very soon after their employment by Peterson, another salesman affiliated with that company traveled from town to town claiming to be Cole Younger.[6] Wolfer wrote a letter to Peterson regarding the imposter, and Peterson, in turn, informed Wolfer that he would see to it that the fraud was discontinued immediately.[7] On August 26, Jim wrote to Wolfer that he was tired of the newspaper speculations that either he or Cole were going to marry soon.[8]

Cole enjoyed working for Peterson and began to feel comfortable as a "free man." His living expenses were paid by Peterson, but Cole had yet to be paid any of the salary he had been promised. In September, Cole again went to the theater, enjoying the complimentary tickets he was given by theaters because of his celebrity. He was amused by a performance of *Kentucky Cal*. He attended a revival and took six days off from his job to attend the Minnesota State Fair. Cole was a happy man. He wrote in his parole report that month, "I have been at peace with all of mankind."[9]

Meanwhile, Jim stayed in his room by himself when he was not working. He continued to complain to Wolfer about the press speculating that he was going to get married.[10] Jim didn't care at all for the newspapers commenting on his personal life. Cole wrote later that Jim stated the following to a newspaperwoman the day of their release:

> When we get out we would like to be left in peace. We don't want to be stared at and we don't want to be interviewed. For twenty-five years now, we have been summoned here to have men stare at us and question us and then go back and write up what they think and believe. It's hard to have people write things about you that are not true and put words in your mouth that you never uttered."[11]

In late September, Jim had an unfortunate accident that caused him to enter the city hospital at Stillwater for a short period of time.[12] Jim's horse walked into some bushes, and when Jim tried to extricate his horse and buggy from the bushes, the horse bolted forward, taking Jim with it. Cole explained: "He worked mostly through Washington County, and with a horse and buggy, but had not been at work more than two months when the sudden starting of his horse as he was getting out of the buggy started anew his intermittent trouble with the bullet that lodged under his spine, and he was compelled to find other employment."[13] Jim sought another job where he would not have to be bounced about by a horse and buggy.

Cole began to settle into his new lifestyle by October. He continued working for Peterson and was an avid theatergoer. He sometimes attended church and claimed that he associated "with honest men and virtuous wimen."[14]

Jim found work as a cigar clerk with Andrew Schoch in St. Paul. His salary continued to be $60 a month. Schoch ran an advertisement in the newspaper announcing that Jim was in charge of the cigar stand. Jim wrote to Wolfer that he found the ad offensive.[15] Dr. Morrill Withrow observed:

> Cole was adaptable and very soon he got his stride. Jim, on the other hand, never could accustom himself to the thought that he was an object of curiosity. It pained him. Moreover, the work he obtained was not that for which he had been trained, and the knowledge that he received it because of a chapter in his life that he would have given anything to forget, only because his employer hoped to receive advertising through that means, was a bitter thought to him."[16]

Jim stayed at home when he was not working and read the newspapers. He did not attend church. He did, however, spend one day at the State Fair, although he did not say in the company of whom.[17] Jim complained that he had trouble with ex-cons asking him for money, and Wolfer encouraged him to deal with such people in his usual forthright manner. Wolfer wrote:

> Do not allow the ex-convicts to bother you. If they ask you to do anything that you think you ought not to do, plainly tell them. I do not think, however, I need to give you this advice as you are very thoroughly grounded in this particular and I know you do not fear to speak up plainly and to the point whenever moral courage is in demand. I am satisfied that you will get along well and that you are sure to prosper."[18]

In November, Cole began to be bothered by minor health problems. He complained that he suffered from rheumatism. He decided to take a "vacation" from his salesman duties, although he continued to attend theatrical performances.[19] His mood seemed less bright than it had been in previous months, but one would expect there would be ups and downs involved in such a change of lifestyle. Cole himself wrote: "I traveled for the Peterson Company until Nov. 1901, covering nearly all of Minnesota. But the change from the regularity of prison hours to the irregular hours, meals and various changes to which the drummer is subject was too much for me."[20]

Jim, ironically, was doing better by late November. On November 15, Jim had written to Wolfer that strange people had been coming around his rooms. He informed the warden that he had told his landlady to keep them away and had also written to Police Chief O'Connor about the situation.[21] By November 20, Jim was much happier and less paranoid. Alix's health had improved and she returned to St. Paul. Jim enjoyed his work at Schoch's store. He wrote in his monthly report that he spent "Sunday dinners with my best Girl."[22] With Alix's return to his life, Jim's spirits were the best they had been since his release from prison. Jim wrote: "Am at peace with every one—am gaining health and flesh and full of good cheer."[23]

On November 25, Jim wrote to Warden Wolfer that he would like to get married but knew that was impossible while he was still on parole. He wondered when the Youngers might be eligible for a full pardon.[24]

Jim and Cole saw each other only periodically in these first few months of freedom. It was undoubtedly important to each of them to establish his own individual identity at this time. Additionally, Cole and Jim displayed their own unique personalities. They did not like to do the same things. Cole continued to enjoy the company of many people and entertained himself with outings at every opportunity. Even with the arrival of Alix, Jim preferred evenings at home alone in his room.

By December, Cole was tired of working for Peterson and began to think he might enjoy employment elsewhere. He complained of being "sick" and wrote that he was bothered by gallstones and his continued rheumatism. He still attended the theater and occasionally went to revival meetings.[25]

Jim was comfortable with his job and especially enjoyed the time he spent with Alix. Alix's family did not like her association with Jim Younger and attempted to persuade Alix not to see him. While the pressure of the situation must have been very difficult for Alix, she and Jim continued to spend most Sundays together. It is likely they shared Jim's first Christmas outside of prison walls. Alix continued to be Jim's world. He did not even try to write relatives back home in Missouri on any kind of a regular basis, if at all.

Cole missed Missouri greatly, especially during the holidays. He had accepted his confinement in prison during the holidays as his fate. Now that he was out in society among families enjoying the holiday spirit, Cole longed to be with his own family. He probably desired to spend some part of the Christmas season with his brother, but Jim preferred to spend that time with Alix. Cole began to resent Alix and told Jim that she was taking up all his time. Jim ignored Cole and continued to spend what little social time he allowed himself in Alix's company.

January, 1902, brought yet another change for Cole. He found employment with Edward J. and Hubert C. Schurmeier. Together with James Nugent, the two brothers owned and operated the Interstate Institute in St. Paul. Their hospital was dedicated to the cure of liquor and morphine addiction. Cole was to work in the office for $1 a day. He did not, however, seem committed to continued employment at the institute. He stated that he was "only here for time being" and that he was looking forward to a new job that (police) "Chief O'Connor is getting for me." January seems to have been a somewhat depressing month for Cole, probably because of his unhappiness during the holidays and his continued wish to return home to Missouri. He complained of suffering from problems with rheumatism, grippe, and his kidney. He didn't attend church often that month, but he did manage visits to the theater. He also was a guest at the annual supper of "Railroad Men" in Minneapolis.[26]

Jim continued working at Andrew Schoch's and managed to get out a little that month. He wrote: "My lady friend and I spent one Sunday at [former deputy warden] Westby's" and at Alix's cousin's home in Minneapolis.[27]

On January 8, 1902, Alix wrote a letter to Governor Van Sant. She asked that Van Sant not view the letter as a formal appeal to the Parole Board but rather as "a woman's prayer for mercy to one whom she loves." Jim had appealed to the governor for a pardon around Christmas. His request went unanswered. Alix believed that she might sway a response from Van Sant if she were to write to him. She wrote the governor of Jim's fine qualities and requested that he grant the couple "a little peace and comfort" by allowing them to live out their remaining years together in marriage. Describing Jim as "the noblest man I have ever met," Alix wrote:

> To be so strong to endure, for the sake of others whom he must protect, a life of ignominy and shame, requires a character of almost superhuman strength and power, and I long for the time when the world will appreciate, and honor, this man as I do.[28]

Governor Van Sant never responded. Somehow, Alix's letter to the governor became common knowledge. Both Alix and Jim began to be hounded by the press for interviews related to their ill-fated love affair. Alix's family was outraged by this rash of unwelcome publicity and encouraged her to return to Boise until interest in the couple waned. Jim reluctantly agreed. He was heartbroken when Alix left. In his parole report he claimed that he was "sick" from his mouth wound from January 29 until February 18.[29] His absence from his job caused him to lose it. Cole later wrote that when he heard about Alix's letter and the uproar surrounding it, he went to Jim in Minneapolis. Cole said that he introduced Jim to several potential employers in the area and claimed that Jim had his pick of places to work. Jim decided to become a clerk at the James Elwin Cigar Store at the Fremont Hotel at 400 Sixth Avenue South in Minneapolis. He was paid $60 a month plus room and board. He claimed that he worked hard and didn't have time even to read.[30]

Cole continued at the Interstate Institute. By February he was assistant manager at $50 a month. He believed that he would get a better job by March and expressed that sentiment in his monthly report to State Agent Whittier. He went to the theater, was present at a few religious lectures, and attended a convention of newspapermen at the Elks Hall in Minneapolis.[31] His activities were virtually unchanged the next month. He still had not found employment elsewhere, although he stated in his report, "I will change work in a few days." Cole went to the theaters and, in addition to the daily newspapers, read "a variety of romance."[32]

Although Jim attended a performance of John Philip Sousa's Band at the Elicum Theater on March 18, his spirits were low and he began to slip back into his familiar melancholy.[33] Cole wrote:

> After our release from prison, Jim's precarious health and his inability to rejoin his family in Missouri combined to make fits of depression more frequent. While he was working for Major Elwin, instead of putting in his free afternoons among men or enjoying the sunshine and air which had so long been out of his reach, he would go to his room and revel in socialistic literature, which only overloaded a mind already surcharged with troubles.[34]

Although his claim that Jim's longing to return to Missouri was more a reflection of his own desires, Cole's assessment of Jim was accurate. Jim continued to read all he could about socialism, women's rights, and metaphysics. Although Jim had always liked to read and study controversial subjects, it's not known exactly why he was interested in these particular topics at this time. He may have simply had a keen interest in current affairs and found that deep knowledge of these subjects enabled him to put distance between himself and most people. If this was Jim's goal, it worked, and he continued to ignore necessary and healthy interaction with the outside world. Jim must have experienced a mood swing by April, however. He attended the Grand Opera in the Palace of the King and stated that his prospects were "very good."[35] Cole wrote about Jim: "When he was up, he was away up, and when down, away down. There was no half way place for Jim."[36]

By April, Cole finally had left the Interstate Institute to take a job with St. Paul chief of police John J. O'Connor. Cole went to work for O'Connor "looking after his home and the laborers" with wages "to be described in the future." He spent his evenings at the O'Connor home or down at police headquarters enjoying the comradery he found there. Cole also kept socially active by attending the preaching of Archbishop Ireland on Easter and going to political meetings, the theater and the Union Railroadmen's Ball.[37]

May seemed to be a routine month for the Younger brothers. Jim followed his solitary routine. Cole continued to enjoy working at O'Connor's and spending his evenings with the police officers downtown. He still didn't know what his salary was and claimed that he hadn't collected any pay since the beginning of his employment. Cole wrote: "I have been disappointed in not getting to work in cigar store before this but all will be well soon."[38] When Wolfer wondered if Cole's apparent idleness was a good thing, Cole had told Wolfer that O'Connor planned to set him up in a cigar and fruit stand near the Union Depot. In June, Cole wrote Whittier that he was the "boss of workmen" and that he performed odd jobs for O'Connor. Wolfer questioned Whittier as to the validity of Cole's job and wondered what was happening with the cigar and fruit stand.[39] Cole wrote Whittier that he was owed $100 by O'Connor and that he had been sick ten days after having "pas (a) gravel stone."

At the end of June, Cole attended a reunion of the 1st Minnesota Regiment.[40] The 1st Regiment proposed a drive for Cole's pardon. Cole remarked to the press: "We don't want to be in a hurry in this matter. I won't have anything to do with the plan, nor will I sanction it. The Board of Control, Warden Wolfer and the State Board of Pardons will be consulted first. When they are ready to act, they will."[41]

When Jim and Alix had earlier appealed to Wolfer, Wolfer told them that the board undoubtedly did not believe that enough time had yet passed to give the matter serious consideration and encouraged them to be patient.

Jim wrote to Wolfer in June that he was often asked about Cole's activities but that he didn't know anything about Cole. The questions left him in "an awkward and foolish position."[42] Wolfer wrote Jim that Cole was working for Police Chief O'Connor and said that he had assumed that Jim knew Cole's whereabouts.

In July, Cole continued work for O'Connor doing odd jobs. He still did not know his salary. He experienced another "gravel stone" but kept busy. He read the newspapers and selections from O'Connor's library. He also attended an old soldier's reunion and both the Republican and Democratic state conventions. He wrote to Whittier: "I am satisfied making a living all right and hoping for better."[43]

July was a terrible month for Jim. James Elwin sold out. The cigar store was closed, forcing Jim out of a job. Although he claimed that his room was paid through September 1, Jim had little money and no prospects for any future earnings. He wrote to Whittier: "I kneed work for I am better contented."[44] Jim wrote that he was plagued by ex-convicts wanting money. By letter, Alix encouraged Jim to try for a pardon again. Jim was once more turned down.

In August, Jim tried to supplement the $2 he had on hand by canvassing for office supplies. He claimed that he had walked thirty miles a day, talked himself "hoarse" and sold nothing. He had quit by August 20.[45] Jim reported his prospects as "gloomy" on his parole report and wrote to Wolfer about his finances. Jim said that he had read in the newspapers where "Bronaugh, Prather and Jones" had sent checks to him to help with his situation. He wrote, "They all talked [to the newspapers] but they forgot the check." He claimed that his nephew Charles Jones had sent him a check for $100 when he was sick but that Jim had heard so much about it in the newspapers that he wished the money had never been sent in the first place. Jim said that he wrote Elkins, Bronaugh, Prather, and "a few others" for money but he hadn't heard from anybody. Jim reported his board was high because of the difficulty he had finding food that he could eat. Additionally Jim wrote: "Cole, I hear, is sick, but I do not know where he lives, and would not like going around inquiring—so keep still."[46]

Since Cole had been living in St. Paul with O'Connor for some time and Wolfer had advised Jim, it is interesting that Jim claimed he did not know where Cole lived. It is likely the two brothers had not seen each other in several months. Cole later wrote to Lizzie Daniel that Jim was involved with no one other than Alix when he lived in Minnesota. Cole claimed that Jim never went out with anyone other than Alix and never went to a picnic, party, theater, or fair. Cole wrote that he attempted to get his brother to be more active and even sent him tickets for the theater. Cole stopped sending the tickets when he realized that Alix was encouraging Jim not to go out and was using the tickets herself.⁴⁷ Jim found little in common with Cole, and rather than listen to Cole's opinions on how he ought to live his life, Jim chose not to keep company with his brother. This bothered Cole, but he elected to leave Jim to his own interests, or lack of them, and tried to enjoy the life he had made for himself over the past year.

Jim wrote Whittier in September that he had taken a job with the Sam Johnston Insurance Company. He was waiting, however, for a license to be granted him and still did not have any money. He stated that a friend had sent him $7, although the friend's name was not mentioned. Jim was getting desperate.

On September 13, Jim invited Bronaugh, who was visiting the state, and B. G. Yates to his room at the Reardon Hotel in St. Paul to discuss his chances for a full and absolute pardon.⁴⁸ Jim told the men that he wanted more than anything to marry Alix (who still had not returned from Idaho) and live with her in Missouri. He had had enough of trying to fit into the Minnesota community and no longer wished to surrender his life and his fate to the Board of Pardons. He asked Bronaugh and Yates to visit Cole and talk to him about what could be done to change their situation. The following day, Bronaugh spent time alone with Jim at his hotel. Bronaugh wrote about Jim that day: "He gave every evidence of being greatly depressed, and appeared utterly broken down in spirit, in hope and in ambition." Bronaugh quoted Jim as saying: "I reckon a fellow might as well cut his throat and be done with it."⁴⁹

On September 29, Agent Whittier wrote to Warden Wolfer that he had at last been able to find a job for Jim with the F. R. Yerxa Company in St. Paul. Jim would either sell cigars or work as a salesman on the floor.⁵⁰ Wolfer was encouraged by this development and wrote Whittier:

> I am glad to hear that you have at last found employment for him and hope he can make a go of it. He seems to be nearly as helpless as a baby. I cannot understand how he has been able to support himself during the long period he has been out of employment unless he receives help from some source other than he has been able to provide for himself.⁵¹

Wolfer had doubts regarding Jim's future, however:

I think it might be well to keep in pretty close touch with him from now on and if he cannot hold his present position or something else that will enable him to support himself, I believe it would be a very good idea for him to return here until such time as something definite may be developed for him.[52]

Jim had moved to St. Paul in anticipation of employment with a company such as Yerxa's. A later article in the Kansas City *Star* mentioned that negotiations for the Yerxa position had fallen through. His hopes were dashed and the loss of work devastated Jim.

Cole said that he visited with Jim on Friday, October 16. How little Cole knew about his brother at that time is revealed in a statement he later made to the Kansas City *Star*: "We had a long talk. He appeared in his usual frame of mind and seemed to have ample money. He never intimated . . . that he considered his predicament sufficiently difficult."[53]

It is possible that Cole did not see Jim on that day or had not seen him for some time. Cole denied that he and Jim had not been on good terms, however. Cole told a reporter that he had not approved of Jim's petition for a full pardon in December and that he also did not approve of Jim's relationship with Alix. He claimed, however, that these feelings did not interfere with the brothers' relationship.[54]

Jim spoke to John Whitaker on Saturday, October 17. Whitaker, himself an insurance agent, said that Jim had told him that he had been ready to become a successful insurance agent when the company for which he was going to work informed him that they could not hire him. The reason for this was that as a paroled but not pardoned ex-convict, Jim's signature on policies could not be honored. According to Whitaker, the insurance company "found that Jim could not write insurance because he was supposed to be dead and his name on an application for insurance cut no more figure than a fly speck." Whitaker quoted Jim as saying:

I am a mere nothing in the world's affairs from now on, old man. I'm a ghost, the ghost of Jim Younger, who was a man, not an extra good one, but I'm nothing. Walkin' around here people might suppose I'm alive, and if it was on the square I could write insurance with the best of them, but I'm as dead as Caesar. The insurance company has informed me that it has satisfied itself of my legal non-existence.[55]

Evidently, Jim held onto the hope that this job would come through. When he was informed of his legal status by the insurance company, he actually felt that he was legally dead. This also was the case in regard to his desire to marry Alix. A paroled ex-convict could not sign his name to a marriage certificate. When Whitaker asked Jim why he didn't just go back to a job selling cigars, Jim replied:

This thing of standing behind a rail and playing polite to a lot of men who are worse at heart than I ever was is not to my liking . . . You see I'm hardly the same man I was when I went into the state prison. In the library I read nearly everything that was ever printed about the soul and its manifestations. The fact is that I believe there is nothing left of me but the soul I started with. I should like to win at something, but all the rest, Quantrill and the old game of fight and war, are just as remote as if they had been another man's experiences. If they would let me be Jim Younger, I'd start under the handicap and beat it before I quit.[56]

Late Saturday evening Jim sent a telegram to Alix in Boise. The message was brief: "Don't write."

At 8:00 the next morning, after having been up all night writing, Jim put a bullet through his head. On October 19, 1902, at the age of fifty-four, Jim Younger died. About 5:00 that evening, when Jim had not showed for either breakfast, lunch, or dinner, the hotel proprietor knocked on his door. Receiving no answer, he broke in the door. There was Jim's body, stretched on the floor beside his bed with a revolver clutched in his right hand. A newspaper account described his wound:

On the right hand side of the head, half-covered by the iron gray hair, was the wound. It was evidently made by an ill-directed shot, being located three inches above and slightly behind the ear. It is probable that Younger did not attempt to shoot himself in the temple, as do most revolver suicides. He secured a rest for his hand on his pillow and sent the bullet, indiscriminately, at his head. It is probable that he lived for some time after the shot had been fired. When the body was discovered the hand which held the revolver was stretched out beside the body. If death had been instantaneous the hand probably would have been found lying on the pillow. Coroner Miller is of the opinion that Younger suffered no pain after the shot, although life, according to all indications, remained in the body for several hours.[57]

On Jim's dresser lay an envelope stuffed with letters from Alix. On one side of the envelope Jim had written: "To all that is good and true I love and bid farewell. Jim Younger."[58] On the other side of the envelope was an additional message: "Oh, lassie, good-by. All relatives just stay away from me. No crocodile tears wanted. Reporters: Be my friends. Burn me up. Jim Younger."[59]

Next to the envelope Jim had placed a letter that he had written the night before. It was not directed to one specific person but seemed to be Jim's way of addressing everyone in his final hour. It read:

"October 18—Last night on earth—so good-by, lassie, for I still think of thee. A. U. G. Forgive me, for this is my only chance. I have done nothing wrong. But politics are all that Van Sant, Wolfer and others care for. Let the people judge. Treat me right and fair, reporters, for I am a square man. A Socialist and decidedly for woman's rights. Bryan is the brightest man these United States has ever produced. His one mistake was in not coming out for all the people and absolute socialism. Come out, Bryan. There is no such thing as a personal God. God is universal, and I know him well, and am not afraid. I have pity for the pardoning board: they do not stop to consider their wives or to think of the man who knows how to love and appreciate a friend in truth. Good-by, sweet lassie.

It is not known who told Cole about his brother's death. Word came down to the newspapers almost immediately that Cole was ill and bedridden. The next day, he would not show his face although he did make the following statement:

It is too bad. We have had so much trouble that it seems unusually hard to bear at this time. I believe Jim was temporarily insane. He had been acting queerly for months. Some of his actions could only be accounted for on the grounds that his mind had become weakened. The criticisms he made about Governor Van Sant and Warden

Wolfer in his last letter are awfully unwarranted. Warden Wolfer was our best friend, both while we were in prison and out. If it had not been for Warden Wolfer we would have still been in prison.[60]

Others who had known Jim the last few months of his life attributed his death to similar circumstances. Wolfer remarked that Jim had acted strangely for a long time and told reporters that he believed the bullet that had lodged near Jim's brain when he got shot in the mouth at Hanksa had caused his mind to slowly give way. John O'Connor claimed that Jim had been going insane slowly for a year. J. H. Schurmeier was quoted as saying that Jim's mind had been long impaired.[61]

Jim's body was taken to undertakers O'Halloran & Murphy. A large crowd gathered, anxious to see the former outlaw's body, but no one was allowed in except those who had a specific purpose. Alix sent a wire from Boise telling the undertakers that it had been Jim's desire to be cremated. Retta Younger Rawlins, however, sent word to those in charge of her brother's body that Jim was to be sent to Lee's Summit by train. Cole apparently deferred to his sister's wishes. The argument of whether or not Jim was to be cremated continued long after Jim's death. Cole later wrote: "I think the 'burn me up' was an admonition to the reporters. Jim always felt that the papers had been bitter to us, although some of them had been staunch supporters of the proposal to our parole."[62]

Alix wrote a letter to Lizzie Daniels in which she claimed that Jim's last wish had been for cremation and she did "not see how his relatives dared to overrule it." She believed that Jim had been consigned to "a lonely, unwished for, grave."[63] While Alix did not return to Minnesota at that time, somehow she was able to get the word to the press that she considered herself Jim's "widow in spirit."[64] Jim's body was claimed by his nephew-in law, C. B. Hull, and his casket was taken to the train station. The following morning, about 10:00, Jim Younger left for Kansas City at last aboard a Chicago, St. Paul, Minneapolis and Omaha baggage car.

After arrival in Missouri, Jim's casket was taken to the home of his niece and nephew, Mr. and Mrs. Nott Fenton in Lee's Summit. Mrs. Fenton was the daughter of Belle and Richard Hall. Jim's body was placed in the parlor of the Fenton home.

The funeral was held on Wednesday, October 22, at the Fenton house. At 10:30 that morning, the front door was closed to all but Jim's sisters and other close relatives. Retta, Laura, Belle, and Emma attended. Sally and Anne were unable to make the trip from their homes in Arkansas and Texas. A short "family-time" was held. Before the doors were opened to the throng of people waiting outside, Retta placed her hands on Jim's casket and remarked: "May God have mercy on the soul of my poor brother."[65]

At 11:00, a twenty-minute service was held. Rev. J. E. Hampton of the Baptist Church and Rev. S. F. Shiffler of the Presbyterian Church officiated. The choir sang "Rest, Weary, Rest" and the Reverend Hampton recited the Twenty-seventh and Ninetieth Psalms. Shiffler said a prayer in which he included Cole and Alix:

And we pray thee to remember the brother, who now sits in his lonely meditation upon the loss of a brother and a companion in the flesh, may he now turn unto thee and find thee as a brother and a friend who sticketh closer than even a brother; and we evoke thy tender mercies upon her who gave this one comfort by imparting unto him the affections of a human tender heart, and as she now grieves his loss, may she turn in her sorrow unto thee and pour out her soul and all that is within her to the praise and glory of thy holy name and may she love thee even greater than him who now has fallen.[66]

The choir then sang the same song that had been sung at Bob's funeral, "We Shall Know Each Other There." About 150 people formed a line and passed Jim's casket. One of the newspapers described what they saw:

Instead of looking upon an unshaven face, with broad and high cheek bones, they saw the features of a meek, mild appearing man, with a growth of beard four inches long tinged with gray. The forehead was high and the head partially bald. The skin back of the right ear, where the fatal bullet entered, was bruised and blackened.[67]

Pallbearers William Gregg, George Wigginton, J. S. Whitsett, O. H. Lewis, Frank Gregg, and Dr. M. C. Miller carried Jim's casket to a waiting hearse. Twenty-two vehicles followed the body to the Lee's Summit Cemetery. Former Quantrill men, marching two abreast, preceded the cortege: Jackson Corder, A. J. Little, Edward Strode, T. W. Webb, Robert Webb, Harrison Trow, James Hulse, Warren Welsh, Samuel Constable, and L. J. Brown.

Reporters remarked later that it was interesting that nothing was really said about the deceased. Neither his virtues nor his shortcomings were discussed. The past was not mentioned. The only relevant comment that was heard was uttered by one of Jim's sisters as the earth was shoveled into his grave: "Poor Jim; he wanted to come back to Missouri, and he had to kill himself to have his heart yearnings gratified."[68]

Alix Muller did not attend, probably because of her disagreement with the handling of Jim's remains. If she had wanted, Jim's sisters were reported to have said they might possibly open his grave for her.[69]

Jim Younger had at last returned home to Missouri. He lay under the shade of the trees and the quiet sounds of the soft Missouri breeze with his brother Bob and their mother Bursheba. Another chapter in the lives of Henry Younger's sons had come to a close.

After Jim's death Alix wrote a letter to Cole's friend Lizzie Daniel asking details about his burial and gravesite. She asked Lizzie to place a wreath of flowers on Jim's grave at Christmas. Lizzie's daughter complied with Alix's wishes.

In February, 1904, Alix joined her step-brother Arthur Muller in Oklahoma City, where she kept house for him. She was writing *Lives of Great Men and Women* when she died there in April of that year.[70]

23

Back to Missouri: Cole Alone

I do not want to be received as a hero for I am a hero of nothing.
    —Cole Younger on receiving word that he could
                    return to Missouri

After Jim's body was safely interred in the family plot in Lee's Summit, Cole began to go about his business, or lack of it, as usual. He stayed in the employ of Chief O'Connor, although he wrote Whittier that he hoped for "better things." The Younger family could not bear the thought of Cole living in Minnesota without family. Jeanette Duncan, eldest of Sally and Jep's children, persuaded her husband, Charles Breed Hull from Knobnoster, Missouri, to move their family to Minnesota so that they would be close to her Uncle Cole. Hull had already bestowed many favors on the Younger brothers while they were in Minnesota. He agreed to take up residence in St. Paul until Cole could obtain a pardon and return home to Missouri. Cole moved in with the Hulls at their home at 551 State Street.

With the death of Jim, Cole's closest friend became his former comrade Frank James. Although Cole and Frank had not spoken or corresponded in twenty-seven years, they kept in touch through mutual friends. One of these contacts was Wal Bronaugh.[1] Bronaugh visited with James on several occasions during the Younger parole drive and also relayed messages from Cole. Writer John Trotwood Moore, Lizzie Daniel's son-in-law, wrote an eloquent and persuasive article for the Nashville *American* in June, 1903, regarding Cole. Frank wrote to Moore, congratulating the author on his true account and closed with these words: "Were I called to deliver a eulogy at your bier, would say among other things, as virtue is to woman as azure to the skys, truth and chivildry is to Trotwood Moore."[2]

Throughout the end of October and during the month of November, Cole claimed that he was ill with his "gravel" condition but expressed the belief that he would "soon be o.k." Cole spent his evenings with his niece and nephew and read the daily newspapers as well as fiction books and magazines. Although he claimed that "all has been peace and good will with [me]," he also wrote that he "would like to return to [my] childhood home."[3] Minnesota had claimed the lives of two of his brothers. Cole was anxious to live out his last days back in Missouri, where the presence of a few of his old friends and many of his relatives would bring him comfort.

Cole continued to have health problems the following month. He wrote that he was plagued by grippe and had also suffered a sinus cold and cough. He believed that the inclement weather of Minnesota was not conducive to good health in a man his age. He claimed that all was "O.K." with his employment but wrote that his work was "nothing at present." He continued to list O'Connor as his employer.[4]

Cole was happy living with the Hulls and spent his first Christmas in twenty-seven years at home with his family, even if that home was in Minnesota. Although Jim certainly must have been on Cole's mind, his holiday was one of the best he had experienced in years. The Hull children adored their Uncle Cole, and Cole was delighted to be in the company of the young people.

By the first of the year, Cole still had not resumed working. He continued to be bothered with grippe, and his rheumatism had flared again. He wrote to Whittier that he had been "doctoring for gravel and grippe." He managed to get out a little more that month and attended meetings of both houses of the Minnesota legislature. He also went to a revival meeting and enjoyed a visit with the Reverend Cressey.[5]

Cole Younger made his final request for a pardon in January, 1903. His request read:

1. Because of ill health and the severity of the Northern climate, which is very hard on him because of his age and infirmities, now being nearly sixty years old.

2. Because he has really and truly reformed and has given evidence of his desire and purpose to live an honest, self-supporting life.

3. For the further reason that he finds it difficult to earn a living in this severe climate, and especially away from his friends and relatives.

4. Because he is ready and willing to submit to any limitations or restrictions that the honorable Board of Pardons, in its wisdom, may think best to impose, so long as he may be permitted to enjoy his freedom and rights of citizenship with his friends and relatives in Missouri.

5. And for the further reason that he now feels more keenly than ever before the loss of friends and relatives since the death of his brother, James H. Younger, and prays that the honorable Board of Pardons may grant this humble petition in order that he may return to his old home and his friends and relatives, there to end his days in peace and quiet.

In January, the quarterly meeting of the Board of Pardons was held. Many in attendance believed that it was time for Cole to be granted a conditional pardon, which would allow him to return to the state of Missouri. Others thought that his employment and activities should continue to be closely monitored. Many felt that the consideration of a pardon for Cole was due to sympathy over the death of Jim. Once again, the Board of Pardons voted against any progressive decisions on Cole's behalf. The meeting caused an uproar in the community, as such lack of action was seen as a backlash against the ex-convict. Cole was now fifty-nine years old. Most people who commented on the situation did not see what harm would come to the state of Minnesota or its people if the older man were now allowed to return to Missouri to peacefully live out his days.

A special meeting of the Board of Pardons was held on February

4, 1903. The board voted unanimously to allow Cole Younger a conditional pardon and the opportunity to return to his childhood home. The conditions of the pardon Cole would sign emphasized that Cole could not place himself on exhibition in any way and that he leave Minnesota for Missouri at once, never to return to Minnesota of his own volition again.

During the morning the Board of Pardons met, Cole decided to engage in some public relations and visited the offices of one of the city's major newspapers. He talked with the staff of the St. Paul *Dispatch* and was headed for other offices when he was approached by a reporter from the Kansas City *Star*. "You're free, Cole," the reporter told him. Cole replied, "Thank God. At last it's come." Cole informed the reporter that he was going to the telegraph office, and the reporter accompanied him. As the two men walked, Cole stated the following:

> I have just as warm friends here as I have in Jackson County. I want you to send my regards to my sister and my friends and especially to H. Clay Daniels of Kansas City. I shall probably not leave St. Paul before Saturday or Sunday, as there are some formalities to be completed yet. Say that I am in good health and feeling jubilant. I expect to engage in business after I reach Lee's Summit and have had a good visit with my sister, Mrs. Hall, and my old acquaintances. I do not want any demonstration when I arrive and will drop in as quietly as possible. I do not want to be received as a hero for I am a hero of nothing.[6]

When Cole arrived at the telegraph office, he sent a wire to his friend Horace Greeley Perry, telling her the good news.[7] The little girl who had ridden with the outlaw when he was breaking in his horse in preparation of the Minnesota robbery had grown up to become a noted newspaper woman. Perry was a champion of the Younger parole and became very good friends with Cole over the years. At one point, there was talk of them being something more than friends, and Perry's family had become alarmed. Both Ms. Perry and Cole insisted this was not the case and the friendship continued. When Cole asked the reporter to send word to "H. Clay Daniel of Kansas City," he was letting Daniel's wife, Lizzie Brown, know his good news. After sending the telegram to the young woman, Cole rushed home to the Hulls to share the good news and make arrangements for his return home to Missouri.

Cole was numb with the news of his pardon. A long, hard battle had been waged, lasting far longer than the Civil War. At last the old guerrilla was going home. He bid his Minnesota friends farewell and boarded a train. He arrived in Missouri on February 16, 1903. Niece Nora Hall and her brother Harry Younger Hall met Cole at the Union Station in Kansas City. There they all boarded a train for Lee's Summit and arrived at the Missouri Pacific Depot there in the afternoon. A large crowd allotted Cole the hero's welcome that he said he shunned. They followed him to Browning's Dry Goods Store, where his niece bought him a pair of rubbers to help him walk through the snow drifts that had formed the night before.[8] He continued on to the hotel run by his niece Nettie Hall and her husband A. G. Donahew. He met with family and friends for the next few days. The town of Lee's Summit was happy to have Cole back. On February 20, that town's paper ran the following editorial:

> Of course the overshadowing local event in Lee's Summit this week has been the presence of the historical Coleman Younger. When he and his brother were paroled from the Minnesota state prison with restrictions, this paper took the ground that the pardon ought to have been full, so they could return to their old friends in Missouri, not that we sympathized with or endorsed any of their misdeeds, but because they were sentenced for those acts, and the punishment having been considered sufficient in the time served it was only just there should be a full pardon.[9]

In telling about Cole's reception, the *Journal* continued:

> Of course he has been kindly greeted by relatives and such few of his old friends yet remaining about the home of his youth. There were also hundreds of the curiously disposed who have sought him. Very modestly and becomingly he has avoided as much as possible any of the latter and is endeavoring as much as possible to comply with the terms of his release.[10]

Cole attempted to settle into yet another new lifestyle and visit with every old friend who was still alive and in the area. He enjoyed the stream of visitors and spent little time discussing himself. Cole was more interested in learning of the changes that had occurred since the last time he had visited Lee's Summit. Former U. S. Senator John Ryder described Cole as he prepared to begin his life anew in Missouri:

> When you see Cole Younger you will see the frame of a robust man. I reckon he must have been a powerful athlete in the vigorous days of old. He looks rather strong yet, but when you get to observing his movements, after you have looked him good in the eye a few times, you will realize that he is a man who has passed through thousands of trying days; that he is aging fast. My notion is that if he can step off the train and greet possibly two or three close and loving ones of his own, go quietly away with only a few lovelighted eyes beaming on him, to a snug hearth in a home full of welcome rest, safety, peace in a satisfied heart—he will do just that thing.[11]

One of the first places Cole visited after catching up with his family was Kansas City. Cole called on his old friend Lizzie Daniel on February 19. He was quoted as having said: "I call her my 'old sweetheart' but that is as far as my attachment ever went. We were good friends, so I want to see her, for until I do I will not be able to realize fully that I am again home."[12] Whether or not Cole and Lizzie ever visited after February, Lizzie's family claims that the next letter she received from Cole was dated June 16, 1914.[13]

Wal Bronaugh met with Cole in April. Bronaugh took Cole down to Clinton, where he visited with a few of his parents' friends and some of the men with whom he had fought the war.[14] This may have been the last time Wal Bronaugh and Cole Younger kept company. Once Cole returned to Missouri, it seemed almost as if he had forgotten Wal Bronaugh's massive efforts to help him and his brothers. Exactly why this might be so is perplexing. Neither Cole nor Jim ever had much to say about Bronaugh or his efforts either while they were in prison or even after their release. Interviews where Cole or Jim publicly thanked Bronaugh or, at the very least, praised him for his efforts on their behalf seem nonexistent. Cole's friend Todd George wrote many years later: "I have often, in later years, wondered why Cole had never mentioned a Mr. Bronaugh of Clinton, Missouri, who did make quite an effort to secure the pardon of the Younger boys. I do not know of anyone who ever heard Cole discuss Mr. Bronaugh."[15]

Harry Hoffman wrote: "Cole said he didn't think much of Bronaugh. 'Jim and I always thought he kept us in prison several years longer than necessary—because he was collecting money from our friends in Missouri, to pay his (supposed) expenses in his efforts to get us pardoned.' Cole was never friendly with Bronaugh after he returned to Mo."[16]

If what Hoffman said was true, it seems a very strange view of a man who worked tirelessly for so many years with very little reward. One would be hard pressed to see how Bronaugh's alleged mismanagement of funds could have been possible given the real expenses he must have incurred through his many visits to various legislators and prominent men both in Missouri and Minnesota.

In 1905, Bronaugh published a book about his trials and tribulations during the years he attempted to help the Youngers entitled *The Youngers Fight for Freedom*. The information contained in the book seems very accurate, and Bronaugh does not focus wholly on his achievements by any means. Neither does he indicate that there was any problem with Cole. His manuscript includes copies of several of Cole's letters to him throughout the years. Cole is quoted as having written very flattering things to Bronaugh, including the following excerpts:

On May 17, 1889: "There are but a few Edwards on earth, neither are there many Bronaughs, for your disinterested friendship has been more Christlike than any man's I ever knew. I regret that I am not more worthy but hope to live to prove that I know how to appreciate the noble friend you have been to us."[17]

On March 26, 1893: "I congratulate myself upon the fact that we have the best friend in the world. No one has a better, and but few his equal."

In a letter dated 1899, the subject of money is addressed. Cole wrote:

> If I had got one or two hundred dollars to pay expenses I would have got out last winter all right, notwithstanding the newspaper talk about the people in Missouri sending forty-five thousand to help me. The facts are as you know, I have never received one dollar from any one in Missouri, except from my nephews to pay ex-

penses. That old mayor that fought us when you were up here, fought us before the legislature in a speech before the committee of the house. He said there was no money being used to corrupt a Minnesota house as they did in Missouri. He said Bronaugh told him he had spent ten thousand dollars, traveled ten thousand miles and worked ten years in Missouri and would put in the same in Minnesota. But I knew he lied and I told them that you never made any such statement; that you would not have made any such statement even if it were true, for you had sense enough to know that such talk would hurt us.[18]

Bronaugh made no reply to this letter in his book. Whether or not there was an actual problem between Cole and Bronaugh remains unclear. Perhaps on that last visit to Clinton, Cole discussed his plans for the future with Bronaugh. Bronaugh may have been aghast at Cole's ideas and firmly told him so.

Todd George formed his own insurance and real estate business soon after Cole arrived back in Lee's Summit. Cole enjoyed sitting around George's office downtown visiting with the men and women of the town as they passed by. George would also take Cole with him as he canvassed the area around Lee's Summit. Cole enjoyed these outings very much. Cole and George were approached by a promoter with an offer to go into business with him financing an electric trolley line between Kansas City and Lee's Summit. However, after much of their work was accomplished, Cole and George never saw the man again.[19] Cole began to realize that he was not just being paranoid when he thought there might be people waiting to approach him with the idea of making a fast buck off his notoriety.

Sometime during the first few months after he returned to Missouri, Cole had been in contact himself with Frank James. The two men considered going into business together although in a manner different from their previous associations. Wild West shows were very popular at this time. In fact, Warden Wolfer had been approached by a couple of these organizations asking that he allow the Youngers to participate while they were on parole. Frank James and Cole Younger seemed like naturals for such a venture. However, the major part of Cole's pardon stipulated that he was not to display himself in public for profit.

Rumors of a Younger-James Wild West Show began to be heard in Minnesota. When Cole's friend and parole champion R. C. Dunn heard them, he wrote Cole a letter. He appealed to Cole to do nothing that would jeopardize his pardon. Dunn cautioned him not to change the feeling of all of the people in Minnesota who had been his friends by blatantly ignoring the conditions upon which he had been allowed to return to Missouri. Cole answered Dunn:

> I have carefully considered the substance of your letter and would certainly feel very sorry if I thought you believed for a moment that I intended to break any promise made to the authorities in Minnesota, or to anyone else. I assure you I shall keep every promise that I have made, and my friends in Minnesota will have no reason to complain of any action which I may take. I do not intend to exhibit myself as an actor or participate in any public entertainment nor do I intend to allow myself to be so exhibited.[20]

If that had been the end of the letter, Dunn and other of Cole's friends and sponsors in Minnesota would have been placated. However, the remainder of the letter demonstrated that not only had the subject of a Wild West show been raised to Cole but that he was already committed to participation:

> I do not believe, however, that the state officials in your state, or anybody in Minnesota want to prevent me from making an honest living. The show with which I will be connected will in no way refer to my life, or the life of any of my associates, but will be of an educational and moral order, very much like Buffalo Bill's Wild West Show, which, as you know, is in every way unobjectionable and has always been patronized by good people.[21]

Cole justified his desire to participate in such a show, regardless of the conditions of his pardon, in the following manner:

> When I returned to my home in Missouri I found myself broken in health and old age rapidly coming on and without any trade or occupation. This was not the worst of it, as I have aged women relatives who have been looking to me for support but instead of being a source of support to them it looked as if I had become to them a source of expense and a burden.[22]

It is unlikely that, after twenty-seven years, any of Cole's sisters expected him to take care of them financially. They all had large families of their own. The matter of Cole joining a theatrical production seems very much in character of the Cole of pre-Stillwater years. Back on his own turf, Cole obviously felt that he could twist the conditions of his pardon to suit his own purposes and desires. In the days of old, when Cole had wanted to do something, he simply did it. In his old age, Cole seemed to be regressing to his former self-centeredness. Cole further stated in his letter to Dunn:

> While I have no occupation or trade, you will realize that my experience with horses and my long army experience of handling bodies of men have in some way fitted me to be manager of such a show as I have described, and in this way enables me to make an honorable and honest living and properly support those who are dependent on me. It was with this intention that I have made the business arrangement which has been spoken of in all the newspapers. It is distinctly stipulated in my contract that I shall do nothing to break the conditions of my pardon, and the people with whom I have connected myself would be the last ones in the world to ask me to break any agreement which I have made. I shall not in any way be paraded or exhibited in public and shall have nothing to do with the giving of entertainment.[23]

To Cole's way of thinking, all he was going to do was lend his name to the production, thus not exhibiting himself or breaking any of the pardon agreements. To Warden Wolfer and the Board of Pardons, however, such an association was exactly what they had in mind when they wrote those stipulations to Cole's release from parole. They did not want Cole to capitalize on his fame. Cole, of course, interpreted the clause differently and made plans for the future.

Cole had been writing his memoirs since his release from prison. During the first couple of months in Lee's Summit, he put the finishing touches to what he called the "true and factual account" of his life. His book, *Cole Younger By Himself*, was published. Very little in the book was true or factual. However, the book made for very interesting reading. It contained many stories related to Cole's glory days during the war and very little about his outlaw days except detailed denials of nearly every robbery in which he had participated. The book included the lecture that Cole had prepared when he was living with the Hulls in St. Paul. Cole had desperately wanted to tour the country with his talk "What My Life Has Taught Me," but Wolfer and the Board of Pardons did not approve the venture. The lecture was saved for publication in Cole's book and later would be given to interested listeners all over the midwest and southwest.

In the meantime, Cole and Frank had decided to lend their names and services to a company formed by entrepreneurs Val Huffman and H. E. Allot. The company became The Cole Younger and Frank James Wild West Company. A tour was planned, and Frank and Cole were called on to act as integral members of the production. Frank James would serve as a master of ceremonies, and Cole, because of his pardon restrictions, would appear "behind the scenes." Cole was given the title of manager, but his work was not entirely behind the scenes. As manager, it was not unusual for Cole to be at the door where he could see all, and where all could see him.

Frank James had been involved in theatrical productions before. Since his acquittals, Frank had held several jobs. At one point, he toured for fifteen months with a production company involved with the play *Across the Desert*. In his autobiography, Cole stated his purpose for becoming involved with the Wild West show: "The 'Cole Younger and Frank James Historical Wild West Show' is an effort on the part of two men whose exploits have been wildly exaggerated, perhaps more than those of any other men living, to make an honest living and demonstrate to the people of America that they are not as they have been painted.[24] The show was billed as a historical Wild West presentation and claimed to be "The World's Greatest Exhibition." The bill included "Russian Cassocks. Bedouin Arabs, American Cowboys, Roosevelt Rough Riders, Indians, Cubans, Western Girls, Mexicans, Broncos, Overland Stage Coach, Emigrant Train, The Siege of Deadwood and the World's Mounted Warriors." The latter were advertised as being "led by the great Cole Younger and Frank James, who will personally appear at every performance."[25] It appears that the folks in Minnesota did have something to complain about.

It doesn't seem likely that Cole and Frank were involved in the selection of talent or the hiring of the crew. The tour began in Chicago.[26] As they traveled the midwest, there began to be trouble with the rowdies associated with the show. On May 24, in Memphis, Tennessee, two of the "Rough Riders" got into a fight after celebrating payday at one of the local saloons. Eugene Scully and Charles Burrows engaged in a fistfight until Scully drew a gun and attempted to shoot Burrows. Their friends tried to pull Burrows out of the path of the bullet but it grazed the man's leg. Scully was arrested on charges of carrying a loaded pistol and for assault with intent to kill.[27] The Younger-James Wild West Show rolled on.

Perhaps Cole had second thoughts about his "exhibition." On May 26, the Memphis *Commercial Appeal* complained that little was seen of either James or Younger and the only involvement between the show and the former outlaws seemed to be the use of their names.[28]

Cole was happy to give interviews while he traveled with the production, although James was more reluctant. Cole had, after all, been giving interviews for the past twenty-seven years. During one such talk with a reporter in Nashville, Cole continued the myth that the James brothers had not been present at Northfield. Cole stated:

> There were eight of us in the party: myself, my brothers Jim and Bob, Chadwell and Miller, those two being killed in the fight at Northfield, Pitts, Woods and Howard. Of course, Woods and Howard were assumed names. The real names of those two men will never be known. They belonged to good families, and their people are now respected and honored, and I will never say a word to hurt them by telling the names of these men. I will say, though, that the James boys were not with me in this raid, and we never were together in any other. Every member of that raiding party except myself is now dead.[29]

During that same interview, Frank James revealed his plans for the future:

> I am going this season with our show, and then I am going to retire. I saw a chance by doing this to feather my nest in my old age. I am

going to buy a farm when this season ends, and then settle down there to pass the rest of my days in peace and quiet.[30]

One Sunday during May in Nashville, police arrested ten men associated with the show for being involved in an illegal crap game on the grounds of the production.[31] Cole and Frank were questioned by the police, as it was assumed that they were the owners of the show. The questioning was discontinued when it was determined that they were not the proprietors.[32]

By June, the entire operation was beginning to fall apart. The men involved with the show were constantly accused of running scams and schemes. The show itself was criticized as being poorly produced and boring. The enterprise continued, though, as the bookings had been arranged many months in advance. The gate, however, was most times slight, and the owners of the show, in addition to Cole and Frank, were not earning a great deal of money. Editorials began to appear condemning the show, the performers, and the operators. Cole and Frank were criticized for allowing themselves to be associated with such an inferior production. Most newspapers who reviewed the show mentioned that the former outlaws, who had been the most feared in the nation, were now reduced to caricatures of themselves. One newspaper wrote: "Such shows should, in our opinion, be suppressed. The younger generation sees men of world wide notoriety as criminals exhibited and hailed as heroes. The influence upon children is undoubtedly bad."[33]

By this time, Cole was once more actively involved in the nightly performances. That same newspaper noted: "Cole Younger did not appear in the performance but walked around in the tent . . . Frank James took a prominent part in the exhibition."[34]

On September 12, Warden Wolfer received a letter from W. F. Wiggens of Studebaker Brothers Manufacturing Company. Wiggins claimed that his company held a bill owed by the Wild West show but didn't know where to find either Cole or Frank.[35] He thought the warden might know. Wolfer was incensed. He had been furious with Cole for becoming involved in the first place and was particularly angered that anyone might think that Cole's actions were sanctioned by the prison officials. He had written to

Cole demanding that he stop his participation in the show but the letters never seemed to reach Cole. Since the production did not enter the state of Minnesota, there was little Wolfer or the Board of Pardons could do. Wolfer, who had been so very helpful to the Younger parole, felt personally offended. Cole had not been home yet a year and already he was cashing in on his notoriety. Wolfer and others who had considered themselves Cole's friends were disgusted by his involvement with the Wild West Show.

By late September, the production had wound its way back to Missouri. Cole visited St. Clair County for the first time in over twenty-eight years when the show played in Osceola. The visit must have been difficult for him, as it had to have reminded him of the brothers lost along the way. Most of the friends Cole had known there were now gone. He visited the old homesteads of his grandfather and uncles to see that much had changed. John Younger's grave remained the same, however. The marker stood where John had been buried at an angle.

Unfortunately, there were problems in St. Clair also. Since the draw was not what was expected, a "scuffle" was arranged between Cole, Frank, and a third man. The third fellow was arrested by Osceola Mayor Housely for disturbing the peace.[36] It was later admitted that the fisticuffs had been planned.

In Appleton City on September 21, Cole and Frank confronted the management of the production with the claim that they were not being paid all that had been agreed upon. Both Cole and Frank "withdrew" from the production and demanded that their names not be used for advertisement. Huffman and Allot swore out a warrant for the arrest of the two on the grounds of breach of contract. Younger and James, claiming the management was committing a fraud, threatened a warrant. Evidently, all charges were eventually dropped and the production continued.

Things came to a head in November when the show played in Illinois. By this time, both Cole and Frank said that they no longer had any complaints against the North and that they didn't even differentiate between Northerners and Southerners any more. Frank James was quoted as having said:

> I have no bitterness against anyone who wore the blue . . . the fierce spirit of the rebellion has all died out of my nature and I am willing

to forgive and forget. My son wore the blue in the Spanish-American War, and when he put it on it looked beautiful and brave. I hated it no longer. For years, I wanted to feel for my pistol when I saw it, but I love everybody. Even my old mother, eighty years old, has forgiven those who caused her to suffer so deeply by the cruel war.[37]

Such sentiments certainly helped the production to play better in the Northern states. Illinois was to be about the last stop of the season for the venture. In a little town there, Allot decided to leave the show for a few days. Huffman was left in charge. According to Allot, the following series of events occurred. Some $9,000 of the production's profits were to be placed in the bank for safe keeping. Cole convinced Huffman that the money would be safer if a draft were made out to Allot. Huffman agreed. Cole was to handle the transaction. Instead of having the draft made out to Allot, however, Cole had it made out to himself. When Allot returned, he called on the bank and was told what Cole had done. Allot confronted Cole, and Cole told him that the draft was safe in one of the production cars. After the conversation took place, Cole took the bank draft, left the production, and went to Mexico, Missouri.

Allot followed Cole and located him in a hotel. When Cole failed to answer Allot's repeated knocks upon his hotel room door, Allot broke the door down. Seeing who it was, Cole dove for a .45 pistol that he had hidden beneath his pillow. He pointed the gun at Allot's head and Allot retreated. Cole then gave the draft to an attorney in the town, telling him that it was the subject of a business misunderstanding. Cole instructed the attorney to give the draft to Allot. The attorney complied. Allot later claimed that Cole had violated his pardon by having the gun and should be arrested. Nothing was ever charged against Cole, for it was his word against Allot's.[38] Allot bought out Huffman's interest in the Wild West show in December, 1903. As far as Cole and Frank James were concerned, the show was over.

24

The War Is Over

I've accomplished one of the things I set out to do at
any rate, and the greatest of them.
            —Cole Younger, 1913

Cole returned to Lee's Summit to live with the Halls in 1904.
Tired of being the main attraction in a circus atmosphere, he
decided to go into business for himself. Briefly, with the backing
of undetermined parties, Cole became the president of the Hydro-
Carbon Oil Burner Company.[1] Cole traveled around Missouri
visiting friends and talking up the company. That seems to have
been the extent of his involvement. He tired of that venture very
soon.

Cole wrote to Warden Wolfer on November 14, 1904, for the
first time in over a year. He mentioned nothing about his ventures
into show business nor acted as if Wolfer might have had any
reason whatsoever to be upset with him. He asked that Wolfer
intercede on his behalf to help him gain an unconditional pardon.[2]
Wolfer did not respond. Cole enjoyed his time back from his
travels by spending the next few months visiting with friends and
family and telling his war stories to a new generation of listeners.

By August, Cole was back in business. He felt that the idea of
an electric railroad was a good one when it had been presented to
him and Todd George in 1903, even if the man who had presented
it had evidently not been legitimate. The Kansas City, Lee's
Summit and Eastern Railroad was created in August, 1905. The

company was chartered in Jefferson City, and Cole was elected president of the construction company. Others involved included W. L. A. Summit, A. Philips, W. F. Johnson, J. J. Appersen, and L. M. Branham.[3] The project had been funded in New York and Chicago and was to become operational by January 1, 1906. Cole stated:

> As a boy, I got acquainted with every foot of the ground which our road will run. Later in life I made a great deal of trouble in that neighborhood and now I want, in a way, to make amends by seeing that my old friends and neighbors have facilities for bringing their hogs, cattle and corn to market.[4]

Cole's involvement in the venture eventually fell through. He found that he was not quite the businessman he thought he could be. He had difficulty keeping up with all the intricacies of the management of the company. Although Cole was brought into the project mainly as a spokesman and a front to gain support in the area, he decided to terminate his association when he began to wonder if the information he was to disseminate was accurate. Cole did not want to be further involved in a business he knew very little about. He did not want to place himself in the position of being taken advantage of again, whether or not that was the intent of the men who owned and operated the railway. Cole decided at this point that perhaps his days as a businessman should end.

Disregarding all the unfortunate incidents that had occurred with the previous production with which he had been involved, Cole decided to continue his career in show business. He joined the Lew Nichols Carnival Company, where he performed most of the same duties he had with the Younger-James venture. Cole stayed with the Nichols show, where he would also appear as a "guest" night after night.

When Bronaugh got ready to have his book published, he solicited photographs of the many people who had been involved in the Younger parole effort. One of the people he approached for this purpose was Warden Wolfer. On February 9, 1905, Wolfer responded to Bronaugh's request with a very interesting letter. Wolfer had been extremely annoyed with Cole's association with the Younger-James Wild West Show and Cole's continued involvement with show business through the Lew Nichols Carnival. He never forgave Cole for disregarding his pardon restrictions and assuming that now that he was free of Minnesota he could do as he pleased. Wolfer felt that Cole had disappointed and made fools of all of the people in Minnesota who had placed their trust in him and worked so hard for his parole and eventual pardon. Wolfer wrote Bronaugh that he did not want his photograph in a book having anything whatsoever to do with Cole Younger or his affairs. Wolfer wrote:

> I am not especially proud of what little I had to do with the release on parole and final pardon of the Youngers. This feeling comes in light of experience I have had since the final release of Cole Younger. To my mind, he has demonstrated very conclusively that he was not entitled to the confidence placed in him by the best friends he ever had in the State of Minnesota.[5]

Wolfer claimed that he was not the only person in Minnesota who felt that way. He wrote:

> If Younger cherishes his freedom and wishes to remain as free as possible without any entanglements, I would advise him, and his friends in Missouri, that he had better keep out of the lines of the State of Minnesota. This frank and blunt statement may come to you somewhat as a surprise but it is a plain statement of my feelings as well as that of thousands of others, and among them some of the best and staunchest friends that Cole Younger ever had in the State of Minnesota.[6]

Since Wolfer had answered Bronaugh's letter, he now thought it only right that he reply to Cole's earlier letter. He sent Cole a copy of the letter he wrote Bronaugh, stating in his letter to Cole, "I think it due you to send you a copy of this letter as I do not believe in saying anything behind one's back that I am not willing to say to his face."[7] Wolfer wrote Cole that he had not answered his letter for two reasons: because he did not want to hurt his feelings unnecessarily and because he hoped that by his silence Cole would get the message that Wolfer was upset with him. Wolfer wasted no words when he wrote:

I see that you are still counting on more help from Minnesota and that you expect those who once took a friendly interest in you to help you still more. I, for one, will not do it. In my opinion, you have already received much more than you are entitled to. You have not only violated the spirit of your pardon but you have, by your conduct, outraged every principle of manhood. Among your old Missouri friends you once had the reputation of being a brave man, but your treatment of Minnesota and your old friends in this state convinces me you are a coward.[8]

Wolfer's letter was evidently released to the press so that his position in regard to Cole Younger would be plainly understood by anyone who may have wished him to be further involved with his former prisoner. Cole was once again a topic of conversation and debate in Minnesota. The warden of the U. S. Penitentiary at Leavenworth, Kansas, R. W. McClaughgary, wrote to the Stillwater warden in support of Wolfer's letter: "He [Cole] deserved a good warming since it is not possible now to give him the good hanging that he ought to have had years ago."[9]

Although Cole didn't really see what all the fuss was about, he decided not to further irritate his former friends in Minnesota who felt that he had disregarded the terms of his pardon. He let the matter of a complete pardon drop. On March 16, the Kansas City *Journal* reported that "Cole Younger has renounced the show business."[10] The reasons stated, however, had nothing to do with Wolfer's letter or the terms of Cole's pardon. Cole is quoted as saying that it was beyond his ability to keep his associates "straight." Cole stated: "I could have made good money out of the show, if I could have kept them fellers straight. I was talking to Pinkerton down at St. Louis the other day, and he told me that they would rather have $1 that they stole than $10 that they had made honestly."[11]

The *Journal* editorialized:

The spectacle of Cole Younger as the champion of ethical business methods and complaining bitterly that he is unable to keep his "fellers straight" is novel and only emphasizes vividly that changes have been wrought in commercial enterprises in the West during the past quarter of a century. There was a time when there had been no trouble in the dividing of profits among his associates.[12]

Although Cole may have claimed to this newspaper that he was giving up show business, he continued to be associated with the Nichols Carnival through 1908. He traveled with Nichols several months out of the year, his job being to introduce "Cole Younger's Coliseum," a display of riders who performed horse-related tricks and feats. Nichols was apparently much more respected than anyone who had been involved with the Younger-James show and Cole never complained about being owed funds from this enterprise. One of his relatives claimed that at one point, when Nichols was running behind with the payroll due to poor attendance, Cole wired home to Lee's Summit for $600, which he loaned Nichols. The loan was repaid.[13]

After he quit the Nichols Carnival for good, Cole would continue to get offers from various Wild West shows to join their productions, as would Frank James.[14] However, both men were through with circus and carnival performances and set their sights on what they really wanted to do with their lives as their final years fell upon them.

By 1909, Cole decided that he was ready to do that which he had planned to do many years before in Minnesota. He talked to his family and decided that the time was right to put together a lecture tour where he could deliver his talk "What My Life Has Taught Me." Cole wrote:

> I had hoped that if my pardon had been made unconditional, to earn a livelihood on the lecture platform. I had prepared a lecture which I do not think would have harmed any one, while it might have impressed a valuable lesson on those who took it to heart.[15]

A fellow by the name of Comstock, who had lived in Lee's Summit while operating the Lee's Summit Flour Mill, arranged a limited tour for Cole. Cole's manager was to be L. A. Von Ericksen. Rowland Marquette, Cole's great-niece's husband, accompanied Cole as his assistant. The small group traveled throughout the midwest, south, and southwest. Although plans to tour Colorado, California, and even the Alaska-Yukon Exposition apparently fell through, Cole did make multitudinous appearances, and his lecture was well received.[16] Postcards came to Cole's family from all over. Every small town and every major city throughout

Missouri, Oklahoma, and Texas was visited. New Mexico, Arkansas, Kentucky, and even Arizona were host states to Cole.[17] He delivered an enlightening and encouraging talk on the pitfalls that must be avoided by youth and the emphasis that must be placed on living a good and decent life serving mankind if one is to be a happy and productive member of society. Apart from quoting "Reno, the famous poet Scout," Cole's original words concluded:

> The farmer who drives to town seven days in the week will soon have his farm advertised for sale. An idle man is sure to go into the hands of a receiver. My friends, glorious opportunities are all before us, with the great Republic's free institutions at our command. Science and knowledge have unlocked their vaults wherein poverty and wealth are not classified. A fitting theater where the master mind shall play the leading role.[18]

Cole not only enjoyed the spotlight that he had created for himself by touring with his words of wisdom and advice, but he also seemed sincerely interested in communicating with youth. Things were now different from what they had been in his early days. Cole was anxious to see the young men and women of the country avail themselves of the many opportunities that were now theirs that had not been his as a young person. He would often take extra time to chat with young people who approached him after his lecture and would listen carefully to what they had to say. Cole, in his last years, had much to share with these young adults. Additionally, he had much to learn.

Cole also took time to lodge his complaints against the "dime novels" and moving pictures that featured the James-Younger Gang or other bands of outlaws. In one interview he stated:

> The trouble with these moving picture and "penny-dreadful" representations of outlaw life is the glamour they throw about it. No mention is made of the hunted, hounded existence, when every man's hand is turned against you; the nights filled with dread and the days of suffering. No mention is made of the end of it all, a violent death or a prison cell. It all looks so easy and heroic to the impressionistic young fellow down in front. And then comes temptation, as it came to me.[19]

Cole finally decided that he had done his best to pay his debt to society, first through the twenty-seven years in Minnesota and second through his lectures. By 1912, he was ready to return home to Lee's Summit to "retire."

With the profits that he made from his lecture tour, Cole was able to move into a lovely two-story white frame house on Market Street in Lee's Summit with his niece, Nora Hall. Nora doted on her Uncle Cole and made a wonderful home for him. Cole would sit out on the porch hour after hour visiting with the many people who passed by or came to call on the old outlaw. Cole's friends from days gone by who had known him as a young man or as a soldier would stop by. Stories would be exchanged and days of adventure would be relived. Cole never told stories of his outlaw days. Frank James would visit and the two men would take long walks where they could be seen in animated conversation and laughter. Whenever anyone approached the two old friends the conversation would be abruptly changed and topics noncontroversial would be discussed.

One of the men who liked to visit Cole was a young evangelist named Charlie Stewart. On one occasion, Cole revealed to the Reverend Stewart that as a young man he had had three goals in his life: to become a Mason (like his brother Richard), to marry a good woman, and to become a Christian. Reverend Stewart encouraged Cole to attend the revival meetings that were being held in Lee's Summit in August of 1913 to perhaps fulfill the one goal still available to him. Cole and his niece Nora attended a few of the meetings, but Cole fell ill and told Nora he didn't feel able to complete the three-week revival. Several days later, however, Cole managed to pull himself together and attend yet another meeting. The church hosting the revival was the Christian Church of Lee's Summit. The church building became too hot to comfortably hold the large crowd of attendees during the simmering days of August. At the east side of the church a huge tent was erected to shield those participating.[20]

On August 21, the fifty-year anniversary of the Lawrence Raid, Cole attended the revival meeting in the tent with Nora. Visiting evangelist Orville Edgar Hamilton called for all sinners to come forward and embrace the opportunity to begin life anew. As the congregation sang the hymn "Just As I Am," Cole Younger kissed his niece on the cheek and rose. As the immense group crowded within the tent watched in astonishment and whispered his name in hushed tones, Cole slowly walked to the front of the congregation and offered his hand to Reverend Hamilton. One hundred and fifty-one people were saved that evening, and Cole stood proud among them as hundreds of people congregated around him to shake his hand.[21]

The newspapers of Missouri and other states as well reported the event. Many expressed a certain suspicion that Cole might have made such a commitment for the sake of publicity or perhaps for the attention. Others supported the former outlaw. Cole was held up as an example of how men can change and how past sins can be put aside in lives devoted to the service of God and Jesus Christ. Cole seemed to be very sincere when he told a reporter a few days after the service: "I've accomplished one of the things I set out to do at any rate, and the greatest of them."[22]

In the following week, Cole was baptized in the Christian Church of Lee's Summit, joined as a member of that church, and attended whenever his health allowed throughout the remainder of his life. Cole continued the life of comfort and peace within his family during the next two years. He continued to visit with friends on a regular basis, and this communion brought him much happiness.

After he was acquitted of all charges brought against him, Frank James returned home briefly to Kearney, Missouri. He soon began a nomadic existence in which he traveled throughout the country in pursuit of employment. From 1888 to 1891 he worked for the Mittenthal Clothing Company in Dallas, Texas. He tended horses for Shep Williams, a livestock importer near Paris, Texas, from 1892 to 1894.

For the next six or seven years James served as the doorman at Ed Butler's Standard Theater in St. Louis. The theater was home to a burlesque production, and Frank became acquainted with managers of other productions. He toured intermittently with the productions *Across the Desert* and *The Fatal Scar*, appearing in minor roles. During the season, James dropped the timer's flag for the horse races at the St. Louis Fairgrounds. He also sold shoes in Nevada, Missouri, for a time.

Then in 1903 James teamed up with Cole Younger for the

Younger-James Wild West Company, traveling with the show for that year and ending his association with the production by 1904. Frank eventually bought a ranch in Fletcher, Oklahoma, where he lived until the death of his mother in 1911. Frank James then moved back to the James farm in Kearney, where he gave tours of the James family home.

Cole's old friend died at his family's home in Kearney on February 18, 1915. When told the news about Frank's death, Cole said nothing but retreated upstairs to his room, where he sat in quiet reflection for the rest of the day. As the last surviving member of the James-Younger Gang, Cole was now alone with his memories.

Cole's health began to be a problem for him, since he was plagued by heart and kidney trouble. He was, after all, over seventy years old. That was an amazing age for a man of his background to reach. He still carried eleven bullets in his body. His niece, Mrs. Frank Hall, wrote to Dr. Morrill Withrow on December 3, 1915:

> He [Cole] has been sick now nearly two years, but has been in bed the last 3 months. He sits up frequently in his room but doesn't try to go downstairs. Some days he feels very well, and on cloudy days he doesn't seem to feel so well. His sickness began with heart and kidney trouble and for eight months now he has been tapped 32 times, drawing 102 gallons of water. It's dropsy of the liver. The swelling mostly in the abdomen. He also has a rupture that gives him a great deal of trouble. We all feel very anxious about him and he seems to think he will be able to get out again, but I hardly think he ever will.[23]

By February 24, 1916, Cole had rallied enough to write to his friend Dr. Withrow himself. He said that he was taking morphine and was relieved enough to put pen to paper. In a shaky hand, Cole wrote of his respect for Dr. Withrow and the other of the prison doctors. He described his various illnesses and invited Dr. Withrow, if he was so inclined, to make suggestions as to his treatment to Cole's Lee's Summit doctor, Thomas J. Ragsdale. He ended the letter with "and believe me your true friend until death."[24] Cole was, by now, suffering from uremia and a combination of diseases, according to Dr. Ragsdale.

On March 7, Cole wrote to his close friend Harry Hoffman. Harvey C. (Harry) Hoffman was born on December 31, 1873, near Smithfield, Illinois. His father was a lumber contractor who relocated his family to Kansas City, Missouri, in the early 1880s. The Hoffmans resided on the east side of Woodland Avenue next to the family of "Tom Howard." Harry became fast friends with little "Tim Howard" and was disappointed when the family suddenly moved. It wasn't until a few months later when Jesse James was assassinated that the Hoffman family realized that their neighbors had been Jesse James and his family.[25]

Hoffman became a telephone lineman for the Central Union Telephone Company and later he was general foreman. Hoffman became acquainted with Cole Younger on the outlaw's return from Minnesota. The elder man enjoyed Hoffman's company, and the two remained close friends. Hoffman became acquainted with "Tim Howard" in later years, and through Jesse Jr., Hoffman became friendly with Frank James. Hoffman was proud of his friendships with the James and Younger families.

In 1909, Hoffman became a deputy marshal for Jackson County. In 1913, he was appointed chief deputy. In 1917, Hoffman served as Jackson County marshal.

Cole had been anticipating a visit from Hoffman, who was living in Kansas City at that time. Cole claimed that he was "feeling well today and I think I will win the fight and get well fast." Cole told Hoffman that he had spent the previous day being visited by "Lee Banks, Jesse James and Zachary Crittenden." Cole reported that he had a nice visit with the men. Jesse James, of course, referred to Jesse Edwards James, and Zachary Crittenden was the son of former governor Thomas Crittenden. This letter may have been the last Cole wrote, for his health did not improve as he had anticipated it would. He began to weaken to the point that he was unable to get out of bed.[26]

On March 19, Cole asked his family, who by this time had gathered in the Market Street house in anticipation of his death, to have Harry Hoffman and Jesse James, Jr. come to his bedside.

Jesse Edwards James, named after John Newman Edwards, was born in Nashville, Tennessee, on August 31, 1875. Because his family lived under the alias of Howard, little Jesse was called

"Tim." Jesse Jr. and his sister Mary were present in their home when their father was assassinated.

Times were not easy for Jesse James's family after his death yet his children grew to be respected members of society. Jesse E. answered an advertisement at the age of eleven so that he might earn money to help support his mother and sister. The ad turned out to be for the law office of Thomas Crittenden, Jr. Jesse was hired as an office boy, and the two sons of fathers who had once been enemies became good friends. At the age of fifteen, Jesse became a clerk at the Armour packing plant, where he worked several years. His mother continued his education during his nights at home. He eventually owned a pawnshop and jewelry store in Kansas City while he attended the Kansas City School of Law.

In June, 1906, Jesse passed the bar exam and entered practice the following year. While in Kansas City, he worked at the law offices of Latshaw & Latshaw, Paul Buzard, and Harold Neibling. Jesse's legal career was primarily involved with the litigation of personal injury cases.

In 1899, Jesse was accused, tried, and acquitted of involvement in the robbery of the Missouri Pacific Railroad at Leeds, Missouri. He wrote a book the following year, *Jesse James My Father*. Also that year, Jesse married Stella Frances McGown. The couple eventually had four daughters: Jo Frances, Lucille Martha, Jessie Estelle, and Ethelrose.[27]

Cole wanted to talk. According to Hoffman, Cole told the two men that he was going to die and that he wanted to ease his conscience. The two men sat with Cole for several hours while Cole talked about his outlaw days, military career, and the time he spent in prison.

Cole spoke of Northfield, identifying the man who killed Heywood but swearing Hoffman and Jesse to secrecy. Cole claimed that it mattered little now, since all of the men who had been in Northfield, except himself, were now dead. Of course Cole had stated that many times before the death of Frank James. Cole requested the two men not reveal the killer as the rider of the "dun horse." Jesse, Jr. understood from Cole that Heywood's killer had been his uncle.[28]

Cole expressed regret that his relationships with so many of his friends in Minnesota had been harmed and told the two men that he had nothing but respect for the prison officials in Minnesota. Jesse and Hoffman were asked by Cole to serve as pallbearers at his funeral. One of the guns that Cole had used at Northfield had been returned to Cole by either Sheriff Glispin or Sheriff Barton upon his pardon. Cole now bequeathed this gun to Marshal Hoffman.

Reminding his visitors to reveal nothing of their final visit with the old outlaw, Cole bid them good-bye. Jesse E. James would never reveal his last conversation with Cole to anyone other than his family. Harry Hoffman, masking the details, wrote accounts of the "true story" of Cole Younger and remained his friend and champion long after Cole's death.

With his family around him, Cole watched the birds outside his upper-story window on March 21, 1916. Unable to express his last thoughts, Cole lay quietly that afternoon. Later dubbed "The Last of The Great Outlaws" by writer Homer Croy, Cole Younger died at 8:45 that evening. He was seventy-two years old.

Cole's funeral was to be held at his church, the Christian Church of Lee's Summit. Only three of Cole's siblings remained alive at that time: Laura, Anne, and Sally. The three sisters were unable either to make arrangements for his service or even to attend. The funeral was organized by the ever-faithful Hall family. All the major newspapers carried articles on Cole's death. Most of them retold the story of the James-Younger Gang, the Youngers' stay in Minnesota, Cole's later life, and his conversion to Christianity. Many newspapers also ran editorials on Cole's character. Jack Lait, a columnist for the Chicago *Herald* wrote:

> My six-shooting idol of stolen hours and "Golden Hours," changed. He closed his eyes in peace with his Maker and his neighbors. He was a dignified old gentleman, respected by his community, wrapped up in religious work, a devout communicant and a valiant exhorter. It was well that I had changed, or I should have been disappointed.[29]

On March 23, Rev. J. T. Webb officiated at the funeral assisted by Rev. Ben J. Lindsey of Clinton. A male quartet sang hymns before the overflow congregation. There were so many people in attendance that the doors of the church were held open to allow the scores of people who had been unable to find a place within the church the opportunity to listen to the service from outside on the church's lawn. The church was filled with floral tributes. One newspaper reported that the largest of these was a wreath from "officials in charge of the Minnesota State Prison" while Cole and his brothers had been incarcerated there.

Among the hundreds in attendance were several of the old guerrillas who were still living. George Shepard, George Noland, and Morgan Maddox were at the church. The James family was represented by Jesse Jr., Frank's widow Annie, and their son Robert.[30]

After the service it started to rain and many of Cole's older friends were unable to accompany the cortege to the Lee's Summit Cemetery. Cole's pallbearers included some of the most promi-nent men in the community: Charles N. Spencer, a druggist; Lee Garvin, assistant cashier of the Lee's Summit Bank; O. C. Brown-ing of Browning Brothers Dry Goods Store; Dr. T. J. Ragsdale; and Harry Hoffman. Some accounts claimed that the sixth pall-bearer was George Crisp of Kansas City while others, including those of members of the Younger family, claim the man to have been Harris Shawhan of Lone Jack. Cole was laid to rest in the Hall family plot, which included his brothers Jim and Bob and his mother, Bursheba.

On March 30, 1916, the following noticed appeared in the Lee's Summit *Journal*:

We wish to thank the many friends and neighbors for favors and kind acts during the sickness and death of our uncle, Mr. Cole Younger. The heart throbs in sympathetic vibration to the love and tenderness shown by the thousand good works and kind expressions tendered in the last trying hours.

The Hall Family
Mr. and Mrs. Nott Fenton
Mr. and Mrs. Peltspring[31]

The lives of the Younger brothers, Cole, Jim, John, and Bob, had now all come to a close. The legend, built and nurtured by their most dramatic and unique experiences and approach to life, however, would continue, perhaps forever.

Genealogy

Charles Lee Younger married: (Patriarch)

Nancy Toney
- Milton T. Younger m. Millie Taylor
- Elizabeth Darlisco m. Thomas Woods

Sarah Sullivan Purcell
- Lucy Sullivan m. James Buster
- Coleman Purcell Younger m. Elinor Murray; Rebecca Smith; Augusta Peters Inskeep
- Henry Washington Younger m. Bursheba Fristoe
- Virginia Lee m. Jacob Creek
- Littleton Purcell Younger m. Eliza Simpson
- Sydney Ann m. George Burnett

Parmelia Dorcus Wilson
- Adeline Lee m. James Lewis Dalton Jr.
- Charles Frank Younger m. Martha Kincaid; Florine Williams
- Sophia Lee m. Tillard Ragan; Charles Braden
- Mary Agatha Lee m. Lock Burden
- Martha Jane m. Travis Morgan
- Thomas Jefferson Younger m. Emma C. Barmour
- Sophronia Lee m. Benjamin Kirkpatrick
- Bruce Younger m. Maibelle Reed (Belle Starr)
- Richard Younger

Elizabeth Simpson
- Simpson Charles m. Florence Higgerson
- Catherine

Richard Marshall Fristoe m. Mary L. Sullivan (Matriarch)
- Bursheba Leighton m. Henry Washington Younger
- Laura Matilda m. Reuben Harris
- Mary Ann m. David Talley
- Thomas John
- Nancy D. m. Isaac Campbell
- Julia E.
- Frances C. m. Lydall Twyman

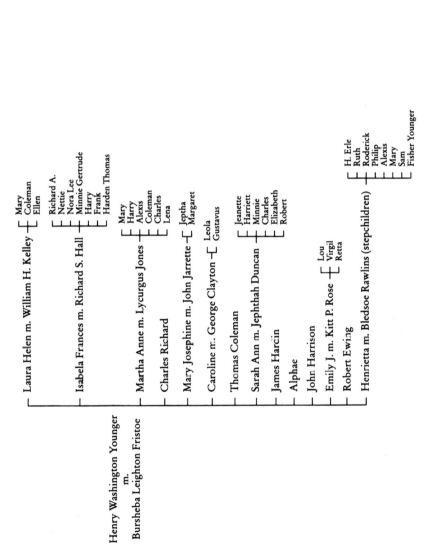

Notes

Chapter 1

1. *Missouri Democrat*, August, 1863.
2. Ibid.
3. *The Families of Charles Lee and Henry Washington Younger*, Marley Brant, 1986.
4. St. Clair County, Missouri, Census records, 1840, 1850.
5. The last will and codicil of Charles Lee Younger.
6. Interview with Charlene Brashier Johnson, granddaughter of Simpson Younger.
7. Ibid.
8. Kansas City *Star*, "Early Segregation Test Here in Annals of the Younger Gamily," Henry A. Bundscher—undated clipping.
9. *The History of Vernon County*, 1887.
10. *The History of Independence*.
11. Personal account of Frances Fristoe Twyman, 1901.
12. Markham Fristoe, brother of Richard, was also influential in the history of Missouri. He served as the first sheriff of Benton County from 1835 to 1836. He also operated the first ferry over the Osage River at Warsaw. Markham's great popularity resulted in the naming of the town of Fristoe, located southeast of Warsaw in Benton County. Bursheba Younger was very proud of this uncle, and it is likely that Bob Younger derived his middle name from Markham's close friend, frontier trapper Ewing Young.

Chapter 2

1. *History of Independence*.
2. *History of Jackson County*, 1888.

3. Records of the Missouri State Assembly.

4. Ibid.

5. Ibid.

6. *The Sims of Virginia*, manuscript held in the Clay County Archives.

7. *History of Vernon County*, 1887.

8. Records of the Kansas State Legislature.

9. *The History of Lee's Summit.*

10. Kansas City *Star*, October 20, 1929.

11. "History of the Truman Medical Center, East."

12. Letter from J. W. Lercher to author.

13. Cass County Recorder, Book K, page 488.

14. Reagan, who later served two terms in the Missouri General Assembly, would issue the first official petition to pardon the Younger brothers for their Minnesota crimes. Although he was disapproving of their postwar activities, Reagan remained their friend.

15. Clayton was active in the Civil War and rode with Cole and John Jarrette as one of Quantrill's guerrillas.

16. From personal accounts of the Younger family. The matriculation records were destroyed when the college was set on fire March 26, 1863.

17. *The History of Lee's Summit.*

18. Ibid.

19. Bill of Sale from Kelley and Younger.

20. Interviews with Delores Reed Fozzard, great-granddaughter of Laura and Will Kelley.

21. During the Civil War Kelley served with Captain Lowe's Company of the Missouri Artillery. He was captured at Vicksburg. (Records of the National Archives, Military Records of William H. Kelley) Upon returning to Cass County, Kelley became a farmer and grocer. Will Kelley is often mistaken for Ed O'Kelley, killer of Jesse James's assassin Bob Ford. They were not the same man. At some point, Laura and Will are said to have been the managers of a boarding house in Westport, Missouri. Sometime during the 1870s, Laura and Kelley parted company. One of the stories that circulates within the Kelley family says Will was transporting a shipment of liquor in a wagon when he was shot in the back. He died soon afterward. Laura relocated from Harrisonville, where Will is buried, to Amoret, Missouri. She died in 1924.

22. Records of the Grand Lodge of Missouri, Ancient Free and Accepted Masons.

23. Records of the Court, Cass County.

24. Harrisonville *Democrat*, August 17, 1860.

Chapter 3

1. Adjutant General's Report, State of Kansas, Seventh Regiment Kansas, Roll.

Chapter 4

1. *They Rode With Quantrell*, Donald Hale.
2. "Quantrill, James, Younger, et al.: Leadership in a Guerrilla Movement, Missouri, 1861–1865," Don R. Bowman in *Military Affairs*, Vol. XLI, No. 1, February 1977.
3. Letter from Cole Younger to J. W. Buel, October 31, 1880.
4. 1860 Cass County Census.
5. *Cole Younger By Himself*, Cole Younger.
6. *Jesse James Was His Name*, William A. Settle.
7. *Cole Younger By Himself*.
8. "A Short History of the Washington Township, Jackson County, Mo.," Rufus Burris, October 11, 1945.
9. "A Jackson County Citizen Writes of the Time of Quantrells and the Jayhawkers," J. T. Palmer.
10. *Cole Younger By Himself*.
11. "The War of the Rebellion: A Compilation of the Official Records of the Union and Confederate Armies," GPO, 1888.
12. Letter from Cole Younger to J. W. Buel.
13. *The History of Cass and Bates Counties, Mo.*, 1883.
14. Records of the National Archives, Military Records of Irvin Walley.
15. Ibid.
16. Ibid.
17. *History of Butler*, Jo Ellen Sears.
18. "Cleared At Last," newspaper clipping from the scrapbook of Hardin Hall.

Chapter 5

1. *Gray Ghosts of the Confederacy*, Richard Brownlee.
2. *Cole Younger By Himself*.
3. Ibid.
4. Personal account of Hiram George.

5. *Youngers Fight For Freedom*, W. C. Bronaugh.
6. Statement of Cole Younger to Harry Hoffman.†
7. Letter from Cole Younger to Lizzie Daniel, 1901.
8. Ibid.
9. "Cole Younger Writes to Lizzie Daniel," William A. Settle, Jr.
10. *History of Cass County, Big Creek Township.*
11. *Cole Younger By Himself.*
12. Ibid.
13. Personal account of Reuban Smith.
14. *Daily Missouri Democrat*, September 1, 1863.
15. *History of Cass County—Big Creek Township.*
16. Ibid.

Chapter 6

1. *Daily Missouri Democrat*, September 1, 1863.
2. White Cloud Kansas *Chief*, September 3, 1863.
3. "General Order No. 11: The Forced Evacuation of Civilians During the Civil War," Charles R. Mink.
4. Lexington *Union*, September 5, 1863.
5. Statement of Cole Younger to Harry Hoffman.†
6. Ibid.
7. *Jim Cummins, The Guerrilla*, Jim Cummins.
8. *Cole Younger By Himself.*
9. Ibid.
10. Years later, David Talley was shot and killed one night by a new hand working at his farm when he was mistaken for a horse thief as he stepped into the barnyard and whistled. David had previously made news when one of his workers "turned reballious" and took after Talley with an ax. Talley was forced to shoot the man. Will and Spence were later Bob Younger's pallbearers.
11. *Cole Younger By Himself.*
12. A "widow" at the age of seventeen, Kate later married Walter Head. She died in a rest home near Kansas City, Kansas, in 1930 and is buried in the same cemetery as Sally Younger Duncan.
13. Interview with Bob Younger by George Craig, 1886.
14. The correspondence of Jim Younger.
15. *Three Years With Quantrill*, John McCorkle.

Chapter 7

1. Interview with Bob Younger by George Craig.
2. Papers of the estate of Henry Washington Younger.

Chapter 8

1. Personal account of "Maggie."
2. Statement of Greenup Bird.
3. *Jesse James Was His Name*, James Ross.
4. Statement of Greenup Bird.
5. Ibid.
6. Statement of Cole Younger to Harry Hoffman.†
7. *Cole Younger By Himself.*
8. Personal account of "Maggie."
9. Newspaper clipping, publication unknown.
10. *Cole Younger By Himself.*
11. Interview with Minnie Padgett by Elizabeth George, October 28, 1959.† Jep, although a farmer, became involved with the Pleasant Hill newspaper and, on occasion, published letters of defense from his brother-in-law, Cole. At some point the Duncans moved south to Arkansas, where they lived for several years. Jep started a "subscription school," since he was the most educated man in the area. He was paid in farm products. The family spent time in Denison, Texas, and eventually relocated to Kansas City, Kansas, where Sally died in 1925.
12. *Jesse James Was His Name.*
13. *Cole Younger By Himself.*
14. Ibid.
15. *Jesse James Was His Name.*
16. Ibid.
17. *Cole Younger By Himself.*
18. *I, Jesse James*, James R. Ross.
19. *Cole Younger By Himself.*
20. Kansas City *Commercial Advertiser*, June 3, 1868.
21. *Jim Cummins, the Guerrilla.*
22. Interviews with June Spicer, great-granddaughter of Josie and John Jarrette.
23. Palm Beach *Post*, July 7, 1986.
24. *Cole Younger By Himself.*
25. Marriage certificate of Maibelle Reed and Bruce Younger.

26. Letter from Minnie Padgett to Harry Hoffman, March 1, 1959.†
27. Interview with Florence Wiley, great-granddaughter of Pearl Reed.
28. Correspondence of Jim Younger.

Chapter 9

1. *Cole Younger By Himself.*
2. Dallas *Morning News*, May 29, 1945.
3. *Texas Legend and Lore*, Edwin Johnson.
4. *Bounty Hunter*, Rick Miller.
5. *Cole Younger By Himself.*
6. Correspondence of Jim Younger.

Chapter 10

1. "James Robbery Integral Part of Wayne History," publication and date unknown.
2. *Jesse James Was His Name.*
3. "James Robbery Integral Part of Wayne History."
4. Transcript of the trial of Clell Miller.
5. Letter of Jesse James to the Kansas City *Times*, July 8, 1872.
6. Letter from Kathleen Bryson of Transylvania University to author, April 13, 1984.
7. Correspondence of Jim Younger.
8. Ibid.
9. *Cole Younger By Himself.*
10. Letters from James W. Oberly of William and Mary College to author, May 1983 and June 1983.
11. *Cole Younger By Himself.*
12. Letter from Wilbur E. Maneray, Tulane University to author.
13. Correspondence of Jim Younger.
14. T. J. was defeated for reelection in 1874 after the Younger-Pinkerton incident at Roscoe but was elected a Missouri state representative on the Greenback ticket in 1878. He was asked to become a congressional candidate on that ticket in the next election but declined, as he didn't feel the party could get elected that year. S. A. Haseltine of Greene County was the party's candidate and led the party to victory. T. J. forever

regretted his decision not to run. In 1882 he was defeated in his bid for the office of county clerk. Although T. J. and Emma lived together until November, 1891, Emma filed for a divorce, which was granted on July 4, 1893. T. J. married his second wife in Ft. Smith, Arkanss. He moved to Pauhuska, Oklahoma, where he died sometime during the week of January 19, 1911.

15. *Jesse James Was His Name.*
16. Letter from Jesse James to the Kansas City *Times*, October, 1872.
17. *Cole Younger By Himself.*
18. *Bounty Hunter.*
19. "Train Robbery!" newspaper clipping, publication unknown.
20. Personal account of "Maggie."

Chapter 11

1. "Welcome to Adair," Adair Community Service Club.
2. Ibid.
3. Appleton City *Democrat*, date unknown.
4. Newspaper clipping, publication and date unknown.
5. Edwards published *Noted Guerillas*, his remembrances of the war, in 1877. John Newman Edwards died in 1889 in Jefferson City and was buried in Dover, Lafayette County, Missouri.
6. *Jesse James Was His Name.*
7. Ibid.
8. Ibid.

Chapter 12

1. *History of Linn County.*
2. Letter from Annapolis to author.
3. Records of St. Clair County.
4. Coroner's Inquest into the death of John Younger and Edwin Daniels, Testimony of Theodrick Snuffer.
5. Coroner's Inquest, Testimony of W. J. Allen (Lull).
6. Coroner's Inquest, Testimony of G. W. McDonald.
7. *Roscoe Gun Battle*, Wilbur Zink.
8. Lee's Summit *Ledger*, March 25, 1874.
9. Records of St. Clair County.
10. Kansas City *Times*, Cora McNeill interview, 1897.

11. Personal account of "Maggie."
12. Letter from Dreat Younger to author.

Chapter 13

1. Drury served ten years as San Luis Obispo County Supervisor and four years as school trustee. He served as president of the board of trustees when the city of El Paso de Robles was incorporated in 1889. Also in 1889, Drury built the Hotel El Paso de Robles, said to be one of the finest of its time. Drury's next venture, the Andrews Hotel, was built later but burned to the ground. Drury and his wife Louisa moved to San Francisco after the Andrews Hotel fire, as the hotel had been uninsured and Drury lost the vast majority of his wealth.

2. *History of San Luis Obispo.* Louisa invested her own money in the Lenox Hotel on Sutter Street in San Francisco, but that hotel was leveled in the San Francisco Earthquake of 1906. Louisa later bought two houses on Pacific Avenue, which were used first as boarding houses and later were turned into a hotel. Drury James died there on July 1, 1910.

3. The Parmers eventually settled in Wichita Falls, Texas, where Susan died in 1889. Parmer's second wife was Sarah Catherine "Kitty" Ogden from Franklin County, Missouri. It has been said that her brother, William Henry Ogden, served with Quantrill. William relocated to Wichita Falls from Missouri in 1875 and brought his sister. Parmer married Kitty on December 24, 1892. It was Kitty who applied for Parmer's widow's pension when Parmer died in 1927. Susan James Parmer, Allen and Kitty are all buried at Riverside Cemetery in Wichita Falls.

4. *Jesse James Was His Name*, William A. Settle, Jr.

Chapter 14

1. *Jesse James Was His Name*, Settle.
2. *I, Jesse James.*
3. *Jesse James Was His Name.*
4. *Cole Younger By Himself.*
5. "Revolvers vs. Croquet Mallets and An Irate Lady," M. C. Eden, *Brand Book*, Vol. 15, No. 4, July 1973.
6. Wheeling *Intelligencer*, September 17, 1875.
7. Huntington *Advertiser*, September 21, 1875.

8. Ibid.
9. Ibid.
10. *History of St. Clair County.*

Chapter 15

1. Personal account of "Maggie."
2. Many years later, Miller's brother Ed was active with the "new" James Gang at least by the time of the Glendale train robbery in 1879. Ed Miller was said to have been ambushed by Jesse James somewhere in Carroll County, Missouri, in 1880 when Jesse became suspicious of Ed's loyalty.
3. Correspondence of Jim Younger.
4. Ibid.
5. Ibid.
6. *Jesse James Was His Name*, Settle.
7. In later years, Bruce became uncharacteristically interested in horse racing. Along with his brother-in-law Lewis Dalton, father of the future outlaws the Dalton brothers, Bruce traveled the horseracing circuit. He lost money and incurred large debts. Bruce's relations with his family and friends became strained as he began to associate more and more with the so-called outlaw elements of the circuit. He relocated to Kansas where he kept company with Belle Reed, later known as Belle Starr. Bruce and Belle were married on May 15, 1880, but for some reason, the marriage appears to have lasted only three weeks.
8. Personal account of Sophia Younger Ragan Braden. Not happy with the direction of his life, Bruce relocated to New Mexico where he hoped to turn his life around. He was never heard from again. A body found in the Guadalupe Mountains in New Mexico was subsequently identified by Sophia as being that of Bruce. The "mummy" was sent to "a museum" in Boston, but the exact whereabouts of the body has never been determined.
9. *Cole Younger By Himself.*

Chapter 16

The names used by the outlaws for aliases during their preparation for the Northfield robbery were taken from the research of Dallas Cantrell.

1. Account of Perry Samuels as told to Harry Hoffman.

2. Written account of Cole Younger given to Dr. A. E. Hedback, 1897.

3. *Youngers' Fatal Blunder*, Dallas Cantrell.

4. St. Paul *Pioneer Press*, undated.

5. *Cole Younger By Himself*.

6. St. Paul *Pioneer Press*, undated.

7. *Cole Younger By Himself*.

8. Interview with Bob Younger by George Craig.

9. St. Paul *Pioneer Press*, undated.

10. Statement of J. Hobbs, September 11, 1876.

11. *Cole Younger By Himself*.

12. Minneapolis *Tribune*, September, 1876.

13. Letter from Mildred Addy, granddaughter of Mads Ouren, to author.

14. Rice County *Journal*, September 14, 1876.

15. Personal account of T. L. Vought, 1876.

16. *The Southern Minnesotan*, "The Gettysburg of the James-Younger Gang," publication and date unknown.

17. Ibid.

18. Letter from F. A. Whittier to J. A. Lawrence, June 18, 1924.*

19. After the Northfield robbery, Adelbert Ames and his wife. Blanche moved to Tweeksbury, Massachusetts. They "wintered" in Ormand Beach, Florida, where Ames played golf often with his friend John D. Rockefeller.

20. *The Southern Minnesotan*, "The Gettysburg of the James-Younger Gang."

21. Le Sueur County Commissioners Report, 1876.

22. Mankato *Free Press*, December, 1876.

23. Account of Cole Younger given to Dr. A. E. Hedback.

24. Ibid.

25. *Robber & Hero*, George Huntington.

26. Ibid.

27. Rice County *Journal*, September 14, 1876.

28. Minneapolis *Tribune*, September 8, 1876.

29. *Robber & Hero*.

30. *The Southern Minnesotan*, "The Gettysburg of the James-Younger Gang."

31. Author's interviews with James Ross.

Chapter 17

1. Dispatch of S. B. Brockway to J. A. Winter, September 14, 1876.*
2. *Youngers' Fatal Blunder.*
3. *Cole Younger By Himself.*
4. *Robber & Hero*, George Huntington.
5. *The Southern Minnesotan*, "The Gettysburg of the James-Younger Gang."
6. *Youngers' Fatal Blunder.*
7. "L. M. Demaray Recalls Story of Narrow Escape by T. J. Dunning and of Raid on Mathews Flock of Chickens," publication unknown.
8. Cole Younger's statement to Harry Hoffman/personal account of "Maggie."
9. Statement of Cole Younger to Harry Hoffman.
10. "The Youngers Last Stand," Harry Hoffman.
11. Account of George Bradford.
12. Personal account of "Maggie."
13. Statement of George Bradford.
14. Account of Charles Armstrong, June 21, 1945.
15. Ibid.

Chapter 18

1. Account of T. L. Vought.
2. Letter from Lillie Le Vesconte to Jacob Hodnefield, February 19, 1945.
3. Letter from Mildred Addy to author.
4. Faribault *Democrat*, September 14, 1876.
5. Statement of George Bradford.
6. Account of Charles Armstrong, June 21, 1945.
7. Ibid.
8. St. Paul *Pioneer Press*, September, 1876.
9. Ibid.
10. Ibid.
11. Faribault *Democrat*, September 22, 1876.
12. Ibid.
13. Ibid.
14. Faribault *Democrat*, October 8, 1876.

Chapter 19

1. *Cole Younger By Himself.*
2. *Convict Life at the Minnesota State Prison*, 1909.
3. Ibid.
4. Interview with Bob Younger by George Craig.
5. "Jesse James in Tennessee," Ted P. Yeatman, *True West*, July 1985.
6. Liberty *Tribune*, November 4, 1881.
7. *I, Jesse James.*
8. *Jesse James Was His Name*, Settle.
9. *Youngers' Fatal Blunder*, Cantrell.
10. *Youngers Fight For Freedom*, Bronaugh.
11. *James Farm Journal*, December 1985.
12. "Convicts Armed As Prison Burned," St. Paul *Pioneer Press* date unknown.
13. *Cole Younger By Himself.*
14. "Convicts Armed As Prison Burned."
15. Ibid.

Chapter 20

1. Letter from Bob Younger to "Aunt," January 25, 1883.
2. *Youngers Fight For Freedom*, W. C. Bronaugh.
3. Letter from W. C. Bronaugh to Frank James, June 13, 1884.
4. After the Youngers were paroled, Bronaugh continued to lead an active life. He served six years as commander of the Missouri division of the United Confederate Veterans and also served on the board of directors of the Confederate Home at Higginsville, Missouri. He wrote a book detailing his involvement with the Youngers' parole entitled *The Youngers Fight For Freedom*. It has been said by some biographers that Wal Bronaugh purchased a home for Frank James when Frank lived in Nevada, Missouri. Bronaugh family members believe that if a Bronaugh was involved in such a transaction it was more likely through Frank Bronaugh rather than Wal, as Frank had a good deal more money than Wal.
5. Personal account of "Maggie."
6. *Youngers Fight For Freedom.*
7. Letter from Patrick Brophy to author.
8. Stillwater *Evening Gazette*, November 9, 1979.
9. Stillwater *Prison Mirror*.

10. Letter from Henry H. Sibley to W. C. Bronaugh, July 8, 1889.

11. In 1892, no longer employed by the penitentiary, Jacob Westby and his family moved to Minneapolis. Westby was in charge of a group of men who surveyed in the northernmost areas of Minnesota. He was living in the St. Paul-Minneapolis area when Jim and Cole were paroled and it is said by members of the Westby family that Cole made frequent visits to the Westby household. Sometime about 1902, Westby relocated to Alaska, where by 1915 he was working as a guard at a prison in that state. Living once again in Minneapolis, Jacob Westby died there on March 19, 1934.

12. *Youngers Fight For Freedom*.

13. Ibid.

14. Ibid.

15. Ibid.

16. Ibid.

17. St. Paul *Pioneer Press*, September, 1889.

18. Butler *Times*, June 12, 1889.

19. St. Louis *Globe*, June 22, 1889.

20. *Youngers' Fatal Blunder*.

21. Ibid.

22. Kansas City *Times*, 1889.

23. Kansas City *Times*. "His Past Sins Forgotten," September 21, 1889.

24. Ibid.

Chapter 21

1. Kansas City *World*, "A Visit to the Youngers," 1895.

2. Ibid.

3. *Youngers Fight for Freedom*, Bronaugh

4. Ibid.

5. Letter from Peter Freligh to Retta Younger.

6. *Youngers Fight For Freedom*.

7. Letter from Cole Younger to W. C. Bronaugh, January 15, 1893.

8. *Youngers Fight For Freedom*.

9. Ibid.

10. Kansas City *Times*, Cora McNeill interview, 1897.

11. *Youngers Fight For Freedom*.

12. Letter from Cole Younger to Bronaugh.

13. *Youngers Fight For Freedom*.

14. St. Paul *Pioneer Press*, "Held Fast In Prison," July 14, 1897.

15. Northfield *News*, July, 1897.

16. Kansas City *Times*, "Doctor Recalls Younger Brothers As Men Above Outlaw Class," October 24, 1958.

17. *Youngers Fight For Freedom*.

18. Ibid.

19. Ibid.

20. Stillwater *Gazette*, July 12, 1901.

21. St. Paul *Pioneer Press*, July 11, 1901.

22. Ibid.

23. Ibid.

24. "Cole Younger Writes To Lizzie Daniel."

25. Grandchildren from Bledsoe's family referred to Retta as "Madra" and accorded her the full privileges of a grandmother. Letter from F. M. Rawlins to author, January 2, 1986.

26. Retta died in Lancaster on March 13, 1915. Bledsoe relocated to Ardmore, Oklahoma, where he once again became a treasured member of the community. When he died on May 13, 1937, the Retail Merchants Association requested that all businesses be closed during Rawlins's funeral.

27. "Withrow Family," account of Dr. M. E. Withrow sent to author by Mary Withrow Division.

28. In 1903, Withrow established a practice in the pioneer community of Koochiching, Minnesota. This community would later be known as International Falls. Withrow married Agatha Mahoney, and the couple had several children. Enlisting in the Army Medical Corps in April, 1918, Withrow served at overseas field and base hospitals until the end of World War I. He was active in the American Legion from its inception and also served as Assistant Surgeon for the U.S. Public Health Immigration Office. Withrow was a Mason and served many years as mayor of International Falls.

29. Letter from Dr. M. E. Withrow to Frank Hall, April 30, 1947.

30. *Youngers Fight For Freedom*.

31. Letters of James Elwin, July 10, 1901; Andrew Schoch, July 1901; J. H. Sthurmeier, July 12, 1901; A. C. Greene, July 13, 1901, addressed to Warden Henry Wolfer.

Chapter 22

1. Letter from George M. Bennett to Henry Wolfer, July 15, 1901.*

2. Letter from Bennett to Wolfer, July 22, 1901.

3. Cole Younger Parole Report, August 1901.*
4. Jim Younger Parole Report, August 1901.*
5. Letter from Jim Younger to Lizzie Daniel, 1901.
6. Letter from Jim Younger to Henry Wolfer, August 14, 1901.*
7. Letter from Henry Wolfer to P. N. Peterson, August 16, 1901 / Letter from P. N. Peterson to Henry Wolfer, August 19, 1901.*
8. Letter from Jim Younger to Henry Wolfer, August 26, 1901.*
9. Cole Younger Parole Report, September, 1901.*
10. Letter from Jim Younger to Henry Wolfer, September 1, 1901.*
11. *Cole Younger by Himself.*
12. Jim Younger Parole Report, September, 1901.*
13. *Cole Younger By Himself.*
14. Cole Younger Parole Report, October, 1901.*
15. Letter from Jim Younger to Henry Wolfer, October 21, 1901.*
16. Kansas City *Times*, October 24, 1901.
17. Jim Younger Parole Report, October 1901.*
18. Letter from Henry Wolfer to Jim Younger, October 24, 1901.*
19. Cole Younger Parole Report, November 1901.*
20. *Cole Younger By Himself.*
21. Letter from Jim Younger to Henry Wolfer, November 15, 1901.*
22. Jim Younger Parole Report, November 1901.*
23. Ibid.
24. Letter from Jim Younger to Henry Wolfer, November 25, 1901.*
25. Cole Younger Parole Report, December 1901.*
26. Cole Younger Parole Report, January 1902.*
27. Jim Younger Parole Report, January 1902.*
28. Letter from Alix J. Muller to Governor S. R. Van Sant, January 8, 1902. Governor's Records, Minnesota Historical Society.
29. Jim Younger Parole Report, February 1902.*
30. Ibid.
31. Cole Younger Parole Report, February 1902.*
32. Cole Younger Parole Report, March 1902.*
33. Jim Younger Parole Report, March 1902.*
34. *Cole Younger By Himself.*
35. Jim Younger Parole Report, April 1902.*
36. *Cole Younger By Himself.*
37. Cole Younger Parole Report, April 1902.*
38. Cole Younger Parole Report, May 1902.*
39. Letter from Henry Wolfer to F. A. Whittier, May 3, 1902.*
40. Cole Younger Parole Report, June 1902.*
41. St. Paul *Pioneer Press*, "Youngers Stop Friendly Move," June 1902.

42. Letter from Jim Younger to Henry Wolfer, June 26, 1902.*
43. Cole Younger Parole Report, June 1902.*
44. Jim Younger Parole Report, July 1903.*
45. Letter from Jim Younger to Henry Wolfer, August 20, 1902.*
46. Letter from Jim Younger to Henry Wolfer, August 24, 1902.*
47. Letter from Cole Younger to Lizzie Daniel.
48. *Youngers Fight For Freedom.*
49. Ibid.
50. Letter from F. A. Whittier to Henry Wolfer, September 29, 1902.*
51. Letter from Henry Wolfer to F. A. Whittier, September 30, 1902.*
52. Ibid.
53. Kansas City *Star*, October 20, 1902.
54. Kansas City *Star*, October 21, 1902.
55. Ibid.
56. Ibid.
57. Kansas City *Star*, October 20, 1902.
58. Kansas City *Star*, October 21, 1902.
59. Kansas City *Star*, October 20, 1902.
60. Ibid.
61. Ibid.
62. *Cole Younger By Himself.*
63. Letter from Alix Muller to Lizzie Daniel, 1902.
64. St. Louis *Republican*, October 26, 1902.
65. Kansas City *Journal*, October 24, 1902.
66. Ibid.
67. Ibid.
68. Ibid.
69. Ibid.
70. St. Louis *Republican*.

Chapter 23

1. Letter from Frank James to W. C. Bronaugh, February 19, 1903.
2. Letter from Frank James to John Trotwood Moore, June 21, 1903.
3. Cole Younger Parole Report, November 1902.*
4. Cole Younger Parole Report, December 1902.*
5. Cole Younger Parole Report, January 1903.*
6. Kansas City *Star*, February 4, 1903.
7. Ibid.
8. "My Twelve Years With Cole Younger," Todd M. George.

9. Lee's Summit *Journal*, February 20, 1903.
10. Ibid.
11. Kansas City *World*, February 9, 1903.
12. Lee's Summit *Journal*, February 20, 1903.
13. "Cole Younger Writes to Lizzie Daniels."
14. *Youngers Fight For Freedom.*
15. "My Twelve Years With Cole Younger."
16. Account of Harry Hoffman. Letter to B. J. George.
17. *Youngers Fight For Freedom.*
18. Ibid.
19. "My Twelve Years With Cole Younger."
20. *Youngers Fight For Freedom.*
21. Ibid.
22. Ibid.
23. Ibid.
24. *Cole Younger By Himself.*
25. Cole Younger and Frank James Wild West Show Flyer.
26. Maryville *Tribune*, 1903.
27. Memphis *Commercial Appeal*, May 25, 1903.
28. Ibid.
29. Nashville *American*, June 1, 1903.
30. Ibid.
31. Ibid.
32. Nashville *American*, June 8, 1903.
33. Nodaway *Forum*, Maryville, September 3, 1903.
34. Ibid.
35. Letter from W. F. Wiggins to Henry Wolfer, September, 12, 1903.*
36. Appleton City *Tribune*, September 22, 1903.
37. Washington *Post*, December 6, 1903.
38. Knoxville *Daily Journal & Tribune*, December 15, 1903.

Chapter 24

1. Kansas City *Journal*, June 1, 1904.
2. Letter from Cole Younger to Henry Wolfer, November 14, 1904.
3. St. Louis *Globe Democrat* August 11, 1905.
4. Ibid.
5. Letter from Henry Wolfer to W. C. Bronaugh, February 9, 1905.
6. Ibid.
7. Letter from Henry Wolfer to Cole Younger, February 9, 1905.

8. Ibid.
9. Letter from R. W. McClaughgary to Henry Wolfer, May 30, 1908.
10. Kansas City *Journal*, March 16, 1905.
11. Ibid.
12. Ibid.
13. Account of Harry Younger Hall.
14. Letter from C. R. Geades to Henry Wolfer, December 17, 1912.
15. *Cole Younger By Himself.*
16. Interviews with Carolyn Hall and Nora Lee Smith.
17. Ibid.
18. "What My Life Has Taught Me," Cole Younger transcript, courtesy Leva Hull Thomas.
19. "Cole Younger Calls Lurid Tales Vicious," publication unknown, June 15, 1909.
20. "From Bandit King to Christian," Wilbur A. Zink.
21. St. Clair County *Democrat*, August 28, 1913.
22. Kansas City *Star*, August 25, 1913.
23. Letter from Mrs. Frank Hall to Dr. M. E. Withrow, December 3, 1915.
24. Letter from Cole Younger to Dr. M. E. Withrow, February 24, 1916.
25. After acting the role of Cole Younger in *Under the Black Flag*, Harry Hoffman became a construction engineer, a job he held until 1939 when he retired. Upon his retirement, Hoffman moved to Oxford, Ohio, where he settled on a ranch he named Trail's End. He died in a nursing home in nearby Hamilton, Ohio, on May 17, 1964.
26. Letter from Cole Younger to Harry Hoffman, March 7, 1916.
27. Jesse James, Jr., his friends, and business partners were involved in the production of the first moving picture on the life of Jesse Woodson James. *Under the Black Flag* was shot on location in Missouri. It premiered in March, 1921, with Jesse starring as his father, Harry Hoffman taking the role of Cole Younger, and Harry Younger Hall portraying Quantrill. Unfortunately, the film did not make the money even to meet its production costs. Jesse and his family moved to Los Angeles in 1926, where Jesse considered involvement in the film industry and practiced law for a few years. Jesse Edwards James died there on May 27, 1951, at the age of seventy-six.
28. Interview with James R. Ross.
29. Chicago *Herald*, Jack Lait, March 24, 1916.
30. Kansas City *Journal*, March 23, 1916.
31. Lee's Summit *Journal*, March 30, 1916.

Sources

Information contained in *The Outlaw Youngers* was researched over a period of fourteen years. Several hundred sources were used, and most of the data presented was cross-checked several times employing all available material. Personal accounts were obtained either from the families of the writers or from historical societies and libraries. Of particular importance to this work were the accounts of Jim Younger, "Maggie," Cole Younger, Bob Younger, Wal Bronaugh, members of the Northfield robbery posse, and the various members of the Younger and Fristoe families. Cole Younger's autobiography was used as an instrument by which clues could be obtained to verify, discount, or shed additional light on information available from other sources. Many errors in relation to chronology and actual events were found in Cole's story when checked against other more reliable sources. It is my belief that Cole wrote this book not as a factual depiction of his life, but rather a vehicle to present his version of the events that brought him to Stillwater Prison, and as an opportunity to provide an alibi for crimes in which he was believed to have been involved. On the other hand, the letters of Jim and Bob Younger and the parole reports of both Cole and Jim provide a very clear and detailed account of many of their activities.

The book *Jesse James Was His Name*, the papers of Dr. William A. Settle, Jr., and the direct involvement of Dr. Settle in this project were great assets in tracking down some of the movements and robberies of the James-Younger Gang. Additionally, each specific robbery was researched and examined as best as time and information available would allow. The James family and the archives of the James Farm provided important information and interesting theories in regard to Frank and Jesse James.

Many of the newspaper articles used came from the Younger family scrapbooks or from personal papers donated to historical societies or libraries. Several were undated, and occasionally the publications in which they appeared were not noted.

The research done by Dallas Cantrell for her book *Youngers' Fatal Blunder* was helpful to me early in my research of the Youngers. Ms. Cantrell's work provided many clues by which I was able to inspect the various files of the counties involved, talk or correspond with the families of those present at many events, and cross-check information using city directories, newspapers, county histories and so on.

When I first started gathering information on the Youngers, it was not with the intention of writing a book but rather to satisfy my own growing curiosity about this fascinating family. Consequently, much of the information I recorded from various county histories has been used without my being able to list the detailed source material. While the data and source were meticulously transcribed, author, publisher, and date of publication were sometimes omitted. For this I sincerely apologize. However, most, if not all, of these books can be found in the historical societies of the counties whose histories have been recorded.

Two sources that were used extensively are presented uncredited as stipulated by the owners of the material. Information referred to as being from the "correspondence of Jim Younger" was perused by me in a private collection of letters Jim Younger wrote to a close friend while in prison. In regard to the accounts of Bob Younger cited as the personal account of "Maggie," a similar situation exists. The information contained in these private letters and accounts has been researched, cross-checked, and authenticated to the best of my ability. I wish to thank those involved for sharing the material and for their generosity in allowing the use of such critical and important information. To have eliminated their use because of the inability to cite them fully would have been grossly detrimental to the final manuscript. It is fervently hoped that in the future these documents and/or the information contained therein will be made public by their owners.

All sources and chapter notes followed by + are contained in the files of the Joint Collection, University of Missouri Western Historical Manuscript Collection—Columbia & State Historical Society of Missouri Manuscripts.

All sources followed by * were found in the files of the Minnesota Historical Society. Since the time of the author's research, the Minnesota Historical Society has made available on microfilm some of the documents and letters pertaining to the Younger brothers. The microfilm is available as " 'Northfield (Minnesota) Bank Robbery of 1876' Selected Manuscripts Collections and Government Records, 1876–1979."

Books

Appler, Augustus C., *The Life, Character and Daring Exploits of the Younger Brothers* (Eureka Publishing Co., 1876).

Bronaugh, W. C., *The Youngers Fight for Freedom* (E. W. Stephens, 1906).

Brownlee, Richard, *Gray Ghosts of the Confederacy* (Baton Rouge, 1958).

Bryan, William S., and Rose, Robert, *A History of the Pioneer Families of Missouri* (1876)

Buel, J. W., *The Border Bandits* (Donnohue, Henneberry and Co., 1893).

Cantrell, Dallas, *Youngers' Fatal Blunder* (Naylor, 1973).

Connelly, William E., *Quantrill and the Border Wars* (Torch Press, 1910).

Crittenden, Henry Huston, *The Crittenden Memoirs* (G.P. Putnam & Sons, 1936).

Croy, Homer, *Last of the Great Outlaws* (Duell, Sloan and Pearce, 1956).

Cummins, Jim, *Jim Cummins the Guerrilla* (1908).

Dacus, Joseph A., *Illustrated Lives and Adventures of Frank and Jesse James and the Younger Brothers* (N. D. Thompson and Co., 1898).

Hale, Donald, *They Rode With Quantrill* (1982).

Helbron, W. C., *Convict Life at the Minnesota State Prison* (W. C. Helbron, publisher, 1909).

History of Benton County.

History of Butler (Jo Ellen Johnson Sears).

History of Cass County, Big Creek Township.

History of Cass and Bates Counties, Mo (1883).

History of Grayson County, Texas (Lucas Publishing).

History of Independence.

History of Jackson County (Union History Co., 1888).

History of Lee's Summit.

History of Linn County.

History of Paso Robles.

History of Ray County, Mo. (Missouri Historical Co., 1881).

History of San Jose.

History of San Luis Obispo.

History of Santa Clara County (National Historical Co., 1883).

History of the Sims Family of Virginia.

History of Vernon County.

Huntington, George, *Robber and Hero* (Christian, 1895).

McNeill, Cora, *Mizzoura* (Mizzoura Publishing Co., 1898).

Miller, Rick, *Bounty Hunter* (Creative, 1988).

O'Flaherty, Daniel, *General JO Shelby: Undefeated Rebel* (Chapel Hill Publishing, 1954).

Ross, James R., *I, Jesse James* (Dragon, 1989).

Settle, William A., Jr., *Jesse James Was His Name* (Bison Books, 1977).

Shirley, Glenn, *Belle Starr and Her Times* (University of Oklahoma, 1982).

Younger, Cole, *Cole Younger By Himself* (The Henneberry Co., 1903).

Zink, Wilbur A., *The Roscoe Gun Battle* (Democrat, 1982).

Correspondence

A. C. Green to Henry Wolfer, July 13, 1901.*

A. W. Hreekler to "Cousin Wm," September 29, 1876.*

Alix J. Muller to Governor Van Sant, January 8, 1902.*

Andrew Schoch to Henry Wolfer, July, 1901.

Ardyce Twyman Haukenberry to Josephine Green, April 19, 1926.

B. G. Yates to W. C. Bronaugh, February 27, 1889.

Bob Younger to "Aunt," January 25, 1883.

Bob Younger to Mrs. McGill, Easter 1887.

C. N. Beandoorz to Henry Wolfer, July 14, 1901.*

C. R. Geades to Henry Wolfer, December 17, 1912.*

Charlene B. Johnson to author, June 27, 1984.

Claude Bronaugh to author, June 24, 1983.

Cole Younger to J. W. Buel, October 31, 1880.

Cole Younger to Fannie Twyman, April 26, 1885.*

Cole Younger to W. C. Bronaugh, March 19, 1891.*

Cole Younger to W. R. Marshall, January 28, 1894.

Cole Younger to Henry Wolfer, September 20, 1901.*

Cole Younger to Henry Wolfer, October 21, 1901.*

Cole Younger to Lizzie Daniels, 1901.

Cole Younger to Henry Wolfer, February 22, 1902.*

Cole Younger to Henry Wolfer, November 14, 1904.*

Cole Younger to Harry Hoffman, April 4, 1907.

Cole Younger to Dr. M. E. Withrow, February 24, 1915.

Cole Younger to Harry Hoffman, March 7, 1916.

Cole Younger to N. L. Norton, February 14, (year unknown).

Cora Deming to W. C. Bronaugh, November 1, 1897.*

Correspondence of Bob Younger to "Aunt," 1877–1888.

Correspondence of Jim Younger, 1899–1901.

Delores Reed Fozzard to author, October 12, 1986.

Donald E. Lambkin to author, November 7, 1986.

Donald Hale to author, June 8, 1983.

Dr. M. E. Withrow to Frank Hall, April 30, 1947.

Dreat Younger to author, 1985.

F. A. Whittier to Henry Wolfer, September 29, 1902.*

F. A. Whittier to J. A. Lawrence, June 18, 1924.*

F. M. Rawlins to author, January 3, 1986.

Frances Butler to Walter Trenerry, November 20, 1962.

Frank James to W. C. Bronaugh, February 19, 1903.

Frank James to John Trotwood Moore, June 21, 1903.

Frank Rose to James Hardin Younger, March 27, 1909.*

George M. Bennett to Henry Wolfer, July 15, 1901.*

George M. Bennett to Henry Wolfer, July 22, 1901.*

Harry Hoffman to B. J. George, June 3, 1958. +

Harry Hoffman to B. J. George, June 25, 1958. +

Harry Hoffman to B. J. George, undated. +

Harry Younger Hall to Henry Wolfer, November 14, 1904.*

Henry H. Sibley to W. C. Bronaugh, July 8, 1889.*

Henry Wolfer to P. N. Peterson, August 16, 1901.*

Henry Wolfer to Jim Younger, October 24, 1901.*

Henry Wolfer to F. A. Whittier, September 30, 1902.*

Henry Wolfer to F. A. Whittier, September 3, 1903.*

Henry Wolfer to J. G. Maertin, February 1, 1904.*

Henry Wolfer to Cole Younger, February 9, 1905.*

Henry Wolfer to W. C. Bronaugh, February 9, 1905.*

J. H. Schurmeier to Henry Wolfer, July 12, 1901.*

J. W. Lercher to author, March 8, 1981.

Jack Hall to author, 1984.

James Elwin to Henry Wolfer, July 10, 1901.*

James W. Oberly of the College of William and Mary to author, May 19, 1983, June 2, 1983.

Jean Forney to author, November 15th, 1983.

Jean Hunsacker to author, October 2, 1986.

Jim Younger to Henry Wolfer, August 14, 1901.*

Jim Younger to Henry Wolfer, August 26, 1901.*

Jim Younger to Henry Wolfer, September 1, 1901.*

Jim Younger to Henry Wolfer, October 21, 1901.*

Jim Younger to Henry Wolfer, November 15, 1901.*

Jim Younger to Henry Wolfer, November 25, 1901.*

Jim Younger to Lizzie Daniels, 1901.

Jim Younger to Henry Wolfer, June 26, 1902.*

Jim Younger to Henry Wolfer, August 20, 1902.*

Jim Younger to Henry Wolfer, August 24, 1902.*

John Mills to author, November 3, 1982, December 6, 1982.

John Wilson to "My dear Sallie," (date unknown).

June Spicer to author, April 13, 1983.

Katherine Kenagy to author, August 9, 1983.

Kathleen Bryson of Transylvania University to author, April 13, 1984.

Lee Smith to author, May 18, 1983.

Leola Mayes to author, December 13, 1983, February 29, 1984, April 17, 1984.

Lillie Le Vesconte to Jacob Hodnefield, February 19, 1945.

Margarette Hutchins to author, July 8, 1983, August 7, 1984, August 31, 1984.

Mildred Addy to author, November 1, 1983.

Minnie Padgett to Henry Hoffman, March 1, 1959. +

Mrs. Frank Hall to Dr. M. E. Withrow, December 3, 1915.

N. O. Tate to Henry Wolfer, July 15, 1901.*

P. N. Peterson to Henry Wolfer, August 19, 1901.*

Patrick Brophy to author, July 9, 1983.

Peter Freligh to Retta Younger, November 11, 1890.*

R. W. McClaugary to Henry Wolfer, May 30, 1908.*

Retta Younger to W. C. Bronaugh, September 22, 1891.*

Retta Younger to Peter Freligh, September 23, 1891.*

Stella James to B. J. George, February 11, 1959. +

Todd George to B. J. George, December 3, 1959. +

W. F. Wiggins to Henry Wolfer, September 22, 1903.*

Wilbur E. Mencray of Tulane University to author, February 11, 1985.

William W. Jeffries, Director, United States Naval Academy to author, March 4, 1985.

W. C. Bronaugh to Frank James, June 13, 1884

Interviews

The author has interviewed the following members of the Younger family:

Robert Brashier (Simpson Younger family)

Sylvia Creek (Creek family)

Le Annis Fox (Younger cousin)

Lena Younger Gilpin (Younger cousin)

Carolyn Hall (Hall family)

Jack Hall (Hall family)

Charlene B. Johnson (Simpson Younger family)

Leola Mayes (Duncan family)

Delores Fozzard Reed (Kelley family)

Lee Smith (Hall family)

June Spicer (Jarrette family)

William Talley (Talley family)
Zudora Von Demfange (Duncan family)
Dorothy Ward (Duncan family)
Ruth Whipple (Duncan family)
Harriet Wickstrom (Duncan family)
Dreat Younger (Younger cousin)

The author has also interviewed:

Betty Barr (great-granddaughter of Jesse James)
Thelma Barr (granddaughter of Jesse James by marriage)
Ruth Coder Fitzgerald (family of Clell Miller)
C. E. Miller (family of Clell Miller)
John Nicholson (grand-nephew of Jesse James)
Ethelrose James Owens (granddaughter of Jesse James)
James R. Ross (great-grandson of Jesse James)
Florence Wiley (great-granddaughter of Pearl [Starr] Reed)

Notes were used from an interview of Minnie Padgett (Duncan family) conducted by Elizabeth George, October 28, 1959.

Articles and Pamphlets

"A Terrible Quintette," John Newman Edwards, 1873.

"Aspects of Slavery in Missouri," Anne Chiarelli, Jackson County Historical Society.

"The Bastille of the Saint Croix Valley," Terrance Keeler, October 14, 1983.

"The Borderland," *Colliers*, September 26, 1914.

The Brand Book, Vol. 16, No. 2, 1945.

Confederate Veteran, Vol. XVIII, No. 4, April 1914.

"Defeat of the Jesse James Gang," Northfield *News*, 1981.

"Denison Texas Centennial, 1872–1972," Denison Kiwanis Club, 1972.

"Edward Noonan Interviewed," Mankato *Spotlight* (date unknown).

"From Bandit King to Christian," Wilbur A. Zink, 1971.

"The Families of Charles Lee and Henry Washington Younger, A Genealogical Sketch," Marley Brant, 1986.

"From the Pen of A Noble Robber: The Letters of Jesse Woodson James, 1847–1882" by Robert Wybrow, The English Westerners Society Vol. 24, No. 2, Summer 1987.

Genealogical notes from the Liberty Tribune, Clay County Archives, Vol. 6.

"General Order No. 11: The Forced Evacuation of Civilians During the Civil War," by Charles R. Mink, *Military Affairs*, December 1970.

"The Gettysburg of the James-Younger Gang," *The Southern Minnesotan* (undated).

"Historical Bank Raid Centered on Ames Family," by Bob Warn for the Northfield Historical Society, 1977.

History of Lee's Summit—Recollections on file in Lee's Summit Library

"History of Lee's Summit," Chamber of Commerce, 1983.

James Farm Journal, December 1985.

"The James Gang in West Virginia," The English Westerners Society.

"Jesse James and Bill Ryan in Nashville" by Ted P. Yeatman, 1981.

"Jesse James in Tennessee," Ted P. Yeatman, *True West*, December 1985.

"The Jesse James Robbery," Adair, Iowa (pamphlet).

"Jim Cummins, the Guerrilla," James Cummins, Excelsior Springs *Daily Journal*, 1908.

Kentucky Ancestors, Volume 16–3, 1981.

"Lancaster, A History, 1845–1945," Lancaster (Texas) Historical Society, 1978.

Marshall-Lovell-Fristoe Genealogy, Josephine N. Green, 1935.

"The Miller Family," by Ruth Coder Fitzgerald, *The James Farm Journal*, 1988.

"Minnesota As It Is," J. W. McClung, 1870.

"Missouri-Mother of the West," Vol. II, 1930 (publication unknown).

"Mrs. Jesse James Jr. Recent Visitor at Museum," Jackson County Historical Society, December 1965.

"Northfield Bank Robbery," Northfield Historical Society.

"Official Report of the Resources and Opportunities of Jackson County, MO.," M. Ballou

"The Prison in Battle Hollow" (undated booklet).

"Quantrell, James, Younger, et al: Leadership in a Guerrilla Movement, Missouri, 1861–1865" by Don R. Bowman in *Military Affairs*, Vol. XLI, No. 1, February 1977.

"Revolvers Vs. Croquet Mallets and An Irate Lady," M. C. Eden, *The Brand Book*, Vol. 15, No. 4, July 1973.

"Robbery of the Ocobock Brothers Bank," Corydon, Iowa (pamphlet).

San Luis Obispo County Pathways, New Paradigm Press, 1981.

"Six Twyman Doctors," Jackson County Historical Society, March 1965.

"Tales of the Amarlugia Highlands of Cass County, Missouri" by Donald Lewis Osborn, 1972.

"Three years with Quantrill," John McCorkle, Armstrong [Mo] *Herald*, 1914.

Truman Medical Center-East History (booklet).

"The Watawon River," Julius Haycraft, Martin County Historical Society, 1945.

"Welcome to Adair," Adair Community Service Club (pamphlet).

Unpublished Manuscripts

"Cole Younger Writes to Lizzie Daniel" by William A. Settle, Jr., 1987.

"Cole Younger" by Harry Younger Hall (undated).

"Interview with Bob Younger by George Craig," 1886.

"The Youngers' Last Stand" by Harry C. Hoffman.†

"What Life Has Taught Me" by Cole Younger, 1903.

Records

1810 Kentucky Census

1830 Howard County Census

1850 Clay County Census, Missouri

1850 Jackson County Census, Missouri

1860 Cass County Census, Missouri

1860 St. Clair County Census, Missouri

1870 Cass County Census, Missouri

1870 Santa Clara County Census, California

1870 St. Clair County Census, Missouri

1880 St. Clair County Census, Missouri

1890 Santa Clara County Census, California

Adjutant General's Report, State of Kansas, Seventh Regiment

Kansas Volunteers-Cavalry Recruits of Co. H Since Veteran Organization

Affidavit of Frank J. Wilcox, September 1976

Affidavit of G. E. Hobbs, September 1876

Affidavit of J. S. Allen, September 1876

Annals of Kansas, 1855

C. R. Younger and Co., Bill of Sale, 1859

C. R. Younger Enrollment Card, Masonic Grand Lodge of Missouri

Campaigns and Battles of the Civil War, Government Printing Office

Cass County Marriage Records, Missouri

Cass County Records, Book K, page 488

Cemetery Records of Cass County

Cemetery Records of Denison Fairview Cemetery, Texas

Circuit Court of Cass County, Book C, Missouri

Claims on Account, Posse in regard to Northfield Bank Robbery

Clelland Miller Trial Transcript, Iowa 1871

Cole Younger manuscript "What Life Has Taught Me"

Complaint, Northfield Robbery, 1876

Consolidated Index, Confederate Soldiers, Government Printing Office

Coroner's Inquest into the Deaths of John Younger and Edwin Daniels, Testimony of Theodrick Snuffer, W. J. Allen (Lull) and G. W. Mc-Donald

Coroner's Inquest, "Heywood and Others," September 1876

Coroner's Report on John Younger and J. S. Allen, 1874

Daughters of the American Revolution, Younger #544072

Death Certificate of James H. Younger, 1902

Death Certificate of Robert Younger, 1889

Employment Request by Andrew Schoch, 1901

Employment Certificate, Jim Younger by Andrew Schoch, 1902

Estate of Coleman Younger, Last Will and Codicil, May 2, 1890

Estate Papers of Henry Washington Younger

Funeral Notice of Bob Younger, 1889

Funeral Notice of Cole Younger, 1917

Grand Lodges of Missouri, Ancient Free and Accepted Masons, enrollment records

Harry Hoffman manuscript "The Fog Amidst the Rumors Cleared Away"†

Indictment against T. C., James and Robert Younger for the Northfield Robbery and Murders, 1876

Indictment for Otterville, Missouri, Robbery, 1876†

Jackson County Marriage Records, Missouri

Jim Younger Parole Reports, (monthly) August 1901, to September, 1902

Land Title Issued to James H. Younger, Texas

Last Will and Codicil of Charles Lee Younger, February 26, 1852

Leva Hull Thomas genealogy

Life Prisoner Roll, Stillwater Prison*

Marriage Certificate of C. A. Pitts and Emma Henderson, December 27, 1874.

Marriage License of Bruce Younger and Maibelle Reed, Kansas

Missouri Rolls of Elected Officials, 1856

National Archives Military Record of Coleman Younger

National Archives Military Record of Irvin Walley

National Archives Military Record of Jephthah Duncan

National Archives Military Record of John Jarrette

National Archives Military Record of Joshua Younger

National Archives Military Record of Richard Marshall Fristoe

National Archives Military Record of William H. Kelley

Ninth United States Census, 1870, Dallas County, Texas

Pardon, Charles and Robert Ford by Thom. Crittenden, 1882†

Pardon petition, Missouri Legislature, 1899

Parole Papers of James Younger, 1901*

Parole Papers of T. C. Younger, 1901*

Parole Reports of Cole Younger, (monthly) August 1901 to January 1903*

Pension Application of Christina Daniels

Pension Application of Cole Younger

Pension Records of Irvin Walley

Pension Records of Jepthah Duncan

Probated Estate of Mary Ringo, California, August 12, 1876

Record of Missouri Confederate Veterans, Coleman Younger

Records of the City of Northfield, Minnesota (miscellaneous)

Resolution of Pardon of T. C. Younger, 1901*

S. B. Brockway Dispatch to J. A. Winter, September 14, 1876*

St. Clair County Circuit Court Records, July 30, 1893, Missouri

St. Paul City Directory, 1901

Statement of Cole Younger in regard to the Stillwater Prison fire, 1884.

Statement of Expenses, Sheriff James Glispin

Stillwater Prison Death Roll*

Stillwater Prison Punishment Record*

Stock Certificate, H. W. Younger

The War of the Rebellion, A Compilation of the Official Records of the Union and Confederate Armies, Government Printing Office, 1888

Transfer papers of T. C., James and Robert Younger from Faribault Jail to Stillwater State Prison, 1876.

Van Buren County Marriage Records, Missouri

Warrant for the arrest of Frank and Jesse James in regard to the Glendale Robbery, 1879†

Warrant for the arrest of Frank James, 1882†

Warrant of Arrest, T. C., James and Robert Younger, 1876

Will of Sarah S. Younger, November 5, 1858, (revised) January 1, 1859

Personal Accounts

"A Jackson County Citizen Writes of the Time of Quantrells and the Jayhawkers," Jacob Teaford Palmer (undated)

"A Short History of Washington Township, Jackson County, Missouri" by Rufus Burris, October 11, 1945

Charles Armstrong, Madelia, June 21, 1945

Charles Pomeroy, 1877

Cole Younger to Dr. A. E. Hedback, 1897

Cole Younger to Harry Hoffman, 1914

Dreat Younger, 1984

G. M. Palmer, Mankato, 1938

George Bradford, 1877

George Hobbs, September 11, 1876

Hiram George, 1900†

Kitty Traverse, St. Paul, 1878

L. M. Demaray, 1876

Leva Hull Thomas (undated)

"Maggie"

Mrs. Louise Thomforde (undated)†

"My Twelve Years With Cole Younger," Todd George

Papers of the Head Family, Kansas City, Kansas

Perry Samuel to Harry Hoffman (undated)†

Robert E. Younger, 1885

Robert H. Cartmell, May 27, 1903*

Sophia Younger Ragan Braden (undated)

Statement of Cole Younger to Harry Hoffman (1914)+

Statement of Greenup Bird re: Liberty Bank robbery, 1866

T. L. Vought, 1876

"The Life of Mrs. Frances Fristoe Twyman by Herself," 1901

"The Sacking and Burning of Osceola" by Owen Snuffer (undated)

The scrapbook of Hardin Hall

W. R. Estes, 1876

William Henry Ogden, Jr. (undated)

"Withrow Family" (sent to author by Mary Withrow Davidson)

Newspapers

Appleton City *Tribune*, September 22, 1903

Butler *Times*, June 12, 1889

Chicago *Herald*, March 24, 1916 Jack Lait

Chicago *Recorder Herald*, May 2, 1909

Cincinnati *Enquirer*, April 17, 1889

Cincinnati *Enquirer*, December 25, 1915

"Cleared at Last," date and newspaper unknown

Clinton *Democrat*, date unknown

Clinton *Democrat*, February 1923 "WC Bronaugh Is Dead"

"Cole Younger Calls Lurid Tales Vicious," June 15, 1909, newspaper unknown

Columbia *Daily Herald*, June 9, 1903

Daily Ardmoreite, May 13, 1937, "AB Rawlins, City Business Man Dies"

Daily Missouri Democrat, September 1, 1863

Daily Oklahoman, April 10, 1904

Dallas *Morning News*, May 29, 1945, "Pillar of Society and Gentleman Bandit"

Faribault *Democrat*, September 14, 1876; September 22, 1876; October 6, 1876

Harrisonville *Democrat*, August 17, 1860, "Sudden Death"

Huntington *Advertiser*, September 21, 1875

Independence *Examiner*, March 23, 1916

Independence *News*, 1868

Jackson County *News*, September 23, 1875

"James Robbery Integral Part of Wayne County History" (date and publication unknown)

"Jesse James Not A Hero To Native Of Northfield, Minnesota," June 26, 1948 (publication unknown)

"Jesse's Jobs," October 17, 1879, newspaper unknown

Kansas City *Journal*, March 17, 1901, "Interview With Reuben Smith"; October 24, 1902; June 1, 1904; March 16, 1905; March 14, 1915; March 22, 1916

Kansas City *Star*, (date unknown), "The Inside Story of the Northfield Bank Robbery"; (date unknown), "Early Segregation Test Here in Annals of the Younger Family" by Henry A. Bundscher; 1895, "A Visit To The Youngers"; October 20, 1902; October 21, 1902; February 4, 1903; February 20, 1903; November 19, 1911, Account of Eliza Harris Deal; August 25, 1913; October 20, 1929; May 16, 1937, "Proud Granddaughters of Jesse James, Bandit"; August 25, 1944, "Cole Younger Served Would be Captors A Dash of Scorn With Morning Coffee"; February 15, 1959; May 18, 1964; November 7, 1987, "The Youngers' Life Story"

Kansas City *Times*, 1897, Interview with Cora McNeill Deming; September 17, 1889; September 20, 1889, "Funeral of Bob Younger"; September 21, 1889, "His Past Sins Forgotten"; March 22, 1916; March 27, 1951, "Jesse James, Jr. Dies"; October 24, 1958, "Doctor Recalls Younger Brothers As Men Above the Outlaw Class"

Kansas City *World*, February 9, 1903

Kingfisher *Times*, January 29, 1925, "Mrs. Adeline Lee Dalton"

Knoxville *Daily Journal & Tribune*, June 15, 1903

"L. M. Demeray Recalls Story of Narrow Escape By T. J. Dunning and Raid on Mathews Flock of Chickens" (date and Mankato publication unknown)

Lee's Summit *Journal*, February 20, 1903; March 23, 1916; March 30, 1916

Lee's Summit *Ledger*, March 25, 1874

Lexington *Union*, September 5, 1863

Liberty *Tribune*, 1875; (date unknown); December, 1879; February 27, 1880, "Bob Younger"; November 4, 1881

Louisville *Courier-Journal*, 1980, "Bank Account . . . Pistol Points to James Gang"

Louisville *Daily Journal*, March 21, 1868

Lowry City *Independent*, February 19, 1931

Madelia *Times-Messenger*, March 27, 1936, "The Inside Story Of The Northfield Bank Robbery"

Mankato *Free Press*, December 1876; September 20, 1979, "The Younger Gang Comes To Mankato"

Maryville *Tribune*, 1903

Memphis *Commercial Appeal*, May 26, 1903

Minneapolis *Tribune*, September 8, 1876; September 25, 1876

Missouri *Democrat*, August 1863

Nashville *American*, June 1, 1903; June 8, 1903

Nodaway *Forum*, September 3, 1903

Northfield *News*, August 2, 1929, "General Ames Too Modest To Tell Part in Northfield Raid"

"Northfield Bank Robbery Is Recalled By Jail Guard's Son," Faribault, (date and publication unknown)

Norton (KS) *Champion*, (date unknown), "One Night With Jim Younger"

Palm Beach *Post*, July 7, 1986, "Grave of Bandit Queen All But Forgotten"

"Quantrill Left Dark Trail Here," (publication unknown), Hardin Hall scrapbook

Rice County *Journal*, "Extra," September 1876; September 14, 1876

San Jose *Mercury Herald*, September 2, 1932, "Gravel With A History"

Spokane Falls *Review*, November 25, 1890

St. Clair County *Democrat*, June 26, 1911; December 14, 1911; August 28, 1913

St. Louis *Globe-Democrat*, September 10, 1893, "Train Robbery"; August 11, 1905

St. Louis *Globe*, June 22, 1889; June 23, 1889

St. Louis *Republican*, February 2, 1874; August 3, 1902; October 26, 1902

St. Paul *Pioneer Press*, (date unknown), "Convicts Armed as Prison Burns"; September, 1876; 1889; July 13, 1897, "Held Fast in Prison"; July 14, 1897; July 11, 1901; June, 1902, "Youngers Stop Friendly Move"; April 2, 1909

Stillwater *Gazette*, July 12, 1901

Stillwater *Evening Gazette*, November 9, 1979

The Southern Minnesotan, (date unknown)

Washington *Post*, December 6, 1903; April 1, 1915

Weekly Border Star, (date unknown)

Wheeling *Intelligencer*, September 17, 1875

White Cloud *Chief*, September 3, 1863

Index